MUSIC
Sound
and
Sense

Second Edition

MUSIC
Sound
and
Sense

Ron Byrnside

Agnes Scott College
Decatur, Georgia

 WCB Wm. C. Brown Publishers

Book Team

Editor *Meredith M. Morgan*
Production Editor *Gloria G. Schiesl*
Art Editor *Gayle A. Salow*
Photo Research Editor *Carol M. Smith*
Permissions Editor *Karen L. Storlie*
Visuals Processor *Jodi Wagner*

Consulting Editor *Frederick W. Westphal*

 Wm. C. Brown Publishers

President *G. Franklin Lewis*
Vice President, Publisher *George Wm. Bergquist*
Vice President, Publisher *Thomas E. Doran*
Vice President, Operations and Production *Beverly Kolz*
National Sales Manager *Virginia S. Moffat*
Advertising Manager *Ann M. Knepper*
Marketing Manager *Kathleen Nietzke*
Production Editorial Manager *Colleen A. Yonda*
Production Editorial Manager *Julie A. Kennedy*
Publishing Services Manager *Karen J. Slaght*
Manager of Visuals and Design *Faye M. Schilling*

Cover and interior design by Mary K. Sailer

Cover Image
Henri Matisse; PIANO LESSON; (1916). Oil on canvas, 8′½″ ×
6′11¾″. Collection, The Museum of Modern Art, New York. Mrs.
Simon Guggenheim Fund. Photograph © 1989 The Museum of Modern
Art, New York.

Table of Contents Photographs
Section 1: © AP/Wide World Photos, Inc.
Section 2: Madonna of the Rose Garden, Stefan Lochner. Wallraf-
        Richartz Museum, Cologne, Germany
Section 3: © AP/Wide World Photos, Inc.

Fold Out End Sheet
Rolin Graphics

Calligraphy by Gary White
Figures 2.3, 2.4, 2.5, 2.6, 5.6 and 8.1; and p. 21 (bottom), p. 64 (top),
p. 76, p. 135, p. 137, p. 154 (bottom)

Library of Congress Catalog Card Number: 88–64182

ISBN 0–697–08368–3

Printed in the United States of America by Wm. C. Brown Publishers,
2460 Kerper Boulevard, Dubuque, IA 52001

10 9 8 7 6 5 4 3 2 1

To my friends
Ellen and Marvin Perry

Sound and Sense Listening Guides   xii
Colorplates   xiii
Preface   xiv
Introduction   3

SECTION 1

Terms and Concepts

1   Time and Music   12

Time Creates Movement and
    Change   14
Rhythm Organizes Time   15
    Beats   16
    Meter   17
    Tempo   18
    Note Values   19
Summary   23
Key Terms   23
Thinking About It   23

2   Sound and Music   24

Pitches and Intervals   27
    The Octave System   27
    Majors and Minors   28
    Melody   29
Harmony and Chords   31
    Harmony Reflects Change   32
    Chords Create Harmony   32
    The System of Functional
        Harmony   33
Texture   34
    Monophonic Texture   35
    Polyphonic Texture   35
Musical Instruments   37
    Voices   38
    The Orchestra Family   39
Summary   45
Key Terms   46
Thinking About It   47

3   Form and Music   48

Music: The Evolving Message   50
Musical Bookkeeping   50
    Ternary: *ABA* or *AABA*   51
    Binary: *AB* or *AABB*   55
    Rondo: *ABACA, ABACADA,* or
        ABACABA   56
    Twelve-Bar Blues: *AA'B*   57
    Sonata-Allegro   58
Theme and Variations: A Process   60
    Creating Variations   60
Song Structures   61
    Strophic   61
    Through-Composed   61
    Modified Strophic   61
Text Setting   62
Additional Examples of the Formal
        Types Discussed in This
        Chapter   62
Summary   65
Key Terms   66
Thinking About It   67

4   Meaning and Music   68

Music Transcends Words and
        Objects   70
The Language of Music   71
    Music and Description   72
    Music and Interpretive
        Description   72
    Program Music   77
    Philosophical Program Music   77
Summary   80
Key Terms   80
Thinking About It   80

Contents

SECTION 2

Styles in Western Art Music

5   Music in the Baroque Era   84

Baroque Art: A Stylistic
        Comparison   87
Music of the Baroque   90
Characteristics of Baroque Music   92
        Functional Harmony   92
        Basso Continuo   92
        Figured Bass   92
Orchestral Music—Genres and
        Composers   94
        The Concerto Grosso   94
        Johann Sebastian Bach   96
        Antonio Vivaldi   97
        Trio Sonata   98
        Keyboard Music   99
Vocal Music—Genres and
        Composers   100
        Opera   101
        George Frederic Handel   105
        Oratorio   106
        Cantata   107
Summary   111
Key Terms   113
Thinking About It   113

6   Music in the Preclassic Era   114

Musical Styles in the Preclassic
        Era   116
        Rococo   116
        Style Galant   121
        Empfindsamer Stil   123
        Sturm und Drang   123
Musical Style as a Reflection of
        Culture   124
        The Symphony   124
Summary   128
Key Terms   129
Thinking About It   129

7   Music in the Classical Era   130

The Symphony in the Classical
        Era   132
The Composers of the Classical
        Era   133
        Franz Joseph Haydn   133
        Wolfgang Amadeus Mozart   138
        Ludwig van Beethoven   139
The Concerto   145
        Mozart's Concertos   145
        Beethoven's Concertos   148
The String Quartet   148
        Haydn's Early Quartets   149
        Haydn's *Sturm und Drang*
                Quartets   150
        Haydn's Later Quartets   151
        Mozart's Quartets   151
        Beethoven's Quartets   151
Piano Sonata   152
        Haydn's Sonatas   152
        Mozart's Sonatas   153
        Beethoven's Sonatas   153
Opera   157
        Comic Opera   157
        The Merging of Comic and Serious
                Opera   158
Summary   166
Key Terms   167
Thinking About It   167

8   Music in the Age of Romanticism 168

Nationalism 171
Music: Language of the Soul 171
    Integration of Music with the Other
        Arts 172
The Composers 172
The Symphony in the Nineteenth
        Century 175
    Felix Mendelssohn 175
    Johannes Brahms 179
    Peter Tchaikovsky 182
    Program Symphony 183
    Hector Berlioz 185
    Choral/Dramatic Symphony 186
Tone Poem 188
Solo Music for the Piano 189
    Piano Sonata 190
    Character Piece 191
    Frédéric François Chopin 191
The Concerto 196
    Robert Schumann 196
Art Song 200
    Franz Peter Schubert 200
    Clara Schumann 204
Opera 205
    Italian Opera 206
    Richard Wagner 220
    German Opera: Wagner's
        Gesamtkunstwerk 220
    Leitmotifs 221
Summary 225
Key Terms 226
Thinking About It 226

9   Music in the Twentieth Century 228

The Evolution of Twentieth-Century
    Art Music 230
Musical Trends at the Turn of the
    Century 231
    Impressionism 231
    Symbolism 235
    Expressionism 238
    Stravinsky's Early Works 243
    Bartók 245
    The Music of Ives 249
Music between the Wars 250
    Dadaism 250
    The French Six 253
    Neoclassicism 255
    The Americana Composers 259
    Gershwin 262
    The Twelve-Tone System 263

Music after World War II 265
    The Rise of Electronic Music 266
    Karlheinz Stockhausen 268
    Chance Music 270
    Minimalism 272
    Adaptions and Expansions 274
Summary 275
Key Terms 277
Thinking About It 277

10   Music in the Middle Ages 278

The Formation of the Gregorian
        Chant 280
    The Nature of the Gregorian
        Chant 281
    The Integration of the Gregorian
        Chant with the Mass 282
The Beginnings of Harmony 285
    The Emergence of Polyphony 286
The Ars Nova: Period of Change 289
    Music of the Ars Nova 289
    Machaut 291
Summary 293
Key Terms 294
Thinking About It 294

11   Music in the Renaissance 296

Humanism Reborn 298
General Characteristics of Renaissance
        Music 299
    Harmony 299
    Counterpoint 299
    Texture 299
    Rhythm 299
Sacred Music 299
Music of the Protestant
        Reformation 299
    Lutheranism 300
    Calvinism 300
    Anglicanism 301
Music of the Catholic Church 302
    The Mass 302
    Josquin des Prez 303
    The Renaissance Motet 305
Secular Music in the Renaissance 306
    The Madrigal 306
    Keyboard and Instrumental
        Music 307
Summary 308
Key Terms 309
Thinking About It 309

SECTION 3

Outside the Sphere of Western Art Music

12   American Popular Music to 1950   312

The Dissemination of American
    Popular Music   314
    The Rise of the Sheet Music
    Industry   314
    Audience Participation   315
The Genteel Tradition   316
    Stephen Foster   317
The Tin Pan Alley Era   318
    Verse and Refrain   319
Popular Music in the 1930s   322
    Song Forms   322
    Lyrics   324
Defining Swing   328
The Big Band Era   329
    Swing Bands   329
    Sweet Dance Bands   331

Singing in the Thirties   332
    Tenor or "Clean" Style   332
    Talking Style   333
    Crooning or "Dirty" Style   333
The Demise of the Swing Era   336
Summary   336
Key Terms   337
Thinking About It   337

13   Jazz   340

The Nature of Jazz   342
    Swing   342
    Improvisation   343
Early Jazz   344
    Blues   344
    Rag   345
    Harmony and Instruments   345
Jazz: A European-African
    Combination   345
    New Orleans Bands   346
1920s Hot Jazz   347
    New Elements in Twenties
    Jazz   348
    Stride Piano   349
Swing in the Thirties and Forties   350
    Jazz Players   350
    Black and White Jazz   351
    The Genius of Ellington   352
Bop and Cool   352
    Characteristics of Bop   352
    Characteristics of Cool Jazz   354
New Jazz   354
Summary   355
Key Terms   357
Thinking About It   357

14   Rock Music   358

The Roots of Rock   361
    R & B   361
    Country   364
Rock and Roll   364
    Rock and Roll Beat   365
    Rock and Roll
    Instrumentation   366
    Soft Rock and Roll   366
From Fifties Rock and Roll to Sixties
    Rock   367
    Motown   367
    The Twist   368
    Surf   368

The Beatles   368
   Sgt. Pepper   370
The Rolling Stones   371
Soul   371
Other Sixties Rock   372
   Folk Rock   372
   West Coast Rock and Acid
     Rock   373
More Recent Rock   374
   Blues Rock   374
   Heavy Metal   375
   Glitter Rock   375
   Punk Rock   375
   Singers/Songwriters   376
   Jazz Rock   376
   Art Rock   376
   Rock in the Late 1980s   377
Summary   377
Key Terms   379
Thinking About It   379

**15   Music in the Non-Western
    World**   380

Africa   382
   North Africa   382
   Sub-Saharan Africa   382
Asia   385
   Indonesia   385
India   389
Japan   392
The West Indies—The Reggae Music
   of Jamaica   393
Summary   394
Key Terms   395
Thinking About It   395

Appendix A *Record/Cassette
 Selections   396*
Appendix B *A Brief List of Composers and
 Their Works   399*

Glossary   403
Index   410
Cultural Time Chart

Sound and Sense Listening Guides

Chapter 3

Chopin Mazurka, op. 67, no. 3 ♪
Chopin Mazurka, op. 63, no. 3 ♪
Haydn Symphony no. 92, Third Movement
Mozart Symphony no. 40 in G Minor, Third Movement
Haydn Piano Sonata no. 37 in D Major, Last Movement ♪
Beethoven Piano Sonata no. 8 in C Minor, op. 13, Second Movement ♪
Beethoven Piano Sonata in F Minor, op. 2, no. 1, Second Movement
Tchaikovsky "March," *The Nutcracker,* op. 71a ♪
Tchaikovsky "Overture Miniature," *The Nutcracker,* op. 71a ♪
Ravel *Pavane pour une Infante défunte*
Mozart Piano Sonata in B^b Major, K. 333, First Movement
Haydn Piano Sonata in E Minor, First Movement ♪

Chapter 4

Mendelssohn *Hebrides* Overture
Beethoven Symphony no. 7, Second Movement

Chapter 6

Stamitz Symphony in D Major
Bach, C. P. E. Symphony in B Minor ♪

Chapter 7

Haydn Symphony no. 45 in F# Minor, *Farewell*
Haydn Symphony no. 101, *The Clock* ♪
Beethoven Symphony no. 3, *Eroica,* First Movement
Mozart Piano Concerto no. 17 in G Major, K. 453
Haydn String Quartet, op. 20, no. 5
Beethoven Piano Sonata no. 12, op. 26 ♪
Beethoven Piano Sonata no. 14, op. 27, no. 2, *Moonlight Sonata*

Chapter 8

Mendelssohn Symphony no. 4, *Italian*
Brahms Symphony no. 2, op. 73, First Movement ♪
Borodin *In the Steppes of Central Asia* ♪
Chopin Polonaise in A^b Major, op. 53, *Heroic* ♪
Chopin Études, op. 10, no. 5 in G^b Major, *Black Key Étude* ♪
Brahms Intermezzo, op. 118, no. 2 ♪
Mendelssohn-Hensel *Andante con moto,* op. 2, no. 2 ♪
Schumann, Robert Piano Concerto in A Minor, First Movement ♪
Grieg Piano Concerto in A Minor

Chapter 9

Debussy "Nuages," Three *Nocturnes*
Stravinsky *Petrushka*
Satie *Parade*
Stravinsky *Octet*
Prokofiev Third Piano Concerto in C Major, op. 26 ♪
Copland *Music for the Theatre*
Barber *Adagio for Strings* ♪
Gershwin, George Piano Concerto in F
Stockhausen *Gesang der Jünglinge (Song of the Youths)*
Glass *Einstein on the Beach* ♪

Chapter 11

Josquin "Gloria," Mass: *Pange Lingua*
Josquin *Ave Maria* ♪

Chapter 13

King Oliver "Dippermouth Blues" ♪
Louis Armstrong "West End Blues" ♪

Colorplates

Plate 1   *The Old Musician*
Plate 2   *Max Schmitt in a Single Scull*
Plate 3   *Mahantango Valley Farm*
Plate 4   *Persistence of Memory*
Plate 5   *The Guitar Player*
Plate 6   *Love*
Plate 7   *Stonehenge*
Plate 8   *Daffodils*
Plate 9   *Basket of Apples*
Plate 10   *Wheatfields*
Plate 11   *Norham Castle, Sunrise*
Plate 12   *Winter (Return of the Hunters)*
Plate 13   *Madonna with Child and Saints*
Plate 14   *Rape of the Daughters of Leucippus*
Plate 15   *Hofkirche*
Plate 16   *A Party in the Open Air*
Plate 17   *A View Near Volterra*
Plate 18   *Liberty Leading the People*
Plate 19   *Forest at Fountainbleau*
Plate 20   *Woman Seated Under the Willows*
Plate 21   Tiffany Lamp
Plate 22   *Three Musicians*
Plate 23   *The Holy Face*
Plate 24   *Twittering Machine*
Plate 25   *Nighthawks*
Plate 26   *Composition in White, Black, and Red*
Plate 27   *Number I*
Plate 28   *Green Coca-Cola Bottles*
Plate 29   *South Rose Window and Lancets*
Plate 30   *Ginevra de'Benci*
Plate 31   *Creation*
Plate 32   *The Sargent Family*
Plate 33   Jukebox
Plate 34   The Beatles
Plate 35   African Musicians
Plate 36   Balinese Gamelan

Preface

The purpose of *Music: Sound and Sense* is to guide students in their search for an understanding and genuine pleasure of many kinds of music. Further, the book suggests ways to think about any kind of music as a part—a very important part—of the cultural context from which it develops. Virtually no one needs to be taught how to "appreciate" music of some kind, but everyone, including the students for whom this book is intended, is enriched by an expansion of personal musical boundaries and tastes. *Music: Sound and Sense* encourages students to engage in such expansions and offers specific guidelines for doing so.

Organization and Scope

There are fifteen chapters divided into three subsections, covering the range from basic terms and concepts (chapters 1–4), to the various periods of Western art music (chapters 5–11), to American popular music, rock, jazz, and an introduction to non-Western musical cultures (chapters 12–15).

For the historical periods (chapters 5–11) I have elected to proceed from the baroque era through the twentieth century and then treat the music of the Middle Ages (chapter 10) and the Renaissance (chapter 11). My feeling is that students new to the subject matter are more likely to be drawn to and involved in the more familiar-sounding music of the baroque than to earlier music, and it is important to actively involve all students from the start.

Professors who prefer a historical approach may wish to start with the earlier music and proceed in chronological fashion. The book is designed to facilitate that approach also. It is simply a matter of the instructor's choice.

All of us who have taught courses of this kind are keenly and, I might add, painfully aware of the limitations of class time; it seems there is never enough time to cover all of the material and rarely is there sufficient time for students to reflect upon what has been presented. The instructor must make some choices concerning the use of class time. It would be a luxury if we could begin classes of this kind assured of student exposure to the basic terms and concepts, but experience has proven that this assumption cannot be made. I believe that some attention and time must be given to basic terms and concepts. After covering the fundamentals, the instructor can proceed to give time and attention to the various chapters as he or she prefers. Ideally, all of the materials should be explored.

Special Features

The artwork featured has been carefully selected and positioned to offer students insights into the cultural context of the music they are learning. "Sound and Sense" listening exercises are found throughout the text. These elements are designed to draw students into active listening. Most instructors doubtless have a collection of works which they regularly use to illustrate various styles and genres of music. Such works can easily be used as supplements to, or in some cases substitutes for, the pieces discussed and analyzed in the text.

Each chapter begins with a "Sounds of the Chapter" element featuring all the musical pieces that will be encountered in the chapter. Within the text special names, terms, and concepts appear in boldface, and margin notes highlight important information.

Each chapter concludes with a comprehensive summary and a list of the key terms. A section called "Thinking About It" poses leading questions that invite creative responses.

Appendix A is a list of the recordings included in the record set, with instructions for the best use of each piece. Appendix B offers a brief list of major composers and their works. The Glossary offers definitions of the key terms and concepts introduced in the text. Finally, a cultural time chart integrating the chronological development of the arts is offered at the end of the book.

The Instructor's Manual to accompany this text contains many diverse components. I suggest alternative course organization formats, goals and means for each chapter, along with outlines, summaries, and a test item file. Further listenings are offered and insights into the "Sound and Sense" listening exercises are provided.

The Record and Cassette Set

The text is accompanied by both a record and cassette set that contain all or part of many of the works discussed and/or analyzed. A list of the works contained on these recordings appears in Appendix A, in the record set itself, and in the Instructor's Manual. The symbol ♪ will be used throughout the text to indicate musical pieces that appear on the record/ cassette set.

Ultimately, the success of courses of this kind is closely tied to the expertise and concern of the instructor, whose role in the learning process cannot be altered by any textbook. I believe, however, that *Music: Sound and Sense* can be a useful tool for the instructor and an informative and challenging book for students.

Acknowledgments

"I wish I had thought of that"—a phrase often expressed by one stimulated or touched by an idea or perspective that comes from someone else. No one can possibly recall the sources of all these ideas. In my case, now, only a few of the most obvious come to mind. To the countless others I extend my honest thanks.

Whatever merit this book may have is due, in large measure, to the expertise of several people who reviewed the manuscript with rigor and compassion:

James M. Anthony
Towson State University

Dan Duncan
Eastern Kentucky University

Neil E. Hansen
Northwest Community College

Judy M. Henderson
Inver Hills Community College

Gary S. Karpinski
University of Oregon

Ben F. Miller
Marshall University

Frank Mueller
University of Wisconsin–Parkside

Mark Alan Taggart
East Carolina University

Paul Taylor
Heidelberg College

Sheree Zalampas
Jefferson Community College

Finally, my thanks go to the fine staff people at Wm. C. Brown who worked on this project, whose intelligence, wit, and patience made my work a joy.

MUSIC
Sound
and
Sense

There is no evidence that people have any physiological need for music, yet throughout history and in all parts of the world, people have everywhere and always had music. It must be concluded, then, that music is very important to humankind. Music is, in fact, one of our self-created treasures.

Throughout the centuries it has been evident that music occupies a special place in our existence. Music has provided a means for expressing something deep inside; it has been a joy, a comfort, and an adjunct to religion. It has been a call to battle, a mnemonic device, and a didactic tool. Mystical, evil, even healing powers have been attributed to music. A given ritual may be invalidated for failure to perform the specified musical accompaniment in some cultures, and in more than one culture a song is viewed as personal property, to be sung only by its possessor. The powers of music have been recognized and jealously guarded by people from many cultures and eras.

In Plato's *Republic,* he suggests some ideas about music that may at first astonish us. While he uses some musical/technical terms that need not concern us at this time, Plato says, in part:

> "What, then, are the dirge-like harmonies? Tell me, for you are a musician."
>
> "The Mixolydian," he said, "and the intense Lydian, and others similar to them."
>
> "These, then," said I, "we must do away with. For they are useless. . . . But again, drunkenness is a thing most unbefitting guardians, and so is softness and sloth."
>
> "Yes."
>
> "What, then, are the soft and convivial harmonies?"
>
> "There are certain Ionian and also Lydian ones that are called relaxed."
>
> "Will you make any use of them for warriors?"
>
> "None at all."
>
> "And gracelessness and evil rhythm and disharmony are akin to evil speaking and the evil temper, but the opposites are the symbols and the kin of the opposites, the sober and good disposition."[1]

Can so fertile a mind as Plato's actually have believed that music is capable of good or evil? He definitely implied that some music is wicked and dangerous to the existence of the state.

Writing in the fourteenth century, Jacob of Liège also made some startling claims about music.

> Would that it pleased the modern singers that the ancient music and the ancient manner of singing were again brought into use! For, if I may say so, the old art seems more perfect, more rational, more seemly,

Introduction

1. Source: Paul Shorey, *Loeb Classical Library Series,* Harvard University Press, Cambridge, MA.

freer, simpler, and plainer. Music was originally discreet, seemly, simple, masculine, and of good morals; have not the moderns rendered it lascivious beyond measure?[2]

Did he really believe that music can be imbued with good morals? Can sounds and rhythms be moral or immoral?

A mythical Eastern prince, concerned that his subjects were not attending to the affairs of state because they were spending too much time making music, proclaimed that music should die before the dawn of a specified day. On the evening before that day, a group of musicians performed a mournful dirge under the prince's balcony. They said to him, "You have decreed that music must die; we have come to bury it." The prince responded, "Bury it deep." Was the prince afraid that music buried in only a shallow grave would somehow arise and again "infect" his subjects?

Music, then, not only offers entertainment, but also reveals characteristics of the culture to which it belongs.

Music does not submit to a singular definition. How music is defined depends upon whom we ask, and also when we ask. For instance, if we were to ask a Tibetan monk, "What is music?" he would produce sounds that many of us in the Western world would be unwilling to call music. At least, it would not be music as we perceive it. But the gravelly, subterranean vocal sounds and the honking of the elongated trumpets are an integral part of the Tibetan monk's spiritual existence. This music is equally important to him as our music is to us.

If we ask a young composer from the 1980s or 1990s to define music, he or she may respond with a series of electronically generated sounds. Some may say, "No, those are squeaks and pops, not music." Still, for the composer and the audience, this is music.

When we listen to "Scarborough Fair" by Simon and Garfunkel, we may say, "Now that's music." This is because our conditioning, our heritage, tells us that this particular piece contains the properties of music and behaves as music should. It is one of tens of thousands of works that we could offer in response to the question, "What is music?" It could serve as our definition of music. But it would be a mistake to assume that our definition is any more valid than the definition offered by the Tibetan monk or the composer of electronic music or a performer from the Kabuki theater or a Pygmie from the Ituri forest or an anonymous ninth-century peasant from northern Europe. Ultimately, there is no singular definition of music. There are many, and each depends on whom we ask and when.

The mention of "Scarborough Fair" suggests another question, namely, "Whose music is it?"

2. From *Source Readings in Music History,* compiled and edited by Oliver Strunk. W. W. Norton & Company, Inc., New York, NY. Copyright 1950 by W. W. Norton & Company, Inc. Copyright renewed 1978. Reprinted by permission.

Tibetan monks with trumpets.
© George Holton/Photo Researchers, Inc.

An anonymous seventeenth-century ballad begins,

Are you going to Scarborough Fair? Savory, sage, rosemary and thyme.

Surely the author of this three hundred-year-old verse would have reason to claim ownership of this song. But we know that Paul Simon and Art Garfunkel, two young men from the twentieth century, composed and recorded "Scarborough Fair." The old song had so moved them that they borrowed it and added to it something of their own. However, it could be argued that "Scarborough Fair" is our music. We listen to it and sing it in the shower; we have made it part of us. So despite the great diversity of music and the many possible definitions of it, it is possible for people from different eras and cultures to derive mutual satisfaction from the same music.

As we approach the study of Western classical music or art music, the question "Whose music is this?" may emerge again. Those who are cautious may fear that art music is simply too foreign to them. But re- member that before you became a computer science major or a French major, those languages were probably foreign to you and seemingly beyond your grasp. Or before you became a math major, differential equations were hopelessly foreign to you. And before you decided to pursue premedical studies, even the simplest organism seemed an un- fathomable mystery. But the desire to know and the willingness to work

at learning helped you to override these obstacles. Now the understanding of many concepts in your field are simple and automatic to you.
Too often we forget that such mastery is acquired cumulatively, step-
by-step over time. The same condition prevails in the study of music,
though the mode of study may be new to you.

In the study of most disciplines the brain, eyes, hands, and ears
are employed. The hearing apparatus is, however, merely a conduit for
the information sought. That which we seek is not what we hear; rather,
what we seek is the meaning behind what we hear. The ear provides a
convenient means of getting to the data, the concept, or the interpretation. It serves only as a means to an end. But in music, what we hear is
what we are after. It is the end, not a means to an end. Thus, our study
is conducted by the ear in cooperation with the brain. Sometimes, students new to this subject believe this isn't enough—that the eyes and
hands ought to be doing something as well. The old adage "seeing is
believing" connotes that if the subject matter is visible, our grasp of it
is more secure. The first step in our study is to rid ourselves of this notion
and to allow the ear to work for us.

Broadly speaking, we can identify four categories of music in the
Western world: (1) art music, or classical music; (2) popular music,
(3) folk music, and (4) jazz. Western art music is a cultivated tradition
as its composers are normally equipped with certain technical/learned

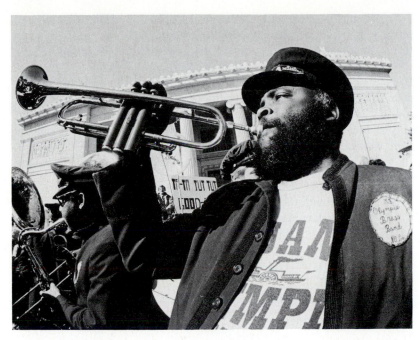

The Olympic Brass Band of
New Orleans performs a jazz
funeral for the King Tut
exhibition.
© AP/Wide World Photos, Inc.

skills, and its audience has acquired the capacity to assimilate lengthy
and often complex musical structures and ideas. The music (or most of
it) is fixed through notation so that it remains approximately the same
each time it is recreated or performed.

Popular music tends to be simpler in some respects, and technically less complex than classical music. The demands on the audience
are different, and the audience is more diverse and vast. Popular music
is generally aimed at commercial success, but, as we shall see, it often
has more redeeming values and makes important sociological commentary.

Folk music in its purest form is generated neither by commercial
nor artistic considerations. It is often functional within the culture, created to accompany or to commemorate certain events important in the
lives of its folk: work songs, lullabies, and accounts of cataclysmic events.
The music lives in oral tradition. It is not notated; instead, it is passed
on from generation to generation through live performances. A folk song
tends to change from time to time, due to the whim and fancy or to the
faulty memory of some purveyor of the song in the chain of its life.

Jazz is an eclectic music whose ingredients are drawn from a variety of sources. These ingredients are reshaped and adapted in unique
ways, so that jazz is distinctly different in some ways from art, popular,
and folk music. Historically, the audience for jazz has been compara-
tively small, but in recent years its appeal has expanded dramatically in
the United States and around the world.

We must also take into account the distinction between sacred and secular music. The difference is evident not so much in purely musical terms, for the two types use or can use essentially the same materials. Rather, the distinction derives from the different functions of the two. In the Middle Ages, the Church fostered and nourished the production of music, some of which exists today in manuscript form. Clearly, this music was designed for sacred purposes. Today, however, we view it not only as the sacred music of the Middle Ages, but also as the art music from that period.

The history of Western art music can be divided into the following stylistic periods:

A.D. 1 through the first millennium	The early Middle Ages. The era of Gregorian chant. All of the music from this era that we will study is sacred music from the early Christian church.
1150–1300	The Gothic period. The emergence of polyphony, a term with which we shall deal later. Thirteenth-century motet.
1300–1450	The Ars Nova period, the late Middle Ages. Sacred music: Mass, motet. Secular music: songs of the trouvères.
1450–1600	The Renaissance. Sacred music: Mass, motet, chorale. Secular music: Italian madrigal, English madrigal.
1600–1750	The baroque. Opera, oratorio, concerto grosso, trio sonata, cantata, keyboard music.
1720–1760	The Rococo or preclassic era. The early symphony and string quartet, keyboard music, concerto, opera.
1760–1800	Classical era. Symphony, string quartet, sonata, concerto, opera, oratorio.
1800–1900	The nineteenth century or romantic era. Symphony, string quartet, sonata, concerto, opera, Lied (art song), tone poem, ballet, music for piano.
1900—	The modern or contemporary era. Symphony, string quartet and other chamber music, sonata, concerto, opera, the emergence of electronic music.

The indicated years of each of these style periods are approximations. The romantic period, for instance, did not begin at 12:01 A.M. on January 1, 1800. One style fades away only gradually and a new one emerges as slowly. Still, however general these dates are, the history of Western art music is a history of periodic stylistic changes and the dates serve as a reminder of these periods.

There are discernible differences between the music of the baroque and the music of the classical periods, and there are reasons for these differences. In part, this study focuses on the characteristics of several styles of music, the differences between those styles and some reasons for the style and taste changes in music. American popular music, rock, jazz, and music of some non-Western cultures are dealt with in section III.

The majority of works discussed in the text are composed by men. Does this mean that women have not been active composers over the centuries? Emphatically no. Indeed there is a long history of women composers that has begun to surface only in recent times. It is clear now that a set of prejudices has historically suppressed such music, or has prevented women from exercising their creativity as composers. It is to be hoped that publication and recordings of women's compositions will increase dramatically in the years just ahead.

To facilitate your study of music, it is necessary to deal with some preliminaries. You will develop a fund of information, terminology, and precepts, both technical and aesthetic, that are common to all music.

The question may arise, "What do I have to do to succeed in understanding these materials?" Regardless of the scope of your background in art music, you should approach this study as a student of music. More than anything else, this will involve listening to music—not simply hearing it, but listening to it—in recorded form and, as often as possible, in live performances. The understanding and love of music are not dependent upon the ability to read musical notation (though of course there is great value in having that ability). Consequently, few examples of musical notation appear in this text. It will, however, be useful to develop some skill in reading rhythmic notation. Particular attention should be given to the discussion of note values and meters in chapter 1.

All of the musical examples mentioned and discussed in the text should be readily available to you in recorded form, and it is important to listen to these recordings. You should have little trouble locating recorded anthologies and song collections of American popular music, rock, and jazz.

SECTION

1

Terms
and
Concepts

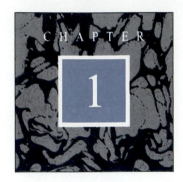

Time
and
Music

Rococo music scene of harpist and two men.

Sounds of the Chapter

J. S. Bach
Brandenburg Concerto no. 2 ♪

Chopin
Waltz, op. 34, no. 2 ♪

Handel
"Halleluja," *Messiah* ♪

Haydn
Symphony no. 101 ♪

Scott Joplin
"The Entertainer" ♪

Time Creates Movement and Change

Buildings, statues, paintings, and even photographs do not stand still. In our memories they may be stationary, immobile objects, but when we actually confront them, we perceive movement. When, for example, we view the magnificent St. Louis Arch, created by Eero Saarinen, we don't see something frozen whole and intact (see fig. 1.1). Rather, our eyes and brain perceive a structure that begins someplace, moves upward and across, then moves on to a landing point elsewhere.

A certain amount of time is required to complete this perception—perhaps only microseconds. Nevertheless, the eyes and brain traverse this span and perceive this structure through a flow of time. Time is the mode of transportation for movement. Movement creates change; thus, time is responsible for both movement and change.

Notice the psychological and emotional changes that occur when time is arrested and movement is thwarted, as in figures 1.2a and b.

a.   b.

Rhythm Organizes Time

Time is a fundamental reality of our existence. The minutes and hours of the clock; the seasons and tides; our every heartbeat, breath, and step; our infancy, childhood, youth, and old age; and all of the countless movements and changes that attend these phenomena—all happen in and are distributed through time. Time is as real to the archaeologist as it is to the hourly employee, as important to the astronomer as it is to the dispatcher.

None of us can ignore, destroy, or will time out of existence. Indeed, we are inclined to make time useful and pleasurable by organizing it in one way or another. When time is organized, it is endowed with **rhythm.** It is rhythm, then, that orders the flow of musical sounds through time. It encompasses all the temporal aspects of music.

Organized time displays rhythm.

Notice that the fence in figure 1.3 has a temporal organization, or a rhythm, consisting of a series of regularly spaced posts of equal size. The series of posts is but one dimension. Notice in figure 1.4 how the personality of the fence changes as we impose another dimension of rhythm upon it: every third post is accented with color.

Rather than being a flat, single-dimensional phenomenon, rhythm has many layers or dimensions. The rhythm of the fence now has two layers: (1) the original series of regularly spaced posts, and (2) the recurring pattern of black, white, white. Each black post marks the beginning of a group of three posts, so it could be called a three-post pattern.

Rhythm has many layers or dimensions, which produce patterns.

In figure 1.5 the fence has yet another rhythmic pattern: each black post marks the beginning of a group of four posts—a four-post pattern.

Figure 1.3

Figure 1.4

Figure 1.5

Beats

The succession of regularly spaced posts of equal size that we see is analogous to a succession of **beats** that we cannot see, but which we hear and feel. Graphically illustrated they appear as:

●   ●   ●   ●   ●   ●   ●   ●

We often respond to these beats in music by tapping our toe or snapping our fingers along with them.

    A succession of beats can be organized into patterns by systematically **accenting** or stressing some beats more than others: the accented beats, which receive more emphasis or force than the other beats, are analogous to the black posts. A three-beat pattern is created by accenting or stressing every third beat:

● ● ●   ● ● ●   ● ● ●   ● ● ●
>   >   >   >

An accented note often has the sign > above or below it.

    By accenting every fourth beat, a four-beat pattern is created:

●●●● ●●●● ●●●● ●●●●
>   >   >   >

By using accenting, some beats are stressed more than others.

Meter

In music, patterns such as we have just described are called **meters.** Each repetition of the pattern is marked off into a **bar,** or **measure,** and in notating music, a **bar line** is drawn at the end of each repetition.

Thus we say that the preceding example displays four bars (or measures) of a three-beat meter. The first beat of each bar is usually the **downbeat** (the accented beat), and the last beat of each bar, the **upbeat.**

The preceding example shows four bars of a four-beat meter.

Many kinds of music—classical, popular, folk, jazz, old, and new—make some use of a rhythmic device called **syncopation.** Syncopation puts the accent on a beat other than the downbeat of a measure or on some portion of a beat other than its beginning. This creates a kind of metrical jerk. Notice how these examples of syncopation put the emPHAsis on the wrong sylLAbles.

Example:

Generally, syncopation seems to work best when it is not overdone; still, the piano rag makes extensive and satisfying use of syncopation in the right-hand part, while the left-hand part steadily plays "on the beat." Listen to Scott Joplin's "The Entertainer."

A meter is a pattern of beats.

Use bar lines to separate each repetition of a metrical pattern.

Syncopation adds interest by accenting a beat other than the downbeat.

The presence of beats and meter in music is almost immediately evident in the first movement of Johann Sebastian Bach's *Brandenburg* Concerto no. 2.

The total rhythmic personality of this piece of music consists of many layers, since time is organized in different ways. The orderly succession of beats of equal duration is merely the simplest and most obvious layer of the music's rhythm. The meter pattern is another layer.

Tempo

In listening to the opening portion of the second movement of the *Brandenburg* Concerto no. 2, a succession of beats and a metrical pattern occurs once more. There is, however, an important and notable difference between the beats of the two movements: the beats of the first movement have a fast pace, while the beats of the second movement have a slow pace. The pace or speed at which music moves is called **tempo.** Tempo is another layer of rhythm. A wide variety of tempos is available in all gradations from very fast to very slow. Here is an abbreviated list of tempo indications commonly used in music.

The tempo of the music is the speed at which it moves.

Term	Translation	Speed or Pace
Largo	Broad	Very slow
Lento	Slow	Slow
Adagio	Slowly	Slow
Andante	Walking pace	Moderately slow
Andantino	Diminutive of andante	A little faster than andante
Moderato	Moderately	Moderate
Allegro	Lively	Fast
Presto	Very quick	Very fast

In some kinds of music it seems somehow "right" to maintain a steady, unflagging tempo from start to finish, perhaps slowing down only at the very end. In other types of music it seems equally appropriate and satisfying to alter the steady tempo by accelerating (**accelerando**) at some points, and by slowing down or retarding (**ritardando**) at other points. This kind of music requires the periodic, purposeful "breaking" of the tempo; the accelerandos and ritardandos seem to add a sense of drama.

Tempo changes within a piece often add drama.

The *Brandenburg* no. 2, first movement, is an example of a kind of music that seems to thrive on and gain its rhythmic vitality from a steady tempo. In contrast, Chopin's *Waltz,* op. 34, no. 2, seems to gain its rhythmic and dramatic punch through the occasional breaking away from a steady tempo. Notice how the tempo speeds up at some points and applies brakes at others. The term applied to a tempo that makes extensive use of accelerando and ritardando is **rubato.** The Chopin *Waltz* is a clear example of the use of rubato.

A rubato tempo speeds up in some places and slows down in others.

A tempo can be temporarily broken with a **fermata** ⌢ , which signifies that a note should be held for longer than its notated duration. Usually a fermata is used for some dramatic purpose, as in "O'er the land of the freeeeeeeeeeeee, and the home of the brave."

Note Values

A piece of music that had only three layers of rhythm—beat, meter, and tempo—would be hopelessly dull and monotonous. To be compelling and satisfying, music requires at least one other layer of rhythm where activity occurs between the beats. In this fourth layer of rhythm, some durations are longer than the basic beat, and some are shorter. The duration of every sound in music, whether it lasts for a beat, for more than a beat, or for less than a beat, has what is called a **note value.** That is, some notes are held through the durational value of two beats, three beats, or more, and some notes last for only a fraction of a beat—one-half of a beat (or toe tap), one-fourth of a beat, one-third of a beat, and so on.

Notes indicate duration of sound.

Organization is achieved on this fourth layer of rhythm with notes. There are several kinds of notes, each having a durational value relative to the others. For example, a figure that looks like a beat with a stem attached to its side ♩ is called a quarter note. A half note ♩ has the durational value of two quarter notes. In other words, a ♩ lasts exactly twice as long as a ♩ lasts. An eighth note ♪ lasts exactly half as long as a ♩ lasts. Thus, it takes two eighth notes, which can be notated as ♪♪ or as ♫ , to equal the value of one quarter note. Allowing for minor changes and refinements, this has been the standard notational system in the Western world since about the late seventeenth century.

Using the quarter note as the standard note value, it is evident from the following chart that all other note values are either multiples or fractions of it.

All notes are either multiples or fractions of quarter notes.

Note values

Quarter notes

Half notes

Whole note

Quarter notes

Eighth notes

Sixteenth notes

Eighth note
triplets

(Here an ♪ = 1/3 the value of a ♩)

Silences between notes are
designated by rests.

Every note value has an equivalent value in silence. In music these silences are called **rests.**

	Note value	Equivalent rest	
Quarter note	♩	𝄽	Quarter rest
Half note	♩	▬	Half rest
Whole note	𝅝	▬	Whole rest
Quarter note	♩	𝄽	Quarter rest
Eighth note	♪	𝄾	Eighth rest
Sixteenth note	♬	𝄿	Sixteenth rest
Eighth note triplets	♫ 3	𝄾 𝄾 𝄾 3	Triplet rests

There are two ways to increase the duration of a note or rest. One method is to place a dot (•) after the note or rest, thereby increasing its duration by fifty percent. For example, a half note has the value of two quarter notes, but a dotted half note has the value of three quarter notes.

Half note   𝅗𝅥 = 𝅘𝅥 𝅘𝅥

Dotted half   𝅗𝅥. = 𝅘𝅥 𝅘𝅥 𝅘𝅥

𝅘𝅥 = 𝅘𝅥𝅮 𝅘𝅥𝅮

𝅘𝅥. = 𝅘𝅥𝅮 𝅘𝅥𝅮 𝅘𝅥𝅮

𝅘𝅥𝅮 = 𝅘𝅥𝅯 𝅘𝅥𝅯

𝅘𝅥𝅮. = 𝅘𝅥𝅯 𝅘𝅥𝅯 𝅘𝅥𝅯

𝄽 = 𝄾 𝄾

The other way to prolong the duration of a note is to join it to another note by means of a **tie** ⌣ . Thus:

𝅘𝅥 ⌣ 𝅘𝅥𝅮 = 3 eighth notes

𝅗𝅥 ⌣ 𝅘𝅥 = 3 quarter notes

     A **meter signature** has two factors—an upper and a lower number. In so-called "simple" meters, such as 4/4 and 3/4, the upper number indicates the number of beats in the metrical pattern; the lower number indicates which note value is the basic beat for the piece of music. Thus, 4/4 indicates a four-beat pattern in which the quarter note is the basic beat. A three-beat pattern, in which the quarter note is the basic beat, is indicated by 3/4. In a compound meter such as 6/8 there are usually only two (not six) beats per bar; each of the two main beats is subdivided into three:

6/8 𝅘𝅥𝅮 𝅘𝅥𝅮 𝅘𝅥𝅮 𝅘𝅥𝅮 𝅘𝅥𝅮 𝅘𝅥𝅮 |

1 2 3 **4** 5 6

The rhythmic notations of the opening few bars of several different pieces of music are illustrated here. They demonstrate a variety of meters, tempos, and note values, the layers of rhythm.

♪ 1. 4/4 Allegro: Handel's "Halleluja" from *Messiah*—simple meter

♪ 2. 3/4 Lento: Chopin's *Waltz,* op. 34, no. 2—simple meter with tempo rubato

♪ 3. 6/8 Presto: Haydn's Symphony no. 101, first movement (following the slow introduction)—an example of compound meter

Begins on an upbeat

♪ 4. 2/4 Moderate: Scott Joplin's "The Entertainer"—simple meter with syncopation

Summary

In chapter 1 you have encountered some of the most basic elements in music—elements that will help you to understand and enjoy the music to come.

Rhythm is the term applied to the organization of time in music, and rhythm is discovered layer by layer. Basic to rhythm are beats. Beats are then organized into patterns called meters. Another layer of rhythm determines the speed, or tempo, at which these patterns progress.

Various types of notes and their durations were presented as either fractions or multiples of the quarter note. If longer duration is necessary, dots and ties can be used. Finally, the method of accenting off of the beat was described and termed syncopation.

Armed with these basics, let's move on.

Key Terms

rhythm	syncopation	presto
beat	tempo	accelerando
accent	largo	ritardando
meter	lento	rubato
bar	adagio	fermata
measure	andante	note value
bar line	andantino	rest
downbeat	moderato	tie
upbeat	allegro	meter signature

Thinking About It

Using some of the terms you have encountered in this chapter, describe some of the rhythmic differences between Handel's "Halleluja" Chorus (example 1) and the Chopin *Waltz* (example 2).

Sound and Music

The Lute Player, Orazio Gentileschi, ca. 1610; canvas; 56½″ × 50⅝″.
National Gallery of Art, Washington, Ailsa Mellon Bruce Fund

Sounds of the Chapter

J. S. Bach
C Minor Fugue, *Well-Tempered Clavier* ♪

Barber
Adagio for Strings ♪

Bartók
Music for strings, percussion and celesta

Beach
"Elle et Moi"

Beethoven
Symphony no. 5
Symphony no. 6, *Pastoral* ♪

Berlioz
Harold in Italy

Borodin
In the Steppes of Central Asia ♪

Boulanger
"Je garde une médaille dèlle"

Britten
Young Person's Guide to the Orchestra

Chopin
Waltz, op. 34, no. 2 ♪

Debussy
Danse sacrée and *Danse profane*
La Mer
Prélude à l'Après-midi d' un faune
Sonata for Flute, Viola, and Harp

Dvořák
Concerto for Cello and Orchestra
Symphony no. 9 (*From the New World*)

Handel
"Halleluja," *Messiah* ♪

Haydn
String Quartet, op. 33, no. 2

Ives
The Unanswered Question ♪

Mendelssohn
Violin Concerto in E Minor

Mozart
Horn Concertos
Queen of the Night aria, *The Magic Flute*

Mussorgsky/Ravel
"Promenade," *Pictures at an Exhibition* ♪

Palestrina
"Agnus Dei," Mass: *Veni sponsa Christi* ♪

Purcell
Variations on a New Ground Bass

Ravel
Boléro

Saint-Saëns
"Elephants," *Carnival of Animals*

Stravinsky
Le Sacre du Printemps

Tchaikovsky
"Dance of the Sugar Plum Fairy," *The Nutcracker*

Varèse
Ionisation ♪

Wagner
Overture from *Tannhäuser*

Stevie Wonder
"Isn't She Lovely"

"Amazing Grace"
"Farmer in the Dell"
"Laudate pueri"
"Laus Deo Patri"
"Scarborough Fair"

Music must have both time and sound.

Music, however defined, has a temporal aspect and a sonorous aspect. Without time and sound, music cannot exist. In chapter 1, some of the ways in which time relates to music were examined. In this chapter something of the nature and uses of sound in music are explored.

When a flexible body such as a taut string, a strip of wood or metal, or a column of air is set into motion, it vibrates until its energy is spent. As it vibrates it displaces the air molecules that rested on its formerly dormant surface. This sets off a chain reaction in which wave after wave of molecules is displaced. If you are situated close enough to such an activity, and if the motion is begun with enough force, your eardrums will pick up the motion and will begin to vibrate. At this moment you experience the sensation of hearing.

Sound is created by vibration.

Unless you have a hearing impediment, your ears pick up sounds more or less constantly: sounds produced by nature, traffic, other mechanical devices, and, of course, music. Fortunately we have the capacity to block out some unwanted sounds while we focus on other sounds that are more interesting and pleasurable at the time. If such were not the case, it would be very difficult for us to listen attentively to music.

Experience tells us that there is a great variety and differentiation of sounds: thunder does not sound like a canary, a snare drum does not sound like a guitar, nor does applause sound like an airplane.

Most *musical* sounds, however, have the following attributes in common:

1. Definite pitch. A given sound is perceived as relatively high or low because of **pitch.** For example, the keys on the far left-hand side of the piano keyboard produce very low pitches; those on the far right-hand side produce high pitches. Every pitch vibrates with a specific **frequency**—it vibrates a certain number of times per second. The higher the frequency, the higher the pitch.

The frequency of the vibration determines the pitch.

2. Timbre, or tone color. **Timbre** is the quality characteristic of and peculiar to a given instrument. A flute playing a given pitch sounds distinctly different from a trumpet playing the same pitch, and the trumpet sounds different from a piano, a banjo, or a bagpipe playing the same pitch.

The same pitch sounds different on different instruments because of timbre.

3. Volume, or amplitude. **Volume** or **amplitude** is the degree of loudness or softness. In music, volume is notated with these symbols:

p (soft)	*mp* (moderately soft)	*pp* (very soft)	*ppp* (softer still)
f (loud)	*mf* (moderately loud)	*ff* (very loud)	*fff* (louder still)

These are referred to as **dynamics.**

Pitches and Intervals

Pitches are the basic units of which musical sounds are created. Every pitch is assigned a letter name, or a letter name plus one of these symbols: ♯ (called a **sharp**), or ♭ (called a **flat**). Both sharps and flats are termed **accidentals.** A ♯ raises the pitch of a letter name; thus C♯ is higher in pitch than C, but lower than D. A ♭ lowers the pitch of a letter name; thus B♭ is lower in pitch than B, but not as low as A.

  The distance that separates one pitch from another (either higher or lower) is called an **interval.** A brief survey of the piano keyboard will help us to identify the names of pitches, and to understand the nature of various intervals used in making music.

An interval is the distance between two pitches.

The Octave System

Refer to figure 2.1, which illustrates a portion of a piano keyboard. Notice that the white keys have been assigned the letter pattern c-d-e-f-g-a-b, followed by the same sequence, C-D-E-F-G-A-B. C is the octave of c, D is the octave of d, and so on. The **octave** is the simplest, purest interval in our tuning system. C sounds almost exactly like c except that its pitch is higher. Similarly, D sounds like d, E like e, and so forth. This is acceptable without knowing its mathematical-acoustic foundations because it is sensed quite naturally. D does not sound like the octave of c, nor do any of the other letter names; only C sounds like the octave of c.

  The black keys, arranged in groups of twos and threes on the keyboard, also have letter names. As seen in figure 2.1, each black key has two letter names such as c♯ and d♭, and d♯ and e♭. This is simply a notational convenience. In some musical contexts it is appropriate to call a given black key c♯; in other contexts it is appropriate to call the same black key d♭. The important point to remember is that a black key (like a white key) produces only one pitch that sounds the same regardless of whether it is called by its ♯ or its ♭ name.

Each piano key produces one pitch.

  Notice, too, that the octave system also applies to the black keys: C♯ is the octave of c♯, B♭ is the octave of b♭.

Figure 2.1

Majors and Minors

If you play any two adjacent keys, you've produced a minor, and if you skip one key in between you've produced a major second.

The smallest interval commonly used in Western music is called a **minor second** (or a half step, or semitone). A minor second can be produced by playing successively or simultaneously any two adjacent keys on the keyboard: for example, c to c♯, or e to f, or g to g♯, or b to c. The next largest interval is called a **major second** (or a whole step, or whole tone). This interval can be produced by playing any two keys that are separated from each other by one intervening black or white key. For example, c to d is a major second, as are e to f♯, g to a, and b to c♯.

Another way of determining the size of a major second is to note that it encompasses the distance of two minor seconds. Thus, the major second, c to d, contains within it the minor seconds c to c♯ and c♯ to d. An octave encompasses the distance of twelve minor seconds: c to c♯, c♯ to d, d to d♯, d♯ to e, e to f, f to f♯, f♯ to g, g to g♯, g♯ to a, a to a♯, a♯ to b, b to C.

This is a convenient way of judging other intervals such as minor third, major third, perfect fourth, augmented fourth, perfect fifth, minor sixth, major sixth, minor seventh, major seventh, as well as those intervals larger than an octave, such as minor ninth, major ninth, minor tenth, and major tenth. Figure 2.2 illustrates various intervals in music notation.

Figure 2.2

As we have just mentioned, an octave contains twelve half steps; for example, the octave c–C contains:

c c♯ d d♯ e f f♯ g g♯ a a♯ b C
   1   2   3   4   5 6   7   8   9 10 11 12

This succession is one kind of musical scale—the chromatic scale—which includes all of the pitches from c to its octave C.

Another very important kind of scale, called the diatonic scale, contains fewer pitches and has a different internal intervallic structure from the chromatic scale. There are, in fact, two kinds of diatonic scales: major and minor. Each has seven pitches plus the octave, for a total of eight pitches; 1 indicates a whole step, and ½ indicates a half step.

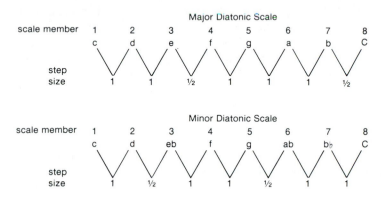

Notice the different placement of whole steps and half steps in the major and minor diatonic scales.

Other arrangements of half steps and whole steps create other scales. For example, each of the ancient church modes contains its own unique scale: the piano's white keys in the octave d to D comprise the Dorian mode, e to E the Phrygian mode, f to F the Lydian mode, and g to G the Mixolydian mode. These modal scales formed the basic pitch materials of Western music for many centuries, but beginning in the seventeenth century, they were abandoned in favor of the major and minor scales.

Modal scales were used for centuries before they were abandoned for major and minor scales.

Modal scales have survived, however, in folk music, and in recent times many jazz and rock musicians have employed them.

Melody

When a series of pitches and its attendant intervals is wedded to a set of note values a **melody** results. A melody has no fixed shape; it may be very active and employ many different pitches and intervals, or it can be fairly static, restricting itself to only a few pitches and intervals. Whatever the case, nearly all melodies have some upward and downward motion, some variety of pitches and intervals. A melody stuck on one pitch invites boredom. Prove this to yourself by singing any song you know (the "Star Spangled Banner," for example), using the correct rhythm, but singing it in its entirety on only one pitch.

We combine a series of pitches and a set of note values to produce a melody.

Figure 2.3

Melody A - Amy Beach: "Elle et Moi" (1895)

Melody B - Chopin: Waltz, op. 34, no. 2

Melodies exhibit both wide and narrow ranges.

The **range** of a melody is the distance between its lowest and highest notes. Without even being able to read the specific pitches notated in figure 2.3, it should be evident that melody A covers a wide range, while melody B has a narrow, restricted range.

There is also no standard or ideal length for a melody. Moving at a moderate tempo in 3/4 meter, "Amazing Grace" takes sixteen bars to unfold (fig. 2.4), while "Farmer in the Dell," moving at a quicker tempo and in 2/4 meter, is complete in only eight bars (fig. 2.5).

Melodies are made up of phrases.

Generally speaking, melodies contain shorter units of activity called **phrases.** The end of a phrase is a temporary resting place—a place to catch a breath, similar to a comma in a sentence. The melody "Amazing Grace" contains four phrases: the first phrase ends in bar four on the word *sound;* the second phrase ends in bar eight on the word *me;* the third phrase ends in bar twelve on the word *found;* and the concluding phrase of the melody ends in bar sixteen on the word *see.*

Very short melodies are termed motives.

An even shorter piece of melodic material is referred to as a **motive.** The opening seconds of Beethoven's Symphony no. 5 present what may well be the best-known motive in the history of Western art music. Like most motives, this one consists of only a few notes, is very brief, and yet is memorable.

In large-scale instrumental works the word **theme** is often used in place of melody. For now, it is wise to accept this as a convention without worrying about the technical differences that exist between a melody and a theme.

Figure 2.4

Amazing Grace

Figure 2.5

The Farmer in the Dell

Harmony and Chords

Thus far we have been talking about pitches that are emitted successively—one after another, one at a time. In conjunction with rhythm these successions create melodies, motives, or themes. These are linear and analogous to the line that defines the horizons observed in nature.

But we know from experience that sounds in music can be emitted more than one at a time. When different pitches are sounded simultaneously they create **harmony.** The building blocks of harmony are **chords.** A chord is a set of three or more pitches sounding together—vertical stacks of pitches. When one chord leads to the next, a **chord progression** is created.

Three or more pitches sounding simultaneously create a chord.

Figure 2.6

Lili Boulanger: "Je garde une médaille d'elle" (1914)

In figure 2.6, notice the diverse natures of melody and harmony. The pitches of the melody are emitted successively (horizontally), while the chords in the accompanying harmony progress as vertical units.

Harmony Reflects Change

The nature of harmony has changed over the ages.

While it is presumed that the earliest music in the Western world was strictly melodic, there is proof that musicians were aware of harmony by at least the early Middle Ages. The history of harmony reveals a series of periodic changes in attitudes and preferences where sonorities, or chords, are concerned. The chords and the harmony preferred by the medieval world differed in some ways from the chords and harmony favored in the Renaissance. Still another set of chordal and harmonic preferences was evident in the baroque, and tastes and preferences have continued to change up to the present.

The notion of what is satisfying and beautiful harmony, then, has not remained constant. Twentieth-century audiences may perceive medieval harmony as crude and filled with displeasing sounds, yet, were it somehow possible for a person from the eleventh century to hear the harmony of "Scarborough Fair," it is safe to assume that the modern rendition would sound chaotic to that person.

Chords Create Harmony

A chord may contain many different pitches. If you gently place your forearm on the keyboard of a piano and depress as many keys as is possible, a chord with many pitches is produced. The sound of the chord may be unpleasant and would not likely be used to accompany any part of the melody "Amazing Grace." If the same operation were performed on only the black keys of the keyboard, the resultant chord might seem less abrasive, but it probably wouldn't sound like the correct accompaniment for "Amazing Grace" either. Only certain carefully selected chords, arranged in a particular order, seem to harmonize the hymn's melody in a satisfactory way.

The System of Functional Harmony

Of the many possible combinations of pitches, relatively few form the basis of the harmonic system that has prevailed and dominated musical practice in the Western world for the past 250 years or so. This system is known as **functional harmony,** or **tonality.** This is a system of organizing chords to produce the sense of being in a key. Music written in accordance with the principles of this system produces a central chord around which all other chords revolve. The chords in this system are built of stacks of major and minor thirds, forming **triads** (consisting of root, third, and fifth), **seventh chords** (consisting of root, third, fifth, and seventh), and other more complex chords.

Properly arranged, these chords produce harmony. A central chord to which all other chords progress—rather like a gravitational system—emerges from this harmony.

In music this phenomenon is referred to as "keyness," or being in a **key.** Every key has seven pitches, which are family members. They belong to the key and can be used melodically and as members of chords. These seven pitches are called **diatonic.** For example, the key of C has the following diatonic pitches:

C D E F G A B (C)
1 2 3 4 5 6 7 (8—octave)

All other pitches—C♯, E♭, F♯, B♭, etc.—are nonfamily members of the key of C and are called **chromatic** pitches in that key. The central or key chord is called the **tonic** (or I). The way in which the chords are arranged in the system of functional harmony gives the tonic a sense of repose and finality. No other chord has this distinct quality, and indeed, a primary function of the tonic chord is to end a piece of music. The piece would not sound as if it were truly ended if it terminated on any chord other than the tonic.

The **dominant seventh** (or V_7) chord has two primary functions: to create harmonic tension by sometimes resisting the gravitational pull of the tonic; and to progress ultimately to the tonic. Thus V_7 resolves into I. The function of the **subdominant** (or IV) chord is to lead to the dominant. Essentially then, the system of functional harmony operates in a cyclical fashion: I leads to IV, which leads to V_7, which leads to I. In practice this simple formula is overlaid and interlaced with a rich diversity of other chords and chord progressions, both diatonic and chromatic, that interrupt, forestall, and greatly enhance this inexorable cyclic flow. The chord vocabulary of functional harmony is thus greatly expanded.

The horizons of functional harmony are also expanded by use of **modulation.** This process makes it possible to shift temporarily in the course of a piece of music from the original, central, overriding key to another key. This allows a piece of music that begins in one key to modulate to one or more other keys and then return to the starting key. The process is different from, but related to, a visual experience called an optical illusion. But a critical difference between a modulation and an optical illusion is that once established, an optical illusion remains unstable, whereas a modulation in music is a temporary move and the return to the original key is both inevitable and stabilizing.

The system of functional harmony is further enriched by two related but differing **modes:** the major and minor mode. A piece can be in the key of C major (major mode) or in the key of C minor (minor mode). In either case, the chord built on the pitch C will be the tonic. If the tonic triad is minor, the key and the mode are minor. If the tonic triad is major, the key and the mode are major. Usually, the minor mode sounds "darker" than the major mode.

Nearly all harmonic systems, including functional harmony, have the conflicting forces of **consonance** and **dissonance** built into them. Consonance, or a consonant chord, is analogous to a state of repose or relaxation, as in sinking into a comfortable chair after running a mile. Dissonance, created by chromatic pitches and chords, is, on the other hand, similar to a state of restlessness and tension, as in the actual heart-pounding, foot-thumping running of the mile. For reasons of health and sanity, this action must eventually wind up in an easy chair. Similarly, the mixture of consonance and dissonance in music is, and always has been, necessary. We must remember, however, that dissonance and consonance are relative terms, and that what is dissonant to the ears of one era or culture might be consonant, or relatively so, to another era or culture.

Texture

Texture refers to the number of lines or voices in a piece of music, and to the quality and activity of those lines. A few technical terms are useful in the description and comprehension of the texture of music. Other descriptive, nontechnical adjectives will also help account for the number and quality of voices, as well as the activity of those voices as they create a musical texture.

Modulation allows changes in key within a piece of music.

Consonant chords convey relaxation, while dissonant chords convey tension. Music demands a combination of the two.

Texture comprises the number of lines or voices in music, as well as their quality and activity.

Love, by Robert Indiana, 1968, aluminum, 12″ × 12″ × 6″, illustrates the dissonance of the letter *O*.

Collection of Whitney Museum of American Art. Purchase with the funds from the Howard and Jean Lipman Foundation, Inc., Acq. #68.71

Monophonic Texture

A texture consisting of only one musical line or voice is called **monophonic.** Singing, whistling, or humming without any accompaniment creates a monophonic texture. It is important to remember, however, that monophony does not necessarily imply a single or solo voice; several people singing the same melodic line without adding any harmony creates a texture that is monophonic.

    If you sing a song alone at a volume level of *p, mp,* or *mf,* the monophonic texture created might be further described as thin or light. If the song is sung at the top of your lungs, the texture will still be monophonic, but a different descriptive adjective, such as full or heavy, would be more appropriate. If ten of your friends sing the song in unison with you, the texture would still be monophonic, but is more accurately described as dense.

A melody with no complementary harmony has monophonic texture.

Polyphonic Texture

When two or more different lines are performed simultaneously, as in harmony, the texture is defined as **polyphonic.** The two major branches of polyphonic music are (1) **homophonic** and (2) **contrapuntal.**

    In a homophonic texture, one line, the melody, predominates any of the accompanying or harmonizing lines. A church hymn in four-part harmony and a solo song with chordal accompaniment are examples of homophonic texture.

    In **counterpoint,** or in a contrapuntal texture, two or more different lines are equally prominent and compelling. Thus, attention is divided between two or more independent melodies rather than focused on one. This kind of texture is also known as **nonimitative counterpoint** because

Two branches of polyphonic music are (1) homophonic, where the melody dominates the harmony, and (2) contrapuntal, where two or more lines are equally prominent.

the voices do not repeat, or imitate, one another. In some contrapuntal
textures, however, a given melody or subject may be stated in one voice
and then restated or imitated in another voice or voices of the texture.
This special kind of contrapuntal texture is imbued with **imitative counterpoint.** The lead voice performs the subject first and then proceeds to
other material while, in succession, a variable number of voices follow
and echo the subject. Graphically illustrated, imitative counterpoint looks
like this:

In imitative counterpoint, the
theme in the lead voice is
restated or imitated in another
voice or voices of the texture.

```
voice 1  XXXXX (the subject)_____(other material)_____
voice 2            XXXXX_____
voice 3                  XXXXX_____
voice 4                  XXXXX_____
```

A **fugue** is a type of composition based on imitative counterpoint.

Some contrapuntal works employ a subsidiary melody or subject
which is combined with and, in fact, competes with the main subject. A
subsidiary subject or melody of this kind is called a **countermelody.**

A countermelody is a
subsidiary melody that adds to
and sometimes competes with
the melody.

The following examples illustrate the various kinds of harmonic
language and textures.

1. Antiphon—"Laus Deo Patri," Psalm 113, "Laudate pueri."
   (Found in the recorded anthology *Masterpieces of Music Before
   1750,* no. 1.) This is an example of monophonic music. The
   rhythm is nonmetrical.

2. Parallel Organum. (Found in the previously mentioned anthology, no. 6.) This is the earliest known type of polyphony in the Western world. It dates from about the ninth century A.D. Notice the hollow, mysterious quality of the harmony.

3. "Agnus Dei" from the Mass *Veni sponsa Christi* by Palestrina. This is a polyphonic texture with imitative counterpoint. We are still not in the realm of functional harmony, but the harmony here has a lovely, almost ethereal quality. This kind of harmonic language and texture was favored in the late Renaissance.

4. Henry Purcell: *Variations on a New Ground Bass* (seventeenth century). (Found in the same anthology, no. 38.) Notice the repetitive nature of the lowest line in the texture, the bass line. This repetitive bass line, called a **ground bass,** is one kind of **ostinato.** An ostinato is a figure, line, or rhythm, usually fairly short, that is repeated doggedly throughout the course of a piece or an extended section of it.

An ostinato is a figure, line, or rhythm used repeatedly in a composition.

5. J. S. Bach: C minor Fugue from the *Well-Tempered Clavier,* Book I. The baroque fugue is considered the soul of imitative counterpoint. By Bach's time, functional harmony definitely had been established as *the* harmonic system of the Western world.

6. Handel: "Halleluja" from *Messiah* (1741). The harmony in this piece is definitely functional. Some sections of the piece are homophonic, as at the beginning, while some sections are contrapuntal, such as, "And He shall reign forever and ever."

7. Dvořák: Symphony no. 9, *From the New World,* second movement (1893). The majestic introduction and the solo that follows are both homophonic. Notice that the harmonic language is more lush, more melancholy, and somewhat more dissonant than the previous examples.

Musical Instruments

Considering the diversity and geographical distribution of the many, many cultures throughout recorded history, and remembering that these cultures have always created music, it should not be a surprise that hundreds, if not thousands, of different musical instruments have been invented. However, only a fraction of these are in consistent use in the Western world today. The modern major symphony orchestra is composed of about one hundred members; still it normally employs only a few types of string, woodwind, brass, keyboard, and percussion instruments. A typical rock group usually employs only one or two kinds of guitar, keyboard, and percussion.

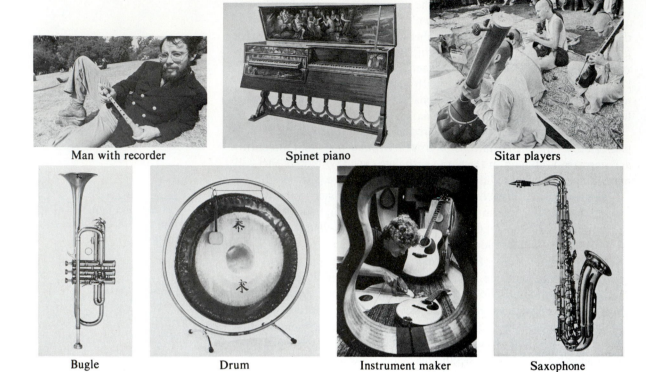

Man with recorder   Spinet piano   Sitar players

Bugle   Drum   Instrument maker   Saxophone

Musical instruments from various parts of the world.

Man with recorder—© Robert Eckert/EKM-Nepenthe; spinet piano—© The Wurlitzer Co.; sitar players—© John Maher/EKM-Nepenthe; bugle—Courtesy, G. Leblanc Corporation; drum—Courtesy, Selmer; instrument maker—© Jill Cannefax/EKM-Nepenthe; saxophone—Courtesy C. G. Conn, Elkhart, Ind.

Consider your voice as an instrument. Which category is it in?

Musical instruments are manifold, and whatever their age, provenance, or type, they have at least one thing in common: they are all manmade, with the exception of the oldest and most universal of all, the human voice.

Voices

This instrument is listed in the plural since there are so many different kinds of voices, all of which produce a nearly infinite variety of timbres and nuances. Consider, for example, the differences between the singing voices of children and those of adults, and the differences between male and female, high and low adult voices.

Adult voices are categorized as follows:

Male		Female	
Tenor	High	Coloratura	Very high
Baritone	Medium	Soprano	High
Bass	Low	Mezzo soprano	Medium
		Contralto (or alto)	Low

Different styles of music require different vocal qualities and techniques. The quality of the rock singer's voice is different from that of the church choir singer, the country/western singer, the folk singer, the jazz singer, or the opera singer. Even within the framework of rock music, voice qualities vary considerably from performer to performer—from Elvis Presley, to Little Richard, to Frankie Avalon, to the Beach Boys, to the Beatles, to Madonna, to Billy Joel, to Tracy Chapman, and so forth.

Human voices are very satisfying as solo instruments, as accompanied soloists, in small and large groups, in groups of men or women, and in mixed groups. The remarkable human voice also blends well with many kinds of instruments.

A spectacular display of the prowess of one human voice is evident in a rendition of the Queen of the Night aria for a coloratura soprano from Mozart's opera, *The Magic Flute*. Equally compelling and electric, in its own way, is Stevie Wonder's rendition of his song, "Isn't She Lovely?"

The Orchestra Family

The concept of the orchestra dates back to the baroque era. At that time the orchestra was considerably smaller than it is today. It employed some instruments that have since dropped from use, and did not include others that have been gradually incorporated since then.

The orchestra was introduced in the baroque era.

The seating arrangement of the modern symphony orchestra, diagramed in figure 2.7, shows the various instruments arranged in groups or families: stringed instruments, woodwinds, brass, percussion, plus the piano and harp. Every family has several members, each with particular capabilities. Some members of a family are designed to play the high part of the texture, some a little lower, some in the middle range, and some at the bottom of the texture. This corresponds roughly to the distribution of human voices: soprano, alto, tenor, and bass.

Strings   Generally speaking, the string family has been the backbone of the orchestra since its inception. This family consists of first violins, second violins, violas, violoncello (or cello), and double basses.

The string family is made up of first violins, second violins, violas, violoncello, and double basses.

The two basic ways of producing sounds from these instruments are: **bowing**—pulling the bow across the strings to produce a smooth or **legato** sound; and **pizzicato**—plucking the strings with the end of the finger. A small wooden device called a mute can be placed over the strings to produce a veiled or muffled sound.

String instruments can be played in two ways: by bowing and by plucking (pizzicato).

The violin, viola, cello, and string bass have proven to be remarkably versatile, and a considerable repertoire of solo, chamber, and orchestral music has been written for them. Listen, for example, to the solo violin in Mendelssohn's Violin Concerto in E Minor; to the solo viola

Figure 2.7
Seating arrangement for orchestra.

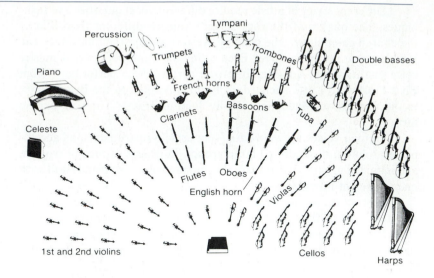

in Berlioz's *Harold in Italy;* to the solo cello in Dvořák's *Concerto for Cello and Orchestra;* and to the string bass in Saint-Saëns' "Elephants" from *Carnival of Animals.* The wonderful way in which the voices of violins, violas, and cellos blend has inspired many composers to write string quartets. Haydn's String Quartet, op. 33, no. 2, is but one glorious example. Samuel Barber's *Adagio for Strings* reveals the warmth and beauty of an entire string section.

The modern chromatic harp, with all its heavenly connotations, has many ancient ancestors who are found virtually all over the world. The harp in today's orchestra was developed in the late eighteenth century, but it came into real prominence only about a century later with works such as Debussy's *Danse sacrée* and *Danse profane,* and his *Sonata for Flute, Viola, and Harp.* Several of Debussy's orchestral scores also feature important and prominent parts for harp, *Prélude à l'Après-midi d'un faune (Prelude to the Afternoon of a Faun),* and *La Mer,* among them.

Woodwind instruments are: flutes, oboes, English horns, clarinets, saxophones, and bassoons.

Woodwinds   The woodwind family is composed of the flute, oboe, English horn, clarinet, various saxophones and bassoon, many of which have historical prototypes. The flute, in one form or another, is an ancient instrument. During the baroque era, the flute entered the orchestra as a permanent member.

The cello lesson

Viola   Violin

Guitar, bass, violin, banjo

Double bass   Cello

String duet

Harp

Stringed instruments.

The cello lesson—© Jill Cannefax/EKM-Nepenthe; viola, violin—Courtesy Scherl and Roth; guitar, bass, violin, banjo—© Jill Cannefax/EKM-Nepenthe; double bass, cello—Courtesy Scherl and Roth; string duet—© Jill Cannefax/EKM-Nepenthe; harp—Courtesy, Salvi Company.

    The oboe, too, has ancient ancestors, but its modern form was developed mainly by the French in the late seventeenth century. The English horn, whose tonal quality resembles that of the oboe, entered the orchestra in the early nineteenth century. The bassoon and its deeper-voiced brother, the contrabassoon, were known in the sixteenth century and were part of the orchestra in the baroque. The oboe, English horn, and bassoon are double-reed instruments. They produce a woody and somewhat nasal sound.

Many woodwinds have long histories.

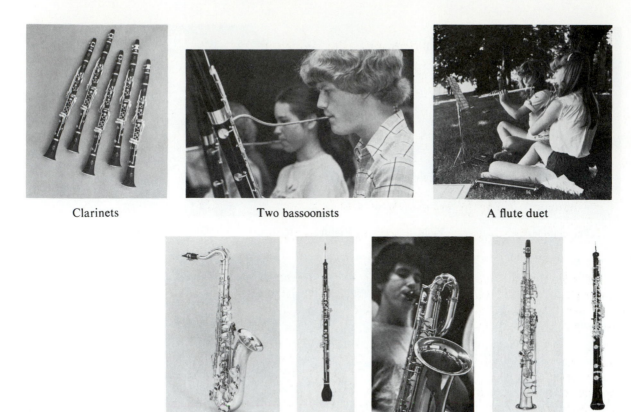

Clarinets   Two bassoonists   A flute duet

Tenor sax   English horn   Jazz on baritone sax   Soprano sax   Oboe

Woodwind instruments.

Clarinet—Courtesy, King Musical
Instruments; two bassoonists—© John Maher/
EKM-Nepenthe; a flute duet—© Jill
Cannefax/EKM-Nepenthe; tenor sax—
Courtesy, Selmer; English horn—Courtesy, G.
Leblanc Corporation; jazz on baritone sax—
© Robert Eckert/EKM-Nepenthe; soprano
saxophone—Courtesy, Selmer; oboe—
Courtesy, King Musical Instruments.

The saxophone is not an official
member of the orchestra.

The clarinet and saxophone are single-reed instruments that produce a more mellow sound, particularly in their middle ranges. Although some composers, beginning in the late nineteenth century, wrote
parts for saxophone, they never became official, permanent members of
the symphony orchestra. However, they found a home in jazz and in
some forms of popular music. The clarinet, on the other hand, became
a permanent member of the orchestra beginning in the very late eighteenth century.

To get acquainted with the timbres of the woodwinds, listen to the
following works in which they are prominently featured.

Flute

Debussy: *Prélude à l' Après-midi d'un faune (Prelude to the
Afternoon of a Faun).*
J. S. Bach: Any of the sonatas for flute and harpsichord.

Oboe
> Beethoven: Symphony no. 6 *(Pastoral),* third movement, ♪
> allegro. After an opening passage, mainly for strings, the
> oboe has a playful solo. The oboe is then joined by a solo
> bassoon, a solo clarinet, and a solo French horn. This
> passage is repeated a little later in the movement.

English horn
> Borodin: *In the Steppes of Central Asia.* ♪
> Dvořák: Symphony no. 9, *From the New World,* second
> movement, largo.

Clarinet
> Borodin: *In The Steppes of Central Asia,* beginning. ♪

Bassoon
> Stravinsky: *Le Sacre du Printemps (The Rite of Spring),*
> beginning.

The woodwind quintet, consisting of flute, oboe, clarinet, bassoon, and French horn, is an integral part of chamber music, especially in more recent times. Woodwind quintets by Anton Reicha, Jacques Ibert, and Walter Piston are available in recorded form.

A woodwind quintet is made up a flute, oboe, clarinet, bassoon, and French horn.

Brass   The brass family of the orchestra includes the trumpet, trombone, French horn, and tuba. In one form or another the trumpet and trombone were known in the late Middle Ages, while the tuba is a more recent invention. By the early nineteenth century these instruments were members of the symphony orchestra, and the trumpet and trombone have become standard instruments in jazz as well. Various mutes can be inserted into the bell end of brass instruments to dramatically alter their tone colors.

The members of the brass family are the trumpet, the trombone, the French horn, and the tuba.

The following examples will help acquaint you with the sounds of the brass instruments.

Mutes can be used to change the tone color of brass instruments.

French horn
> Mozart: Any of the *Horn Concertos*

Trumpet
> Mussorgsky/Ravel: *Pictures at an Exhibition,* beginning ♪

Trombone
> Wagner: Overture from *Tannhäuser*
> Ravel: *Boléro*

Tuba
> Britten: *Young Person's Guide to the Orchestra*

Tuba   The high school concert band   French horn

Trumpet   Trombone

Brass instruments.

Tuba—Courtesy, King Musical Instruments;
Concert band—© Jean Claude Lejeune/EKM-
Nepenthe; French horn, trumpet, trombone—
Courtesy, Selmer

Percussion instruments include
the timpani, glockenspiel,
chimes, xylophone, vibraphone,
snare drum, bass drum,
cymbals, gongs, triangle,
tambourine, wood blocks,
castanets, gourds, and
maracas.

Percussion   Some percussion instruments are among the oldest musical instruments known, and yet in the Western world at least, the percussion family has only recently received the special attention that other
instrumental families have enjoyed for some time. In this respect many
African and Asian musical cultures are far ahead of the Western world,
and have been for a very long time. Fortunately, in our century some
composers have begun to tap the rich, manifold vein of percussion instruments.

   Of the percussion instruments most commonly employed in the
modern symphony orchestra, some have definite pitch and some do not.
Those with definite pitch include the timpani (tunable "kettle" drums),
glockenspiel, chimes, xylophone, and vibraphone (having either wooden
or metal bars or tubes that are struck with mallets). The snare drum,
bass drum, cymbals, gongs, triangle, tambourine, wood blocks, castanets, gourds, and maracas have indefinite pitches. These latter are essentially rhythm instruments.

   Edgard Varèse's *Ionisation* (1931) is an excellent introduction to
the special qualities and capabilities of percussion instruments. The piece
requires thirteen players and thirty-seven percussion instruments. Bartók's *Music for Strings, Percussion and Celesta* provide other excellent

Gettin' into it

Cymbals of various sizes

Trap set with bass drum, snare drum, side drums, two tom-toms, ride cymbal, high hat cymbal

examples. Technically, the celesta is a member of the percussion family even though it is a keyboard instrument, and in practice is usually played by the pianist in the orchestra. The most celebrated celesta solo is Tchai-kovsky's "Dance of the Sugar Plum Fairy" from *The Nutcracker.*

Percussion instruments.

Trap set—Courtesy, Remo, Inc.; playing drums—Frank Sitemen/EKM-Nepenthe; cymbals—Courtesy, Avedis Zildjian Company

Summary

This chapter is essentially about two things: musical sounds and the instruments that produce these sounds.

Pitches are the basic sound material of music. Every pitch has certain characteristics including frequency (highness or lowness), volume (loudness or softness), and timbre or tone color (determined by the instrument playing the pitch). In cooperation with rhythm, pitches can be combined in several different ways to create melody, harmony, and texture.

A melody, motive, or theme consists of a rhythmized succession of pitches and intervals. The texture of an unaccompanied melody is called monophonic.

When three or more pitches are sounded together, they create a chord. A succession of chords produces harmony. Most of the music with which we are most familiar adheres to the principles of a system called functional harmony. In that system certain kinds of chords and chord progressions are used to produce the sense of being in a key. The tonic, dominant seventh, and subdominant chords are central to this "keyness," and all chords, consonant and dissonant, must ultimately resolve to the tonic.

A contrapuntal texture is a special type of polyphonic texture in which two or more musical lines are equally compelling. Imitative counterpoint consists of a lead voice or line and one or more following voices. The following voices, each in turn, imitate or echo the subject first presented by the lead voice.

In addition to the various ranges of the human singing voice, every instrument has its special tone quality or timbre. The instruments of the modern symphony orchestra are divided into the following groups or choirs: strings, woodwinds, brass, and percussion.

Key Terms

pitch	theme	texture
frequency	harmony	monophonic
timbre	chord	polyphonic
volume (amplitude)	chord progression	homophonic
dynamics	functional harmony	contrapuntal
sharp	(tonality)	counterpoint
flat	triads	nonimitative
interval	seventh chords	counterpoint
octave	key	imitative
minor second (half	diatonic	counterpoint
step, semitone)	chromatic	fugue
major second	tonic	countermelody
(whole step,	dominant seventh	ground bass
whole tone)	subdominant chord	ostinato
melody	modulation	bowing
range	modes	legato
phrase	consonance	pizzicato
motive	dissonance	

Thinking About It

In terms of texture, what is the difference between Bach's C Minor Fugue ♪ (from the *Well-Tempered Clavier*) and Borodin's *In the Steppes of Central Asia*? ♪

Henry Purcell's *Variations on a New Ground Bass* features an ostinato. How would you describe an ostinato? Can you think of a rock song or songs that contain an ostinato? What is a modulation?

CHAPTER

3

Form
and
Music

The Boston Ballet's production of "Swan Lake."

© AP/Wide World Photos, Inc.

Sounds of the Chapter

J. S. Bach
French Suite no. 1 in D Minor ♪
St. Matthew Passion

Beethoven
Piano Sonata in F Minor, op. 2, no. 1
Piano Sonata no. 8 in C Minor, op. 13 ♪
Piano Sonata in Ab Major, no. 12, op. ♪
  26
Symphony no. 3 (*Eroica*)

Brownie and Sonny
"I'm a Stranger Here" ♪

Ray Charles
"Someday"

Chopin
Mazurka, op. 63, no. 3 ♪
Mazurka, op. 67, no. 3 ♪

Debussy
"Beau Soir"
"La Flute de Pan" ♪

Rudolph Friml
"Indian Love Call"

Handel
Messiah
"Tonami a vagheggiar," *Alcina*

Haydn
"Minuet," Symphony no. 92
Piano Sonata no. 37 in D Major ♪
Piano Sonata in E Minor ♪
String Quartet, op. 76, no. 3

Billy Joel
"Just the Way You Are"

Scott Joplin
"The Entertainer" ♪
"Maple Leaf Rag" ♪

Little Richard
"Tutti Frutti"

Glen Miller
"In the Mood"

Mozart
Piano Sonata in Bb Major, K.333
Symphony no. 40 in G Minor ♪

Elvis Presley
"Hound Dog"

Ravel
Pavane pour une Infante défunte

Jimmy Reed
"I Was So Wrong"

Schubert
Die Erlkönig ♪
"Gute Nacht," *Die Winterreise*
"Who is Sylvia?"

Clara Schumann
"Liebst du um Schönheibt" ♪

Pinetop Smith
"Pinetop's Boogie Woogie"

Stephen Sondheim
"Send in the Clowns"

Otis Spann
"Good Morning Mr. Blues"

Tchaikovsky
"March," *The Nutcracker* ♪
"Overture Miniature," *The Nutcracker* ♪

"A Froggie Would A-Courtin' Go"
"Amazing Grace"
"Battle Hymn of the Republic"
"Down in the Valley"
"My Country 'Tis of Thee"
"The Star Spangled Banner"
"Wondrous Things of Thee Are
  Spoken"

Music: The Evolving Message

It has been said that "Time ensures that everything doesn't happen all at once." This quote is applicable to the experience of listening to pieces of music, as well as to life in general.

If a piece of music were really a "piece" in the ordinary sense of the word, then it should be tangible and observable as a whole. Clearly, "piece of" is not the intended meaning where musical compositions are concerned, for a piece of music is neither tangible nor something that happens all at once. Music unfolds over a span of time; it does not appear as an entity that is visible as a whole. It becomes meaningful to us as we absorb the content of each passing phase of the span and relate each phase to the others. The more fully we grasp the contents and sense the interrelationships of a given piece of music, the more intimately we know it. In essence, then, knowledge of the form or structure of a given work rests on the perception and understanding of its various parts and how they relate to one another.

The composer's work involves piecing together the various separate musical ideas he or she invents to form a larger musical whole that has continuity. We as listeners do not have the burden of inventing these ideas, but our grasp of a piece is dependent upon our ability to perceive its continuity. Musical chaos would result without this ability. Where the true appreciation of music is concerned, it would be difficult to overrate the importance of being able to hear form.

> To grasp a piece of music, we must be able to perceive its continuity.

It is important to analyze form on more than one level. If a landscape were observed from 10,000 feet in the air, its structure is perceived in one light. From an altitude of 500 feet, the perception of the structure begins to change in some ways: the general outlines observed from 10,000 feet are out of sight (but not out of memory), but new and significant information is gained. For example, the shaded areas are now revealed as patches of trees, and the snakelike line comes into focus as a river. A walking tour of the landscape presents an infinite variety of detail and the interrelationships of the many parts, large and small, are visible.

Similarly, the structure of musical compositions can be examined. This examination can proceed from the general to the particular or vice versa. Either the whole piece or merely individual movements of a multimovement work can be examined, as can the sections that make up the piece or movement, the subsections, the phrases, or even the motives.

Musical Bookkeeping

To assist these analyses, a kind of musical-structural bookkeeping method is employed. Capital letters designate sections of a piece, and lowercase letters designate subsections. If a section or subsection is repeated exactly or nearly exactly during a piece, its letter is repeated in the analysis. For example, the diagram *ABA* indicates that there are three sections

> Capital letters designate sections of a piece, and lower case letters designate subsections.

in the piece, the last of which is a repetition of the first. When a nonliteral repetition occurs, the analysis reads: *ABA'*. The *A'* indicates that the repetition is nonliteral but nevertheless recognizable as the content of *A*.

A' indicates a nonliteral repetition of *A*.

There is no fixed length for a section of music; in a large-scale work, such as a symphonic movement, a section may be lengthy. In a small work, such as a song or a short piece for the piano, a section of music may be brief. Whatever the scale, a section can be loosely defined as a musical unit that has internal cohesion and reaches a conclusion. A section can terminate with a momentary pause or it can run directly into the next section. In either case, the beginning of a new and contrasting section is usually marked by some notable change in content. Many popular songs such as "Send in the Clowns" (Stephen Sondheim) and "Just the Way You Are" (Billy Joel) have the form *AABA* on the level of the section.

A section is a musical unit that has internal cohesion and reaches a conclusion.

Lowercase letters are used to mark the constituents of sections. Again, the length and duration of a subsection is variable. In some works a subsection can be a short phrase; in others it can consist of several phrases. A diagram of the formal structure of "Send in the Clowns," and the corresponding length of these sections, looks like this:

level of the section	*A*	*A*	*B*	*A*
level of subsections	*abc*	*abc*	*def*	*abc*
	(:27)	(:24)	(:34)	(:34)

Some forms have been used consistently through long periods of music history: the ternary, binary, rondo, twelve-bar blues, and sonata-allegro forms.

Ternary: *ABA* or *AABA*

The simple **ternary** form *ABA* is found in many kinds of music spanning centuries. It has proven to be not only aesthetically pleasing, but also psychologically rewarding. The reiteration of *A* creates a pleasing sense of symmetry. Moreover, the restatement of *A*, given its particular location within the form, has another value: it reintroduces the familiar. When confronted with a series of events, each of which is new and unpredictable, we tend to become uneasy or bored. But the recurrence of one or more of the events has a reassuring effect.

It is true that in a fine piece of music each component has a purpose, but it does not necessarily follow that every element is as important as others. In most ternary forms, the content of *A* is the most important material. In a sense it is ultimately what the piece is all about, and so it lingers in our memories. In an *ABA* form, *A* is clearly in a position of prominence: the *A* section is stated twice; it is the first thing we hear as well as the last.

In the *ABA* form, the content of *A* tends to be of primary importance.

The presence of *B* is a necessary diversion.

However, *B,* too, is important in the ternary form. It must be present to ensure the success of the form. If *B* were not included, nothing would remain but a succession of *A* statements. No musical material, however compelling and gripping, can stand alone for very long. The presence of *B* interrupts *A* and focuses our attention on something new before we begin to get "too much of a good thing." The *B* section is designed to be diversionary, but not reactionary. It contains enough interest and contrast to attract our attention, yet it does not overpower *A*. The return to *A* is all the more satisfying precisely because of the diversionary activity of *B*.

Listeners find the ternary form *ABA* especially pleasing.

Composers have made frequent use of the *ABA* form, and audiences from different cultures and eras have long found it satisfying. The ternary form, for example, is found in the literature of nineteenth-century piano music. The form of Mazurka, op. 67, no. 3, by Frederic Chopin, is diagramed and discussed in the following "Sound and Sense." (The term **opus** [or op.] means work or composition. Many composers, including Chopin, used opus numbers in ordering their compositions chronologically.)

Many of the Sound and Sense listening guides in this text are accompanied by a "time line" indicating the length of the sections or subsections. These approximations are given in minutes or seconds and appear under or next to the letters used in the graph. These may be of assistance when listening to a given work for the first time or two. But they should be abandoned as soon as they have served their purpose, for the ultimate goal is not to "watch the clock," but to listen to, correctly perceive, and enjoy the music.

Sound and Sense
ABA **Form**

Title: Mazurka, op. 67, no. 3 (1846)
Composer: Chopin
Meter: 3/4
Tempo: Allegretto
Key: C major

A Closer Look

A		*B*	*A*
aa'	*aa'*	*bb'*	*aa'*
(:25)	(:25)	(:14)	(:27)

This is a brief example in which *A* is dominated by a single idea, and the short *B* section consists of a single, contrasting idea.

Notice that the material in *B* of this piece contrasts with that in *A* in terms of harmony, melody, rhythm, and, to some extent, range, although its range is more restricted than the range in *A*.

Mazurka, op. 67, no. 3, concludes with a section called a **coda** (Italian for "tail"). A coda is simply an ending formula or a musical stop sign. (A more extensive examination of the nature of the coda at various stages of history appears in chapter 7.)

Coda means tail—and acts as a musical stop sign.

Chopin's Mazurka, op. 63, no. 3, is a longer and somewhat more complex example of ternary form.

Sound and Sense
Complex *ABA* Form

Title: Mazurka, op. 63, no. 3 (1846)
Composer: Chopin
Meter: 3/4
Tempo: Allegretto
Key: C♯ minor

A Closer Look

A	*B*	*A'*	*Coda*
aa' bb'	*cc' (or d)*	*aa''*	___
(:45)	(:25)	(:25)	(:21)

The two subsections of *B* resemble each other, yet the second of them seems to grow organically and develop a unique structure from the first. Hence, we have the option of calling it either *c'* (if we feel strongly about its relationship to *c*) or *d* (if we feel it is more autonomous).

The return to the *A* section includes a subsection that is a nonliteral repetition of neither *a* nor *a'*. Still it is clearly derived from the content of *a*, so it is designated *a''*.

Large compositions—symphonies or concertos—consist of a number of individual entities called **movements.** For example, a classical symphony normally consists of four movements.

A large-scale ternary form was used as the third movement of most eighteenth- and nineteenth-century symphonies. Beethoven and other romantics used a dance in 3/4 time called the **scherzo** for this purpose. Classical composers, Haydn and Mozart among them, preferred another triple-meter dance called a **minuet.** The minuet has the form minuet-trio-minuet *(ABA)*. The third movement, "Minuet," from Haydn's Symphony no. 92, is diagrammed here.

Classical symphonies usually contain four movements.

The minuet has an *ABA* form.

Sound and Sense

Minuet

Title: Symphony no. 92, third movement (ca. 1788)
Composer: Haydn
Recording: Szell, Cleveland Orchestra
Meter: 3/4
Tempo: Allegretto
Key: G major

A Closer Look

A (minuet)	*B* (trio)	*A* (minuet)
aa'ba'ba'	*ccdc'dc'*	*aba'*
(2:17)	(2:28)	(1:08)

As you listen to this example you will notice that the diagram does not list everything that happens. For example, four smaller segments are subsumed under *a*. Notice, too, that the most notable change in content occurs at section *B* with the entrance of the French horns.

The third movement of Symphony no. 40 in G Minor by Wolfgang Mozart (1756–91) is another minuet-trio-minuet.

Sound and Sense

Minuet-Trio-Minuet

Title: Symphony no. 40 in G Minor, third movement (1788)
Composer: Mozart
Meter: 3/4
Tempo: Allegretto
Key: G minor

A Closer Look

A (minuet)	*B* (trio)	*A* (minuet)	
aa'a''a'''	*bcb*	*a*	
(1:34)	(1:52)	(:48)	(Dorati, London Symphony)

This movement is somewhat more compact than the Haydn example, as all of the material of Section *A* is derived from a single idea—*a*—and several nonliteral repetitions of it. Here again, the most notable change in content begins at *B,* a section that is largely dominated by the woodwinds. This contrasts with the two *A* sections that are dominated by the string instruments.

The third movement of Beethoven's Symphony no. 3, the *Eroica* symphony, is a scherzo-trio-scherzo—*ABA* design. Once more, the most obvious change in content occurs at the trio *(B)* with the entrance of the French horns.

Ternary form is also found in the field of vocal music. A special kind of operatic song called a da capo aria was particularly favored by opera composers in the baroque era. "Tonami a vagheggiar," from the opera *Alcina* by George Frederic Handel, is a da capo aria having the formal structure *ABA*. The same is true of the arias, "He was despised" from Handel's *Messiah,* where the *B* section begins with the words "He gave his back to the smiters," and of "Grief and pain" from J. S. Bach's *St. Matthew Passion,* where the *B* section begins with the words, "May the anguish of my spirit." (Additional examples of ternary form, as well as other forms discussed in this chapter, are listed at the end of this chapter.)

Beethoven's *Eroica* symphony exhibits the *ABA* form in its third movement.

Binary: *AB* or *AABB*

Although it seems logical that a two-part structure would be easier to grasp than a three-part structure, it is generally not true in music. The impact of **binary** *AB* is very different from that of ternary *ABA*. Binary form lacks the return to *A* and the psychological comfort that accompanies this return. *A* must make its point without the benefit of a restatement. *B* must be equal in force with its partner *A;* otherwise the piece would have a lame ending and would lack justification.

The dance suite from the baroque era contains many examples of binary form. The French Suite no. 1, in D minor, by J. S. Bach, contains six short dance movements: allemande, courante, saraband, menuet I, menuet II, and gigue. All are cast in the binary form *AABB* (the menuet II does not repeat *B*). In most cases, *A* begins on tonic and ends on dominant, and *B* begins on dominant and ends on tonic.

In these pieces, one of the functions of *B* is to provide contrast to *A*. The degree of contrast, however, presents a problem. If the contrast is violent and overpowering, the piece loses all sense of unity, particularly in view of the fact that *A* is not repeated. *A* and *B* would sound like two different pieces rather than as partners in a single work. It is the composer's difficult task, then, to make *A* and *B* sound like separate entities that are recognizable as related parts of a larger entity.

Binary form means two-part structure, in which *A* and *B* are of equal importance.

The composer must make the *A* and *B* sections in binary form work as partners in the piece.

Bach provided an ingenious solution to this problem in the six movements of the French Suite no. 1, in D minor. The *B* section begins with a variation of the opening material of the *A* section in each case. In the allemande, the opening gesture of *A* is inverted (turned upside down) at the beginning of *B*. The same is true of the courante and the gigue. In the saraband, the opening gesture of *A* is in the highest part; the same gesture at the opening of *B* is found in the lowest part. Once this unifying connection is made, the *B* section is free to proceed to contrasting material.

Rondo: *ABACA, ABACADA,* or *ABACABA*

It is evident from the **rondo** diagram that it keeps "coming 'round to" the *A* section. The recurrences of *A* are separated by sections of contrasting materials. In many rondos, the *A* sections are all in the tonic key and the contrasting sections are in some other key(s). Two movements, one by Haydn and another by Beethoven, both diagrammed below, illustrate how the rondo works.

The rondo form is characterized by the recurrence of *A*.

Sound and Sense ♪

Rondo

Title: Piano Sonata no. 37 in D Major, last movement (1780)
Composer: Haydn
Meter: 2/4
Tempo: Presto
Key: D major

A Closer Look

A—aabb, tonic key		(:35)
B—ccdd, tonic key		(:35)
A—aabb, tonic key		(:35)
C—eee'e'f, subdominant key		(:42)
A—a'b'b', tonic key		(:35)

Sound and Sense ♪
Rondo

Title: Piano Sonata no. 8 in C Minor, op. 13, second movement
(in A♭ Major) (1799)
Composer: Beethoven
Meter: 2/4
Tempo: Adagio
Key: A♭ major

A Closer Look

A—aa	(:58)
B—bc	(:47)
A—a	(:33)
C—dd'	(:48)
A'—a'a'	(:54)
Coda	(:38)

Many American rags have a structure that is reminiscent of the rondo. The typical rag, like the rondo, has five or more sections. But unlike a rondo, the sections are often all in the tonic key, and the *A* section is repeated only once instead of two or more times. On the section level, both "The Entertainer" and "Maple Leaf Rag" have the form *ABACD*, compared to a common rondo form *ABACA*.

"The Entertainer" has a ♪ slightly different rondo form.

Twelve-Bar Blues: *AA'B*

The **twelve-bar blues** probably developed as a poetic form in the late nineteenth century. Early in its history, however, singer-musicians and instrumentalists breathed music into it and created an extraordinarily versatile musical form.

All twelve-bar blues have the melodic and poetic structure *AA'B*.

Both the melodic and poetic structures follow the same format. The poetic structure consists of an opening line in which a problem or situation is presented, a second line in which, for the sake of emphasis, the problem or situation is repeated, and a third line in which a conclusion or outcome is introduced.

A Well, I'm feelin' so bad all the live long day.
A Well, I'm feelin' so bad all the live long day.
B Think I'll go down to the river and throw my poor self in.

The melodic form, likewise, has the same melodic phrase for both the first and the second *A;* a different melodic phrase is sung to *B*. Examples of this poetic/melodic form are plentiful in the three record anthology,

The Best of the Blues (Sine Qua Non 103/3), one of several fine recorded anthologies of blues readily available to the public. A few of the twelve-bar blues from this collection are "Good Morning Mr. Blues" (Otis Spann), "I Was So Wrong" (Jimmy Reed), "I'm a Stranger Here" (Brownie and Sonny) and "Someday" (Ray Charles).

Most twelve-bar blues are in 4/4 time—all of the above examples are in 4/4. Return to the examples and determine the length of each of the three sections: How many measures or bars long is *A?* the second *A? B?* When it has been determined that *AAB* equals four bars plus four bars plus four bars, the reason this form is called the twelve-bar blues is obvious. There are also blues patterns of eight bars, sixteen bars, and others, but the twelve-bar blues is employed most often.

The twelve-bar blues also has a basic harmonic formula:

Content	*A*				*A'*				*B*			
Bar	1	2	3	4	1	2	3	4	1	2	3	4
Chord	I	–	–	–	IV	–	I	–	V_7	–	I	–

With only slight modifications, the twelve-bar blues form and its attendant harmonic scheme are found in a variety of music that succeeded the blues. The scheme is often found in boogie woogie, of which "Pinetop's Boogie Woogie" by Pinetop Smith is a good example. It is also found in the big band repertoire of the swing era, as in Glenn Miller's "In the Mood." Little Richard's "Tutti Frutti," and Elvis Presley's "Hound Dog" are examples of the twelve-bar blues format in early rock and roll music. Contemporary rock music, too, often employs the twelve-bar blues form.

Sonata-Allegro

The word sonata has two meanings in music. It can designate a genre of musical composition, such as a piano sonata, a violin sonata, or in the baroque era, a trio sonata. Or, as it is used in this text, the **sonata-allegro** form (for short, sonata form) refers to a specific musical structure.

As the twelve-bar blues is to blues, jazz, and some types of popular music, so the sonata-allegro form is to Western art music of the past two hundred years. The form is ubiquitous; it is found in one or more movements of the symphony, the concerto, the string quartet, and the sonata.

The form crystallized in the classic era of the mid-eighteenth century after a period of experimentation. With some modifications, the sonata-allegro form has survived to the present day.

The form has the following elements: exposition-development-recapitulation-coda.

The **exposition** section introduces the principal thematic materials of the movement. Often, but not always, there are two contrasting themes—*A* and *B*—and a closing theme—*C,* which frequently is reminiscent of the *A* theme. The themes don't follow one another back to back, but are joined by a connective non-thematic section called a **bridge.**

Twelve-bar blues format is found in boogie woogie, big band, early rock and roll, and today's rock music.

The sonata-allegro form contains: exposition-development-recapitulation-coda.

In the sonata-allegro form, the exposition introduces the dominant themes.

The exposition section is normally repeated verbatim. Materials bracketed by these signs, [: :] , are repeated literally. Thus the exposition section of the sonata form is diagramed:

A _____ B
(Tonic key) (modulatory bridge   (Dominant key or   (Bridge) C (or A')
            section)   relative minor)

This diagram is obvious in the exposition section of the first movement of Mozart's Symphony no. 40 in G Minor. When listening to the piece, note the contrasting characters of *A* and *B*. *A* is rather jagged, whereas *B* is more lyrical.

After the repetition of the exposition section, the form proceeds to the development section wherein one or both of the themes introduced in the exposition section are developed. The **development** section has no set length, nor does it behave in any prescribed way, but it usually deals with thematic materials from the exposition section. These materials are developed so that new characteristics are revealed.

A theme can be developed in any or all of the following ways:

1. All or part of a theme can be cast in a series of different keys. The development section is usually harmonically restless and is marked by frequent changes of key.
2. A theme can be tossed about the orchestra (in the case of instrumental works), played first by one group of instruments, then by another.
3. A theme can be combined with a countermelody that vies equally for attention.
4. A theme can be pulled apart or broken into fragments. Notice that in the Mozart example an extended patch of the development plucks the first three notes from the *A* theme and repeats them several times at different levels. It is as if this fragment of the theme were being put under a microscope.

The development section is filled with tension and struggle; the developing theme seems to fight for its life. This turmoil is resolved with the **recapitulation,** where everything is reordered. This section is very similar to the exposition in terms of content and the order of events. A major difference, however, is that in the recapitulation, both *A* and *B* are in the tonic key, so the movement ends in the tonic rather than the dominant.

The sonata-allegro form concludes with a coda. Sometimes the coda is little more than the ending formula mentioned earlier. Often, though, in large-scale movements such as the Mozart example, the coda is extended. In fact, the coda has nearly the proportions and the activity of another development section in the Mozart Symphony, no. 40. in G Minor.

In the development section of the sonata-allegro form, new characteristics of the theme are revealed.

The turmoil experienced in development is resolved in the recapitulation.

Sonata-allegro form ends with a coda.

Theme and Variations: A Process

All of the forms discussed thus far are means of organizing musical ideas to make them comprehensible. Theme and variations is not so much a set structure as it is a process, but, like any useful form, it too is a means of organizing musical ideas. In a theme and variations, there is no set length, no prescribed number of sections, and no established policy governing repetition and contrast. The process allows considerable freedom so composers from the Renaissance to the twentieth century have displayed great affection for it.

Creating Variations

The theme comprises not only the melody but also the harmony and formal structure of the theme section.

Variations are created by changing note values, adding notes or rhythmic devices, and changing the environment.

A theme and variations begins with a full statement called, logically, the theme. **Theme** in this case implies not only the melody, but the harmony and the formal structure of the section called the theme. A number of other sections, called **variations,** follow. These variations are created in two basic ways: the melody itself is varied (through ornamentation, change of note values, other added notes, or rhythmic devices); or the melody is retained in its original state, but its environment is changed from one variation to the next.

The second movement of the Haydn String Quartet, op. 76, no. 3, is an example of the environmental variation. Listen first to the theme section itself—the melody may be familiar as the hymn "Wondrous Things of Thee are Spoken." This section has the form *aa'bcc,* which is retained in each of the four variations that follow the theme section. In each of these four variations, the melody is stated in its original form and is clearly recognizable. However, the environment in which the melody is found changes. In the first variation, the texture is reduced to two instruments, one carrying the melody, the other weaving a countermelody around it. In the second variation the melody is given to the cello, and two of the other strings carry a new countermelody. All four instruments are active in the third variation: the viola has the melody and there are new countermelodies above and below it in the texture. In the fourth and last variation, the melody is returned to the first violin which quietly carries it to a high singing range. The movement concludes with a brief coda.

The first movement of Beethoven's Piano Sonata in A♭ Major, no. 12, op. 26, is an example of a theme and variations in which the melody itself is varied. The theme section has the ternary form *aa'ba'.* Notice as you listen to the five variations that this structure is retained throughout. Each of the variations has a traceable relationship to the melody of the theme section, although some are more clearly discernible than others. For example, in the first variation, the quick notes added in the right-hand part do not obliterate the original melody; in the second variation, the left-hand part is closely related to the melody; but the third variation only faintly echoes the melody.

Song Structures

There are two basic types of song structure: strophic and through-composed. These terms apply only to songs, not instrumental or keyboard music.

Strophic

"O'er the land of the free and the home of the brave" are usually the last words heard in "The Star Spangled Banner" although they are not the last words in the song. They are merely the final words in the first stanza. The other four stanzas are rarely sung, but when they are, they are sung to the same music as the first stanza. This structure, where multiple stanzas are all sung to the same strand of music, is called **strophic.** Many hymns, art songs, folk songs, and popular songs are strophic. "Amazing Grace," "Battle Hymn of the Republic," "Down in the Valley," "A Froggie Would A-Courtin' Go," and "My Country 'Tis of Thee" are all strophic, as are the art songs "Who is Sylvia?" by Franz Schubert and "Beau Soir" by Claude Debussy.

A strophic song has multiple stanzas, all sung to the same strand of music.

Through-Composed

The opposite of strophic is **through-composed,** a type of song in which new music is composed for each stanza of the poem and no section of music is repeated. Through-composed songs are not numerous outside the field of art song, but Schubert's *Erlkönig* and Debussy's "La Flute de Pan" are fine examples of the type.

New music is composed for each stanza of a through-composed song.

Modified Strophic

A third type of song structure—**modified strophic**—combines aspects of both strophic and through-composed. In Schubert's "Gute Nacht" from the song cycle *Die Winterreise,* the first two stanzas are sung to the same music, the third stanza is sung to a slightly different version of the same music, and the fourth and last stanzas employ the same music, changed from the minor mode to the major.

Modified strophic combines the strophic and the through-composed types of song structure.

Text Setting

There are two basic ways of setting a text to a melody—syllabic and melismatic. A **syllabic** setting is one in which there is one note of the melody for each syllable of the text, as, for example, in "My Country 'Tis of Thee." A **melismatic** setting uses two or more melodic notes with several syllables of text, as in "Indian Love Call" (on the words "you" and "too").

Additional Examples of the Formal Types Discussed in This Chapter

Sound and Sense

Ternary *ABA* Form

Title: Piano Sonata in F Minor, op. 2, no. 1, second movement (1795)
Composer: Beethoven
Meter: 2/2
Tempo: Allegro
Key: F minor

A Closer Look

A—aa'ba''
B—cc'd
A—aa, both ornamented
ba, both ornamented
Coda

Sound and Sense ♪
Ternary *ABA* Form

Title: "March" from The Nutcracker, *op. 71a (1891–92)*
Composer: Tchaikovsky
Meter: 4/4
Tempo: Allegretto
Key: G major

A Closer Look

A—a, trumpets; *b*, strings; *aba'*, low brass *abab*	(:58)
B—c, flutes; *c*	(:14)
A—a''b'aba''abab	(:58)

Sound and Sense ♪
Binary *ABAB* Form

Title: "Overture Miniature" from The Nutcracker, *op. 71a (1891–92)*
Composer: Tchaikovsky
Meter: 2/4
Tempo: Allegro guisto
Key: B♭ major

A Closer Look

A—aaba	(:45)
B—cc	(:47)
A—aaba	(:45)
B—cc	(:35)
Coda	(:15)

Sound and Sense ♪

Rondo Form

Title: Pavane pour une Infante défunte (orchestral version) (1910)
Composer: Ravel
Recording: Slatkin, St. Louis Symphony
Meter: 4/4
Tempo: Lento
Key: G major

A Closer Look

A—a, French horn dominates	(1:05)
B—b, oboe and winds dominate; *b*, strings	(1:20)
A—a, clarinet and flute dominate	(1:07)
C—c, flute; *c′*, clarinet; *c* and *c′* repeated	(1:30)
A—a, flute dominates	(1:23)

Sound and Sense

Sonata-Allegro Form

Title: Piano Sonata in B♭ Major, K. 333, first movement (ca. 1779)
Composer: Mozart
Recording: R. Cassadesevs, piano
Meter: 4/4
Tempo: Allegro
Key: B♭ major

A Closer Look

Exposition

    A—a (:16)   *a′* tonic key
    Bridge (:19)   modulates to

    B—b (:39)   *b′* dominant key

    C—c (:41)

Development
The *A* theme is developed and there are several changes of key (:50)

Recapitulation
A—a, tonic key; *a'*
Bridge
B—b, tonic key; *b'* ⎤
Bridge   ⎥— (2:02)
C—c   ⎥
Coda   ⎦

Sound and Sense
Sonata-Allegro Form

Title: Piano Sonata in E Minor, first movement (1778)
Composer: Haydn
Recording: Arthur Balsam
Meter: 6/8
Tempo: Presto
Key: E minor

A Closer Look

Exposition
    A—a, tonic key; *a'*   (:17)
    Bridge   (:21)
    B—b (new key of relative major), *b'*   (:21)
    (repeat entire exposition verbatim)

Development
The *A* theme is developed and there are several changes of key (:47).

Recapitulation
    A—tonic key
    Bridge   ⎤
    B—b, tonic key; *b'*   ⎥— (1:05)
    A—a fragment of *a* closes the movement ⎦

Summary

In this chapter you have been exposed to various forms composers use to organize their musical ideas. You've learned to identify and record many of the most frequently used forms.

    Musical bookkeeping allows us to record the intangible forms of the music we hear. Capital letters designate sections of pieces and lower case letters designate subsections. The ternary form *ABA* indicates a piece of music made up of three sections, with section three repeating section one. This repetition offers reassurance and satisfaction to the listener.

Binary form, *AB* or *AABB*, offers no repetition. In this form the two sections must work hand in hand to create cohesion within the piece.

In rondo form we return to the *A* section repeatedly. Rondos can be composed in a variety of ways, including *ABACA, ABACADA,* and *ABACABA.*

Twelve-bar blues form has the common poetic and melodic structure *AAB,* along with a basic harmonic formula. You've probably heard this form in current rock music.

The sonato-allegro form is recognized by its structure: exposition, development, recapitulation, and coda. Mozart's Symphony no. 40, first movement, is a good example of this form.

Using theme and variations, the composer establishes a theme and then employs numerous devices to vary that theme. The note values or the rhythm or the environment might change from one variation to the next.

Songs usually display one of two basic structures. If a song has several stanzas sung to the same music, the structure is strophic. If each stanza of the song is sung to a different music, and no music line is repeated, the structure is through-composed. A third structure alternative is merely a combination of the two basic forms: modified strophic shows characteristics of both.

Your newly acquired knowledge of form, and the method for recording this nontangible aspect of music, will help you to improve your listening skills and to appreciate similarities and differences found in various types of music.

Key Terms

ternary	rondo	theme
opus	twelve-bar blues	variations
coda	sonata-allegro	strophic
movement	exposition	through-composed
scherzo	bridge	modified strophic
minuet	development	syllabic
binary	recapitulation	melismatic

Thinking About It

Construct a Sound and Sense listening guide for Simon and Garfunkel's
"Scarborough Fair." Include a formal analysis on the level of the section
and the subsection, and comment on meter and other rhythmic details,
texture, and instrumentation.

    Repeat the assignment for Joplin's "The Entertainer."   ♪

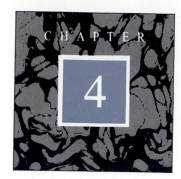

Meaning
and
Music

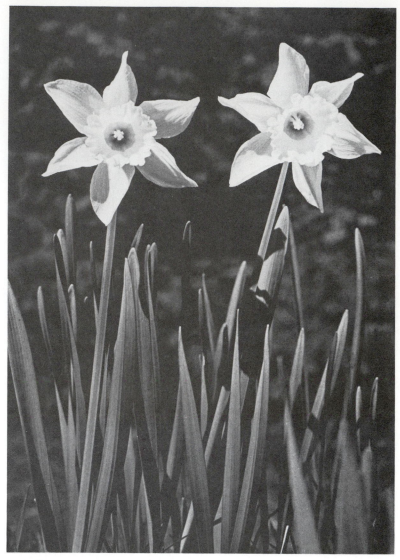

Daffodils.
© Tim Jewett/EKM-Nepenthe

Sounds of the Chapter ♪

Barber
Adagio for Strings

Bartók
"The Night's Music," *Out of Doors*

Beethoven
Symphony no. 6 (*Pastoral*) ♪
Symphony no. 7

Debussy
"Nuages," *Nocturnes*

Ives
The Unanswered Question ♪

Mendelssohn
Hebrides Overture
Italian Symphony
Violin Concerto

Vivaldi
"Spring," *The Seasons* ♪

von Weber
Der Freischütz ♪

Music Transcends Words and Objects

Emotions, thoughts, and visions are difficult to express without stumbling over too many words or groping for a single word that escapes consciousness. Yet some individuals are capable of expressing their thoughts with an economy of words and an accuracy that invites others to thrill in the emotion.

William Shakespeare undoubtedly possessed this capability. The following extract exemplifies the superior quality of his work.

> . . . daffodils,
> That come before the swallow dares, and take
> The winds of March with beauty . . .
> (Shakespeare: *The Winter's Tale* IV, iv. 118–20)

Is this *only* an assemblage of words? If the answer is yes, then perhaps there is no such thing as poetry. If the answer is no—this is not *only* an assemblage of words—then perhaps it is true that there is something meaningful beyond the words: something inspired by the words, but not limited to them. The meaning transcends the words themselves.

But what is the meaning? Does this pair of lines mean something about daffodils? About swallows? About the winds of March? The lines speak of all three, but ultimately they evoke a condition, a season, an atmosphere, and a mood to which the daffodils, swallows, and winds are only accessories.

In a context other than this poetry, the daffodil has its own phenomenological identity that is observable, knowable, and appreciable. The same is true of the swallow and the wind. But in the context of this poetry, something of the separate identities is lost or forgotten—they are no longer *only* phenomena. The separate identities are surrendered to a larger entity having a meaning of its own.

Perhaps then, the special magic of the poet is that he or she can take well-known phenomena, such as daffodils, swallows, and wind, and blend them together to produce a more profound meaning.

The great French painter, Paul Cézanne, once exhibited a painting entitled *Apples*. A critic chided him, saying, "That doesn't look like apples." Cézanne replied, "It's not apples, it's appleness." Clearly the larger essence was more important than the objects, and the meaning of Cézanne's painting far exceeded the boundaries of the objects.

The profundity of Shakespeare's poetry cannot be explained by words beyond a very general level. The impact of the poetry and the meaning it communicates is undeniably real. The fact that we cannot always express it in so many words does not deny its existence, it merely demonstrates the occasional poverty of words.

It is possible to speak of meaning in generalities. For example, a particular piece of music might evoke tears in most listeners. Obviously,

The force of poetry often cannot be expressed in words.

Basket of Apples, by Paul Cézanne, ca. 1895, oil on canvas, 65.0 cm × 80.0 cm, described by the artist as "appleness" (see colorplate 9).

sadness is embedded in the meaning of the piece. But certainly the specific meaning, the reason for the sadness, will vary from listener to listener. Each listener brings a unique set of experiences, memories, associations, and expectations to the piece. The listeners are alike enough to recognize the general quality of sadness, but sufficiently individual to have personal, particular interpretations of it.

The meaning of music varies with each listener.

The Language of Music

Many of the temporal and sonorous aspects of a piece of music are exposed with careful study—its meter, tempo, melody, harmony, texture, form, and instrumentation. It is also possible to speak confidently about the style, genre, date of composition, and composer of a given piece. The fact that a piece is in 4/4, is essentially homophonic, is in rondo form, and is played by a string quartet can be verbalized, but it is impossible to state with certainty what the piece means even when the composer states the meaning. Only individual interpretations or a general consensus is possible.

Structural aspects of music can be identified, but the meaning is individualized by the listener.

In an age and a culture so dependent on proof, it seems strange that the inability to identify the specific meaning of a given poem or composition does not matter. In fact, the pleasure and the profound experience of the poem or the composition is not depreciated by this inability. This is perhaps the magic, not of the poet, but of poetry itself—

Not all feeling evoked by music should be confined to words.

the experience is so real that any attempted explanation would only be an interference. Felix Mendelssohn wrote, "The thoughts which are expressed to me by music that I love are not too indefinite to be put into words, but, on the contrary, too definite."

Music is a special kind of language, but like any language, it is merely a conduit for communication. Some of these messages are explored here.

Music and Description

Music has the capacity to produce believable **descriptions** or imitations of things beyond itself. These things are found primarily in nature and possess sound and motion, such as babbling brooks, bird calls, thunder, breezes, falling rain, and lightning. The attempt to describe these things in music has intrigued composers for a long time: pieces with bird call imitations were performed at least as long ago as the fourteenth century. But music made exclusively of these descriptions is very limited, and tedium develops quickly. The music is impoverished and robbed of its more profound functions. The meaning of the music is evident, but it quickly induces boredom.

Music composed to imitate nature's sounds exclusively becomes tedious.

Used judiciously and sparingly, however, descriptions of this kind can be useful and meaningful in music. Writing in the mid-eighteenth century, the British critic Joseph Avison said, "If the composer uses imitation [i.e., description] in a general way, it should succeed in bringing the object before the hearer, rather than in forcing a comparison between the object and the sound."

Judicious use of descriptive music is found in Vivaldi's "Spring."

Vivaldi's "Spring" from *The Seasons* is a delightful piece of music that uses descriptions judiciously. Listen to the first movement of this work in which bird calls, gentle breezes, a rainstorm, and the calm after the storm are described. Another convincing use of descriptive music is found in the Wolf's Glen Scene from act 2 of Carl Maria von Weber's opera, *Der Freischütz*. In the last four minutes of the scene, a series of magic bullets is cast. The casting of each is followed immediately by patches of extraordinary music, describing in succession a flock of night birds, a wild boar, a hurricane, wheels, cracking of whips, trampling of horses, barking of wild dogs, and thunder and lightning. Here the descriptions are ingenious, not so much because they are so strikingly realistic, but because they add so much to the overall atmosphere of the scene.

Music and Interpretive Description

Music has the additional and more subtle capacity to rise above a simple description of nature to an interpretation of, or commentary upon, it. Interpretive description does not offer the "musical photograph" of birds, raindrops, or lightning, but rather expresses the density of the forest, the majesty of the mountains, the depth and action of the sea, or the force of the storm. This appears to be Beethoven's intent when he produced his Symphony no. 6, or *Pastoral Symphony.* On the back of the title page of the first violin part of this symphony, and in one of his sketchbooks, Beethoven wrote:

Beethoven employs interpretive description in his *Pastoral Symphony.*

> Pastoral symphony, or recollections of country life (expressive of feeling rather than painting). . . . All painting in instrumental music, if pushed too far, is a failure. Anyone who has an idea of country life can make out for himself the intentions of the author without many titles.[1]

Beethoven, adhering to this belief, provided only a brief title for each of the five movements of this symphony: (1) "Cheerful feelings aroused on arrival in the country"; (2) "Scene at the brook"; (3) "Joyful gathering of the peasants"; (4) "Thunderstorm"; and (5) "Glad, thankful feelings after the storm."

Ironically, another great composer, Claude Debussy, a lifelong admirer of Beethoven's music, felt that this particular work was less successful than many of Beethoven's others because it was, in his view, too imitational. Debussy wrote:

> How much more profound an interpretation of the beauty of a landscape do we find in other passages in the great Master, because, instead of an exact imitation, there is an emotional interpretation of what is invisible in Nature. Can the mystery of a forest be expressed by measuring the height of the trees? Is it not rather its fathomless depths that stir the imagination?[2]

1. Extract from "Programme Music in the Last Four Centuries" (Frederick Niecks). Reproduced by courtesy of Novello and Company, Ltd.

2. *Three Classics in the Aesthetic of Music,* by Claude Debussy, Ferruccio Busoni, and Charles Ives, 1962, Dover Publications, Inc., New York, NY. Reprinted by permission.

Breakers on the Headland at Granville 1853, Paul Huet illustrates the active sea, as at Fingal's Cave.

Courtesy, The Louvre

Mendelssohn depicted his impression of Fingal's Cave through music.

In 1829, Felix Mendelssohn visited Fingal's Cave, located on one of the Hebrides Islands off the coast of Scotland. In August of that year he wrote to his beloved sister, Fanny:

> . . . in order to make you understand how extraordinarily the Hebrides affected me, the following came into my mind there.[3]

Figure 4.1 shows the opening measures of the *Hebrides* Overture by Mendelssohn.

Three years later he wrote to Fanny concerning the *Hebrides* Overture or, as it is sometimes called, *Fingal's Cave*:

> I cannot bring the *Hebrides* to a hearing here because I do not consider it finished as I originally wrote it. The middle section in D major is very stupid, and the whole so-called development smells more of counterpoint than of whale blubber, gulls, and salted cod.[4]

Mendelssohn was often very critical of himself and his work. Several of his best known and most admired works, including the *Italian* Symphony and the Violin Concerto, displeased him. The composer's opinion notwithstanding, the *Hebrides* Overture has thrilled audiences for more than a century and a half. The piece is cast in a sonata-allegro form, as seen in the following Sound and Sense.

---

3. Extract from "Programme Music in the Last Four Centuries" (Frederick Niecks). Reproduced by courtesy of Novello and Company, Ltd.

4. Extract from "Programme Music in the Last Four Centuries" (Frederick Niecks). Reproduced by courtesy of Novello and Company, Ltd.

Figure 4.1
This is what came to
Mendelssohn's mind as he
viewed Fingal's Cave.

© EKM-Nepenthe, From Felix Mendelssohn
Letters "The Hebrides Overture from Fingal's
Cave"

Sound and Sense
Sonata-Allegro Form

Title: Hebrides *Overture (*Fingal's Cave)*, 1830*
Composer: Mendelssohn
Recording: C. von Dohnany, Vienna Philharmonic
Meter: 4/4
Tempo: Allegro moderato
Key: D major

A Closer Look

Exposition (not repeated)

    A—theme in the tonic key of B minor—in violas   (1:00)
       and cellos at start, then higher strings
    Bridge section—woodwinds are featured;   (:48)
       modulates to the key of D major

B theme in cellos at start, then in higher strings   (1:00)
A'—first in flute, then brass, leading to a climax   (:47)
      and then falling off

A theme

B theme

Development (2:57)
Begins with several statements of this rhythm in brass and winds:

The *B* theme is developed, followed by the *A* theme which leads to a climax.
The flute then enters; a build-up to a second climax follows.
      This rhythm is then developed in marchlike fashion: which leads to a
third climax that ends on a trill, ushering in the recapitulation.

Recapitulation
      A theme in violas and cellos in the key of B minor   (:53)
      B theme in clarinets in the key of B minor/major   (:49)

Coda (1:39)

Many musical pieces cleverly combine imitation and interpretive description to bring a scene to life.

Béla Bartók's "The Night's Music," from the piano suite *Out of Doors* both describes and reflects upon nature's sounds. Once more, the occasional chirping of insects is not as fascinating as is the overall atmosphere and eeriness of night that the piece evokes.

From an extensive list of works that operate this way, listen to one more: Claude Debussy's "Nuages" ("Clouds"), from the Three *Nocturnes* for Orchestra. Debussy said of this piece:

"Nuages" represents the unchanging aspect of the sky, with the slow and melancholy passage of the clouds dissolving in a gray vagueness tinged with white.

Program Music

Instrumental music that is alleged to be inspired by or connected to a story, painting, poem, character, or scene, is often referred to as **program music.** The program, or extramusical idea behind the piece, may consist of nothing more than a title, or it may consist of a fairly detailed verbal sketch. When a composer provides such a program, he or she is emphasizing that the program is intimately tied to the meaning of the piece. Given foreknowledge of the program, listeners may be persuaded to find a similar meaning in the piece. Without knowledge of the program this may not happen, but the audience may still be moved by and find meaning in the piece.

Some have persistently held that program music is somehow "cheaper" than **absolute music** (music without an indicated program). It is argued that the verbal program is a crutch used to support wobbly music, and that absolute music stands on its own, nobler legs. Our task here is not to defend or to attack program music, but rather to try to understand what it is.

Obviously, the composer intends the program to serve as a means of focusing attention on the general meaning he or she feels is expressed in the music. The good composer knows that no written program can be devised that will add to or detract from the quality of the music. The program may, however, invite a perception of the music and its general meaning that is more closely related to the *composer's* perception.

Program music is based upon a story, painting, poem, character, or scene.

Absolute music has no program.

The program may bring our perception of the music closer to that of the composer's.

Philosophical Program Music

Charles Ives, an American composer, expressed his opinion of program music in *Essays Before a Sonata.* Some of his statements from that publication appear here:

> Does the success of program music depend more upon the program than upon the music? If it does, what is the use of the music, if it does not, what is the use of the program? Does not its appeal depend to a great extent on the listener's willingness to accept the theory that music is the language of the emotions and *only* that?[5]

Ives continues, suggesting that descriptive program music that plays only on the sensuousness of raw emotion is shallow. He seeks, rather, meaning and emotions in a deeper sense "which may be a feeling influenced by some experience perhaps of a spiritual nature in the expression of which the intellect has some part." For him the ideal music must bring to bear the cooperation of heart and mind in the production of meaning

The American composer Charles Ives questioned the purpose of program music.

---

5. Quotation from: *Three Classics in the Aesthetic of Music,* by Claude Debussy, Ferruccio Busoni, and Charles Ives, 1962, Dover Publications, Inc., New York, NY. Reprinted by permission.

in this deeper sense. He suggests that our conception of program music should not be limited simply to descriptive pieces. He understands program music in a broader sense, for he says:

> On the other hand is not all music, program-music—is not pure music [absolute music], so called, representative in its essence?[6]

Thus another type of program music in which imitation, interpretation, and description have little or no role is introduced. This is **philosophical program music,** which attempts to relay the essence and power of ideas and attitudes, and is not content merely to describe objects or scenes. Ives himself produced such a work in *The Unanswered Question* (1908). Ives's program appears here:

> The strings play *ppp* throughout, with no change of tempo. They are to represent "The Silences of the Druids" who speak, see, and hear nothing. The trumpet intones "The Perennial Question of Existence" and states it in the same tone of voice each of the seven times it enters. But the hunt for the "Invisible Answer" undertaken by the flutes becomes gradually more active, faster, and louder. The "Fighting Answerers," as time goes on, seem to realize a futility, and begin to mock "The Question"—the strife is over for the moment. After they disappear, "The Question" is asked again for the last time, and the "Silences" are heard beyond in undisturbed solitude. . . .[7]

But can a composer communicate something meaningful to us in instrumental music for which he provides no program, descriptive or otherwise? It is possible, but to paraphrase Mendelssohn, the specific meaning is too definite to put into words. The possible meaning of a given work can be approached, however, in a general way. This vantage at least assists audiences in thinking about the work in an active rather than a passive manner. The first listening of the piece is likely to make an impact. But on repeated listenings, the nature of that impact, indeed, the sense of meaning in the piece, may change and evolve.

Unlike Symphony no. 6, Beethoven provided no program at all for Symphony no. 7, and yet there is something in this music that suggests a program. In the second movement of this symphony, for example, a sense of weakness transformed into great power, and a sense of humility transformed into glorification and great dignity, are created.

The following Sound and Sense illustrates the formal structure of this movement on the level of the section and subsection.

Imitation, interpretation, and description play little or no role in philosophical program music.

Your sense of meaning in a piece of music will evolve during repeated listenings.

6. Ibid.
7. Ibid.

Title: Symphony no. 7, second movement (1812)
Composer: Beethoven
Recording: Szell, Cleveland Orchestra
Meter: 2/4
Tempo: Allegrette
Key: A minor

A Closer Look

The dominant theme—*a*—whose environment is varied with each repetition, is notated:

A	*B*	*A'*	*B'*	*A''*
aa'a''a'''	*bcc'*	*a''''*-fugue	*b'*	*a*
(2:37)	(1:21)	(1:52)	(:35)	(1:00)

Notice first of all the rather common or humble nature of this theme that spends so much time on one pitch and traverses only a very limited range. Its plodding rhythm is restricted to two note values— ♩ and ♪ . This would appear to be the commonest, most unpromising musical clay, but Beethoven has a magnificent destiny in mind for it.

The theme is first heard in *a*, where it is placed at the bottom of the texture and played by violas, cellos, and double basses. It enters almost apologetically at a very quiet dynamic level. Notice in *a'* that the theme rises in the texture to the second violins and speaks no longer in a whisper, but in a clearly audible voice. Further, a lovely countermelody is wound around it. In *a*, the theme may seem ridiculous, but something happens to it in *a'* that eliminates this possibility.

In *a''* the theme continues its ascent in the texture, and it is sung in a higher, louder voice by the first violins. It is joined by another equally compelling countermelody. Metaphorically speaking, it is as if the theme has gotten off its knees, risen, and begun to walk in a steady, dignified gait.

The full-voiced orchestra takes the theme in *a'''* while the first violins wrap a high, soaring countermelody around it. Moving from its humble, unpretentious beginning, the theme has achieved magnificence.

The *B* section provides the necessary contrast and diversion. Notice, however, that the cellos and double basses retain the rhythm of the *a* theme in the background. Upon its reentry in *A'*, the theme becomes the subject of a fugue. Beethoven has now bestowed upon this theme the ultimate musical dignity.

The movement ends with *A''* almost as quietly as it began, but in the course of the movement the theme has been completely transformed. It bids its noble, though understated, adieu.

Summary

In the first three chapters you learned to analyze the special nature of rhythms, themes, harmonies, textures, instruments, and forms. When these elements are joined together to create music, however, they collectively produce the sense of something beyond themselves. In this chapter, we identified that essence as meaning.

When music merely imitates, its meaning is quite clear. When music begins to describe, the meaning we find is colored by our individual experiences. To bring our perceptions closer to theirs, composers such as Vivaldi, Beethoven, Mendelssohn, Berlioz, Debussy, and Ives provided a set of clues regarding the meaning of their music. These clues are termed programs.

Programs may influence our interpretation of musical pieces. But in each piece of music, whether program or absolute, we are likely to discover meanings both universal and unique to ourselves.

Key Terms

musical description
program music
absolute music

philosophical
  program music

Plate 1
Music, the universal language.

The Old Musician; Edouard Manet; (French, 1832–1883); Date: 1862; canvas; 1.874 cm × 2.483 cm; National
Gallery of Art, Washington, Chester Dale Collection.

Plate 2

Motion, time, and rhythm are discussed in chapter 1. Despite this painting's seemingly placid surface, these three elements are apparent in the water, bridge, clouds, and oarsmen.

Max Schmitt in a Single Scull; Thomas Eakins; The Metropolitan Museum of Art, Purchase 1934. Alfred N. Punnet Fund and Gift of George D. Pratt (34.92).

Plate 3
Rhythmic patterns and meters are discussed in chapter 1. Notice the many
patterns and repetitions in this visual image.

Mahantango Valley Farm; American; Date: late 19th century; window shade; 0.711 cm × 0.899 cm; National
Gallery of Art, Washington; Gift of Edgar William and Bernice Chrysler Garbish.

Plate 4
Time, rhythm, and memory have been universal sources of inspiration in all of the arts. Musical time is different from so-called real time: a fascinating piece of music may seem to be all too brief, while a dull piece may seem annoyingly long and drawn out.

The Persistence of Memory; Salvador Dali; 1931; oil on canvas; 9½″ × 13″; Collection, The Museum of Modern Art, New York. Given anonymously.

Plate 5
The nature and quality of musical sounds are discussed in chapter 2. Notice
how the player listens with great care.

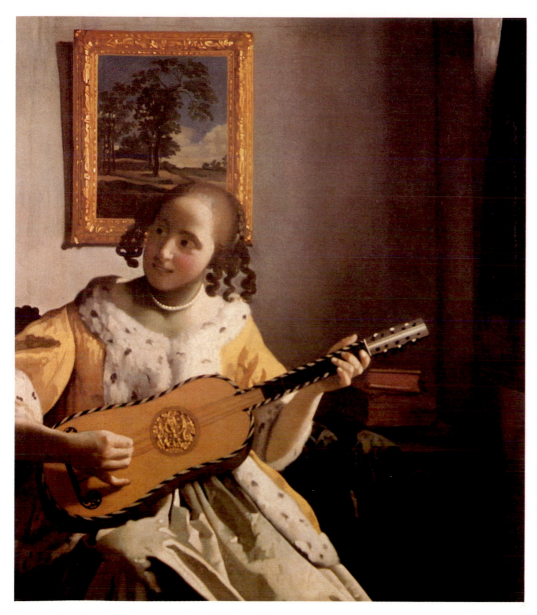

The Guitar Player; Vermeer; The Greater London Council as Trustees of the Iveagh Bequest, Kenwood.

Plate 6
Consonance and dissonance are discussed in chapter 2. Notice how the letter
O creates dissonance.

Love; Robert Indiana; 1968; aluminum; 12″ × 12″ × 6″; Collection of Whitney Museum of American Art;
Purchase with funds from the Howard and Jean Lipman Foundation, ACQ #68.71.

Plate 7
Form, as discussed in chapter 3, makes a given work perceptible and
memorable.

Stonehenge; © Jill Cannefax/EKM-Nepenthe.

Plate 8
. . . daffodils,
That come before the swallow dares, and take
The winds of March with beauty . . .
(See meaning as discussed in chapter 4.)

Daffodils; © John Maher/EKM-Nepenthe.

Plate 9
As mentioned in chapter 4, Cezanne said that this painting is not about
apples—it is about appleness.

Basket of Apples; Paul Cezanne; ca. 1895; oil on canvas; 65.0 cm × 80.0 cm; Helen Birch Bartlett Memorial
Collection, 1926.252; © 1989 The Art Institute of Chicago. All Rights Reserved.

Plate 10
The long, lonesome stretches of land, the sky, with its mixture of heaviness and lightness, dark, cool trees, and the solitary traveler combine to create a mood. How would you describe that mood? How do motion and texture contribute to the mood? (For a discussion of meaning and mood, see chapter 4.)

Wheatfields; Jacob Isaacksz Ruisdael; The Metropolitan Museum of Art; Bequest of Benjamin Altman 1913 (14.40.623).

Plate 11
Color, shape, and texture combine to create the mood of this painting (see chapter 4).

Norham Castle, Sunrise; J. W. N. Turner; The Tate Gallery, London.

Plate 12
Can you detect the motion, meter, rhythm, tempo, texture, form, and mood in
this painting?

Winter (Return of the Hunters); Pieter Brueghel; Scala/The Art Resource, New York.

Thinking About It

Grappling with meaning can be difficult since there are no clear-cut answers to questions. Still, it seems to be in our nature to seek meaning in music. Even after you have firmly established in your own mind the meaning of a given piece of music, you may discover that the meaning changes, sometimes dramatically, as you discuss the work with friends who also know the work. As time permits, you should involve yourself in such discussions. Samuel Barber's *Adagio for Strings* could form the basis for one such discussion.

SECTION

2

Styles
in
Western
Art
Music

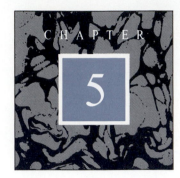
Music in the Baroque Era

Musical soiree at Montague House in London at the time of Handel. Heidegger, Handel's impressario, is at the piano, 1736.

© The Bettmann Archive

Sounds of the Chapter

J. S. Bach
Brandenburg Concerto no. 2 ♪
Brandenburg Concerto no. 5
Cantata no. 80 (*Ein' feste Burg ist unser Gott*)
"Jesu, Joy of Man's Desiring"
Saint Matthew Passion
Six English Suites
Six French Suites ♪
Fugue in C Minor, *Well-Tempered Clavier* ♪

Caccini
Le Nuove musiche

Corelli
Trio Sonata in F Minor, op. 3, no. 9

Handel
Alcina
"Halleluja," *Messiah* ♪
Israel in Egypt
Messiah
Trio Sonata in F Major, op. 2, no. 5 ♪

Haydn
Surprise Symphony

Lully
Alceste

Monteverdi
Orfeo

Mozart
Symphony no. 40 in G Minor ♪

Purcell
Dido and Aeneas
Variations for Harpsichord (*Variations on a New Ground Bass*)

Vivaldi
"Spring," *The Seasons* ♪

The road leading back through history is expansive but much of the terrain as far back as the seventeenth century is familiar to us. Beyond this time, the road narrows dramatically, and familiar signposts become scarce. The music and the philosophical foundations of the Renaissance and pre-Renaissance eras may intrigue and inspire us, but they still seem foreign to us, as if they belong to the history of another world. The music, especially, seems alien. Its rhythm is difficult to appreciate because our appetite for upbeat/downbeat and meter is not satisfied; melodies and themes may not emerge in a clear fashion; the sense of key, and of tonic or dominant, is not present, and the formal structure of much of the music does not coincide with our notions about how music is put together.

Baroque music seems modern to us.

The baroque, on the other hand, seems somehow modern. The music from the baroque (ca. 1600–1750), though clearly different from ours in some ways, is nonetheless music with which we can empathize. This is because many of our twentieth-century musical practices and genres were born in the baroque, were nurtured through the years, and have survived into our time. Meter and functional harmony, discussed in chapters 1 and 2, became the standard means of organizing musical time and chords in the baroque and remain the standard today. Opera, chamber music, orchestral music, keyboard music, and the concerto, all of which are staples of Western art music today, were invented in the baroque. Even the concept of the ticket-buying public is traceable to the baroque era.

The Enlightenment includes the middle and late baroque, the preclassic, and classic eras.

It sometimes happens that catch words or phrases from a certain period in history are retained to identify the character or summarize the accomplishments of a given age. Thus, the period comprising the second half of the seventeenth and all of the eighteenth centuries is frequently called the age of the Enlightenment, of which the middle and late baroque, preclassic, and classic eras are elements. This age placed the highest premium on reason and viewed rationality, rather than experience or tradition, as the true source of knowledge. Because sensory perceptions vary greatly from person to person or from culture to culture, the leaders of the Enlightenment viewed the senses as unreliable sources of knowledge. Rather, the detached and unyielding proofs of mathematics and the wisdom accumulated by empirical investigation were viewed as the unquestionable sources of human knowledge. Consequently, the sciences and mathematics flourished during the Enlightenment.

The Enlightenment era stressed emperical proof.

A spirit of inquiry and a drift toward individual liberty characterized the enlightened baroque.

This spirit of inquiry and the slow but steady drift toward individual liberty were characteristics of the enlightened baroque. Indeed, the Enlightenment represented a fundamental shift in the Western world. Culture was reoriented, from deeply entrenched authority to the establishment of the modern republic that became manifest in the late eighteenth century with the success of both the American and the French revolutions.

For a time, however, the forces of the Enlightenment had to share the stage with a power that was very nearly the antithesis of the Enlightenment. This power was the absolute monarch, of whom France's Louis XIV is the most notable example. All power, all authority, and, by extension, all knowledge were invested in the person of the monarch. Individual liberties were minimal or nonexistent in such a situation.

The baroque was thus witness to a titanic struggle between these two opposing forces—Absolutism, representing the old order, and the Enlightenment, a new order that eventually won the battle. Oftentimes, the arts of the baroque period reflected this conflict between these major forces and their ideologies.

Baroque arts reflect the struggle between Absolutism and the Enlightenment.

Because of the change and conflict characteristic of the baroque, the artistic style that emerged was distinctly different from its predecessor, the Renaissance style. Baroque art was first viewed as wild and undisciplined; the term baroque originally meant "anything in bad taste." Flourishes, extravagance, and intricate detail characterized this new art style, and though wild and undisciplined, it soon shed this unfavorable connotation and was legitimized as a stylistic label for music and the other arts of the seventeenth and early eighteenth centuries.

Baroque originally meant "anything in bad taste."

Baroque Art: A Stylistic Comparison

Two paintings—one by Giorgione, the other by Rubens—shown in figures 5.1 and 5.2, illustrate this drastic change in art forms from the Renaissance to the baroque. The former is a product of the Italian Renaissance; the latter of the early baroque. Even a cursory examination of the two paintings reveals some marked stylistic differences characteristic of the eras during which they were painted.

Compare Renaissance and baroque styles in art.

Perhaps the most striking element of the Renaissance work is the abundant use of geometric shapes: the squares on the floor, the superimposed rectangles of the throne and the circle at the base of the throne, the triangles formed by the banner held by St. George (left front), the one formed by the head and hand positions of St. Francis (right front), and the larger triangle formed by the heads of Mary, St. George, and St. Francis. These are all firm, even self-confident, shapes, where everything is fixed in place, giving the painting a stable and static quality.

The characters are neither overweight nor underweight; they are, in fact, ideally proportioned, healthy, and beautiful. Their countenances reflect no fear, no desperation, nothing trivial. Rather, they are faces that reflect thoughtfulness, serenity, and, once more, self-confidence. Mary's left hand grips the throne with assurance and comfort; there is no suggestion that she is holding on out of fear; no chance that she will fall. She is in control.

Renaissance figures appear ideally proportioned.

Figure 5.1
Madonna with Child and Saints by Giorgione—
Renaissance serenity and
control (see colorplate 13).

Nature is visible, though secondary in importance to the characters in the painting. Notice that nature is contained by the wall behind
Mary and the others. Aside from the symbolic content of the painting,
it is clear that the characters are the subject of a passive, serene, self-
contained world.

The Rubens presents a very different vision. The painting exudes
action. Everything—the people, the horses, even the sky—strain with
motion and threaten to burst beyond the frame and escape the canvas.
The horse at the left arches its head to one side revealing huge, tense
muscles. The front legs of the horse at the right are also tense with action.
There is a sweeping, spiraling quality running from the lower left-hand
corner to the woman's outstretched hand near the top right corner. The
generous swatches of cloth echo this motion; the material is heavy and
dense.

Baroque figures exude action.

The figures are all muscular and fleshy, their robustness sharply
contrasting with the cool, ideally proportioned figures in the Giorgione
painting. The faces, particularly the eyes, of these characters are animated rather than coolly passive. The eyes of the central woman peer
beyond the bounds of the frame in an entreaty for assistance. The world
of this baroque painting is charged with drama, unlike the Italian Renaissance Giorgione.

Figure 5.2
Rape of the Daughters of Leucippus by Rubens—baroque action and voluptuousness (see colorplate 14).
© The Art Resource, New York

The human affections were of particular interest to baroque artists. René Descartes (1596–1650), one of the most influential thinkers of the seventeenth century, described the baroque concept of emotion, or "passions," in his treatise *The Passions of the Soul* (1649). The following is a paraphrase of an excerpt.

Descartes wrote on human passion in *The Passions of the Soul* in 1649.

> The human soul is located in a small gland in the middle of the brain. The body creates one variety of passions, the soul itself creates another variety. When the two varieties work together in a common effort they create a response to some object. The principal effect of the passions is that they incite the soul to desire those things for which they prepare the body. So it is that the feeling of fear incites a desire to fly; the feeling of courage incites a desire to fight. There are six basic passions: wonder, love, hatred, desire, joy, and sadness. All other human passions are related to one or more of these.

Philosophers, artists, and music theorists of the time codified the many works on this topic and compiled them in the *Doctrine of Affections*. The ideas contained in the *Doctrine of Affections* became the aesthetic creed for baroque artists, composers, and others in the arts.

Charles LeBrun (1619–90), an artist and aesthetician, spoke to the artist in terms of the *Doctrine of Affections*. The proper expression of a given passion was, as far as he was concerned, measurable: the precise tilt of the head, the opening of the eyes, and the line of the mouth all had to be properly proportioned in order to incite in the viewer the desired passion (see fig. 5.3).

Descartes: Spokesman for the *Doctrine of Affections*.
Free Library of Philadelphia

Figure 5.3
Prescriptions for painters, in
accordance with the *Doctrine
of Affections*.
© The Bettmann Archive

Attention   Desire   Rapture   Simple Bodily Pain   Laughter

Terror or Fright   Anger   Despair   Sadness   Hatred or Jealousy

Music of the Baroque

The music of the baroque, like the art, reflected the Enlightenment characteristics of ornamentation and extravagance. Furthermore, it was the
pleasure of the composer, as well as an obligation, to find the musical
means to express various states of the soul so as to involve the emotions
of the audience. The composer was not seeking self-expression, but the
expression of generalized states to which any rational person could respond. During the baroque, a whole catalog of **musical recipes** was developed; a collection of musical figures, rhythms, and chord progressions,
each of which was the means of expressing one or another affection. The
intent was to create a one-to-one relationship between a given musical
configuration and a specific affection.

The baroque composer
expressed various states of the
human soul.

It seems likely that the most convenient means of achieving this goal would be with the type of musical description discussed in chapter 4, where, for example, a rippling figure would represent water. But the baroque composer and his audience were interested in something much more profound than mere description, although this, too, abounds in baroque music. Nor were they concerned simply with imitation of natural phenomena such as bird calls, water, or thunder. They strove to imitate states of the soul such as wonder, love, joy, and sorrow.

The composer's job was to present these passions in the clearest and most forceful way. In vocal music, the composer sought the dominant affection of a passage of text, combined it with the appropriate musical configuration, and retained that configuration throughout the duration of that portion of the text. There are countless examples of these movements or sections generated by one figure. Handel's oratorio, *Israel in Egypt,* provides some striking examples. Listen first to the air for alto, based on the text "Their land brought forth frogs, yea, even in the king's chambers. He gave their cattle over to the pestilence. Blotches and blains broke forth on man and beast." Notice that the opening figure, the little hopping motive presented by the violins, runs throughout almost the entirety of the air, and is even incorporated into the singer's vocal line. The following chorus, "He spake the word and there came all manner of flies and lice in all their quarters," is similarly dominated by the initial whirling figure presented by the violins, and the chorus subsequent to this, "He gave them hailstones for rain . . ." is built the same way.

The opposite approach to this kind of text setting involves spotlighting every individual word in a text that is rich with word-painting possibilities. This approach is frequently encountered in the sixteenth-century Italian madrigal and was one of the principal items against which the emerging baroque composers reacted most strongly.

> One (bright) day we all went (up) the hill,
> There we heard the sweet (song of the bird.)
> (Suddenly) (lightning) flashed and the (rain) came.
> We all ran (down) the hill and were (very sad)
> that the weather had stopped our (happy time.)

For each of the circled words a musical figure or device could be invented that would sound like the thing represented by the words. The baroque composer would consider such a setting a hopeless mishmash from which no central or dominant affection could arise. Rather, he or she would determine the general feel of the whole text and invent one musical figure to serve the entire passage.

Description and imitation were not enough for the baroque composer.

Characteristics of Baroque Music

Functional Harmony

The principles of functional harmony are a product of the baroque period.

In the examination of harmony in chapter 2, the nature of functional harmony was described as a systematic ordering of chords from which the sense of key and also of tonic, dominant, and subdominant emerge. This harmonic system, still in use today, is a product of the baroque. It is not possible to say precisely when the system first came into existence, but from the mid-to-late seventeenth century onward, functional harmony was universally employed. In 1722 the French composer Jean-Philippe Rameau published his *Treatise on Harmony* in which most of the basic principles of functional harmony are explained and codified, and in which the terms tonic, dominant, and subdominant are introduced. Rameau did not invent the system, but his treatise describes harmonic practices that were prevalent before and during his time. Tonality is a unifying factor in nearly all music from the middle and late baroque, despite composers' individual styles.

Basso Continuo

Basso continuo is common to nearly all baroque music.

Another feature common to nearly all baroque music is the **basso continuo,** or thorough (meaning throughout) bass. The continuo was played on a keyboard instrument, either harpsichord or organ, or on a lute, and it was usually joined by a cello, bassoon, or some other instrument capable of playing a bass line. Thus, the continuo employed an instrument that could play chords supported by an instrument that could play the lowest single line in the musical texture. The two instruments served essentially as accompaniment, fleshing out the harmonies and supplying the underlying bass line that supported the solo singers or instrumentalists. As the name continuo implies, the basso continuo played nonstop for the duration of a work. It usually did not call attention to itself; it unobtrusively supplied the necessary harmonic backdrop. Handel's Trio Sonata in F Major, op. 2, no. 5, will introduce you to the basso continuo.

Figured Bass

The figured bass noted the bass line of the composition, as well as the chords to be played.

The keyboard player of the continuo was expected to play or "realize" a fully fleshed-out part. The instrumentalist had to rely on his or her ability to read and interpret a baroque musical shorthand called a **figured bass.** This consisted of the bass line of the composition written out in musical notation, above which were written various numbers and symbols telling the performer which chords to play above the bass line. Figure 5.4 shows a figured bass for the opening phrases of the chorale: "Was bist du dock, o Seele." Figure 5.5 shows the realization of the same figured bass.

Figure 5.4

Figure 5.5

Some of the adjectives applied to the Rubens painting are also descriptive of baroque music. Most music from the baroque could be described as dramatic, active, ornamental, and virtuosic. Composers at that time were fond of the vivid contrast between loud *(f)* and soft *(p)*, and the contrast in volume that results from playing a small group of instruments against a larger group. Precise tempo indications are not plentiful in baroque manuscripts, but evidence suggests that composers were also fond of dramatic contrasts between fast and slow.

Dramatic contrasts typify baroque music.

A great deal of baroque music is infused with what a jazz musician would call "a beat"—a steady, relentless pulsation. It has been suggested that this music has an atomic rhythm; an ever-present smallest note value, beyond which there is no further significant subdivision. This is evident in J. S. Bach's *Brandenburg* Concerto no. 2. Notice as you listen to the opening minutes of the first movement that there is a constant tick-a-tick-a-tick-a in the rhythmic background. As the concerto progresses to the slow movement, notice that the atomic unit slows down dramatically but is still present.

Can you hear the atomic rhythm in Bach's *Brandenburg* Concerto no. 2?

This kind of beat is present in all of the movements of the six *Brandenburg* Concertos. Listen for it also in the Fugue in C Minor from Bach's *Well-Tempered Clavier,* book 1. Indeed, this sense of action derived from atomic rhythm is found in a great many works by Bach and other composers from the late baroque.

There is action, too, in prototypical melodies from the baroque. Baroque melodies tend to be long, spiraling and complicated, unlike those from the classical era which will be covered in chapter 7. The length and expansive quality of baroque melodies can be tested by taking a deep breath as the melody begins and attempting to hold it until the first major

Baroque melodies are expansive.

stopping place. The opening statement from *Brandenburg* Concerto no. 5, or Bach's well-known melody "Jesu, Joy of Man's Desiring," are excellent pieces with which to experiment.

Compare, for example, the Bach melodies just mentioned with the opening theme of Mozart's G Symphony no. 40 in G Minor, and the theme from the second movement of Haydn's *Surprise* symphony. In contrast to the baroque themes, these classical melodies are expended in short bursts of energy—small bits that create a larger whole. Graphically illustrated the two types appear thus:

Baroque melodic type

Classical melodic type

Baroque melodies are marked also by a profusion of such ornaments as trills, mordents, and turns. In contrast to some other styles, the ornamentation in baroque music seems to grow organically from the spiraling character of the melody. It does not seem to be an afterthought or something pasted on to the melody; it is, rather, a natural part of the action of the melody.

Many works from the baroque, whether vocal or instrumental, are designed for performance by highly skilled master musicians. Baroque music has a regal quality and the sense of a style somehow "bigger than life." This idea automatically calls for performers with better than average skills. Some sense of the vocal prowess demanded of an opera singer in the baroque era is apparent in the aria "Tonami a vagheggiar" from the opera *Alcina* by Handel.

Thus, the general stylistic ingredients of baroque music are drama, activity, ornamentation, and virtuosity. These ingredients are evident in most genres and forms of the era.

Orchestral Music—Genres and Composers

The Concerto Grosso

The **concerto grosso** was the dominant form of orchestral music in the baroque era. It emerged in the second half of the seventeenth century as a multimovement piece. Usually, it alternated a number of fast, slow, and dance movements, and it featured a small group of soloists (usually two or three) called the **concertino.** The concertino was pitted against and played in alternation with a larger group of instruments called the **tutti.** The basso continuo discussed earlier completed the ensemble.

Important composers of early concerto grossi include Alessandro Stradella (1645–82), Arcangelo Corelli (1653–1713), Georg Muffat (1645–1704), and Giuseppe Torelli (1658–1709). The genre underwent

---

Margin notes:

Compare the classical and baroque melodic types.

The spiraling character of baroque melodies creates natural ornamentation.

Baroque music exhibits drama, activity, ornamentation, and virtuosity.

Concerto grosso dominated orchestral music in the baroque era.

some changes in the course of its history, and as it evolved in the hands of Vivaldi, J. S. Bach, and Handel in the late baroque, it normally had three movements: fast-slow-fast. (There are, however, some important exceptions to this general rule.)

In an earlier chapter we discussed the various effects and information that emerge from viewing a landscape from 10,000 feet in the air, from 500 feet in the air, and from ground level. As our perspective changes so does the scene. The *Brandenburg* Concerto no. 2, a glorious ♪ example of the concerto grosso as it existed in the late baroque, can be examined from these same perspectives.

This metaphorical view from 10,000 feet reveals the fast-slow-fast superstructure of the work and the presence of an atomic rhythm. Return to the first few minutes of the opening movement to pick up the rhythm. We feel more comfortable when we are able to tap our toes, snap our fingers, or in some other way empathize with the rhythm of the music at hand. From 10,000 feet we may be aware that other, more complex things are happening in this movement. As we feel at ease with the rhythm of the piece our curiosity will likely begin to wander to some of them. At that point, we will want a closer look at the work.

Bach's *Brandenburg* Concerto no. 2 reveals a fast-slow-fast structure.

Keeping the rhythm in mind, descend to 500 feet and listen to the same excerpt again. Now we detect that sometimes the tutti plays, and sometimes one or more members of the concertino play. Our view from this perspective confirms that the concertino consists of four members— violin, oboe, flute, and trumpet—which enter successively, each solo entrance being preceded by a statement from the tutti. A pattern emerges: tutti-concertino-tutti-concertino-tutti-concertino-tutti-concertino.

In the *Brandenburg* Concerto no. 2, the concertino consists of the violin, oboe, flute, and trumpet.

As we approach ground level and listen to the piece once more, we may be prompted to ask specifically what the tutti plays each time it enters, and what the four members of the concertino play. Careful listening should reveal that the tutti plays the same or essentially the same material each time it enters—A or A'. Also, each member of the concertino plays B or B'. This formal process has the special name **ritornello**. In the case of the *Brandenburg* no. 2, both the tutti and the concertino have unique ritornellos. The repetitive nature of the ritornello process creates formal cohesion and unity. But it is only one way of creating formal cohesion.

Formal cohesion is created by the ritornello.

A large number of concerto grosso movements have ritornello structures, but they also contain a variety of formal types. Moreover, there is diversity in both the roles and the positions of tutti and concertino. In contrast to the *Brandenburg* no. 2, some movements lead with the concertino and follow with the tutti. In other movements the concertino passages may be of equal length to the tutti passages; in still others, some of the concertino passages may be quite protracted. In short, a great diversity of internal workings and structure are possible within the general framework of baroque concerto grosso movements.

Baroque concerto grosso movements show diversity in internal workings and structure.

But we left the first movement in midstream, at the point where all four members of the concertino had entered the action.

The remainder of the movement consists essentially of a series of varied repetitions of the tutti's material. These repetitions have the following rhythm:

The concertino's material has the rhythm:

The slow and fast movements are in direct contrast.

The slow movement provides a dramatic textural contrast to the first movement: the tutti and the concertino trumpet are silent, and the movement is carried by the other three concertino instruments and the basso continuo. The continuo provides the harmonic backdrop and the slow but constant atomic rhythm, over which the violin, oboe, and flute weave an intricate contrapuntal web.

The trumpet heralds the opening of the concluding fast movement. Here, in contrast to the first movement, the tutti is silent until each of the concertino members has entered the texture.

Johann Sebastian Bach

Bach (1685–1750) composed this and the other five *Brandenburg* Concertos around 1721; he dedicated them and "humbly offered" them as a gift to a petty nobleman, the Margrave (Governor) of Brandenburg. Undoubtedly, the Margrave was unaware that these concertos were masterworks and that his "humble servant" was destined to be one of the greatest composers in the history of Western art music.

Johann Sebastian Bach (1685–1750).
Free Library of Philadelphia

Bach's style was out of step with the musical trends of the day.

Interestingly, J. S. Bach was not among the most widely celebrated composers of his day and his musical style was viewed by many of his contemporaries as stodgy and old fashioned. Indeed, the musical styles of two of his sons, Carl Philipp Emanuel and Johann Christian, were more favorably regarded than his own. After his death in 1750, Bach's music was largely forgotten until early in the nineteenth century when Felix Mendelssohn rediscovered it and mounted a now famous performance of the *Saint Matthew Passion* (in 1829). That performance and other contemporaneous revivals of his music at last established for Bach the lofty position he richly deserves in history.

The long and difficult road to musical immortality was matched by the difficulties and tragedies of his own life. Bach was orphaned at the age of about ten. His first wife died in 1720; she had borne him seven children, four of whom died as infants or young children. The following year he married a cousin, Anna Magdalena, and their married life seems to have been a happy one. Still, they endured the loss of seven of their thirteen children.

Bach's troubles in private life mirrored the difficulties he faced in his musical career.

A deeply religious man, Bach spent the greater part of his career in the service of the Lutheran church in the roles of composer, organist, and conductor. Petty squabbles with church officials, dealings with unruly or uninspired choir members, regular pleas for proper financial support (so that he might care for his large family), and the tedious task of copying his own music were part of his daily life.

His last year or so was spent in the darkness of blindness, though there are reports that his sight was restored just days before his death. He died of apoplexy in July of 1750, leaving behind a prodigious legacy of sacred and secular music, the quality of which remains unsurpassed.

Antonio Vivaldi

Vivaldi (1678–1741) is forever associated with the colorful city of Venice. He was himself a colorful character with a shock of bright red hair which earned for him the affectionate nickname "the red-headed priest." (He was ordained a priest but was dismissed from his duties for health reasons.) His many sacred choral works, as well as his concerto grossos, made him an extremely popular figure in the cultural life of eighteenth-century Venice.

Vivaldi was the most prolific composer of concerto grossos: approximately 450 of them are extant, of which the majority are solo concerti. These solo concerti have a concertino consisting of only one instrument. Particularly charming and colorful is a set of four programmatic concerti called *The Seasons,* published about 1725. Each of the four has the standard fast-slow-fast arrangement of movements, and each is prefaced by a sonnet for one of the four seasons. The program and structure of the first movement of the "Spring" concerto reads as follows:

Vivaldi was a prolific composer of concerto grossos; about 450 are still in existence.

Opening tutti ritornello	Spring has come back again, and joyously
Concertino	The birds salute him with their merry song;
Tutti ritornello followed by some new material	And streams, by zephyr's gentle breath set free, With a sweet murmur swiftly flow along.
Tutti ritornello followed by agitated material	With veils of darkness covering the sky, Come thunder and lightning, to proclaim him king;

Tutti ritornello with
concertino

But when their fury's spent, and
      passes by,
Sweetly once more the birds are
      heard to sing.[1]

Trio Sonata

The trio sonata was the
dominant form of chamber
music in the baroque era.

The **trio sonata,** a multimovement work usually written for two solo instruments plus basso continuo, was the dominant form of chamber music in the baroque era. (**Chamber music** calls for a few instruments rather than an entire orchestra, and it is designed for intimate surroundings, such as one's home, rather than a concert hall.) The trio sonata was developed in the mid-seventeenth century and raised to a high artistic level by, among others, Arcangelo Corelli (1653–1713), and later in the era by Handel, J. S. Bach, Georg Philipp Telemann (1681–1767) and others.

Trio sonatas often show the
slow-fast-slow-fast movement
plan.

In the closing years of the seventeenth century, Corelli published four volumes of trio sonatas. The third of these, Opus 3, contains twelve trio sonatas, most of which follow the four movement plan: slow-fast-slow-fast. Generally speaking, the slow movements tend to be homophonic and the fast movements contrapuntal.

The keyboard player fleshes
out the harmony in Corelli's
Trio Sonata in F Minor, op. 3,
no. 9.

Corelli's Trio Sonata in F Minor, op. 3, no. 9, for two solo violins and basso continuo, is a particularly lovely example of the genre. The keyboard part of the basso continuo is played on an organ. The figured bass of the opening measures of the initial movement is provided here so that you can appreciate how the keyboard player fleshes out the harmony and adds appropriate improvisation by interpreting the numbers and symbols.

Handel's Trio Sonata in F
Major, op. 2, no. 5, exhibits
mixed solo instruments and a
fifth movement—a gigue.

Handel's Trio Sonata in F Major, op. 2, no. 5, for flute, violin and continuo (published 1731), is a fine example of the late baroque trio sonata. The composer mixed his solo instruments, a common procedure

1. Extract from "Programme Music in the Last Four Centuries" (Frederick Niecks). Reproduced by courtesy of Novello and Company, Ltd.

Harpsichord with elaborate decoration.
Courtesy, D. Jacques Way and Zuckermann Harpsichords

in the late baroque, and combined a woodwind with a string. In contrast to the earlier Corelli sonata, Handel's sonata has five movements, the last of which is a dance called a gigue. The keyboard member of the continuo is played on a harpsichord. Notice that the other member of the continuo, the cello, has a very active part in the texture and is not restricted merely to presenting the bass line.

Keyboard Music

There were several kinds of keyboard instruments in use during the baroque, but by far the most popular were the harpsichord and the organ. The history of the harpsichord dates back to the fifteenth century, but the widespread use of the instrument and the creation of a large body of literature for it did not develop until the seventeenth century. In the late baroque, both the mechanics of the instrument and the music composed for it reached a zenith. In fact, to today's audiences the harpsichord is probably the instrument that sounds the "most baroque."

Baroque composers were fond of arranging various kinds of dances for harpsichord. Usually such dances were grouped into a collection and termed a **suite** or a **dance suite** for harpsichord. The binary structure of most baroque dances, as discussed in chapter 3, is an *AABB* design. The

George Frederic Handel (1685–1759).
Free Library of Philadelphia

Dance suites were arranged for harpsichord, an instrument that reached its zenith in the baroque era.

Most of the dances in a baroque suite have binary structure.

core of the dance suite consisted of four dances with contrasting tempos and/or meters: **allemande** (moderate tempo, duple time), **courante** (moderate tempo, triple meter), **saraband** (slower tempo, triple meter) and **gigue** (lively tempo, usually in the compound meter 6/8).

Later in the baroque, this basic core of dances was expanded to include other dances and sometimes an opening movement that was not a dance, the **prelude.** Examples of this type of baroque suite for harpsichord are found in the six English Suites and the six French Suites, by J. S. Bach.

Throughout the baroque, composers of keyboard music expressed a special fondness for variations (see chapter 3), either a theme with variations or a set of improvisatory melodic variations over a ground bass. An example of the latter type is found in Henry Purcell's *Variations for Harpsichord,* sometimes called *Variations on a New Ground Bass* (no. 38 in *Masterpieces of Music Before 1750*).

The organ was another important baroque keyboard instrument.

The other important baroque keyboard instrument, the organ, has been a part of music making for a very long time. In the course of its history, it has undergone numerous changes in size, mechanism, and basic sound. The baroque was witness to a major change in the organ: it became larger, more powerful, more versatile, and tonally richer than any of its ancestors. The marvels of this instrument were matched by a body of organ music which, in the opinion of many, is unparalleled in the history of Western art music.

Organ improvisation was popular in baroque.

A variety of organ music was produced by many composers during the baroque era. The toccata and the fantasia were flashy, virtuosic types of organ music written with no set form. They contained something of the spirit of improvisation, whereas the fugue was much more rigorously structured and usually more sombre in mood. The chorale prelude was another important type of organ music that was raised to the highest artistic level by J. S. Bach.

Vocal Music—Genres and Composers

The opera, oratorio, and cantata emerged as vocal genres during the baroque era.

The baroque created and developed three large-scale genres of vocal music with instruments: opera, oratorio, and cantata. These have proven to be enduring, for composers throughout the baroque, the classical era, and the nineteenth and twentieth centuries have continued to produce them. The elements that these three have in common are solo singing in the form of recitatives and arias, small ensemble numbers for a duet or trio of singers, choruses, and orchestra.

Opera

The most dramatic musical genre, the **opera,** emerged early in the baroque era. It has undergone numerous changes throughout its history, but regardless of the time, the place, or the composer, opera has always been the synthesis of drama and music intended for the stage. The visual aspect of the genre cannot be overestimated; the full impact of an opera can only be experienced by witnessing a performance. Obviously this cannot be produced in the format of a book and we are thus at a disadvantage to fully understand what opera is and how it works. However, we can explore some aspects of opera that will be useful when we actually attend opera performances.

Opera blends music and drama.

The Operatic Structure   On the largest structural level, an opera, an essentially secular genre, is divided into a number of acts. In the middle baroque the standard was five acts, and in the late baroque the standard was three acts. Each act comprises a number of scenes—usually two or three, though acts with several scenes were not unusual in the baroque. A scene is a unit in which a character may be introduced and developed, some new facet of the story may be presented, or a given scene may be presented for more or less purely musical reasons.

The text of an opera is called a **libretto** and is normally written by someone other than the composer—the librettist.

The libretto is the text of an opera.

The opera composer and the librettist must constantly be aware of the flow of three basic lines: the story line, the line of character development, and the musical line. The drama or story line must have some innate interest and must unfold at an appropriate pace or the audience will become disinterested. The characters must continue to evolve and develop to assure audience involvement with them. Not everything that happens in an opera is the equivalent of a hit song, but there must be enough vocal "treats" along the way to satisfy the strictly musical palate. And it becomes an even more complicated and difficult undertaking to make sure that one of these three lines doesn't steal the limelight from the others.

The story, the characters, and the music develop simultaneously.

The composer must also be concerned with the arrangement of the musical forces—solos, small ensembles, chorus, and orchestra. Working within the limits imposed by the libretto, the opera composer strives for an agreeable mixture of these forces and tries to avoid long stretches in which only one is present.

Solo Singing in the Opera   There are two basic types of solo singing in opera: **recitative** and **aria**. The word recitative suggests singing in the manner of a recitation, and indeed the typical recitative from baroque opera is such. Recitatives tend to be wordy, syllabic, and loaded with information about the characters and the unfolding story. Frequently they are musically static, and the audience's attention is focused more on the text than on the melodic line. In contrast, the aria—the songlike phenomenon—is very active musically. It may be greatly embellished and may traverse a wide vocal range. An aria may revolve around a very few lines of text or single words that are repeated. The story line may stand still when this happens, but its pace will pick up again in an ensuing recitative.

Recitative singing provides much of the opera's story line.

An aria is musically active.

Opera History   The oldest examples of opera are products of early seventeenth-century Florence, Italy. A group of Florentine noblemen called the Camerata were among those responsible for the creation of opera. In 1602 a Camerata composer, Giulio Caccini (ca. 1550–1618), published a collection of songs under the title *Le Nuove musiche* (the new music). The title was well-chosen, for the style of Caccini's music was new and contrasted sharply with the late Renaissance choral contrapuntal style. It consisted of solo singing with minimal homophonic accompaniment called monody.

Their fascination with classical antiquity led the Camerata quite naturally to the production of librettos based on Greek mythology. They were particularly interested in the drama and in the clear, affective, uncluttered presentation of the text. In their opinion, word painting and counterpoint interfered with such a presentation. Here, in part, is what Caccini said in the preface of *Le Nuove musiche:*

The first operas were based upon subject matter drawn from Greek mythology.

> [I was] convinced . . . with the clearest reasons not to follow that old way of composition whose music, not suffering the words to be understood by the hearers, ruins the conceit and the verse . . . a laceration of the poetry. . . . I have endeavored in those my late compositions to bring in a kind of music by which men might, as it were, talk in harmony, using in that kind of singing . . . a certain noble neglect of the song. . . .[2]

What the Camerata lacked was a truly expert composer, one thoroughly grounded in the craft and techniques of musical composition and possessing a fertile musical and dramatic imagination. Such a composer was Claudio Monteverdi (1567–1643). His earliest opera *Orfeo* is generally regarded as the first operatic masterpiece.

The first operatic masterpiece, Orfeo, was composed by Monteverdi.

2. From *Source Readings in Music History,* compiled and edited by Oliver Strunk. W. W. Norton & Company, Inc., New York, NY. Copyright 1950 by W. W. Norton & Company, Inc. Copyright renewed 1978. Reprinted by permission.

Based on the Greek myth of Orpheus and Euridice, *Orfeo* was first performed at Mantua in 1607. Unlike the operas of the Camerata, Monteverdi's *Orfeo* skillfully blended solo singing with choruses, small ensembles, and an orchestra of about forty players. It is a musical palette of great richness and diversity, as is evident in act III (the entire act contains but one scene).

The setting is the entrance of the underworld where Orfeo has come, guided by Speranza, the goddess of hope. He is in search of his beloved Euridice. Orfeo sings a recitative in syllabic style with basso continuo accompaniment. He is answered by another recitative sung by Hope (Speranza). Notice how gloom pervades Hope's recitative. In Orfeo's next recitative we learn that he must continue his pursuit without the company of Hope.

Charon is introduced next, and with him a new vocal range. He is a bass, while Orfeo (tenor) and Hope (alto) are higher voices. At the conclusion of his recitative the orchestra plays the prelude to Orfeo's extended aria which follows. This is a strophic aria with a variety of instrumental accompaniments. It should be immediately obvious that the style of the aria, "Possente spirto," is markedly different from the recitatives: it is fancier, more elaborate, and imbued with virtuosity. Clearly the aria is the center of gravity in this act.

After another statement from Charon, Orfeo sings an active and impassioned recitative that approaches the quality of an aria. The act concludes with a fatalistic statement from the chorus. Again, the chorus adds an ingredient to the mix of musical forces employed by Monteverdi.

Operatic Forms   Opera rapidly gained popularity, and during the seventeenth century it spread over western Europe and England. In many of these nations the opera developed unique characteristics.

A distinctly French brand of opera called **tragedie lyrique** was developed in the 1670s under Jean Baptiste Lully (1632–87). In Lully's operas, the French dual loves of drama and ballet became central features. Lully also created an orchestral preface called a French overture for his operas. Other composers were attracted to this, and the French overture was widely employed later in the baroque era as the frontispiece of operas as well as a separate orchestral piece. The French overture consisted of two sections: the first was slow, majestic, and in dotted rhythms; the second was livelier and imitative. An example of French overture is found in Lully's *Alceste*. Another is the "overture" to Handel's oratorio, *Messiah*.

The British imported Italian opera but developed their own operatic style in the English language. The central composer of English opera was Henry Purcell (1659–95), whose masterpiece is the short opera

Orfeo blends solos, choruses, small ensembles, and orchestra.

In the seventeenth century, opera spread from Florence across Europe and to England.

French opera, which combined drama and ballet, featured an overture made up of one slow and one fast section.

The central composer of English opera was Purcell.

Dido and Aeneas (1689). The work begins with a French overture and contains a lovely aria called "When I am Laid in Earth," which occurs near the opera's conclusion.

Italian opera continued to change, and during 1700–1725 it evolved into a highly formalized type called **opera seria.** Almost without exception the subject matter of opera seria was drawn from classical antiquity. Particularly favored were those stories or legends in which there are three pairs of lovers and a minimal number of secondary characters. Attention was thus focused on individual characters caught in dramatic situations; in musical terms the attention was focused on solo singing. Small ensemble numbers were few and the chorus, if there was one at all, played a very minor role. In essence, then, an opera seria consisted of a sequence of arias connected by recitatives and embellished with an occasional ensemble. The opera seria was always presented in three acts with one, two, or three scenes per act.

The highly formalized opera seria focused on individual characters, downplaying the chorus.

Unquestionably the central features of an opera seria, and the most popular with the audience, were the incredible singers. The art of singing in **bel canto** (beautiful singing) style was raised to an unprecedented height. The primary vehicle for the singer was a special type of aria called **da capo aria.** The da capo aria is a three-part form *ABA* in which the repetition of *A* is greatly embellished by the singer.

A da capo aria is in *ABA* form.

Act I, scene 2, from Handel's *Alcina* (1735) illustrates how these forces work together. Alcina, the enchantress, capable of turning people into wild beasts or rocks, is infatuated with Ruggiero. Ruggiero is similarly infatuated with Alcina, though he is betrothed to Bradamante. Ruggiero has been evading Bradamante for some time, and Bradamante, disguised as her own brother Ricciardo, has come with her tutor, Melisso, to search for her lost lover. The story, though farcical, provides an excellent vehicle for the singers to display their voices and a variety of passions.

In this scene there are five arias, four of which are da capo arias; one for Oronte, another character in the opera, two for Alcina, and two for Ruggiero (whose part is often sung by a female despite the fact that Ruggiero is a male character). The remainder of the scene is given to connective recitative accompanied only by basso continuo. Notice how the recitatives move the story line and seem to build or lead directly to the arias. Notice also that the orchestral accompaniment to each aria revolves around a single idea. This is, of course, a reflection of Handel's involvement with the *Doctrine of Affections.* The text of the opening recitative and da capo aria follows.

An anti-chamber to Alcina's apartments

Ruggiero   **Ruggiero**

Recitative

Vo cercando la bella cagion delle   I go in search of the lovely cause of
mie pene;   all my woes;
vieni, deh! vieni a me, caro mio   come, oh come to me, my dearest
bene!   dear!

Da capo aria

A

Bramo di trionfar   I long to triumph
sol per piacer d'amor,   only for the pleasure of love,
ma non contento ancor   but all unsatisfied yet
m'agita l'alma.   my heart aches within me.
Bramo di trionfar, ecc.   I long to triumph, etc.

B

Suol gloria accompagnar   Glory should attend
un generoso ardor,   a noble passion,
ma senza amor il cor   but, lacking love, my heart
non può aver calma.   cannot rest in peace.

A

Bramo di trionfar, ecc.   I long to triumph, etc.
La cerco in vano, e la crudel non   I seek her in vain, and the cruel
torna.   woman does not return.[3]

George Frederic Handel

Like J. S. Bach, Handel (1685–1759) was born in northern Germany in
1685. But beyond that their lives and musical styles were dissimilar.
Whereas Bach was a church musician whose travels and fame were severely restricted, Handel was essentially a composer of operas and oratorios, a man who had an international reputation and amassed a
considerable fortune. Bach's style, as mentioned earlier, was rooted in
northern German traditions in which rigorous counterpoint was a central feature. Handel was trained in the lighter, less complex Italian style.
Bach was a family man whose personality could be described as serious
and brooding. Handel remained a bachelor who was much at home among
the high society.

3. From Handel's *Alcina* reprinted through the courtesy of PolyGram Special Products, a Division of PolyGram
Records, Inc.

Handel was a well-known composer of opera seria, much in vogue for several decades.

Handel settled in London in 1712 and quickly became a favored composer of opera seria. For more than a generation the English public eagerly supported Italian opera seria. In fact, it would be difficult to exaggerate its popularity. Handel was one of several composers who rode the wave of this popularity, but in the 1720s the affections of the audience began to shift to an emerging brand of opera—comic opera (discussed in chapter 6). Before long opera seria, which could not withstand the competition, was no longer in vogue. At this time Handel became very active as a composer of oratorios.

Oratorio

Elements of the oratorio are: recitatives, arias, small ensemble numbers, choruses, and orchestra.

The **oratorio,** though a concert piece rather than a staged work, has some elements in common with opera: recitatives and arias, small ensemble numbers, choruses, and orchestra. As we have seen, the chorus played a very minor role in opera seria, but in the oratorio the chorus became a central feature. Unlike the opera, the oratorio does not have a plot or characters per se, but it does utilize a central theme.

Handel's *Messiah* is an example of an oratorio.

Messiah   Handel's most renowned work, and one of the best known works in the entire history of Western art music, is the oratorio *Messiah* (1742). *Messiah* is an extended work for vocal soloists, chorus, and orchestra. It is more in the nature of a narrative than a drama, having fifty-three individual numbers. The piece is divided into three large parts and is based on the Old and New Testament texts. There is no story line per se, but each of the three parts develops a theme.

The first part deals with the coming of Christ and with the manifold glory of God. The general spirit is one of rejoicing. The second part concerns the crucifixion of Christ. Its mood is darker, in sharp contrast to part one. The third part revolves around the theme of humanity's redemption through Christ.

There are twenty choruses in *Messiah.* It is obvious that Handel devoted much of his talent to these choruses, just as he had to the arias in his operas. Handel did, however, include a number of beautiful arias in this work, also.

Messiah begins with a stately French overture and immediately proceeds to a recitative and aria for tenor.

Recitative: Comfort ye, comfort ye my people, saith your God. Speak comfortably to Jerusalem, and cry unto her that her warfare is accomplished, that her iniquity is pardoned. The voice of him that crieth in the wilderness, Prepare ye the way of the Lord, make straight in the desert a highway for our God.

Aria: Every valley shall be exalted, and every mountain and hill made low; the crooked straight, and the rough places plain.

Most of the recitatives in this work are, like this first one, adorned with orchestral accompaniment, not just the basso continuo. This has a softening effect that seems appropriate, given the nature of the text. The aria is truly an exaltation and Handel makes the most of the word "exalted," by spinning a fine melismatic web over it each time it occurs.

Not all recitatives feature orchestral accompaniment.

The chorus makes its triumphal entrance in no. 4 on the text "And the glory of the Lord shall be revealed." It is a vigorous and powerful chorus that alternates between imitative and homophonic textures. There is a dramatic and deafening silence just before the last words are sung. Elsewhere in the first part there are arias for bass, alto, and soprano, but there is nothing more compelling than the choruses, especially no. 12, "For Unto Us a Child is Born," with its virtuosic lines and quick tempo.

The triumphant, powerful chorus alternates between imitative and homophonic textures.

The choruses from part two provide an explicit contrast to the joyful mood of part one. Listen in particular to no. 24, "Surely he hath borne our griefs." Notice the extreme, wrenching dissonances that occur on the words "grief," and "He was wounded for our transgressions, He was bruised for our iniquities." But the gloom that pervades this section is dispelled completely with the final number of that part, no. 44, the famous "Halleluja" chorus.

The overriding optimism of the work is nowhere more obvious than in the lovely aria for soprano that opens part three—"I know that my Redeemer liveth."

Cantata

In some respects a **cantata** resembles both opera and oratorio since it contains arias, recitatives, small ensemble numbers, a chorus, and an orchestra. Some secular cantatas even resemble opera in terms of story line and character development; sacred cantatas, however, do not. Like oratorio, but unlike opera, the cantata (both secular and sacred) is not intended for the stage, nor is it divided into acts and scenes. Generally speaking, the cantata is a shorter work than an oratorio. *Messiah,* for example, lasts more than two hours, whereas the average cantata may last from twenty to forty-five minutes.

A cantata has characteristics of both opera and oratorio.

Of the many church cantatas composed by J. S. Bach, about 200 have survived from all stages of his musical career—from his earliest compositions for the Lutheran church to those he composed late in life. Many of his church cantatas make extended use of a chorale (see chapter 11) and for that reason are called chorale cantatas. A **chorale** is a hymn melody (and text) used in the Lutheran worship service. A **chorale prelude** is a composition for organ based on a chorale melody.

J. S. Bach composed both church and secular contatas.

Figure 5.6

Ein' feste Burg ist unser Gott   Cantata no. 80, *Ein' feste Burg ist unser Gott (A Mighty Fortress Is Our God)* is a chorale cantata. There are eight numbers in this cantata and part of the chorale (melody and text) is used as the substance of numbers 1, 2, 5, and 8. The chorale melody is shown in Figure 5.6.

Cantata No. 80:
Ein' Feste Burg Ist Unser Gott

(Text by Luther; Melody by Crüger for the Reformation Festival)
1. Choral Motet

Ein' feste Burg ist unser Gott,	A stronghold sure is God our Lord,
ein' gute Wehr und Waffen;	Whose strength will never fail us;
er hilft uns frei aus aller Not,	He keeps us free from all the horde
die uns jetzt hat betroffen.	Of troubles that assail us.
Der alte böse Feind,	Our ever evil foe
mit Ernster's jetzt meint,	Would fain work us woe,
gross Macht und viel List	With might and deep guile
sein grausam Rüstung ist,	He plans his projects vile,
auf Erd' ist nicht seinsgleichen.	On earth is not one like him.

A basic theme of Cantata no. 80 is the conflict between good and evil; one's struggle with the temptations of evil and the power and eventual triumph of God in one's life.

Using the chorale tune and the first verse of the chorale text, Bach created a magnificent, intricately detailed musical tapestry for chorus and orchestra. It is a big, imposing number that reflects the might and majesty of God. Notice that Bach provides a free and florid treatment of the chorale tune, sometimes augmenting its note values, sometimes adding musical embroidery of his own invention.

The structure of both tune and text is *AAB*. The two *A* parts of the text speak of God as a stronghold, a liberator of earthly troubles. The *B* part of the text speaks of Satan in vivid terms. The *A* and *B* parts, then, present the sense of conflict in the text.

2. Choral Duet (Soprano, Bass)
Soprano

Mit uns'rer Macht ist nichts getan,	Standing alone are we undone,
wir sind gar bald verloren.	The Fiend would soon enslave us;
Es streit't für uns der rechte Mann,	But for us fights a mighty One
den Gott selbst hat erkoren.	Whom God has sent to save us.
Fragst du, wer er ist?	Ask ye, who this be?
Er heisst Jesus Christ,	Christ Jesus is He,
der Herre Zebaoth,	Lord God of Sabbaoth,
und ist kein andrer Gott,	There is no other God;
das Feld muss er behalten.	He can and will uphold us.

Sopranos sing the second stanza of the chorale, speaking alternately of Satan (the fiend) and Christ, once more staging the conflict. A very active and florid bass solo that speaks of liberation and victory acts as an anchor for this number. Notice that the orchestral accompaniment revolves around a single, initially stated figure.

Bass

Alles, was von Gott geboren,	Every soul by God created,
ist zum Siegen auserkoren.	Has by Christ been liberated.
Wer bei Christi Blutpanier	They who Jesus' standard bear,
in der Taufe Treu' geschworen,	To His service dedicated,
siegt im Geiste für und für.	All will in His victory share.

A bass soloist sings a reflective recitative accompanied only by basso continuo, in this case organ and cello. The text dwells on the devil and human sin, and is in a sense a warning.

3. Recitativo (Bass)

Erwäge doch, Kind Gottes die	Thou child of God,
so grosse Liebe,	Consider what complete devotion
da Jesus sich mit seinem	The Savior showed for you
Blute dir verschriebe,	In His supreme atonement,
womit er dich zum Kriege wider	Whereby He rose triumphant
Satans Heer und wider Welt	Over Satan's Horde, and human sin
und Sünde geworben hat.	And error and all things base.
Gib nicht in deiner Seele	Let not, then, in your being,
dem Satan und den Lastern statt!	The Evil One have any place.

Las nicht dein Herz,	Let not your sins
Den Himmel Gottes auf der Erden,	Convert the Heaven there within you,
Zur Wüste werden,	Into a desert.
Bereue deine Schuld mit Schmerz,	Repent now of your guilt in tears,
dass Christi Geist	That Christ the Lord
mit dir sich fest verbinde.	To you be fast united.

A modified da capo aria for soprano and continuo follows the admonition in the preceding number. The text responds to the admonition, commanding evil and sin to depart. In this and the preceding numbers, notice that the original chorale tune is absent.

4. Aria (Soprano)

Komm in mein Herzenshaus,	Come dwell within my heart;
Herr Jesus mein Verlangen.	Lord Jesus, I adore Thee.
Treib' Welt und Satan aus,	Bid evil all depart
und lass dein Bild in mir erneuert prangen.	And let Thine image ever shine before me.
Weg, schnöder Sündengraus!	Out, sin, how base thou art!
weg, weg.	Begone away, away.

5. Unison Chorale (Soprano, Alto, Tenor, Bass)

Und wenn die Welt voll Teufel war	Though fiends appear on every hand
Und wollten uns verschlingen,	All eager to devour,
so fürchten wir uns nicht so sehr	We need not fear; we can withstand
es soll uns doch gelingen.	And baffle all their power.
Der Fürst dieser Welt	The Arch-Fiend of all,
wie saur er sich stellt,	Shall not us appall,
tut er uns doch nichts,	His might is laid low,
das macht, er ist gericht't,	He cannot strike a blow;
ein wörtlein kann ihn fallen.	One Word from God will fell him.

The chorale tune makes a triumphant reentry in this number, as does the orchestra. The text is aggressive and defiant of Satan.

6. Recitativo (Tenor)

So stehe denn bei Christi blutgefärbter Fahne,	So take thy stand with Jesus' blood-be-spattered banner,
O Seele, fest,	O soul of mine,
und glaube, dass dein Haupt dich nicht verlässt,	And trust thee ever in His power divine.
ja, dass sein Sieg auch dir den Weg zu deiner Krone bahne.	Yea, He will lend His might To gain for thee thy crown of glory.
I ritt freudig an der Krieg!	Go joyous forth to fight!
Wirst du nur Gottes Wort	If thou but hear God's Word
so hören als bewahren,	And do as He command thee,

so wird der Feind gezwungen
auszufahren,
dein Heiland bleibt dein Heil
dein Heiland bleibt dein Hort.

No foe, however mighty can
withstand thee,
Salvation now is sure,
Thy refuge is secure.

The texture and mood change dramatically in this number. Here the text is resolute. The recitative is sung by a tenor, and we are aware that Bach has carefully mixed his musical forces and vocal types.

7. Duet (Alto, Tenor)

Wie selig sind doch die,
die Gott im Munde tragen,
doch sel'ger ist das Herz,
das ihn im Glauben trägt.
Es bleibet unbesiegt
und kann die Feinde schlagen,
und wird zuletzt gekrönt,
wenn es den Tod erlegt.

Blessed is he who praises God,
Whose Words will sanctify him;
More blessed still is he
Who bears Him in his heart.
With Him will grace abound
Nor can the foe come nigh him;
At last will he be crowned,
When death shall set him free.

This is a small ensemble number, a duet for a high male voice and a low-register female voice. The mood of the text is pious and reflective.

8. Chorale

Das Wort sie sollen lassen stahn
und kein Dank dazu haben.
Er ist bei uns wohl auf dem Plan
mit seinem Geist und Gaben.
Nehmen sie uns den Leib,
Gut, Ehr', Kind und Weib,
lass fahren dahin,
sie haben's kein Gewinn;
das Reich muss uns doch bleiben.

The Word of God will firm abide
Against our foes assailing,
For He will battle on our side,
An Ally never failing.
Tho' they take from me here
All that I hold dear
I will not complain,
Their vantage will be in vain,
God's might is all-prevailing.

This is a straightforward, unadorned setting of the chorale tune sung to the last verse of the chorale text. It is likely that, when Bach lived, the entire congregation would have joined the choir in singing this number.

Summary

Our study of the baroque era began with a look at its position in history. The baroque experienced the rise of the Enlightenment and its successful challenge of Absolutism. This major struggle between old and new marked the beginning of the modern democratic nation state. At first termed "baroque" to emphasize its wild, undisciplined nature, the arts of this period now carry the title as a stylistic label.

Baroque art, exemplified by the works of Rubens, show a sweeping, spiraling quality barely contained by the canvas. Figures are robust, muscular, and animated.

The baroque composer felt an obligation to express the various states of the human soul. These can be expressed through means that became characteristics of baroque music. The most important of these characteristics are functional harmony, basso continuo, and figured bass. Stylistic ingredients include drama, activity, ornamentation, and virtuosity. These are found in both the orchestral and vocal music of the period.

The baroque era produced several genres of instrumental music: the concerto grosso, the trio sonata, and keyboard music. Concerto grosso, the dominant form of orchestral music, was a multi-movement piece, featuring a small group of soloists called concertino, alternating with a larger group of instruments called tutti. A basso continuo completed the group. J. S. Bach's *Brandenburg* Concerto no. 2 is a good example.

The trio sonata, the dominant form of chamber music in baroque, was a multi-movement work featuring two solo instruments and a basso continuo. Corelli's Trio Sonata in F Minor, op. 3, no. 9, and Handel's Trio Sonata in F major, op. 2, no. 5, are two examples.

Keyboard music, both harpsichord and organ, flourished during the era. Harpsichord music featured dance suites while organ music focused on the toccata, the fantasia, the fugue, and the chorale prelude.

Three large-scale genres of vocal music were created during the baroque: opera, oratorio, and cantata. All three genres include the elements of solo singing in recitatives and arias, small ensembles, choruses, and orchestra.

In opera, several acts are divided into scenes that present a story line through music and drama. Simultaneously, the story, the music, and the characters are developed. While early opera focused on Greek mythology, opera developed during the baroque period in the hands of the Italians, French, and British.

The baroque oratorio was a concert piece with the chorus as the central feature. The oratorio also developed a theme, as evidenced by Handel's *Messiah*.

The cantata resembled both the opera and the oratorio, though the cantata is usually a shorter work than the oratorio. J. S. Bach composed both church and secular contatas.

By now, you should feel quite familiar with many elements of baroque—its historical significance, its artistic characteristics, and its musical genres.

Key Terms

musical recipes	dance suite	aria
basso continuo	allemande	tragedie lyrique
figured bass	courante	opera seria
concerto grosso	saraband	bel canto
concertino	gigue	da capo aria
tutti	prelude	oratorio
ritornello	opera	cantata
trio sonata	libretto	chorale
chamber music	recitative	chorale prelude

Thinking About It

This is the first of several chapters in which we deal with the concept of style. Be sure you can adequately describe baroque style and list its characteristics. Above all, be sure that you can hear these characteristics in the musical examples included in this chapter. Your ability to identify stylistic baroque features will eventually facilitate your understanding of style in other eras of music and allow you to compare and contrast one style with another.

It is also important to know the types of music written during the baroque era, not only for the purposes of this course, but for future involvement with art music. The term concerto grosso should suggest certain things to you and bring forth a set of expectations—what the musical forces will be, who will play what and when, how many and what types of movements there will be. Similarly, the terms suite, trio sonata, opera seria, and cantata should be suggestive and develop a set of expectations and predictions.

Knowledge of baroque genres will tell you *what* is being played, knowledge of style will tell you *how* it is being played, and an understanding of the *Doctrine of Affections* will tell you *why* the music is the way it is. Explore the *what, how,* and *why* in Bach's *Brandenberg* Concerto no. 2.

CHAPTER

6

Music
in
the
Preclassic
Era

Conversation in the Park, Thomas Gainsbourough.
Cliché des Musées Nationaux, Paris

Sounds of the Chapter

C. P. E. Bach
Fantasia in C Minor, K. 475
Symphony in B Minor ♪

J. C. Bach
Symphony in D Major, op. 18, no. 1 ♪

J. S. Bach
Brandenburg Concerto no. 2 ♪
French Suite no. 1 in D Minor ♪

Couperin
"Le Croc-en-jambe" ♪

Stamitz
Symphony in D Major (*Sinfonia a 8*)

Musical Styles in the Preclassic Era

The preclassic era roughly spanned the years 1720–70. This period was witness to many changes—social, aesthetic, philosophical, and artistic—and to the collapse of the baroque world.

During this period, a number of stylistic movements evolved, and with some reshaping, many characteristics of these styles became part of the classical Viennese style that blossomed about 1770–1810. The first of these contributing movements was essentially a French phenomenon known as **rococo.**

Rococo

Louis XIV died in 1715 after a reign of more than half a century. Politically, his death signaled the end of the absolute monarchy in France. Psychologically, his death forced both the aristocracy and the citizenry to consider the future without their father figure. Artistically, the Sun King's death heralded the decline of baroque ideals in France. The dramatic opulence, virtuosity, and passion of royal baroque art began to crumble as rococo gained popularity with its refinement, grace, wit, simplicity of texture, and a reduction from monumental to more human and natural proportions.

The heir to the throne was Louis's seven-year-old great-grandson, Louis XV. However, the child could not assume command of the government until 1723, when he became of legal age. During the interim (1715–23), the government was run by a board of regents, headed by Philip, Duke of Orleans. This period is known as the Regency.

The spirit of rococo began to imprint itself on French culture during the Regency. Louis XV, influenced by Philip, encouraged the popularity of rococo, rather than the baroque his great-grandfather had endorsed.

Two dominant trends evident in the French rococo are the quests for pleasure and for personal liberty. Both Philip and Louis XV espoused this hedonistic trend as they were men of weak and dissolute character whose appetites for pleasure exceeded their sense of responsibility toward the country and the people. In fact, their disinterest in governing the country was a contributing factor to the revolution that occurred in the late eighteenth century.

The great palace of Versailles epitomized the grandeur of the French baroque and stood as a visible symbol of the power and majesty of the Sun King for whom it was built. The fact that Versailles was situated eleven miles from Paris presented not only a physical gap between the king and his people, it also symbolized the psychological chasm between them.

The preclassic period followed the baroque.

With the death of Louis XIV came the end of baroque.

Rococo introduced refinement, grace, and wit.

Rococo exhibits the quests for personal liberty and pleasure.

Rococo exterior.
© The Bettmann Archive

Philip left all of the baroque grandeur of Versailles behind when he ascended the throne and reestablished the court in Paris. He was a city man, and the style of painting, decoration, and music that flourished around him was charming, elegant, tasteful, and lighthearted. His style was aristocratic, but not regal; snobbish, but not pompous. His tastes and ideas were refined and clever, but not profound.

The rococo was an age of collectibles. Sea shells displayed in delicate glass cases, porcelain figurines, and snuff boxes were subtly and tastefully displayed in the drawing room. There was also evidence of the love of nature and the out-of-doors as the picnic and the "outing" are common motifs in some of the best paintings from the rococo. This love of nature was not passionate, but rather a delight in nature and a desire to be comfortable with it. Gardens were neatly trimmed and often formed into unnatural shapes, reversing the usual order of art imitating nature. The decoration of the interior of the houses typically featured vines, small

Many rococo paintings show a delight in nature.

Figure 6.1
The decorative rococo.
© Historical Pictures Service Inc., Chicago

Watteau was the central
French painter during the
rococo period.

birds, and butterflies. It appeared as though efforts were made to make
outdoors look like indoors, and indoors look like outdoors—the garden
filled with furniture, the house filled with plants.

The decorative panel shown in figure 6.1 is by Jean Antoine Watteau (1684–1721), the central French painter of the time. Notice the
out-of-doors motif and the use of vegetation as ornamentation.

This *was* an age of ladies and gentlemen; an age in which proper
manners and good taste were highly valued. The coquette, the flirtatious,
and the risqué were elements of this era, evidenced by the many suggestive seminude paintings and the behavior of many an aristocrat. Rococo
ladies and gentlemen, as subjects of rococo art, are beautifully, ideally
proportioned.

Women occupied a new and important position during the rococo period. They were responsible for the creation of the *salon,* an intimate gathering of educated men and women where fine conversation and the exchange of ideas were encouraged. Later in the century, when Madame Pompadour became the mistress of Louis XV, her impeccable taste and refinement formed a lasting influence on French culture.

Rococo music reflected many characteristics of the era. The central composer of the French rococo was Francois Couperin (1668–1733). He composed several sets of **ordres** (suites) for the harpsichord, or in French, *le clavecin.* Many individual pieces from these *ordres* have fanciful, playful titles, such as the names of women or the names of moods or states of mind. One piece from the twenty-second *ordre* has the title "Le Croc-en-jambe" or "The Dirty Trick." Its playful mood, light texture, short-breathed melody, and delicate ornamentation identify it as a product of the French rococo.

The Grand Ball—an elegant ball in the rococo.
© The Bettmann Archive

Women made an impact on intellectual and social development during the period.

Couperin was the central composer of French rococo.

Madame Pompadour—a
dominant figure in the French
rococo.
The Victoria and Albert Museum

A Party in the Open Air, J. A.
Watteau (see colorplate 16).
Bildarchiv Preussischer Kulturbesitz

Figure 6.2

Figure 6.3

Figure 6.4

The music from this period displays a clear preference for homophonic rather than contrapuntal, and light rather than dense textures. Careful listening to this Couperin piece should reveal that the melody is made up of short phrases that are easily sung, despite the delicate ornamentation. Figure 6.2 illustrates the basic outline of the first phrase of the "Croc-en-jambe" melody in unadorned form. Figure 6.3 shows us the phrase as Couperin notated it, complete with markings for the ornamentation. Figure 6.4 illustrates the "realization" of the ornamentation, or how the piece actually sounds.

Rococo musical texture is homophonic and light.

Style Galant

The light, elegant style of music from the rococo was not limited to France. A more general term for this musical style is **style galant.** It can be used interchangeably with rococo as a stylistic label for much of the music from 1720 to 1760, and even later.

The terms "rococo" and "style galant" are interchangeable.

The minuet, Tiepolo.
Museo de Arts Decorativas

J. C. Bach   Johann Christian Bach (1735–82), the youngest son of J. S. Bach, composed music that typifies the style galant. He was invited to London in 1762 to take the position of music master to the court. He produced a large number of symphonies and concertos in the style galant, and beginning in 1765, became coproducer of a very successful series of public concerts known as the Bach-Abel concerts. Because his own works were frequently featured in these concerts, he became an enormously popular composer both in Britain and on the continent.

J. C. Bach's pieces are examples of style galant.

His Symphony in D Major, op. 18, no. 1, first movement, provides an excellent illustration of the temper and ambience of the style galant.

In the 1750s a British journalist wrote: "More and more people are turning to the delightful art of music." The statement may at first seem silly, but on reflection it suggests some important points. For one thing, it informs us that music was regarded as delightful at this time. This information agrees with a basic tenet of the style galant: it is designed to please.

Style galant music was composed for the listener's pleasure.

Secondly, one can infer that music was no longer the exclusive property of the noble and wealthy. Increasingly, it became a public art with "more and more people turning to it." A rising middle class, economically bolstered by the industrial revolution in England and elsewhere in Europe, could now afford to participate in and learn about art music. In a real sense the masses were being liberated from a cultural

The masses had access to style galant music.

prison. They were free to partake of a kind of music that in earlier times was either denied them or beyond their comprehension and hence, enjoyment. Beginning in 1725 with the **concerts spirituels** in Paris, public concerts became common in many European metropolitan centers.

Public concerts became popular in England and France.

Empfindsamer Stil

There were also centers of creativity scattered about Europe where gifted young composers and musicians interested in new styles of music gathered. The galant was but one of these styles. Some composers found the style galant too limiting, too facile, and lacking in natural, human qualities. The Germans in general, and Carl Philipp Emanuel Bach in particular, were purveyors of a style that leaned heavily on sentiment, even sentimentality. This style emerged in the 1750s and took the German name *empfindsamer stil,* the "sensitive style," and was filled with weeping motives, sighs, fluctuations in tempo, and flights of emotional improvisation. C. P. E. Bach (1714–88), the older brother of J. C. Bach, was for a time an exponent of this sensitive style. His Fantasia in C Minor, K. 475, is an excellent example of *empfindsamer stil* (found in *History of Music in Sound,* vol. VII). Note the abrupt changes in mood, tempo, and activity.

The Germans created a sentimental style of music termed empfindsamer stil.

Sturm und Drang

A few years before the eruption of the American Revolutionary War, another preclassic style developed in Europe, again principally in Germany. It was an emotional, sometimes violent style called **Sturm und Drang** ("Storm and Stress"). This style attempted to revitalize music, scourging it of rococo pleasantness and *empfindsamer stil* melancholy. It emphasized crunching dissonance, minor keys, and jagged themes that contrasted sharply with more lyrical ones. Counterpoint, which played such a minimal role in both galant and *empfindsamer* styles, became an important feature of *Sturm und Drang* style. C. P. E. Bach's Symphony in B Minor, written in 1773, twenty years after his Fantasia in *empfindsamer stil,* is a good example of the fiery and passionate *Sturm und Drang* style.

Another offering of Germany at this time was Sturm und Drang style music.

Sturm und Drang was in direct contrast with rococo and empfindsamer styles.

The middle decades of the eighteenth century experienced a multitude of forces and counterforces. J. S. Bach and Handel, the supreme masters of the late baroque, lived into the 1750s. Other vestiges of baroque style and aesthetics survived and were favored by a segment of the population. To them, it was as if nothing were changing or nothing of consequence was developing. But things were changing, and two of J. S. Bach's own sons, each in his own way, figured prominently in these changes. Further changes were yet to come in the eighteenth century,

While J. S. Bach adhered to the baroque style, his two sons personified new directions of music.

brought about by Joseph Haydn (1732–1809) (born in the midst of the style galant), Wolfgang Mozart (1756–91) (whose birthdate coincides with the development of the *empfindsamer stil*), and Ludwig van Beethoven (1770–1827) (born as the *Sturm und Drang* movement was taking shape).

Musical Style as a Reflection of Culture

Music, then as now, did not operate in a vacuum. The changes in musical style and content that occurred in the eighteenth century, the preclassic era, reflect and complement various changes in the larger cultural context.

The Enlightenment influenced both the baroque and the preclassic eras.

The American Revolution (1776) and the French Revolution (1789) represent the dramatic quest for personal liberty that, as mentioned earlier in this chapter, was a dominant trend throughout most of the eighteenth century. The philosophical basis of this trend is traceable to a number of studies, treatises, and ideas that fall under the broad umbrella of "The Enlightenment," discussed in chapter 5. Two words—rational and natural—were at the core of this intellectual movement. The French Encyclopedists created a monumental 35-volume work that investigated the whole field of knowledge. In the process, virtually everything, including religious doctrines and authority at all levels, was reassessed in the light of reason. Reason was king, and rationalism was proclaimed:

> A new way of life, entirely factual, to be lived in the light of nature and reason, in political freedom, religious tolerance, and emancipation from the shakles of metaphysics.

Voltaire and Montesquieu led the movement toward rationalism.

Voltaire and Montesquieu were leading forces in the rationalist camp. They and other rationalists decried the "unnatural" authority of organized religion and the "unenlightened" monarchy in France. Rousseau deviated from pure reason into the realm of "naturalness." In his *Social Contract* (1762), Rousseau declared that people are born free, and that the state must serve the interests of the individual. Civilized society was, for him, the archenemy of the human soul, and he called for "a return to nature," the fountainhead of true humanity.

Rousseau called for a return to nature.

Just after the midcentury, there was a rediscovery of, or at least a renewed interest in, the artistic models of classical antiquity. These models were the most rational and the most natural to the enlightened mind.

The Symphony

The orchestra, as stated earlier, developed during the baroque era. It was used to accompany large-scale vocal works such as operas, oratorios, and cantatas. Composers also produced a strictly instrumental repertoire for it, including the concerto grosso, which was the dominant form of baroque orchestral music. During the preclassic era, the orchestra maintained this role in opera, oratorio, and other forms of sacred music. With some modifications, the concerto also flourished during the classical era. Most notably, however, preclassical composers and musicians laid the groundwork for the supreme accomplishment of the classical era, the **symphony.**

The orchestra maintained a position of importance during the preclassic era.

The fully developed classical symphony of the late eighteenth century did not appear overnight. It was the result of an evolutionary process that began in the early years of the century—first in Italy, then in Vienna, Mannheim, Berlin, Paris, London, and elsewhere. Composers of various nationalities were a part of this process. Giovanni Sammartini (1701–75), Alessandro Scarlatti (1659–1725), Matthias Georg Monn (1717–50), Maria Margherita Grimani (fl. 1713–18), Georg Christoph Wagenseil (1715–77), Johann Stamitz (1717–57), William Boyce (1710–79), Francois Joseph Gossec (1734–1829), Marianne von Martinez (1744–1812), C. P. E. Bach, J. C. Bach, Luigi Boccherini (1743–1805), and others.

The groundwork for the pure classical symphony was laid during the preclassic era, and it evolved gradually.

The Mannheim School   Johann Stamitz was the leading force of the Mannheim school of symphonists. This school, founded in the 1740s, produced compositions and performances that developed a widespread reputation for excellence. In terms of ensemble (ability to play together) and expressiveness, the Mannheim court orchestra became the model for other European orchestras.

The Mannheim court orchestra was the model for its time.

One of the distinguishing features of this orchestra was its skill in performing **crescendos** and **decrescendos.** A crescendo ($\diagup$ in musical notation) is a gradual, systematic increase in volume. Thus, instead of moving directly from *p* to *f* in the dramatic baroque manner the increase in volume was achieved gradually—in an orderly, well-mannered way. A decrescendo ($\diagdown$), the opposite of a crescendo, is a gradual decrease in volume. It is recorded that audiences literally rose from their chairs in the excitement of a crescendo and had their breath taken away with a decrescendo.

A crescendo indicates an increase in volume, while a decrescendo indicates a decrease in volume.

Stamitz himself wrote over seventy symphonies, and those in the Mannheim circle composed hundreds of symphonies from the years 1740–60.

The Mannheim orchestra was small by today's standards, probably numbering about thirty-eight to forty-five players, including, in addition to the string family, two players of the flute, the oboe, the French horn, and the bassoon.

Stamitz's Symphony in D Major (actually called *Sinfonia a 8*) is in four movements: presto, andante, minuetto, and prestissimo. He was very innovative, since the majority of preclassic symphonies, including some of the early ones by both Haydn and Mozart, had but three movements.

Stamitz, unlike many preclassical composers, wrote symphonies in four movements.

Sound and Sense
Preclassic Symphony

Title: Symphony in D Major (ca. 1748)
Composer: Stamitz
Recording: Archive Production
Meter: 4/4
Tempo: Allegro
Key: D major

A Closer Look

First Movement

The first movement of the Stamitz Symphony in D Major is the longest and most dramatic. Its form suggests sonata-allegro without achieving that status; some development exists, but there is no real development section and no bona fide recapitulation. Instead of the *A*-bridge-*B* layout of a real sonata form exposition this work presents a series of thematic scraps linked together. Notice that the movement begins with three "hammer strokes" by the orchestra, that a long dramatic crescendo connects *b* to *c,* and a brief section of imitative counterpoint leads to *e.*

a—hammer strokes, *a* repeated	(:11)	
b—French horns enter, builds to	(:10)	
cccc'	(:09)	
d—dominant key, more lyrical gesture, *d* repeated	(:10)	(1:04)
Bridge containing bits of imitative counterpoint	(:08)	
e—oboes, *e* repeated	(:16)	

These thematic scraps then reappear in scrambled order as a quasi development (:42).

Recapitulation (1:15)

Second Movement

The slow movement in 4/4 is essentially homophonic and is scored only for the strings. This movement also presents a series of short thematic bits: *abcd,* which is then repeated nonliterally.

Third Movement

The third movement is a minuet, the texture is homophonic, and, as expected, the meter is 3/4. The form of this movement is diagrammed at the section and the subsection:

A (minuet)	*B* (trio)	*A* (minuet)
aabb	*ccdede*	*ab*
(:45)	(1:04)	(:22)

Notice that the trio section features the woodwinds—first the oboes, then the French horns.

Fourth Movement

The last movement is the shortest and the fastest, with the simple structure:

A—wide-ranging theme	(:25)
B—more lyrical theme	(:28)
A'	(:32)
B'	(:32)

The Berlin School   Carl Philipp Emanuel Bach was the premier composer of the Berlin school that flourished at about the same time as the Mannheim school. Bach's Symphony in B Minor, mentioned earlier in connection with the *Sturm und Drang* movement, deserves another, more detailed, listening at this point. The work is in three movements (there is no minuet), as were many symphonies at this time. It is scored for strings and continuo. The continuo existed in the symphony well into the eighteenth century, although it appeared more out of habit than necessity. It no longer served any real purpose, and, in time, it disappeared entirely.

C. P. E. Bach was the foremost composer of the Berlin school.

The preclassic symphony featured a continuo.

Sound and Sense ♪
Berlin School

Title: Symphony in B Minor (1773)
Composer: C. P. E. Bach
Meter: 4/4
Tempo: Moderato
Key: B Minor

A Closer Look

First Movement

As you listen, notice that the first movement, like that of the Stamitz Symphony in D Major, is the longest and weightiest. It contains a string of small thematic bits, not a large *A* theme and a contrasting *B* theme. Each of the small thematic bits presented in the exposition has a different emotional character:

a—limpid	(:08)
b—furious	(:09)
c—soaring	(:08)
d—playful	(:16)
e—weeping and dissonant	(:12)
f—angry	(:07)
g—lyrical	(:09)
h—sad, weeping	(:13)

Pockets of rather stern counterpoint appear later in the movement.

Second Movement

The second movement commences without pause. Its thematic materials are lyrical and the harmonic language is at times aggressively dissonant. This creates a rather haunting effect, far too passionate and emotional for the style galant. This work is solidly in the *Sturm und Drang* style.

Third Movement

The concluding movement begins with an angry outburst, then continues with a great deal of counterpoint.

The Vienna School was a contemporary of the Mannheim and the Berlin schools.

The Vienna School   The symphonic school at Vienna is geographically and musically closest to Haydn's background. Several stylistic elements at various times commingled in the symphonies from the school, laying the groundwork for what would eventually become, in the hands of the mature Haydn, the Viennese classical style. The pure classical symphony was a mixture of some galant characteristics, some *empfindsamer stil, Sturm und Drang* characteristics, a stabilized orchestra, and the slow but certain expansion of the genius of Haydn.

Summary

We've termed the period around 1720–75 the preclassic era. The baroque was in retreat while the first signs of the Viennese classical era were emerging. The preclassic era was one of transition in politics, philosophy, and the arts. This transition was shaping eighteenth-century Europe.

The rococo style, which developed in France under King Louis XV, showed a refinement, a naturalism, and a simplicity of texture not seen in the baroque. The paintings of the period's greatest painter, Jean Antoine Watteau, exude a comfort with nature and the propriety of the age.

Rococo music, sometimes termed style galant, is exemplified by the compositions of Francois Couperin. This music shows homophonic, light texture superimposed with ornamentation. The European masses were exposed to style galant through public concerts offered in several metropolitan centers. J. C. Bach's Symphony in D Major, op. 18, no. 1, is a good example of style galant.

Rococo was only one style of music popular during the preclassic era. A German sentimental and emotional style, *empfindsamer stil,* was popularized by C. P. E. Bach in the 1750s.

In the 1770s the *Sturm und Drang* style emerged. In contrast to the other preclassic styles, *Sturm und Drang* features dissonance, minor keys, counterpoint, and jagged themes.

As the philosophers of the time expounded upon the enlightenment, doctrines of reason, and social contract, the composers were in the earliest stages of developing the classical symphony. Schools of symphonists grew up in both Mannheim and Berlin, Germany, and in Vienna, Austria. The Mannheim court orchestra, however, became the European model.

We'll continue our investigation into the evolution of the symphony in the next chapter.

Key Terms

rococo	*concerts spirituels*	symphony
ordres	*empfindsamer stil*	crescendo
style galant	*Sturm und Drang*	decrescendo

Thinking About It

A good way to distinguish the late baroque style from rococo style is to listen again to the Couperin "Le Croc-en-jambe" and then to the "Allemande" from J. S. Bach's French Suite in D Minor. Notice that the Couperin is almost entirely homophonic and that its theme is expended in short little bursts. The Bach, on the other hand, always seems to have some inner part moving, creating the illusion of counterpoint. The theme is long and spiraling.

How would you characterize the differences between the Rubens painting in chapter 5 and the Watteau painting, *A Party in the Open Air,* in this chapter? Think in terms of texture, colors, subject matter, and physique of the characters in the two paintings. How do the changes in art coincide with changes in musical styles?

What differences do you find among these three works?

      J. S. Bach's *Brandenburg* Concerto no. 2, J. C. Bach's Symphony in D Major, op. 18, no. 1, and C. P. E. Bach's Symphony in B Minor?

Music in the Classical Era

House Concert, eighteenth century, by V. Reggianini.

© Historical Pictures Service, Inc., Chicago

Sounds of the Chapter

J. S. Bach
Brandenburg Concerto no. 2 ♪

Beethoven
Piano Concerto no. 1
Piano Concerto no. 4
Piano Sonata in Ab Major, no. 12, op. ♪
26
Sonata no. 13
Piano Sonata no. 14, op. 27, no. 2
  (*Moonlight Sonata*)
String Quartet, op. 18, no. 1
Symphony no. 1
Symphony no. 3 (*Eroica*)

Gay and Pepusch
The Beggar's Opera

Handel
Trio Sonata in F Major ♪

Haydn
The Creation
String Quartet, op. 3, no. 5
String Quartet, op. 20, no. 5
String Quartet, op. 33, no. 2
String Quartet, op. 50, no. 1–6

String Quartet, op. 54, no. 1–3
String Quartet, op. 76, no. 1–6
String Quartet, op. 77, no. 1–2
Piano Sonata no. 37 in D Major ♪
Symphony no. 10 in D Major
Symphony no. 45 in F♯ Minor
  (*Farewell*)
Symphony no. 101 (*The Clock*) ♪
The Seasons

Mozart
Cosi fan tutte
Don Giovanni
The Magic Flute
The Marriage of Figaro
Piano Concerto no. 17 in G Major,
  K. 453
Piano Sonata in Bb Major, K. 333
Symphony K. 16
Symphony no. 26, K. 184
Symphony no. 40 in G Minor, K. 550 ♪
Symphony no. 41, K. 551 (*Jupiter*)
Violin Concerto in A Major, K. 219

The term "classical," when used in music, has a specific meaning.

The music of the classical era, however, does not resemble the music of classical antiquity.

All music conveniently categorized as "classical" is not from the classical era.

The terms "classic" and "classical" must be approached with some caution. These terms have been used in so many different ways that confusion about their meaning can arise. For example, we speak of a classic joke, a classic beauty, a classic novel, and we also speak of classical antiquity, the classical era, and classical music. There are, however, distinctions to be made between the various uses of the terms.

Since the early Renaissance the arts of the ancient Graeco-Roman civilizations have been considered models of superiority; hence the title, classical antiquity. We might expect, then, that any succeeding era described as classical would manifest an affinity to the arts of classical antiquity. This is true of some architecture and literature of the later eighteenth century, but in virtually no way does the music of the classical era resemble that of classical antiquity. Nor is it true that the arts of the late eighteenth century are superior to those of other eras simply because they are labeled classical. Not every classical symphony is "a classic," nor is it necessarily superior to a symphony from the nineteenth or twentieth centuries.

The confusion is further compounded by the Western world's tendency to label all music other than popular, jazz, or folk as classical music. Many large record companies issue popular music on one label and classical music on another. These companies also cater to a rock market, a jazz market, and a classical music market. But this does not imply that a record label or a particular market is devoted exclusively, or even primarily, to music from the classical era. They merely use the term classical in a much larger sense: it encompasses all art music, including that from the classical era.

The Symphony in the Classical Era

Figure 7.1 diagrams the number, order, and character of movements in the typical classical symphony of the late eighteenth century.

The shapes suggest the character of the movements. In terms of what is called "musical weight," the first movement is the heaviest. It is normally the longest of the four movements, contains proportionately more of the most profound ideas, and has the most involved development. The slow second movement provides lyrical balance for the drama of the first movement. The third movement, the dance (minuet and trio), is in some respects the least complicated. The presence of the minuet proved to be a valuable tool for eighteenth-century audiences. Its familiarity encouraged them to feel more comfortable with the complete symphony. Because it was a familiar element, it is diagrammed here as a comfortable round shape. The squiggly line representing the final movement indicates this is the shortest of the four movements and is often playful in mood.

The final movement of the classical symphony is the shortest.

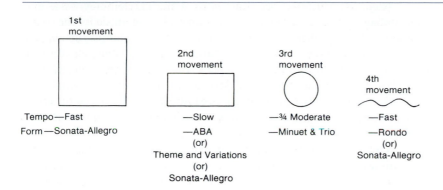

Figure 7.1

1st movement

Tempo—Fast
Form—Sonata-Allegro

2nd movement

—Slow
—ABA
(or)
Theme and Variations
(or)
Sonata-Allegro

3rd movement

—¾ Moderate
—Minuet & Trio

4th movement

—Fast
—Rondo
(or)
Sonata-Allegro

The tempo of the first movement is reasonably fast, although not so fast as to violate the classical sense of good taste. Similarly, the slow second movement is not too slow. Irrational exaggerations of anything, including tempos, may have suited the baroque ideal, but they were avoided in the classical age. The minuet, or third movement, again moves at a moderate tempo. The last movement usually takes a tempo just a little faster than that of the first movement; if the first movement is allegro, the last movement is likely to be presto.

The relative tempo of each movement has been standardized.

Haydn in particular was fond of prefacing his late symphonies with a brief, slow introduction. This solemn frontispiece leads directly to the first movement proper.

The Composers of the Classical Era

Franz Joseph Haydn

Haydn (1732–1809) was born into a peasant family at Rohrau in southern Austria, but this inauspicious birth hardly suggests the magnitude of his destiny. When he died seventy-seven years later, Haydn was unquestionably regarded as the greatest composer of his time. This fame and success, however, were not easily won.

Haydn's formal education ended when he left the Cathedral of St. Stephen in Vienna at the age of sixteen. For about the next twelve years, he scratched out a meager existence in Vienna, primarily as a street musician.

The Esterhazy Estate   At the age of twenty-nine, Haydn was employed by the wealthy and artistically discriminating Esterhazy family. He took up residence at the family palace in Eisenstadt, Austria, where he remained for the next thirty years. Haydn worked in virtual isolation, away from the mainstream of musical activities in Vienna and other important centers.

Franz Joseph Haydn
(1732–1809).
Free Library of Philadelphia

Haydn's responsibilities while in the Esterhazy employ were very demanding. He was expected to compose and rehearse music for the court orchestra, for chamber music, for the opera theater, and for the chapel, as well as to manage administrative tasks. Despite all this, Haydn had complete liberty to compose and experiment as he wished. He learned by trial and error the effects and procedures that were successful and discarded those that were not. Slowly, steadily, Haydn mastered the craft of composition and learned to harness and channel his enormous creativity.

These years of experimentation, growth, and self-fulfillment were rewarding eventually. Haydn spent the last twenty years of his life basking in the sunshine of worldwide acclaim. His works were performed widely, resulting in Haydn's being much celebrated, honored, and sought after.

Haydn's Compositions   Haydn's output was prolific: he composed 104 symphonies, 83 string quartets, 52 piano sonatas, 2 major oratorios—*The Creation* and *The Seasons*—operas, church music, concertos, and chamber music. The symphonies were written throughout his creative years and so serve as a vehicle to trace both Haydn's development as a composer and the metamorphosis of the symphony from its playful galant beginnings to its magnificent classical arrival.

Haydn's Symphony no. 10 in D Major was probably composed during his first eighteen to twenty-four months at the Esterhazy palace, from 1761–62. Its demeanor, size, and scope are completely galant in style. The orchestra numbers about twenty players (four each of first and second violins, four violas, two cellos, and two basses, two flutes, and two French horns). This early work follows the three-movement format: fast-slow-fast. The entire symphony is only about twelve minutes in length, roughly half that of most of Haydn's mature classical symphonies.

Haydn wrote about forty-three symphonies during his first ten years at the Esterhazy estate. All except one of these are in major keys. These works all stay within the general limits of the style galant, although Haydn continued to experiment, expand, and move steadily in the direction of the four-movement format.

A major stylistic shift is evident in the next six symphonies (nos. 44–49). Here Haydn is in the midst of his *Sturm und Drang* years. Many of these symphonies are in minor keys and contain some striking dissonances. The thematic content also reveals some violent contrasts. Typically, a *Sturm und Drang* theme is either very energetic and angry or it is quiet and introspective. Established forms, such as the sonata-allegro, are sometimes twisted out of their customary shapes in these *Sturm und Drang* symphonies.

Haydn had complete freedom to experiment musically.

Haydn achieved fame and glory during his lifetime.

Haydn's symphonies trace the development of his talents and the metamorphosis of the genre.

Haydn's earliest style galant symphonies had only three movements.

Haydn's symphonies numbered 44 through 49 feature *Sturm und Drang* characteristics.

Haydn's Symphony no. 45 in F♯ Minor, subtitled *Farewell*, illustrates several of these features. It is composed in four movements, fast-slow-minuet-fast, all of which are in sonata-allegro form except the minuet.

Sound and Sense
Sturm und Drang **Features**

Title: Symphony no. 45 in F♯ Minor, Farewell *(1772)*
Composer: Haydn
Meter: 3/4
Tempo: Allegro
Key: F♯ Minor

A Closer Look

First Movement

The first movement is the most violent of the four. The exposition begins with several varied repetitions of the *A* theme. This is a jagged, restless theme that stretches over two octaves in eight measures, and it contains a great deal of startling interplay between *f* and *p:*

A Theme

Oddly, there is no *B* theme in the exposition, and the lack of one serves to make the *A* theme even more prominent. The angry character of the *A* theme dominates. Stranger still, a *B* theme appears in the middle of the development section. The *B* theme is as melancholy as the *A* theme is violent.

Second Movement

This is quiet and reflective, yet there are many unexpected dissonances and changes of key.

Third Movement

The minuet, normally a mild-mannered movement, has a number of harmonic jolts beginning in the third measure.

Fourth Movement

The presto finale (last movement) begins with a quiet but furious *A* theme, leading to a contrasting *B* theme that features some pockets of imitative counterpoint. The extended coda that follows has an interesting history. Whether fact or fancy, the story illustrates Haydn's creative genius.

The court orchestra musicians were anxious for a holiday and had been pestering Haydn to speak to the prince on their behalf. Haydn, not wanting to be brash or undiplomatic, refused to do so. Instead, he devised a musical plan to accomplish this end. The coda to the *Farewell* symphony was written so that one by one, the various parts of the orchestra ceased playing. As a player reached the end of his part, he packed up his instrument and exited. Thus, during the coda, the orchestra got smaller and smaller, until at the end there were only two violins left playing. The prince understood the message and is reported to have said: "I see what you're after—the musicians want to go home! Very well, we'll pack up tomorrow." Where words had failed, Haydn's music had succeeded.

The charm of this story does not diminish the character of the coda. Like the rest of the work, it has an urgency, a dissonance not found in Haydn's style galant symphonies.

Haydn's zenith as a symphonist occurred in the 1780s and 1790s.

The creative and emotional storm of the *Sturm und Drang* years waned, but the experience was necessary for the composer's growth. The most beneficial aspects of the experience greatly influenced Haydn's crystallized classical style. The symphonies from the 1780s and 1790s are in this more mature style and reflect Haydn's zenith as a symphonist. The last twelve symphonies (93–104) were commissioned by an entrepreneur named Salomon for a London concert series. Any one of the collection is a model of classical music style.

Sound and Sense   ♪
Classical Style

Title: Symphony no. 101 (The Clock) *(1794)*
Composer: Haydn
Meter: 3/4–6/8
Tempo: Adagio-presto
Key: D minor–D major

A Closer Look

The four movements (fast-slow-minuet-fast) are prefaced by a majestic, slow introduction. The work is scored for a full-scale classical orchestra (the usual strings but in greater numbers than in earlier times), plus two flutes, oboes, clarinets (found only in Haydn's late symphonies), bassoons, French horns, trumpets, and timpani.

Several of Haydn's symphonies were given nicknames by someone other than Haydn. In this case, *The Clock* is derived from the tick-tock motion of the accompaniment of the second movement.

Introduction and First Movement

The slow introduction is dignified and serious, laced with some startling dissonances—a perfect foil for the playfulness of the first movement proper. The introduction is in 3/4 and marked Adagio, but after a brief pause at the end of the Introduction, it switches to 6/8 and presto as the first movement proper begins.

Exposition

    A—has the rhythm: (:23)

    It is played first by the violins, then by the flute, and then
       by the full orchestra. The texture is generally light and
       airy except when the full orchestra plays ff

    Bridge—again featuring violins and flutes   (:26)
    B—The rhythm of the *B* theme has some similarities to the   (:19)
      A theme:

    C   (:26)

Development

The opening portion features a contrapuntal dialogue between first and second violins, and then with all the strings. It builds to a climax near the end with the entire orchestra (1:24).

Recapitulation (:53)

Coda (:58)

Second Movement

Andante; a large *ABA* form, sometimes called song form. Two bassoons supply the tick-tock under the theme played by the violins.

Third Movement

Minuet and trio.

Fourth Movement

Vivace, rondo form.

Haydn and Mozart were contemporaries on the musical scene in Europe in the late eighteenth century.

Wolfgang Amadeus Mozart (1756–91).
The New York Public Library

Mozart's acclaim came in his childhood.

Mozart composed his first symphony at the age of eight or nine.

Wolfgang Amadeus Mozart

Franz Joseph Haydn and Wolfgang Amadeus Mozart (1756–91) met for the first time in the winter of 1781 when Haydn was forty-nine and Mozart was twenty-five. A profound and long-lasting admiration and friendship developed between them, as evidenced by Haydn's remark to Mozart's father:

> Before God and as an honest man, I tell you that your son is the greatest composer known to me either in person or by name. He has taste, and what is more, the most profound knowledge of composition.

By the time of this meeting, Mozart had already been acknowledged as a child prodigy, having played the piano before many European heads of state who adored and coddled the amazing child. But after the joy and success of his childhood, Mozart endured an adulthood haunted by frustration, financial woes, ill health, and a discouraging lack of widespread acclaim for his music.

Even though Mozart and Haydn are often coupled by music historians, their lives were strikingly different. Haydn's peasant childhood, youthful years of scuffling, acceptance of a role in the patronage system, and slow, steady artistic growth leading to widespread acclaim vividly contrasts with Mozart's life.

Born into a musical and educated (though not wealthy) family, Mozart enjoyed public adulation during his childhood. But his inability to enter the patronage system denied him solid, steady employment and led to financial ruin. He lived less than half as long as Haydn and was buried in a pauper's common grave, without ceremony or friends. The bright promise of Mozart's youth was never fulfilled in adulthood.

Mozart's works are catalogued by Köchel or K. numbers, not by opus numbers. Ludwig von Köchel was a nineteenth-century author-historian who undertook the chronological cataloguing of all of Mozart's more than 600 works. Each work was assigned a K. number, such as Symphony no. 40 in G minor, K. 550. Though there are exceptions to the rule, generally a high K. number indicates that Mozart composed the work later in his life. K. 550 is thus a late work.

Mozart wrote his first symphony, K. 16, at the age of eight or nine. This is a miniature galant piece in three movements (fast-slow-fast) that is about eleven minutes in length and is filled with galant charm. It is, of course, a marvel that a nine-year-old child could compose such a piece, but his earliest symphonies are separated from his later work by a wide artistic gulf. You can appreciate the scope of this gulf by listening to the first symphony (K. 16), and then to the G Minor Symphony, K. 550, the first movement of which was discussed in chapter 3.

At the age of 17 or 18 (1773–74) Mozart encountered the *Sturm und Drang* movement. Some of his symphonies from those years reflect the movement's influence. Mozart's no. 26, K. 184, is especially representative of this.

Mozart's later symphonies, together with Haydn's London Symphonies, are the crowning glory of the late eighteenth-century symphony. Symphony no. 41, K. 551, subtitled *Jupiter,* was written during the last few years of Mozart's life when his health was failing rapidly. And yet, this work is filled with youthful energy and sunny spirits.

Both the first and second movements of *Jupiter* are in sonata form. The first, as expected, is longer and weightier. The second movement presents a songlike *A* theme and a *B* theme which, with its touching dissonances, suggests tragedy. The third movement (minuet and trio) is a gem among eighteenth-century minuets. The minuet theme consists of a series of short, descending phrases, each starting on a different pitch. When properly performed, the rhythm has an easy, billowing effect, unlike the stiff, pompous character of so many other classical minuets. The fourth movement, also in sonata-allegro form, is larger, more complex, and more dramatic than most symphonic final movements. This last movement is also highly contrapuntal.

Ludwig van Beethoven

Ludwig van Beethoven (1770–1827) is probably the most famous of all composers of Western art music. He is also extremely complex in terms of both his personal life and musical compositions. In fact, the image of Beethoven as a lonely genius who accomplished musical miracles in an aggressively individual way is essentially accurate.

It is not true that Beethoven was a starving, penniless artist who labored in some hovel producing masterworks that only future generations would appreciate. In reality, his music sold very well and afforded him a comfortable living. During his lifetime he was a much-celebrated composer, but, unlike Haydn, was not an approachable person, and so he distanced himself from the adoring musical public.

Beethoven knew and greatly admired the works of Haydn and Mozart; in fact he moved to Vienna for the purpose of studying with Mozart, but that plan was interrupted by Mozart's death. In 1792, Beethoven left Bonn to study with Haydn, but it was not a happy teacher-student relationship, and so it ended quickly. The two composers went their separate ways, but Beethoven never lost his enthusiasm for Haydn's music, and the influence of that master is evident in much of Beethoven's early work.

Mozart was influenced by Sturm und Drang *at the age of about seventeen.*

Mozart's Jupiter *symphony does not reflect his failing health and low spirits of the time.*

Complexity is common to Beethoven's music and personality.

Haydn's influence is evident in Beethoven's early work.

Neither Beethoven nor Mozart
entered the patronage system.

Beethoven's early career was nurtured and in part financed by a
group of noblemen who recognized the composer's genius. Although
Beethoven was grateful for the help, he did not let this association dictate his actions: he refused to enter the patronage system.

As we mentioned before, Haydn was able to accommodate himself
to the patronage system, and profited by staying with it for nearly thirty
years. Mozart's more temperamental and quarrelsome personality prevented him from fitting into the system. But Beethoven, in contrast to
his two great contemporaries, simply *would not* enter the system, although he realized it was beneficial for some. On that issue alone he
battled formidable odds—and won decisively. Beethoven's fierce independence of the patronage system, coupled with the fact that he did not
fit into any neat stylistic or sociological pigeonholes, helps explain his
reputation as a complex personality.

In the late 1790s and early 1800s, a malady that had been stalking
Beethoven for several years finally caught up with him: he realized that
he was becoming deaf. A more devastating affliction for a composer is
hardly imaginable. And yet, the majority of Beethoven's monumental
works, many of which are numbered among the richest musical treasures
we possess, were written in the silence of deafness. Once more, Beethoven had triumphed against the odds.

Many of Beethoven's most
significant works were written
after he became deaf.

Classifying Beethoven's Compositions   Beethoven lived the first half of his life in the eighteenth century, so by the time he became a young man, the classical style was fully formed. But by the time he had reached middle age, nearly all of the philosophical bases and many artistic manifestations of nineteenth-century romanticism had appeared. Since Beethoven's music is a product of his experiences, it is difficult to classify it as classical, romantic, both, or neither.

A fine sense of proportion and balance, a mastery of the developmental process, and the creation of large, organically solid edifices are characteristic of musical classicism. Inasmuch as Beethoven was a consummate master of these, he is a classical composer. Romanticism is characterized by wizardry in the expression of emotions and subtle nuances of mood, the musical presentation of ideals and programs, and the harnessing of an expanding functional harmony. Beethoven was equally masterful of these, and so he can legitimately be called a romantic.

Still, Beethoven does not strictly conform to these hallmarks of the two eras—the man and much of his music transcend chronological and stylistic boundaries. As a result, Beethoven's music must be examined as a unique entity, only generally related to one style or another.

Beethoven's Symphony no. 1 (ca. 1798) is the most Haydnesque of the nine symphonies he composed. But his Symphony no. 3 (subtitled *Eroica*) is the epitome of those characteristics of classicism listed previously. At the same time, the work completely transcends all previous conceptions of a symphony.

Beethoven's life spanned the end of the classical era and the beginning of the romantic age; he was influenced by both periods, but he developed a unique style.

Beethoven's *Eroica* set new standards for symphony.

Sound and Sense
Musical Classicism

Title: Symphony no. 3, Eroica, *first movement (1803)*
Composer: Beethoven
Recording: Szell, Cleveland Orchestra
Meter: 3/4
Tempo: Allegro con brio
Key: E♭ Major

A Closer Look

Symphony no. 3 has the standard number and order of movements found in classical music: fast-slow-dance-fast. Its structure is created from a few, rather than many, ideas. The process of development, so important to the classical style, is fully realized.

But the work extends beyond the limits of the late eighteenth-century classical symphony. The length of *Eroica* is atypical of a classical symphony. Usually, a classical symphony will run about twenty-five minutes; *Eroica* is nearly twice that length. Another difference is the replacement of the courtly

minuet of the classical symphony with a rough-and-ready peasant dance called
a **scherzo.** No lady in a long, flowing gown could possibly dance to the tempo
of this scherzo. And the codas to the first, second, and particularly fourth
movement, are greatly protracted. They amount almost to additional
development sections.

First Movement

The first movement, in sonata-allegro form, begins after two loud and vicious
hammer strokes. The *A* theme comprises three subthemes that are
interrelated. Notice that the subthemes can be reduced to simple triads.
Members of the triads to which these themes are reducible are marked here
with an x.

Similarly, the *B* theme comprises three subthemes, one of which, *e,* is also
triadic.

The long exposition section that contains these themes is diagramed as
follows:

(:17)	(:11)	(:14)	A (:10)	(:14) (:30)	=	(1:36)
a	*a*	*a*	*a*	*b* *c*		
in the	in the	marked by	key of E♭,			
cellos	woodwinds	syncopation	then C			
			minor,			
			then A♭			

(:35)	(:29)	B (:20)	(:10) = (1:34)
d	*e*	*f*	*a'*
in clarinets, then violins, then woodwinds	derived from the triadic natures of *a,b,c*	includes a passage of extreme dissonance	

The long development section that follows is charged with energy and violence; the *a* theme is ripped apart note by note. Toward the middle of the development there is a fugal section; this is followed by an extended passage of shattering dissonance that raises the listener to a state of near frenzy and leaves little doubt that the composer is enraged. The supreme tension finally reaches a peak and collapses into a quiet section that provides the necessary antidote to the preceding violence.

This diagram serves as a road map through the battlefield of the development section:

a'—the theme is twisted slightly out of shape
b—appears accompanied by some figuration in the violins
a—is presented four times in succession beginning each time on a different note: C C♯ D E; this series of entrances generates tremendous power
a—is further developed as it is combined with *c*
b—is developed
fugal section
shattering dissonance
b—the antidote; note the change of orchestration that creates a complete change of mood
a—further and new development
b—more of the antidote
a—is dismantled as its pitches are torn, one by one, off the torso of *a*. Finally there is but one pitch left quivering in the violins

Recapitulation
Before the orchestra can conclude the development section on the V₇ chord, a solo French horn enters with *a* on the tonic chord. The juxtaposition of the orchestra's V₇ and the horn's I chord creates an odd harmonic jolt that may at first sound like an error by Beethoven. But it is not a mistake; Beethoven intended the jolt. This moment provides us with the first clue that the French horn has a special and symbolic role to play in the *Eroica* symphony. The horn is the symbol of the hero. Notice that when the rest of the orchestra is content to linger in the ashes of the development, the French horn pulls it out of the development and into the recapitulation wherein the battered *a* theme is reconstructed. After only a few measures into the recapitulation, the *a* theme is restored to its original shape, using the French horn for its voice. The remainder of the recapitulation parallels the order of events in the exposition.

Coda
Perhaps one of the things that most startled the early nineteenth-century audience was the length and character of the coda. No longer a mere musical "stop sign," in Beethoven's hands it is prolonged and assumes the character of an additional development where new facets of the *a* theme are revealed. Notice the prominence of the French horn in the coda, also.

Second Movement

The slow movement—Marcia funebre (funeral march)—is solemn and dramatic. It is cast in a very large *ABA* form with an extensive coda. The *A* sections are in C minor, and the *B* section in C major. The principal themes from these sections are, like those of the first movement, easily reduced to triads.

Third Movement

The third movement is a scherzo, having the form *A* (scherzo)-*B* (trio)-*A* (scherzo). The theme of the trio is also triadic. Notice that the trio is played by the French horns, the voice of the hero.

Fourth Movement

After a brief dramatic flourish, the last movement quickly proceeds to a set of seven variations based on the triadic theme:

and its bass line:

A long, brilliant coda featuring the French horn concludes the movement and the work.

Eroica captures the essence of classicism while foreshadowing romanticism.

The *Eroica* is a landmark composition. It appears to be the essence of musical classicism; providing a final glorious exclamation point to that noble creation of the eighteenth century—the symphony. But simultaneously, the piece is an example of a newly emerging style—musical romanticism—with all its echoes of heroism, symbolism, formal and emotional expansiveness, and the urge to interrelate in a close and unmistakable way all the parts to the whole.

A typical late eighteenth-century symphony is a collection of four agreeable movements. For a symphony of this kind, any minuet and trio (provided it is in the appropriate key) could serve as the third movement; one minuet can be substituted for another without damaging the integrity of the symphony as a whole. This is not true of the *Eroica,* where no such substitutions can be made. These specific four movements belong together; they share thematic, rhythmic, and instrumentational interconnections that are critical to the sense of the whole work. Each of the movements has its being, makes sense, and is in part explained by the others. Beginning with the *Eroica,* the symphony acquired a narrative sense, and every major symphonist who came after Beethoven in the nineteenth century built upon this premise.

The Concerto

The concerto was an important part of the legacy bequeathed by the baroque to succeeding ages. Composers of the classical era were quick to claim this inheritance and to remodel it to conform to their own tastes and needs.

The classical composers reshaped the baroque concerto grosso to form the concerto.

The new age made use of the basic three-movement plan (fast-slow-fast) of the old concerto grosso, but the concertino (with its usual complement of two, three, or four performers) was replaced with a single soloist—one violin, one piano, or some other solo instrument. Thus, whereas in the baroque the genre is referred to as the concerto grosso, in the classical era it is called a **concerto**—a piano concerto, a violin concerto, or a horn concerto.

The classical composers, so fascinated with the sonata-allegro, put the form to use in the concerto. Typically, the first movement of the concerto was cast in this form. Immediately, though, a problem arose: How should the materials of the exposition section be distributed between the orchestra and the soloist? Who gets to play what, and when? Should the orchestra be allotted the *A* theme and the bridge, and the soloist be given the *B* theme? Or should this be reversed? The ingenious solution was found in the double exposition.

The first movement of the concerto was usually in sonata-allegro form.

Mozart's Concertos

As previously explained, the exposition section in a sonata form is repeated literally. However, in the double exposition of the concerto, the repetition is nonliteral. When listening to the first movement of Mozart's Piano Concerto no. 17 in G Major, K. 453, notice that the orchestra alone plays the exposition in its entirety once. But instead of the expected verbatim repetition of the exposition, the soloist enters and, with the cooperation of the orchestra, performs a varied repetition of the exposition.

This is a **double exposition.** It was an ingenious, aesthetically satisfying, and well-mannered solution to the problem. Neither soloist nor orchestra felt slighted; both were allowed to deal with the entire substance of the exposition.

In the classical concerto, the orchestra and the soloist share the development and recapitulation. At the end of the recapitulation, and before the coda, a special section played only by the soloist occurs. This section is called the **cadenza.** In the cadenza, the soloist improvises and develops one or more themes from the movement. Often (but not always) the cadenza concludes with a trill or series of trills. The trills are a signal to the orchestra that the soloist is ready to finish the improvisation and is requesting the orchestra's cooperation in playing the coda that ends the first movement.

The classical concerto features a solo between the recapitulation and the coda called the "cadenza," a solo improvisation.

Sound and Sense
Classical Concerto

Title: Piano Concerto no. 17 in G Major, K. 453 (1784)
Composer: Mozart
Recording: Rudolph Serkin with the London Symphony
Meter: 4/4
Tempo: Allegro
Key: G Major

A Closer Look

First Movement (Allegro)

First Exposition (Orchestra)
  A—a gentle, playful theme played first by violins, then by   (:29)
      winds
  Bridge—a denser texture as the whole orchestra joins in   (:30)
  B—a more lyric theme; texture thins as violins take over,   (:31)
      answered by woodwinds
  Bridge—several *ff* chords   (:16)
  C—a quiet theme played by soft violins with flute and oboe   (:31)
      providing filigree

Second Exposition
  A'—piano enters and dominates texture; woodwinds answer   (:40)
      the piano at ends of phrases
  Bridge—piano with orchestra   (:30)
  B'—piano alone, then orchestra joins in   (:31)
  Bridge—woodwinds with piano filigree   (:24)
  C'—piano with strings and then with woodwinds   (1:16)

Development (1:58)

Recapitulation (3:12)

Cadenza
Solo piano—(1:22)

Coda
Orchestra with piano (:50)

Second Movement

In addition to being hauntingly beautiful and harmonically eccentric, andante, this movement has a most unusual shape. It is in sonata-allegro form, but, as the graph below illustrates, the *C* theme does not reappear in the recapitulation as expected; instead it is held in reserve until the coda, which appears after the cadenza. The *A* theme is also presented in an unusual way: it consists of a five-measure phrase followed by silence, almost as if it were cut off from the rest of the movement. The effect is startling and dramatic.

First Exposition
    A—orchestra, woodwinds are featured prominently   (:23)
    B—oboe solo joined by flute, French horn, bassoon, and   (1:12)
      strings
    C—orchestra   (:20)

Second Exposition
    A—solo piano   (:23)
    B'—begins with piano and strings; a dialogue among   (1:12)
      woodwinds follows
    C'—orchestra is answered by piano   (:40)

Development (1:46)

Recapitulation
    A   (:24)
    B''   (1:52)

Cadenza (1:34)

Coda
    A'   (:30)
    C''   (:32)

Third Movement

The concluding movement consists of a set of variations on a simple, folklike theme. This is the kind of variation in which the theme itself is varied. Notice, too, how Mozart varies his performing forces. The movement is diagramed as follows:

Theme section	*aabb* (orchestra)
First variation	*aabb* (piano with light orchestral accompaniment)
Second variation	*aabb* (piano and woodwinds)
Third variation	*a* (woodwinds)
	a (piano)
	b (woodwinds)
	b (piano)
Fourth variation	*a* (strings and winds shift to minor mode)
	a (piano)
	b (strings and woodwinds)
	b (piano)

Fifth variation	*a* (full orchestra, shift back to major mode)
	a (piano)
	b (full orchestra)
	b (piano)

Bridge leading to an extended coda. Variations continue.

Now is an appropriate time to listen to Mozart's Violin Concerto in A Major, K. 219, and to any of his four horn concertos.

Beethoven's Concertos

Beethoven performed his Piano Concerto no. 1 in public, dazzling his audience with the cadenza.

Beethoven's Piano Concerto no. 1 was composed in 1798 when Beethoven was better known as a concert pianist than as a composer. Frequently, Beethoven performed the work in public, dazzling audiences with his playing, particularly his ability to improvise in the cadenzas of piano concertos. The form of his Piano Concerto no. 1 is very straightforward, beginning with a fast movement in a clearcut, though lengthy, sonata form, followed by a quiet and lyrical slow movement, and a fast third movement in rondo form.

The great length of the work is the most obvious departure from the classical norm; the first movement alone is nearly as long as entire late eighteenth-century concertos. When listening to the first movement, notice the double exposition with its three distinctly different themes, the lengthy development, and the standard recapitulation. The cadenza grows to monumental proportions, systematically calling into play each of the dominant themes. It also features an elaborate set of trills near the very end.

Beethoven began his Piano Concerto no. 4 with a solo.

Beethoven broke new ground with his Piano Concerto no. 4 (1805), for the first movement begins, not with the orchestra, but with the soloist who gently enunciates the dominating theme of the movement. Only after the initial statement from the soloist does the orchestra enter. Later in the nineteenth century, this procedure of soloist followed by orchestra was so prevalent that it became the norm.

The String Quartet

The string quartet was the dominant form of chamber music in the classical era.

During the classical era, the string quartet, consisting of two violins, a viola, and a cello, became the dominant form of chamber music. Like the symphony, the string quartet slowly evolved during the preclassic period and finally assumed its classical shape in Haydn's hands.

Appreciation of the string quartet is often an acquired taste, since it lacks the pizzazz of the full orchestra and the dazzle of soloistic music. Many audiences find the magic of the string quartet genre is slow to materialize, but once the taste is acquired, the appetite is insatiable.

Haydn rehearsing a string quartet.
© The Bettmann Archive

Haydn's Early Quartets

Haydn's first string quartets were written several years before his first symphonies. The earliest of these are in true galant style, and some may, in fact, be arrangements of other instrumental pieces written while he was a street musician in Vienna. These quartets are lighthearted, essentially homophonic, and harmonically subdued. Some are in three movements, some in four, and some in five. As with Haydn's symphonies, it is possible with the quartets to trace his evolution as a composer and to monitor his changes from galant, to *Sturm und Drang,* to pure classicism.

Many of Haydn's string quartets were composed and published in sets of six. Thus, Opus 1 contains six individual quartets: Opus 1, no. 1; Opus 1, no. 2, and so on. Opus 3, no. 5 was probably written in the middle 1760s, when Haydn had already composed a dozen or more quartets. This work is not indicative of his early efforts, but is, nonetheless, still solidly entrenched in the style galant.

The work has four movements (fast-slow-dance-fast). The first movement is cast in a miniature sonata-allegro form; the charming second movement is in the form of a serenade, the dance movement is a standard minuet-trio-minuet, and the last movement is a playful rondo. The whole quartet is only about eleven minutes in length. This order and number of movements became the standard in the classical era; notice

Haydn's first string quartets were composed before he began to write symphonies.

Haydn's string quartets evolved from style galant through *Sturm und Drang* to pure classicism.

Opus 3, no. 5, is a good example of Haydn's style galant string quartet.

In Haydn's early string quartets, the first violin dominates the second violin, viola, and cello.

that it corresponds precisely with the classical symphony. In this quartet, as in most of Haydn's early ones, the first violin is clearly dominant, and the second violin, viola, and cello serve primarily as accompaniment. But with time and experience, Haydn learned to integrate the four instruments equally.

Haydn's *Sturm und Drang* Quartets

Haydn composed the String Quartet, op. 20, no. 5 in the midst of the tumultuous *Sturm und Drang* years. The same kind of passion, dissonance, and raw energy we found in the *Farewell* symphony of the *Sturm und Drang* years are evident in this quartet, too. *Sturm und Drang* works deviate from classical models in some forms and the order of movements. Such is the case with this work: it has the standard four movements, but in the order fast-dance-slow-fast.

Sound and Sense

***Sturm und Drang* Quartet**

Title: String Quartet, op. 20, no. 5 (1772)
Composer: Haydn
Meter: 4/4
Tempo: Moderato
Key: F minor

A Closer Look

The first movement is in sonata form but is somewhat misshapen. The opening *A* theme is followed by a bridge that modulates to the proper key for the *B* theme, but before we hear the *B* theme, *A* appears again in the new key. The development section is followed by the recapitulation in which the second statement of *A* does not appear. The movement concludes with a long, complicated coda that amounts to an additional development section.

The minuet is also in the principal key of the work (F minor). Here there is none of the galant charm; instead, there is a brooding, agitated quality. The mood brightens a little in the trio section, but is more bittersweet than cheerful.

The slow movement, adagio in 6/8, is dominated by a single theme that is played against a succession of countersubjects, producing some jarring dissonances and several unexpected twists in the harmony.

The last movement is an angry-sounding fugue filled with stern, serious counterpoint. The movement is much too serious and rigorous for rococo ears.

Haydn's Later Quartets

With the six quartets, Opus 33 (1781), Haydn arrived at the threshold of string-quartet mastery. Now listen to Opus 33, no. 2 in its entirety, for here, fully formed, is the classical string quartet that Haydn worked thirty years to perfect. Other important purely classical quartets by Haydn that deserve listening attention include Opus 50 (six quartets), Opus 54 (three quartets), Opus 76 (six quartets), and Opus 77 (two quartets).

Haydn's Opus 33 exemplifies his fully matured classical string quartet.

Mozart's Quartets

The early string quartets of Mozart are, like those of Haydn, mostly in the style galant. But in the 1780s Mozart, again like Haydn, began to produce purely classical string quartets of the highest quality. The last ten quartets include a set of six (K. 387, 421, 428, 458, 464, and 465) that Mozart composed in 1783–85 and dedicated to Haydn. Mozart said it was from Haydn that he first learned the art of string quartet writing. Any of this group of six will serve as a model for Mozart's mastery of the classical string quartet.

Mozart mastered the classical string quartet after first composing in style galant.

Beethoven's Quartets

The earliest of Beethoven's string quartets (the six quartets of Opus 18), which date from 1798–99, were composed at a time when musical classicism was in full bloom. Beethoven kept track of various musical ideas in sketchbooks, of which several are extant. One of these sketchbooks reveals the difficulty he had and the numerous trials and errors he had to endure in order to create the first theme of Opus 18, no. 1. When listening to the theme, it seems to have been composed with ease, but the numerous entries in the sketchbook indicate this was not the case.

  The first movement is the longest and is dominated by this theme that caused Beethoven such grief. The second movement is slow and has an air of tragedy about it. The third movement is a scherzo-trio-scherzo. And the last movement is an allegro in rondo form.

Beethoven began composing string quartets at the height of the classical period.

Piano Sonata

The piano was invented in the early eighteenth century, but it did not come into real prominence and widespread use until the second half of that century. When it did arrive, however, the piano quickly displaced the harpsichord as the primary keyboard instrument. Composers devoted their energies to creating a repertoire of solo and ensemble music for it.

Once the piano rose to prominence, it replaced the harpsichord as the primary keyboard instrument.

The reasons for the piano's popularity are many. As its name *pianoforte* (Italian for "soft and loud") implies, the instrument can produce a range of volume levels, something the harpsichord cannot do. The piano also can sustain sounds, whereas the sounds produced by a harpsichord decay and disappear quickly. The piano is a versatile and powerful instrument. It is so powerful that it can be heard over an entire symphony orchestra, making the piano concerto possible. Since the instrument blends well with other instruments, classical composers developed a rich body of chamber music involving the piano. Finally, the piano is a fine solo instrument, worthy of the body of solo music created especially for it during the classical era: the piano sonata.

Piano music has these advantages: range, sustenance of sound, versatility, power, and ability to blend well with other instruments.

Since the vogue for solo piano recitals did not develop until the second quarter of the nineteenth century, there was no demand to create solo sonatas in the classical era. Nevertheless, Haydn, Mozart, Beethoven, and others composed piano sonatas. Perhaps they did so for their private entertainment, for those who commissioned them, or out of a love for and fascination with the marvelous new instrument. Regardless of their motivation, Haydn wrote fifty-two sonatas, Mozart nineteen, and Beethoven thirty-two.

During the classical era a body of music was created for the piano—the piano sonata.

Haydn's Sonatas

The earliest Haydn sonatas date from the 1760s and, for the most part, are lightweight homophonic works consisting of three or four movements in the style galant. Some of the sonatas from the 1770s are in minor keys and have other *Sturm und Drang* characteristics. Increasingly, the tendency was toward a three-movement plan, fast-slow-fast, and no dance movement. The last of Haydn's sonatas, some of which were written during his final productive years, are models of classical grace and inventiveness. These are the Haydn sonatas most frequently heard in recitals today. Listen, for example, to the last movement of his Sonata no. 37 in D Major.

Haydn's sonatas evolved from style galant through *Sturm und Drang* to classical.

Mozart's Sonatas

All of the Mozart piano sonatas were written around 1774–89, and all are in three movements. This music is so rich and diverse that it is difficult to pick a single favorite or even to say what constitutes a "typical" Mozart piano sonata. The Sonata in B♭ Major, K. 333 (1778) is but one of many exquisite examples of Mozart's sonatas. The first and second movements of this sonata are in sonata-allegro form; the last movement is a rondo.

Beethoven's Sonatas

Throughout the nineteenth and twentieth centuries, Beethoven's piano sonatas have been among the most widely performed. In terms of technical and performing difficulty, they range from pieces suitable for gifted amateur piano students to works so devilishly difficult that they nearly defy performance. Stylistically, they range from classical to romantic to those which transcend all stylistic labels and enter a kind of mystic realm. The thirty-two sonatas are as diverse in terms of overall shape: some are in four movements, some in three, some in two, and no. 13 has but one movement with frequent internal changes of tempo and mood. Variation also exists in the order of movements in Beethoven's sonatas. Even more so than with Mozart, it is not easy to identify a "typical" Beethoven sonata.

Beethoven's piano sonatas are among the most popular, and they vary widely in both style and shape.

The Sonata in A♭ Major, no. 12, op. 26, the first movement of which was encountered in chapter 3, is an appropriate listening selection. Opus 26 has four movements: andante-scherzo-funeral march-allegro.

Sound and Sense
Sonata

Title: Piano Sonata no. 12, op. 26 (1800–1801)
Composer: Beethoven
Meter: 3/8
Tempo: Andante
Key: A♭ major

A Closer Look

First Movement
The first movement consists of a theme with five variations. The opening segment of the theme is simplicity itself, stressing repeated notes. The structure of the theme is *aaba',* and this structure is retained in each of the variations except the last variation—it has an addendum that serves as a coda.

Theme

a	(:20)
a	(:20)
b	(:25)
a'	(:24)

Variation I	(1:15)
Variation II	(1:05)
Variation III	(1:12)
Variation IV	(1:03)
Variation V	(1:38)

Second Movement

This movement, scherzo-trio-scherzo, is propelled almost entirely by a simple rhythm:

Scherzo

a	(:10)
b	(:30)
b	(:30)

Trio   (:33)

Scherzo

Third Movement

The third movement, entitled "Marcia funebre sulla morte d'un Eroe" ("Funeral march on the death of a hero"), is related to the second movement of the *Eroica* Symphony. This movement has the shape *ABA*. The *A* sections are mostly in the minor mode, and the *B* section shifts to the major mode. This is similar to what occurs in the second movement of the *Eroica*. This movement, too, is dominated by one rhythm—in this case, a dotted rhythm:

A—scherzo	(1:18)
B—trio	(1:00)
A'—scherzo	(2:50)

Fourth Movement
Rondo

A	(:25)
B	(:25)
A	(:25)
C	(:25)
A	(:30)

Coda (derived from *A* and *B*) (:38)

During the years 1800–1801, Beethoven composed his most popular sonata, *Moonlight Sonata* (Piano Sonata no. 14, op. 27, no. 2). However, many people know only the first movement of this work.

This haunting movement is effective in and of itself, which accounts for its popularity, but its full impact is lost when it is taken out of the context of the whole sonata. The three movements that comprise the sonata span an incredible emotional range. The first movement has the mysterious, brooding quality, foiled perfectly by the gentle, quietly playful second movement. The third and last movement, with its agitation and fire, presents another facet in the emotional spectrum.

Sound and Sense

Sonata

Title: Piano Sonata no. 14, op. 27, no. 2 (Moonlight Sonata) *(1800–1801)*
Composer: Beethoven
Recording: Rudolf Firkusny
Meter: 4/4
Tempo: Adagio
Key: C♯ minor

A Closer Look

First Movement

The first movement is loosely constructed along the lines of a sonata-allegro. In Beethoven's day it was most unusual to begin a sonata with a slow movement, particularly one so moody and atmospheric. Its mood is created in part by numerous shifts from minor to major mode and back to minor: from dark into light and then back into darkness. The quiet but relentless triplet figure, which runs throughout the movement, contributes a sort of ghostly quality to the movement, as does the fact that the music is designed to be played *pp*. The *A* theme uses repeated notes as its opening gesture, a feature of several other works by Beethoven.

A—the triplet figure establishes the mood, and the *A*   (1:11)
  theme enters about twenty seconds later
B—begins with a long, painful, quiet dissonance   (:40)
A'—in a different key   (:26)

Development   (1:07)
The development is made entirely out of the triplet
  figure, which runs the gamut from high to low

Recapitulation
   A   (:45)
   B   (:40)

Coda
The *A* theme is now placed at the bottom of the texture   (:55)

Second Movement

This movement introduces a complete change of mood; it is the sunshine
between the darkness of the first movement and the storm of the last
movement. It is a little scherzo-trio-scherzo.

Scherzo
   a—alternates short legato phrases with answering   (:16)
     staccato phrase
   b—the texture is broadened slightly   (:21)
   b   (:22)

Trio
Texture of the right hand consists wholly of octaves   (:48)

Scherzo
Without repeat of *b* phrase   (:40)

Third Movement

Exposition
   A—quick, agitated theme   (:29)
   B—more lyrical theme but with some syncopation   (:32)
     that makes it somewhat restless
   C—an agitated theme, once more featuring repeated   (:21)
     notes
(The exposition is then repeated verbatim.)

Development (1:03)

Recapitulation (2:33)

Coda (:17)

Opera

The attitudes and tastes of the preclassic era differed greatly from those of the baroque. It is not surprising that the baroque opera seria, with its virtuosic musical style and the pompous gods and goddesses of its contrived plots, could not survive in the breezy atmosphere of the new age. The opera seria was a perfect vehicle for the royal baroque age, but the democratically oriented Enlightenment called for a more accessible musical style and more down-to-earth characters and plots.

The opera seria fit the style of the baroque age but was not suitable for the classical age.

Comic Opera

After the opera serias of Handel and his generation, Mozart assumed a position of importance in opera history. But between the decline of opera seria and the rise of Mozart's ideal, the most important development was the creation of **comic opera.** Although its origins were humble, it caught the public's fancy rapidly and soon displaced opera seria all over Europe. There were, in fact, several national forms of comic opera: in Italy it was called opera buffa; in France it was called opéra-comique; in Germany, singspiele; and in England, ballad opera. By the middle of the eighteenth century, all of these types were alive and flourishing.

Comic opera was an important element in the development of the opera.

Recall that an opera seria has three acts, interspersed with long intermissions during which the audience visited, dined, played cards, and conducted business. Some composers developed the idea of supplying light musical entertainment to fill these intermissions. Increasingly, this entertainment was organized into acts. Thus the evening consisted of the three acts of the opera seria plus the two acts of the light entertainment, called **intermezzo.** The opera seria consisted of: Act I, Intermezzo (act i), Act II, Intermezzo (act ii), and Act III. When the intermezzo was extrapolated from this context and given individual attention, the comic opera was born.

In opera seria, the intermezzo was light entertainment organized into two acts; the comic opera grew out of the intermezzo.

The Beggar's Opera   The most famous and widely performed ballad opera is *The Beggar's Opera,* written and compiled in 1728 by John Gay and Johann-Christoph Pepusch. This short comic opera does not concern gods and goddesses; instead street people are its characters: highwaymen, jailers, pimps, and trollops. Spoken dialogue is interspersed with ballads or popular songs. Clearly, bel canto is inappropriate for this style; indeed, virtuoso singers would be hopelessly out of place in this opera. Unlike opera seria, this music with its more mundane content was very accessible to the public at large.

Comic opera themes were popular with the general public.

Comic opera featured ballads.

During the first act of *The Beggar's Opera,* two of the main characters, Peachum and his common-law wife, are enraged at the news of the marriage of their daughter, Polly. They sing the following ballad text:

> Our Polly is a sad slut! nor heeds what we have taught her.
> I wonder any man alive will ever rear a daughter!

The characters, plot, and language definitely bespeak the commoners.

The Merging of Comic and Serious Opera

Eighteenth-century composers were able to create a compromise between opera seria and comic opera.

The Beggar's Opera and other similar pieces are distinct opposites of opera seria; they are an unmistakable, perhaps shocking reaction against it. But in the later decades of the eighteenth century, some composers reworked the comic opera to conform to some of the conventions of more highbrow opera. These composers believed that arias, recitatives, and ensemble numbers could be absorbed into the fabric of comic opera and would enrich their works. They also determined that comic opera need not be slapstick, nor even truly comic, but that serious subject matter and characters could be employed.

Several of Mozart's operas illustrate that compromise— *Don Giovanni,* for example.

Several of the operas of Mozart—including *The Marriage of Figaro, Don Giovanni, Cosi fan tutte,* and *The Magic Flute*—synthesize the comic and the serious. These operas, so rich with marvelous music, are also credible dramas with real characters who emerge, come to life, and develop personalities.

Mozart's *Don Giovanni*   The very first scene of *Don Giovanni* (1787) illustrates that the story line, character development, and music are on a very high plane.

Don Giovanni[1]

Atto I	*Act One*
Scena I	*Scene I*
Piazza. Da un lato il Palazzo del Commendatore; dall'altro una locanda.—S'appressa l'alba.	*(A Garden. Night.)*
Leporello	**Leporello**
(indi Don Giovanni e Donna Anna.)	*(wrapt in a dark mantle, impatiently pacing to and fro before the steps to the palace)*
Notte e giorno faticar,	
Per chi nulla sà gradir;	On the go from morn till night,
Pìova e vento sopportar,	Running errands, never free,
Mangiar male e mal dormir.	Hardly time to snatch a bite;
Voglio far il gentiluomo,	This is not the life for me.
E non voglio più servir;	I would like to play the master,
Nò, nò, nò, non voglio più servir.	

1. Copyright © 1962, by G. Schirmer, Inc. International Copyright Secured. Reprinted by permission.

Oh che caro galantuomo:
Vuol star dentro colla bella,
Ed io far la sentinella!
Voglio far il gentiluomo,
E non voglio più servir,
Nò, nò, nò, non voglio più servir.
Ma mi par, che venga gente,
Non mi voglio far sentir, Ah!
*(Entra Don Giovanni, e Donna
Anna.)*

Donna Anna
Non sperar, se non m'uccidi,
Ch'io ti lasci fuggir mai.

Don Giovanni
Donna folle, indarno gridi!
Chi son io tu non saprai.
(Taci, e trema al mio furore.)

Donna Anna
Scellerato!

Don Giovanni
Sconsigliata!

Donna Anna
Genti, servi! Al traditore!
Come furia disperata
Ti saprò perseguitar.

Would no more a servant be,
No, no, no, no, no, no,
I would a master be.
(facing the palace)
What a difference between us!
Warm you lie in arms of beauty
While I freeze on sentry duty;
I would like to play the master,
Would no more your servant be,
No, no, no, no, no, no,
I would your master be.
What was that? We're in for
trouble.
This is not the life for me,
No, no, no, no, no,
This is no life for me.
*(Hides himself. Enter Donna Anna,
holding Don Giovanni firmly by the
arm.)*

Anna
No, you won't, you shan't escape
me!
I will never let you go!

Giovanni
(trying to conceal his features)
Do not scream! You'll wake the
household.
Kiss me, dear, and let me go!
Now! Now let me go.
*(almost hissing; covering his
mouth)*
Stop that noise or I shall hurt you.
Stop, I tell you!
(seizing her roughly)

Must I hurt you?

Anna
No, you won't, you shan't escape
me,
I shall never let you go!
Fire and murder! Save me! Seize
him!
Fire and murder! *(freeing herself)*
Try to stop me!
(turning to the palace)

(The three sing at once)   Help me! Save me!
                                                                From my unrelenting fury
                                                                You shall never get away.
                                                                From my unrelenting, my avenging
                                                                fury
                                                                You shall never get away.
                                                                Fire and murder! Try to stop me!
                                                                Save me! Help me!

                        (Esce Donna Anna.)   *(During this action the
                                                                Commendatore enters, hastily, a
                                                                torch in his left hand, a sword in
                                                                his right. Seeing the
                                                                Commendatore approach, she runs
                                                                into the house.)*

Don Giovanni   **Giovanni**
(Questa furia disperata   From her unrelenting fury
Mi vuol far precipitar.)   I had better get away.
                                                                Stop, I tell you!
                                                                I shall hurt you.
                                                                How am I to get away?

(Don Giovanni, il Commendatore,   *(He haughtily confronts the
Leporello.)*   Commendatore.)*

Leporello   **Leporello**
(Che tumulto! oh, ciel, che gridi)   Master cursing, the lady screaming,
Il padron in nuovi guai!   How am I to get away?
(Sta a veder ch'il malandrino   Well, we're in a pretty pickle;
Mi farà precipitar.)   How am I to get away?
                                                                Yes, we're in a pickle this time,
                                                                Yes, a very pretty pickle,
                                                                And I cannot get away
                                                                From this pretty pickle this time,
                                                                And I think that I can say
                                                                For this pretty pickle this time
                                                                There will be the deuce to pay!

Commendatore   **Commendatore**
Lasciala, indegno;   Where is the villain? Draw, sir, and
Battiti meco.   fight me!

Don Giovanni   **Giovanni**
Va, non mi degno   No! Pride forbids me to draw on
Di pugnar teco.   greybeards.

Commendatore   **Commendatore**
Così pretendi   Faint-hearted coward! I challenge
Da me fuggir?   you.

                                                                Giovanni
                                                                Force me not!

Commendatore   **Commendatore**
Battiti!   Draw, I say!

Don Giovanni
Misero! Attendi,
Se vuoi morir.

*(Si battono—il Commendatore
cade)*

Leporello
(Potessi almeno
Di quà partir.)

Commendatore
Ah soccorso! Son tradito.
L'assassino m'ha ferito,
E dal seno palpitante
Sento l'anima partir.

Don Giovanni
Ah, già cade il sciagurato,
Affannoso e agonizzante;
Già dal seno palpitante
Veggo l'anima partir.

Leporello
(Qual misfatto! qual eccesso!
Entro il sen dallo spavento
Palpitar il cor mi sento—
Io non so che far, che dir!)

Giovanni
Force me not!
(draws his sword)
Dotard, on guard, then!
Your death is near.
*(He strikes the torch out of the
Commendatore's hand. The
Commendatore attacks. They fight
and the Commendatore falls
mortally wounded.)*

Leporello
If I could only get out of here!
*(The moon rises slowly; lights
appear in the palace windows;
great excitement within; servants
hasten with torches behind the
closed gates.)*

Commendatore
Ah, I'm wounded! Ah, I'm dying!
God, protect my child from evil!
From this mortal scene of sorrow
My immortal soul must fly.
(He dies.)

Giovanni
Ah, he's fallen! Ah, he's dying!   *(The three sing at once)*
Paying dearly for his folly.
On this world of love and beauty
He must close his aged eye.
*(Servants return with Don Ottavio
and hasten with him from the
street into the palace.)*

Leporello
Who has fallen? Who is dying?
How I shiver, how I shudder!
Rooted to the spot by terror,
I can neither move nor cry.

Recitative

Don Giovanni *(Sotto voce)*
Leporello, ove sei?

Giovanni *(softly)*
Are you there, Leporello?
*(He sheathes his sword and dons
his cloak.)*

Leporello
Son quì per mia disgrazia, e voi—

Leporello
I only wish I wasn't. Are *you*
there?

Don Giovanni
Son quì.

Giovanni
Of course.

Leporello
Chi è morto—voi, o il vecchio?

Don Giovanni
Che domanda da bestia! Il vecchio!

Leporello
Bravo! Due imprese leggiadre: sforzar la figlia ed ammazzar il padre!

Don Giovanni
L'ha voluto suo danno.

Leporello
Ma Donn'Anna cos'ha voluto?

Don Giovanni
Taci! Non mi seccar, vien meco—se non vuoi qualche cosa ancor tu— *(Minacciandolo)*

Leporello
Non vo' nulla, Signor! Non parlo più.
(Partono. Donna Anna, Don Ottavio, e Servi con fiaccole.)

Donna Anna
Ah, del padre in periglio in soccorso voliam!

Don Ottavio
Tutto il mio sangue verserò, se bisogna. Ma dov'è il scellerato?

Leporello
Are you a ghost? Is *he* one?

Giovanni
What an imbecile question! He's done for.

Leporello
Bravo! Pretty good for one evening. To rape the daughter and then skewer the father!

Giovanni
He compelled me; I had to.

Leporello
And Donn'Anna . . . also compelled you?

Giovanni
Silence! No more from you. Remember, *(threatening to strike him)* you can join the old man if you wish.

Leporello
From now on I'll be dumb as any fish.
(Exeunt. Donna Anna enters; she agitatedly descends the steps with Don Ottavio and servants bearing torches.)

Anna
Quick! His life is in danger. We must come to his help.

Ottavio
(raising his drawn sword)
I will defend him. I will save him or perish.
But I see and hear no one.

Anna
I fear some evil.

Recitative and Duet

Donna Anna
In questo loco. *(Vedendo il corpo di suo padre.)* Ma qual mai s'offre, oh Dei, spettacolo funesto agli occhi miei! Padre mio! Mio caro padre!

Don Ottavio
Signore!

Anna *(seeing the corpse)*
What, O God, do I see! What spectacle of horror appears before me! *(She sinks down beside the body.)* It can't be! Not my father! *(She throws herself upon the corpse.)* Speak to me, father!

Ottavio
Who did this?

Donna Anna

Ah, l'assassino mel trucidò! Quel sangue, quella piaga—quel volto tinto e coperto del color di morte! Ei non respira più—fredde le membra! Padre mio! Caro padre! Padre amato! Io manco—io moro!

Anna

Ah, the assassin has struck him down! He's wounded! Look, he's bleeding! So silent, so still and so unnaturally pallid! *(Don Ottavio offers to raise her; she refuses.)* So icy to the touch, breathing no longer! *(She rises.)* Tell me, father, that I'm dreaming! Answer me, father! *(She reels.)* Have mercy! Have pity!
(Don Ottavio supports her, and leads her to the stone seat.)

Don Ottavio

Ah soccorrete, amici, il mio tesoro! Cercatemi, recatemi qualche odor, qualche spirito. Ah non tardate! Donn'Anna, sposa, amica! Il duolo estremo la meschinella uccide.

Ottavio *(to the servants)*

Help! Do not stand there gaping, but help your mistress! Bring smelling salts immediately. Go at once, get some brandy. Be quick, I tell you! Donn' Anna! Dearest! Beloved! O Grace of Heaven, let her not die of sorrow!
(A maid hurries into the palace and returns immediately with a smelling-bottle which she offers to Donna Anna.)

Donna Anna

Ahi!

Anna

Ah!

Don Ottavio

Già riviene! Datele nuovi aiuti.

Ottavio

Look, she's stirring! Give her a sip of brandy!

Donna Anna

Padre mio!

Anna *(with a deep sigh)*

Let me dream it.

Don Ottavio

Celate, allontanate agli occhi suoi quell'oggetto d'orrore. Anima mia! Consolati, fa core!

Ottavio *(to servants)*

And quickly! Remove this blood-bespattered body! She musn't see it again. *(Serving-men raise the Commendatore, and bear him into the palace.)* Wake, Donna Anna! I love you! Be comforted!

Duet

Donna Anna

Fuggi, crudele, fuggi!
Lascia che mora anch'io!
Ora ch'è morto, oh Dio!
Chi a me la vita diè!

Anna

(springing up, and repulsing Don Ottavio as if insane)

Heartless tormentor, leave me!
Leave me to die beside him.
Cold is he now and lifeless
Who gave my life to me.

Don Ottavio
Senti cor mio, deh senti!
Guardami un solo istante!
Ti parla il caro amante.
Che vive sol per te!

Donna Anna
Tu sei, perdon, mio bene!
L'affanno mio, le pene!
Ah, il padre mio dov'è?

Ottavio
Hear me, dear heart, Donn' Anna,
Turn to your faithful lover
Whose heart is in your keeping,
O turn your eyes to me!

Anna
*(perceiving her error and giving
Don Ottavio her hands)*
Let me once more embrace him.
Once more! Once! Father! My
father!
*(approaching the spot where the
Commendatore fell)*
But where, O where is he?

Don Ottavio
Il padre lascia, o cara!
La rimembranza amara:
Hai sposo e padre in me!

Ottavio
Donn' Anna, weep no longer.
Time will abate your sorrow.
Your husband and father I'll be.

Anna
Gone! Forever! O where, O where is
he?

Ottavio
Weep no longer!
Time will abate your sorrow.
Both husband and father,
Both husband and father I'll be.
*(Donna Anna stands with lofty
demeanor opposite Don Ottavio.)*

Donna Anna
Ah, vendicar, s'il puoi,
Giura quel sangue ognor!

Don Ottavio
Lo giuro agli occhi tuoi.
Lo giuro al nostro amor!

Anna
Ah! Will you swear to avenge him?
Blood must for blood be poured.

Ottavio
*(raising his hand as for taking an
oath)*
I swear it. I swear it.
By the eyes I love, I swear it.
I swear it on my sword.

Duet

Che giuramenti oh Dei!
Che barbaro momento!
Fra cento affanni e cento
Vammi ondeggiando il cor!
(Partono)

Anna
Though cunning as the serpent
He fly from retribution,
Our righteous wrath shall find him,
Blood shall for blood be poured.
Blood for blood is calling.
Vengeance!
No ocean deep shall hide him

Nor subterranean cavern;
Our righteous wrath shall find him,
Death be his just reward,
At last his just reward.
Ottavio
Though cunning as the serpent
He fly from retribution,
Our righteous wrath shall find him,
Blood shall for blood be poured.
I swear it! By love I swear it. I
swear it on my sword.
No ocean deep shall hide him
Nor subterranean cavern,
Our righteous wrath shall find him,
Death be his just reward.
*(Exeunt slowly into palace. The
curtain falls rapidly.)*

This scene is about twelve minutes in length. During that brief span, five different characters—a soprano, a tenor, a baritone, and two bass voices—are all introduced. Each is sharply drawn, unique. Leporello is a manservant who, it is clear, is accustomed to abuse and is afraid of his own shadow. The music that Mozart creates for him has a comic air. But to an attentive listener, it becomes clear that he is not a simple buffoon, but rather a bitter, cynical person who would surely turn on his master if only he could. He says, "I would like to play the master, would no more your servant be."

All facets of Don Giovanni's character are not exposed in this one scene, but it is obvious that he is ruthless and cruel.

Donna Anna's complicated personality begins to unravel in this opening scene. Though certainly in this first scene she appears to hate Don Giovanni, eventually there is some doubt as to her true feelings toward him. Some of her comments to her fiancé, the weakling, Don Ottavio, indicate some uncertainty about her love for him.

The musical forces are distributed so as to provide maximum variety:

Aria—bass
Recitatives
Trio—soprano, baritone, bass
Recitatives
Trio—baritone, two basses
Recitatives
Duet—soprano and tenor

Mozart develops the characters quickly.

Mozart's music provides diversity.

The story line holds the interest of the audience by moving quickly from incident to incident.

The story moves as briskly as the character development and music: an alleged rape, a fight, a murder, and a vow of vengeance are all packed into the short scene.

Summary

The classical era was dominated by three powerful and distinctly different personalities: Haydn, Mozart, and the young Beethoven. It is principally from the works of these three composers that our perception of musical classicism is formed. At the root of this classicism is a sense of proportion and balance, a mastery of the developmental process, and the creation of large, organically solid edifices out of few musical raw materials. These large edifices took the shape of the symphony, the concerto, the string quartet, the piano sonata, and the opera.

The symphony of the classical era was in four movements, with each movement designed to perform a specific function and to carry a certain musical weight. Haydn's symphonies clearly reflect his evolution as a composer. His early works are in style galant, his next symphonies exemplify *Sturm und Drang* influence, and his compositions from the 1780s reveal him at his zenith as a classical symphonist.

Mozart composed his first symphony at an early age. He, like Haydn, began writing in three movements. Later, however, he fell under the influence of *Sturm und Drang,* and by the time he had reached his twenties was writing some of the most beautiful classical symphonies ever created. Beethoven, unlike the other two, never settled into the purely classical pattern. His symphonies exuded characteristics of the classical and romantic eras but transcend them both.

The concerto emerged in the classical era, having evolved from the baroque concerto grosso. The classical concerto featured one solo instrument to partake in the repetition of the exposition and to add improvisation. Beethoven, not stylistically confined to the classical era, composed concertos that deviated from the classical norm as standardized by Mozart.

The string quartet was the dominant form of chamber music in the classical era. It assumed its classical form in Haydn's hands and was masterfully developed by Mozart and Beethoven.

Once the piano achieved prominence in the second half of the eighteenth century, the classical composers created a body of solo music to feature the instrument's qualities. The piano sonatas of Haydn evolved over time, revealing the stages of his musical development. Mozart's sonatas show a wide diversity of styles while Beethoven's piano sonatas transcend all stylistic labels.

The classical era witnessed the birth of a new type of opera. The popularity of the baroque opera seria declined in favor of a light, down-to-earth opera that had evolved from the intermezzo. The first comic operas included simple themes, spoken dialogue and ballads or popular songs. Later in the eighteenth century, Mozart and other classical composers reworked the comic opera to create credible drama and more sophisticated music. These composers created a middle ground between the extremes of opera seria and the early comic opera.

Key Terms

scherzo	double exposition	comic opera
concerto	cadenza	intermezzo

Thinking About It

It is important to have a solid understanding of the major genres of the era. Using the text, your notes, and recorded examples, answer the following questions.

1. What is a symphony? What are some of the differences between a style galant symphony and Haydn's Symphony, no. 101, *The Clock*?
2. What are the differences between the Bach *Brandenburg Concerto no. 2* and the Mozart Piano Concerto, no. 17, in G Major, K. 453, discussed in this chapter?
3. What are the differences between Handel's Trio Sonata in F Major (see chapter 5) and the Mozart Piano Concerto no. 17 in G Major, K. 453?
4. How is a dance suite different from a piano sonata?

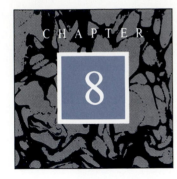

Music
in
the
Age
of
Romanticism

The Valley Farm: Willy Lots House, J. Constable
The Tate Gallery, London

Sounds of the Chapter

Beethoven
Symphony no. 3 (*Eroica*)
Symphony no. 5
Symphony no. 6 (*Pastoral*) ♪
Symphony no. 9

Bellini
Norma

Berlioz
Roméo et Juliette ♪
Symphony Fantastique

Bizet
Carmen

Borodin
In the Steppes of Central Asia ♪

Brahms
Academic Festival Overture
Intermezzo, op. 118, no. 2 ♪
Symphony no. 2, op. 73 ♪

Chopin
Études, op. 10
Étude, op. 10, no. 5 in G♭ Major ♪
Polonaise in A♭ Major, op. 53 (*Heroic*) ♪
Twenty-Four Preludes, op. 28
    Prelude no. 1 in C Major
    Prelude no. 4 in E Minor
    Prelude no. 7 in A Major
    Prelude no. 20 in C Minor
    Prelude no. 21 in B♭ Major

Donizetti
Lucia di Lammermoor

Dukas
L' Apprenti Sorcier

Dvořák
Slavonic Dances for Orchestra

Grieg
Piano Concerto in A Minor

Liszt
Années de Pèlerinage
Hungarian Rhapsodies

MacDowell
Woodland Sketches

Felix Mendelssohn
Fingal's Cave
Songs without Words
Symphony no. 4 (*Italian*)

Fanny Mendelssohn-Hensel
Andante con moto, op. 2, no. 2 ♪

Mozart
Symphony no. 40 in G Minor ♪

Mussorgsky
Night on Bald Mountain
Boris Godunoff

Puccini
La Bohème

Rossini
Il barbiere di Siviglia ♪

Schubert
An die Musik ♪
Die schöne Müllerin
Die Erlkönig ♪
Moments musicaux
Trout Quintet
Unfinished Symphony
Die Winterreise
Clara Schumann–"Liebst du um ♪
   Schönheit"

Robert Schumann
Kinderscenen
Papillons
Piano Concerto in A Minor ♪

Strauss
Also sprach Zarathustra

Tchaikovsky
The Nutcracker ♪
Romeo and Juliet
Symphony no. 6 (*Pathétique*)

Verdi
Rigoletto

Wagner
Der fliegende Holländer
Der Ring des Nibelungen
Lohengrin
Tristan und Isolde

von Weber
Der Freischütz ♪

"Romantic" is the stylistic label applied to the philosophy and the arts of the nineteenth century.

The term "romantic" had different connotations during the nineteenth century than it does in the twentieth. To us, the word romantic conjures visions of moonlight and soft music. But romantic is also the stylistic label applied to the arts and philosophy of the nineteenth century.

The nineteenth-century artist had a strong personal relationship with nature. We can see this in the writing of those who shaped romantic philosophy, the canvases of the great nineteenth-century landscape painters, the poetry, and the music of the nineteenth-century romantics. These people were not content merely to observe nature. For them, there was a sort of mystical bond that existed between the earth and the soul. Self-discovery and inner peace resulted from this communion with nature.

Self-discovery and inner peace resulted from the nineteenth-century artist's relationship with nature.

The following lines by Phillip Otto Runge exemplify this special relationship between artist and nature:

> When the sky above me abounds with countless stars, when the wind rushes through the wide space . . . when above the woods the sky turns red; the valley steams and I fling myself upon the grass under the glittering drops of dew, each leaf and each blade of grass teems with life, the earth lives and stirs beneath me, all resounds together in a single chord, then the soul jubilates aloud and soars into the boundless space around me, and there is no below and no above, no time, no beginning and no end. . . .
> *(Phillip Otto Runge, 9 March, 1802)*

The mystery of nature is reflected in the artistic works of the nineteenth century.

The romantic also loved the mystery of nature. The darkness of the night or the dense, sun-forsaken forest, where shapes and images are either invisible or blurred, were often integrated into the arts of the time. These environments unleashed the imagination and stimulated the creativity of the artist, sometimes producing works considered macabre or horrifying. The reading public of the nineteenth century, whose numbers had swelled with the spread of public education, devoured the literature of the romantics. Mystery stories (such as Mary Shelley's *Frankenstein*), novels set in faraway, exotic places, or historical tales (especially from the Middle Ages) were particular favorites.

The nineteenth-century romantic studied the past.

The expansive spirit of the romantic was attracted to, and sometimes tortured by, the attempt to achieve the unattainable—to comprehend infinity. Some romantics sought to achieve this by delving into the past. In Germany, particularly, the nineteenth century was an age of historicism that mined the past in search of cultural roots. This search was beneficial in terms of the literature produced: the first German dictionaries were compiled, along with important collections of German folklore and tales, such as the tales compiled by the brothers Grimm.

The romantic period was one touched by escapism.

This journey into the past could be interpreted as an attempted escape from the present. And the concurrent fascination with utopia and the infinite confirms this escapist theory. Indeed, the nineteenth century was a troubled and frightening time. The old rationalist order of the eighteenth century had begun to decay, and there were few reliable clues about what would replace it. It is understandable that people sought stability, even if this meant backtracking into the past or speculating about the future.

The people of the romantic era sought stability.

Nationalism

The search for identity was, in part, responsible for the rise of nationalism in the romantic age. The use of folk songs, or of freshly composed melodies fashioned after true folk songs, could provide a work with a nationalistic or regional flavor. Or, in the case of some operas, ballets, and tone poems, the use of folklore, folk stories, or folk mythology could accomplish the same end. The urge to create music with a nationalistic bent may have been triggered by a variety of impulses, but surely one of these was the composer's desire to celebrate and demonstrate pride in his or her national origins.

A sampling of nationalistic works from the nineteenth century includes Dvořák's *Slavonic Dances for Orchestra,* Borodin's tone poem *In the Steppes of Central Asia,* Mussorgsky's *Boris Godunoff,* Liszt's *Hungarian Rhapsodies,* the Mazurkas and Polonaises of Chopin, Weber's *Der Freischütz,* the *Woodland Sketches* of MacDowell, and many others.

An emphasis on nationalism was another aspect of the romantic era.

This interest in nationalism, as well as in nature, resulted in the romantic notion that "There is no longer any above or below, no longer any beginning or end," but rather a continuity in which "Everything is in tune with everything." Let's now take a look at the music of the romantic era to see how this philosophy applies.

Romanticism influenced all of the arts.

Music: Language of the Soul

Music occupied a very important position in the romantic era. To the romantic, words were the language of the intellect, but music was the language of the soul. Painting provided the clearest vision of the exterior, but music provided the clearest vision of the interior—the world of emotions, the heart, and the soul. The intangible, invisible nature of music made it the most expressive of the arts, and its awesome power intoxicated the romantic mind. The romantics believed that words somehow limited experiences, but music had the power to break the shackles of these limitations and free the imagination and emotions to realize an experience completely. Whereas painting and poetry were descriptions of an experience, music and the experience were nearly one and the same thing.

Music was thought to be the most expressive of the arts in the romantic era.

Integration of Music with the Other Arts

Several romantic composers
wrote literature also.

Even some romantic poets recognized this critical difference and suggested that all the arts should "aspire to the mysterious condition of music." Several romantic composers, however, did not restrict themselves to music but undertook literary endeavors as well. Robert Schumann, Berlioz, Mendelssohn, and Wagner were authors as well as composers. Schubert, Brahms, and others created a vast repertoire of solo songs because of their personal fascination with words. So although music was the most appropriate romantic vehicle, the other arts were also attractive to the composers, helping them to define or enhance their work.

A movement to synthesize the
arts arose in the nineteenth
century. Mendelssohn
attempted this type of
synthesis in *Fingal's Cave*.

An urge to blend the arts was a natural outgrowth of this situation. Program music, discussed in chapter 4, reached an unsurpassed level in the romantic age as a result of this movement to synthesize the arts. (As you recall, words were provided with the music to ensure full audience appreciation of the work.) Remember, too, that Mendelssohn was displeased with his composition, *Fingal's Cave,* because it had too much counterpoint (a strictly musical phenomenon) and too little of the smell of salted cod and whale blubber (things that can be perceived through visual images and words). To him, the desired synthesis of the sonorous, the visual, and the verbal arts failed to materialize in this piece.

The nineteenth century was an age of extremes and paradoxes. No experience was too small or too subtle to escape the attention of the romantic artist, nor was any so vast that the artist feared trying to express it. Thus, the nineteenth-century composer created on the one hand the art of the miniature, like the piano preludes of Chopin (some of which last less than a minute) and the brief *Moments musicaux (Musical Moments)* of Schubert. Yet, the nineteenth century was also the age of gigantic works when some symphonies were four or five times the length of their classical counterparts. In fact, some of Wagner's music dramas lasted nearly six hours!

The Composers

Much of the art music we hear
today was created during the
nineteenth century.

Many of the works performed by modern symphony orchestras, chamber ensembles, opera companies, and solo recitalists are products of the nineteenth century. In fact, art music audiences of today listen to far more music composed during the nineteenth century than from any other time period. Nineteenth-century music is not necessarily superior; rather, sociological, practical, and even political concerns endowed it with a popularity unexceeded in other musical periods.

In the nineteenth century, artists were believed to possess a greater depth of feeling than ordinary mortals, and presumably their ability to express their thoughts and ideas was somehow inspired. For this reason, the composer and the virtuoso performer were regarded as wizards or prophets. They were heroes in an age that sought heroes. A great wealth of music issued from the romantic age and many of these revered composers—some of the highest artistic genius, as well as some with more modest talent—contributed to this musical treasure chest. A list of some of the most prominent composers of the nineteenth century follows.

Composers and performers were considered heroes of the romantic era.

Hector Berlioz (1803–69) French
Georges Bizet (1838–75) French
Alexander Borodin (1834–87) Russian
Johannes Brahms (1833–97) German
Frédéric Chopin (1810–49) Polish
César Franck (1822–90) Belgian
Edvard Grieg (1843–1907) Norwegian
Franz Liszt (1811–86) Hungarian
Edward MacDowell (1861–1908) American
Gustav Mahler (1860–1911) Austrian
Felix Mendelssohn (1809–47) German
Fanny Mendelssohn-Hensel (1805–47) German
Modest Mussorgsky (1835–81) Russian
Giacomo Puccini (1858–1924) Italian
Sergei Rachmaninoff (1873–1943) Russian
Gioacchino Rossini (1792–1868) Italian
Franz Schubert (1797–1828) Austrian
Clara Schumann (1819–96) German
Robert Schumann (1810–56) German
Richard Strauss (1864–1949) German
Peter Tchaikovsky (1840–93) Russian
Giuseppe Verdi (1813–1901) Italian
Richard Wagner (1813–83) German

This extraordinary group of composers brought to nineteenth-century romanticism a diversity of cultural backgrounds, temperaments, and artistic creeds. Some, like Chopin, Liszt, Clara Schumann, and Rachmaninoff, were virtuoso performers in addition to being composers. Others, like Berlioz, never mastered a musical instrument. It was mentioned earlier that some romantic composers were active in literature or journalistic fields. Others—Schubert, for instance—found verbal expression difficult, yet he is among the most significant and prolific song composers of the romantic era.

The Romantic composers had diverse backgrounds and talents.

Verdi and Wagner were primarily opera composers; Chopin wrote almost exclusively for the piano. Borodin and Mussorgsky added the flavor of the exotic East to the pool of nineteenth-century music. Rossini continued the Italian tradition of bel canto singing in his operas; Brahms and Franck, each in his own way, continued and expanded the contrapuntal traditions of northern Europe. Tchaikovsky's lovely and personal

Each composer developed his or her own specialty.

Hector Berlioz (1803–69)

Johannes Brahms (1833–97)

Frédéric Chopin (1810–49)

Clara Schumann (1819–96)

Felix Mendelssohn (1809–47)

Franz Schubert (1797–1828)

Robert Schumann (1810–56)

Giuseppe Verdi (1813–1901)

Richard Wagner (1813–83)

harmonic language stayed within the bounds of functional harmony; Liszt, Wagner, and Mahler composed works that almost entered the realm of keyless music.

Many of these composers knew one another or knew one another's music. Robert Schumann, for example, actively supported the music of young composers. Liszt supported, conducted, and to some extent funded performances of Wagner's music. Robert Schumann and Brahms were close friends but Wagner and Brahms, largely due to Wagner's temperament, were bitter enemies.

Several of these contemporaries knew of each other's works.

The accomplishments of some of these composers are even more incredible considering their tragically short lives. Chopin died of consumption at the age of thirty-nine; Mendelssohn, whose life was otherwise happy and comfortable, died of exhaustion at thirty-eight; Mussorgsky died of alcoholism at forty-six; Schubert died of venereal disease at only thirty-one; and Robert Schumann died in an insane asylum at forty-six.

Many romantic composers died at an early age.

The Symphony in the Nineteenth Century

A singular symphonic ideal did not exist after Beethoven began working with the form. Instead, there were several different symphonic ideals. For example, Beethoven's Symphony no. 5 demonstrated that the Viennese developmental approach was still a viable and powerful symphonic ideal. On the other hand, the *Eroica* symphony demonstrated that this same ideal could be broadened to include a philosophical program laden with symbolism. Symphony no. 6 *(Pastoral)* created a new symphonic ideal, one of whose bases was descriptive program music. The final movement of Beethoven's last symphony, Symphony no. 9, has extensive parts for vocal soloists and chorus with lines from Friedrich Schiller's *Ode to Joy.* Thus, the choral symphony was established as yet another symphonic ideal. All of the great nineteenth-century symphonists employed one or another of these symphonic ideals as a point of departure for individual experimentation. Some of those ideals and the composers' interpretation of them are examined here.

A number of different symphonic ideals existed.

Felix Mendelssohn

Felix Mendelssohn (1809–47), grandson of the renowned eighteenth-century philosopher, Moses Mendelssohn, was reared in a comfortable and cultured environment: intelligent conversation and regular performances of chamber music were staples of his parents' household. Even as a child he performed at home with the adults in these recitals. As a young teenager he composed music for them, and by the age of fifteen he had written a considerable quantity of music.

Mendelssohn is called the
"romantic classicist" because
his music exhibited
characteristics of both styles.

He was a gentleman, scholar, conductor, performer, and composer. Throughout his tragically brief life, he remained close to his family, especially his gifted sister, Fanny, whom he adored.

Mendelssohn was a classically educated man in a romantic age, and his music partakes of many of the best qualities of both those worlds. He has been called the "romantic classicist," meaning that his classical background, training, and general disposition were fanned by the flames of nineteenth-century romanticism.

Mendelssohn's *Italian*
symphony is rooted in
classicism.

Mendelssohn's Symphony no. 4 (subtitled *Italian*) exemplifies the nineteenth-century symphony that is modeled on the classical symphony perfected by Haydn, Mozart, and Beethoven. Mendelssohn created the colorful harmonic language of *Italian,* but the general shape of the symphony, the developmental process, and the manipulation of simple, effective thematic materials are rooted in classicism. The *Italian* symphony has the standard classical four movements: fast-slow-minuet-fast.

Sound and Sense
Nineteenth-Century Symphony

Title: Symphony no. 4, (Italian) (1830–32)
Composer: Mendelssohn
Recording: C. von Dohnanyi, Vienna Philharmonic
Meter: 6/8
Tempo: Allegro vivace
Key: A major

A Closer Look

Mendelssohn wrote the bulk of this work in 1830, then revised and completed it in 1832 at the age of twenty-two. He conducted its first performance in London of that year, but he was so dissatisfied with it that he would not allow it to be published during his lifetime. Understanding that Mendelssohn was his own severest critic, it is still difficult to understand his disappointment with this piece. It is a work of youthful exuberance and joy, but at the same time it reveals consummate mastery of form and orchestration. Because Mendelssohn was widely traveled, certain locations were an inspiration to his music (e.g., *Hebrides* Overture, *Scotch* Symphony). He did not quote folk materials from those locales, though it is possible that the themes from the last movement of the *Italian* symphony—labeled a *saltarello*—were built upon tunes associated with this Italian folk dance.

First Movement

This movement is in sonata-allegro form and 6/8 meter. The principal thematic materials are derived from manipulations of the long (♩) and short (♪) note values of 6/8 meter as illustrated at the top of page 177.

A Theme = short to long

B Theme = long to short

C Theme, which appears for the first time in the development section, juxtaposes
the long value with a group of short values.

Exposition

A and bridge—Fluttering woodwinds supply the   (1:29)
background, then the violins announce the *A* theme:

The first five pitches of *A* are stated several times by
various instruments. A crescendo leads to a second full
statement of *A*. A decrescendo occurs just before the
arrival of the *B* theme
B—clarinets and bassoons announce this theme first: (:42)

Other woodwinds and strings then join in
A—a clarinet heralds the return of *A;* then the whole   (:36)
orchestra joins in
(The exposition is not normally repeated)

Development

C—this new theme is introduced and becomes the basis for   (:36)
a fugal section:

A'	(:23)
C'—a marchlike section	(:30)
X—a quiet section leads to the recapitulation	(:31)

Recapitulation

A	(:30)
B'	(:44)
C	(:23)
Coda—comprised mainly of the *A* theme	(1:19)

Second Movement

The second movement creates the atmosphere of a quiet, dignified procession: cellos and basses establish a relentless walking motion throughout, while each of the movement's two lovely themes float above. The *A* theme has two parts, a prefatory gesture:

which leads to the heart of the *A* theme:

The contrasting *B* theme uses somewhat quicker note values:

It is a binary form with coda and is in the key of D minor.

A—a prefatory phrase by woodwinds, violins, and violas. The heart of the theme is stated first by oboe, bassoon, and viola, then it is answered by flutes and violins. A second phrase is stated and answered similarly	(2:00)
Bridge	(:32)
B—clarinets and French horns are featured	(:40)
A'—orchestration as before	(1:00)
B—as before	(:37)
Coda—drawn chiefly from *A*	(:58)

Third Movement

The third movement is a minuet and trio with brief coda. Its ambience is reminiscent of Mozart; its orchestration is sheer elegance.
Minuet

A—devoted mainly to elegantly scored strings (with repeat)	(:57)
A'—strings continue, but flutes, oboes, clarinets, and bassoons become more active	(1:14)

Trio—French horns, and later trumpets and timpani,   (1:30)
   dominate

Minuet
   A   (:49)
   Coda—elements of *A* and the trio theme are blended   (:30)
      together

Fourth Movement

The movement—saltarello, presto—is dominated by this rhythm that is
typical of the Italian saltarello:

It moves at a whirlwind pace and reveals Mendelssohn's utter wizardry as an
orchestrator. His is a very democratic approach to orchestration for, as this
movement amply demonstrates, Mendelssohn slights no member or section of
the orchestra; each instrument and instrumental group is featured in the
spotlight.

   For reasons perhaps known only to himself, Mendelssohn elected to end
this A major symphony in the minor mode, thus casting a bit of a shadow over
this otherwise bright and sunny work.

Johannes Brahms

Brahms (1833–97) was born in Hamburg, Germany's only major port
city. As a teenager he studied music (piano and composition) and eked
out a living as a piano player in bars and clubs. By his twentieth year
he was traveling the concert circuit as pianist with an undistinguished
trio.

   The traveling did pay some dividends, however, for it brought him
into contact with Robert Schumann who became an important champion
of Brahms's music. Brahms admired Schumann's work and obviously
was grateful for the professional boost Schumann's public praise afforded his career. Yet his personal life, too, was forever to be affected
by the Schumann family. Though Clara Schumann was fourteen years
older than Brahms, he nevertheless was hopelessly and passionately attracted to her. After Robert Schumann was committed to an asylum in
1854, Brahms became more or less a permanent member of the Schumann household; he helped look after the six Schumann children when
Clara was away on concert tours. While it is clear that Clara loved
Brahms in her own way, any proposals of marriage at this time were
declined.

   Brahms' inability to win Clara as his wife periodically led him to
moods of darkness and despair. At one point he even proposed marriage
to Clara's daughter, Julie, who was of course several years his junior.

Brahms benefited from the
public praise of contemporary
Robert Schumann.

Frustrations in Brahms's
personal life led him to moods
of darkness and despair.

But despite Brahms's somewhat gloomy and, at times, cantankerous personality, he was much celebrated and honored. In 1879 the University of Breslau conferred upon him an honorary doctoral degree, at which time he wrote the *Academic Festival Overture*. The event triggered an unpardonably vicious attack on Brahms by Richard Wagner which may have been motivated by jealousy. This caused a rupture in the musical world that came to be known as the "Brahms-Wagner controversy," though Brahms had virtually nothing to say on the matter. In the closing decades of the nineteenth century Wagner was viewed as the champion of musical radicalism; Brahms was viewed as the arch conservative, the defender of classical ideals in music.

Brahms and Classicism   Brahms continued and greatly expanded the structural and developmental principles of the classical symphony later in the nineteenth century. Early in his career, Brahms was considered a radical composer, but when he tempered that radicalism and unleashed the power of his innate classicism, he found his true personality as a composer. This, however, did not occur until later in Brahms's musical career.

Brahms composed symphonies in the classical style.

In awe of Beethoven's symphonies, Brahms was reluctant to try his own hand at composing one. Indeed, he waited until he was forty-three years old to write the first of his four symphonies.

Brahms's classical orientation is not immediately apparent in his symphonies. His music sounds far too full in terms of texture to be termed such. In fact, Brahms's harmonic language is more exotic than Mendelssohn's and is even laced with more dissonance. But these dissonances assume a softer quality with repeated listening. This harmonic language has been described as "autumnal."

Brahms's harmonic language has been described as "autumnal."

Brahms's symphonies show a dense texture.

In contrast to Mendelssohn's work, Brahms's textures are very dense and some inner part is always in motion. Mendelssohn's airy orchestral textures are reminiscent of Haydn and Mozart, but the density of Brahms's textures is far different. Mendelssohn's *Italian* symphony is about the same length as a late Haydn symphony; the symphonies of Brahms are about twice that length.

Brahms was a romantic composer who had mastered classical structure and organization.

Once we see beyond the lush harmonic language, the dense textures, and the great length of Brahms's symphonies, we see a composer who is a master of the sonata form, counterpoint, and the developmental process. And like Haydn (and Mendelssohn), Brahms created organic themes out of small units of material. Ultimately, Brahms is considered a thoroughly romantic composer who mastered and adhered to classical principles of structure and organization. His Symphony no. 2, op. 73, serves to illuminate this.

Sound and Sense ♪
Romantic Symphony

Title: Symphony no. 2, op. 73, first movement (1872)
Composer: Brahms
Meter: 3/4
Tempo: Allegro non troppo
Key: D minor

A Closer Look

Symphony no. 2 has four movements: fast-slow-dance-fast. The first
movement is cast in a very large, but clear-cut, sonata form. In this
movement, and in fact, in Brahms's sonata forms in general, there is no one *A*
theme or *B* theme in the exposition, but rather several themes are grouped
under *A* and several under *B*. These themes form theme groups: the *A* theme
group and the *B* theme group.

Before proceeding to a diagram of the movement, look at the *A* theme
group of this movement. Notice at the top of page 182 that each of the
themes evolves from an initial descending half step (marked by brackets); this
is the seed from which these themes grow in organic fashion. The themes are
unique but are obviously very closely related to one another.

Exposition

		A Theme Group		
(1:24)		(:24)	(:42)	
a1	bridge	*a2*	*a3*	bridge
French	trombones	high violins,	woodwinds	
horns		then woodwinds		

		B Theme Group		
b1	*b1*	*b2*	*b3*	*b1*
cellos	woodwinds	dotted rhythm	low strings	strings,
		loud (*ff*)	syncopated	then
(:35)	(:27)		accompaniment	woodwinds
		(:28)		
			(:30)	(:48)

(Brahms indicates that the exposition is repeated. Some recordings, however,
do not honor this repeat but go instead directly to the development section.)

Development
An extended fugal section begins about 30 seconds into the development and
is followed by a brief section filled with sharp dissonance that is played by the
low brass (3:04).

Recapitulation
The recapitulation closely follows the order of events in the exposition. The
movement then concludes with a lengthy coda based mostly on theme *a1*.

The second movement (adagio) is cast in a large song form—*ABA*—and
demonstrates Brahms's considerable skill with counterpoint.

The third movement has the shape of a rondo: *ABACA*.
The last movement is the fastest of the four. It is in sonata-allegro form and features an *A* theme that has a folklike quality.

Peter Tchaikovsky

It is probably accurate to say that of all the romantics, Tchaikovsky (1840–93) is the one whose music has the broadest appeal. Even people with little or no background in art music are likely to be familiar with some of his melodies. Several of his themes from symphonies and ballets were incorporated into popular songs in the 1930s and 1940s; a theme from his tone poem *Romeo and Juliet* was used in a popular television commercial in the 1980s; and various themes from his ballet *The Nutcracker* have been used in the popular media. These melodies are eminently memorable and singable, and for many people they have an emotional appeal. Oddly, they are the products of a tortured soul.

Tchaikovsky grew up in St. Petersburg (now Leningrad), Russia. Much of his music has a distinctly Russian flavor, though it is not as obviously nationalistic as, for example, the music of Borodin or Mussorgsky. He was trained in the legal profession and did not turn to music until the age of about twenty. He studied and then taught at the St. Petersburg Conservatory of Music.

Despite his successes, Tchaikovsky was haunted by self-doubt.

But despite these successes, his entire life seems to have been haunted by self-doubt and irrational fears. In czarist Russia his "crime"—homosexuality—was punishable by public whipping and permanent exile to Siberia. Perhaps in an effort to hide his sexual orientation he married one of his students in 1877. The marriage was a disaster; Tchaikovsky reported to his brother that it was "torture." Within weeks he attempted suicide; immediately thereafter he separated from the young woman and never saw her again.

At about that same time he received a handsome stipend from a woman he didn't know, and whom he was destined never to meet. Mdme. von Meck, an extremely wealthy widow, was so enamored of Tchaikovsky's music that she decided to support him annually. Her only stipulation was that the two of them should never meet, though there was a voluminous correspondence between the two. She supported him for fourteen years and then, without any warning or explanation, withdrew her support. In addition to his devastation, Tchaikovsky was guilt-ridden for having accepted her money for all those years.

For fourteen years Tchaikovsky received financial support from an admirer of his music.

Despite his misfortunes, Tchaikovsky developed an international reputation and came to the United States in 1891 to conduct several of his works. Back in St. Petersburg, he conducted the first performance of Symphony no. 6 (*Pathétique*) in October 1893. He died shortly thereafter, apparently a victim of cholera.

Program Symphony

Pathétique   Tchaikovsky's Symphony no. 6 *(Pathétique)* is different from Brahms's Symphony no. 2 in both conception and result. Though it is a symphony and has four movements, *Pathétique* otherwise has little connection with the classical symphony model.

Tchaikovsky's Symphony no. 6 includes a philosophical program.

In February of 1893, Tchaikovsky wrote to his nephew, saying:

On the way to Paris last December the idea for a new symphony came to me, this time a symphony with a program, but a program that will remain an enigma to all. Let them guess for themselves; the symphony will be called merely 'Programmatic Symphony' [6]. But the program is indeed permeated with subjectiveness, so much so that not once but often, while composing it in my mind during my journey, I shed tears.

It is clear—from the music itself as well as from these words—that this is not a descriptive program symphony. Rather, the program is philosophical or subjective in character. The subtitle, *Pathétique,* does not mean pathetic; it translates as pathos, the Greek term for suffering. The subtitle, as well as Tchaikovsky's personal problems, may be a clue to the meaning of the program.

Pathétique begins with a slow, moody introduction, in which the bassoon is the principal voice. The introduction moves immediately to the first movement proper: allegro and sonata form. An *A* theme is introduced in the exposition, after which a bridge leads to a change of tempo (andante) and to the *B* theme. Oddly, the *B* theme is so compelling and is repeated so often in the course of this movement that it completely overshadows the *A* theme. It is as if Tchaikovsky wanted to save the best theme for last. This is not a classical procedure, and there is something even more "unclassical" about this sonata form. There is a

In *Pathétique* the *B* theme overshadows the *A* theme.

Liberty Leading the People by
Frederick Eugene Delacroix—
a heroic theme (see colorplate
18).
© Alinari/The Art Resource

so-called development section, but there is no real development in *Pathé-tique*. There are merely repetitions, primarily of the lovely *B* theme.

The developmental process lies at the foundation of the classical or the classically oriented symphony. Haydn, Mozart, and Beethoven, as well as Mendelssohn and Brahms, created themes that were capable of being developed for their symphonies. Such themes became even more fascinating and multidimensional as they were developed. In a sense, these themes acquired their full personalities and potential only after being developed. This is true of theme *A* of the first movement of Mozart's Symphony no. 40 in G Minor, and also of the *A* theme (first movement) of Beethoven's *Eroica* symphony.

The dominant theme in
Pathétique needs no
development.

This is not the case, though, with the dominant theme (the *B* theme) of the first movement of Tchaikovsky's *Pathétique*. It is a theme so complete and self-contained that it requires no development; in fact, any conceivable development of it would detract from, rather than add to, its personality and potential. It is a melody that would suffer a great loss if it were dissected or forced to compete with a countermelody in a contrapuntal environment. The ♪ ♪♪♪ | ♩ |, which dominates the first movement of Beethoven's Symphony no. 5, was made for and purposely designed for development. It has been suggested that this is a kind of musical seed whose flowering is achieved only through development. In contrast, Tchaikovsky's theme is already a flower. Since Tchaikovsky started with a flower rather than a seed, there was neither the necessity for nor even the possibility of a germinating (developmental) process. Continuing along this line, we might think of a classical theme and its development as a phenomenon in a state of becoming, whereas Tchaikovsky's theme is in a state of being.

Tchaikovsky further departs from classical models by using an allegro rather than a slow tempo in the second movement of *Pathétique*. The movement is in the rare 5/4 meter throughout and is cast in a large song form *(ABA)*. It is dominated by two full-blown themes and contains virtually no counterpoint.

The third movement begins with scherzolike material (though it is not in 3/4). This leads to a much longer section that is dominated by a loud and forceful march theme. (As in the first movement, the second theme dominates.) The scherzolike material returns briefly but is then completely overshadowed by the march for the remainder of the movement.

The last movement is slow (adagio). This represents yet another departure from a classical model. This movement has an *ABA* form with coda. Both the *A* and *B* themes have an air of tragedy about them; they establish a mood that seems to suggest grief. Since they are the concluding statements of the symphony, they may perhaps be clues to the overriding quality of Tchaikovsky's unspoken program.

Hector Berlioz

Berlioz (1803–69) is clearly the giant among French romantic composers: his conceptions were on a grand, dramatic scale and his tastes ran the gamut from Shakespeare to the macabre and diabolic. Like Tchaikovsky, he began serious music studies at about the age of twenty. And though Berlioz never mastered a musical instrument, he became one of the greatest orchestrators of all time.

He burst upon the Parisian scene at the age of twenty-six with the first performance of his *Symphonie Fantastique* (or "Fantastic" Symphony), a five-movement work with an elaborate program that is autobiographic in some respects. Each of the movements is preceded by explanatory program notes, and the entire symphony is prefaced by this general statement:

> A young musician of abnormal sensitivity and ardent imagination poisons himself with opium in a fit of amorous despair. The narcotic dose, too weak to cause death, plunges him into a heavy sleep accompanied by the weirdest visions, in which his sensations, emotions, and memories . . . are transformed into musical images and ideas. The beloved one herself becomes a melody, an *idée fixe,* which haunts him everywhere.[1]

The tempo, meter, and form in the second movement of *Pathétique* depart from the classical model.

The third movement of *Pathétique* is dominated by a march theme.

Berlioz's *Symphonie Fantastique* has an elaborate program that is partially autobiographical.

1. Extract from "Programme Music in the Last Four Centuries" (Frederick Niecks). Reproduced by courtesy of Novello and Company, Ltd.

The "beloved one" was an Irish Shakespearean actress named Henrietta Smithson; Berlioz was wildly in love with her though he had never met her. Berlioz eventually met and later married Smithson, but the marriage lasted only about two years due, no doubt, to Smithson's alcoholism and aberrant behavior.

Berlioz's works, primarily operas and symphonies, were composed on a grand scale.

Berlioz was primarily a composer of large-scale works—operas and symphonies—nearly all of which have literary and programmatic bases.

Choral/Dramatic Symphony

Some Romantic composers followed Beethoven's lead in creating choral symphonies.

A number of nineteenth-century composers emulated Beethoven in his ninth Symphony and incorporated the human voice into the once instrumental form. In doing so, they broke with classical tradition and transformed the symphony into a romantic phenomenon—the **choral** or **dramatic symphony.**

Berlioz composed a symphony based upon Shakespeare's Romeo and Juliet.

Roméo et Juliette   Berlioz's profound interest in Shakespeare and literature in general undoubtedly affected the creation of *Roméo et Juliette* (Romeo and Juliet) (1839). The work, scored for a large symphony orchestra plus chorus and vocal soloists, has the following formal divisions:

> *Part 1*
>> 1. Introduction: Tumult and strife; the Prince intervenes (orchestra).
>> 2. Prologue: Three sections for chorus and vocal soloists with orchestral accompaniment.
>
> *Part 2*
>> 1. Romeo alone; his sadness (orchestra).
>>   Concert and ball; fete at the Capulets (orchestra).
>> 2. Calm night; the young Capulets, as they leave, sing recollections of the ball music (chorus with orchestra).
>> 3. Love scene between Romeo and Juliet (the orchestra).
>> 4. Queen Mab or the Dream Sprite (orchestra, scherzo).
>
> *Part 3*
>> 1. Funeral march for Juliet (chorus and orchestra).
>> 2. Romeo at the tomb of the Capulets (orchestra).
>> 3. Finale (bass solo, two choruses, and orchestra).

Berlioz abandoned the classical four-movement plan.

Obviously, the basic classical four-movement plan, fast-slow-dance-fast, is discarded in favor of three large parts that contain various subparts. A drama is presented here, told in part by words and voices and in part by the wordless orchestra. The work is long and complicated, but some idea of how these various forces work together is gained by examining Part 2. (Time permitting, you should listen to the work in its entirety.)

In Part 2, no. 1, Romeo is alone with his thoughts: thoughts that are reflected in the orchestra's music. Eventually the tempo quickens and ballroom music begins to intrude and then to dominate the scene. This leads to no. 2, where the chorus sings strains of the dance music as they disappear into the late night. The chorus sings:

Ohé! Capulets—bonsoir, bonsoir!	Ho ho! Capulets, good-night all!
Cavaliers, au revoir!	Gentlemen, farewell!
Ah! Quelle nuit, quel festin!	Ah! what a night, and what
Bal divin!	A glorious ball!
Que de folles paroles!	What mad, enchanting talk!
Belles Véronnaises	Oh, girls of Verona,
Sous les grands mélèzes,	Can't you go now and dream of
Allez rêver de bal et d'amour,	love
Allez rêver d'amour	Under the evergreens till dawn?
Jusqu'au jour!	Go dream of love
Tra la, la la la la, la le ra la!	Til dawn,
	Tra-la, la la la . . .

The famous love scene between Romeo and Juliet then follows (Part 2, no. 3). Significantly, Berlioz directs the orchestra to recount this part of the story. Although the words between Romeo and Juliet in this scene are among the most famous in the English language, Berlioz relies upon the power of the wordless orchestra to convey the meaning. A cello is prominently featured in an impassioned solo, answered by a flute—the voices of Romeo (cello) and Juliet (flute). Toward the end of this section there is some activity involving cello and flute that suggests the excitement of heartbeats. The section then ends very quietly.

Berlioz chose a cello and a flute to represent the voices of Romeo and Juliet in the love scene.

Queen Mab is depicted by the orchestra in Part 2, no. 4. Berlioz described this section to his friend, the poet, Heinrich Heine:

> . . . Queen Mab in her microscopic car, attended by the buzzing insects of a summer's night and launched at full gallop by her tiny horses, fully displayed to the Brunswick public her lovely drollery and her thousand caprices. . . . You, the poet of fairies and elves . . . know only too well with what slender thread their veil of gauze is woven, and how serene must be the sky beneath which their many-colored tints sport freely in the pale starlight.

Part 2, no. 4 has the form scherzo-trio-scherzo, so structurally it is not too far removed from Beethoven's model. The orchestration is quiet and dazzling throughout. The close resemblance between the music and Berlioz's programmatic basis is strikingly apparent when listening to the movement.

Tone Poem

The **tone poem** (or symphonic poem) was the special contribution to the field of orchestral music by some nineteenth-century composers. The juxtaposition of the words "tone" and "poem" suggests once again the romantic's desire to synthesize the arts. The tone poem is usually a one-movement piece for orchestra and is usually programmatic.

> *The tone poem resulted from the romantic composers' attempt to synthesize the arts.*

There is no set form or length for a tone poem. Some are cast in a loose sonata form, and many are cast in "homemade" forms (forms that are freshly invented by the composer to accommodate the program behind the tone poem). Some tone poems are only about eight minutes in length, while others last an hour or more.

Franz Liszt is generally credited with the invention of the tone poem in the 1840s, but many other composers in the nineteenth and twentieth centuries were attracted to the genre. A tone poem by the Russian composer Borodin is examined in this section. It provides a good idea of how a tone poem functions.

> *Liszt is usually credited with the invention of the tone poem.*

Sound and Sense ♪
Tone Poem

Title: In the Steppes of Central Asia *(1880)*
Composer: Borodin
Meter: 2/4
Tempo: Allegretto con moto
Key: A minor and major

A Closer Look

Borodin provided the following program for this haunting tone poem.

> Out of the silence of the sandy steppes of Central Asia come the sounds of a peaceful Russian song. Along with them are heard the melancholy strains of Oriental melodies, then the stamping of approaching horses and camels. A caravan, accompanied by Russian soldiers, traverses the measureless waste. With full trust in its protective escort, it continues on its long journey in a carefree mood. Onward the caravan moves. The Songs of the Russians and those of the Asiatic natives mingle in common harmony. The refrains curl over the desert and then die away in the distance.

The musical structure of this tone poem is simplicity itself; it is one of the homemade forms mentioned earlier. Two themes, *A* (introduced by a clarinet):

A theme

and *B* (introduced by an English horn):

B theme

are presented. These themes recur and eventually are combined contra-
puntally. In the background cellos and violas perform a plucking figure
suggestive of footsteps. Here is a graphic illustration of the order and content
of this work after a brief, mysterious-sounding introduction played by high
strings and flute:

A—clarinet, answered by French horn	(:42)
Footsteps—low strings	(:22)
B—English horn	(1:08)
A—clarinet, answered by French horn	(:45)
A—full orchestra	(:24)
Footsteps	(:21)
B—English horn and cellos	(:34)
B—violins answered by violas and cellos	(:30)
A & B—combined contrapuntally; *A*-oboe, *B*-violins	(:51)
A & B—combined contrapuntally; full orchestra	(:28)
A—fragmented in French horn, clarinet, English horn, oboe	(1:08)
A—solo flute with high violins	(:20)

The nineteenth century bequeathed a rich body of orchestral tone
poems. Some of these are long and serious in nature, such as Strauss'
Also sprach Zarathustra (Thus Spake Zarathustra), the dramatic
opening of which was used as the soundtrack for the movie *2,001, a Space
Odyssey.* Other tone poems are more playful and entertaining, like Paul
Dukas's *L'Apprenti Sorcier (The Sorcerer's Apprentice)* and Mussorgsky's *Night on Bald Mountain.*

Nineteenth-century tone poems
vary in length and nature.

Solo Music for the Piano

Nineteenth-century advances in piano construction and quality vested
in the instrument thunderous power and also enabled it to play the sub-
tlest and most delicate nuances. The piano became an instrument for
both virtuosos and amateurs—for the large concert hall and the intimate
drawing room. And it was useful in churches, schools, and social clubs.

Because of its versatility and expressive power, the piano was the
romantic instrument par excellence. The instrument was also a positive
factor in the economic climate of the nineteenth century. In London,
Vienna, and elsewhere in Europe, piano factories were established that
employed craftsmen and laborers in significant numbers. As the demand

Romantic composers were
attracted to the piano's
versatility and expressive
power.

Liszt at the piano with friends:
Musset, Victor Hugo, George
Sand, Berlioz, Rossini, and
Countess D'Agoult.
© The Bettmann Archive

for tutoring of amateurs increased, more teachers joined the work force.
The music publishing industry also benefited from the increased interest
in the piano, since instruction books for the amateur pianist were in
demand.

   Because of this fascination with the piano, a demand for piano music
of a high quality arose. Composers such as Chopin, Liszt, Robert Schumann, and many others fulfilled this need.

In the nineteenth century the
formal solo piano recital
became an institution.

   Each of these changes contributed to the nineteenth-century establishment of the formal solo piano recital as an institution.

Piano Sonata

Two major branches of nineteenth-century solo piano music developed:
the **sonata** and the **character piece.** Several of the era's major composers
wrote piano sonatas, such giants as Schubert, Chopin, Liszt, and Brahms.

Piano sonatas of the nineteenth
century are generally long,
complex, and technically
demanding.

The piano sonatas, which were generally long and complex pieces in two,
three, or four movements, were technically very demanding.

Character Piece

The other branch of solo piano music, the **character piece,** embraces a much wider variety of music. The typical character piece is shorter and less complicated (in terms of form) than the piano sonata. Often, character pieces were published in groups or collections, and frequently they had fanciful and programmatic titles. Schubert's *Moments musicaux,* Chopin's *Polonaises and Preludes,* Brahms' *Intermezzos,* Mendelssohn's *Songs without Words,* and Robert Schumann's *Kinderscenen (Scenes from Childhood)* and *Papillons* are all collections of character pieces.

There is no prescribed length for a character piece. Chopin's Ballades last from eight to ten minutes, while seven of his Twenty-Four Preludes last less than a minute each. There is also no definite formal structure for a character piece, though the great majority are cast in straightforward two- or three-part forms. The emotional content of these nineteenth-century character pieces ranges from stormy and dramatic, to quiet and introspective, to playful. These character-piece traits are especially evident in works by Chopin, Liszt, MacDowell, Brahms, Clara and Robert Schumann, and other romantics.

Frédéric François Chopin

Someone in the nineteenth century dubbed Chopin (1810–49) "the poet of the piano." The description is apt, for nearly all of his works, save for two concertos and four sonatas, are brief, poetic character pieces for the piano: Nocturnes, Mazurkas, Ballades, Preludes, and others. And contemporary accounts tell us that Chopin played the piano in a most exquisite and poetic manner. Unlike other romantic virtuosos such as Franz Liszt and Clara Schumann, Chopin's shy and reserved personality were best suited to intimate gatherings rather than the concert stage.

Chopin was born in Poland to a French father and a Polish mother (note his French middle name), both of whom were cultured people with a fine sense of taste. The frail child flourished in this comfortable atmosphere. At the age of twenty-one he moved to Paris, then the cultural capital of Europe, the city where he was to reside for the remainder of his brief life.

He became the darling of Parisian society and counted among his friends many of the most influential and artistically important persons of the day. One of them, Madame Aurore-Lucie Dudevant (who wrote provocative novels under the name of George Sand) became his lover

> Character pieces are shorter and less complicated than piano sonatas.

> There is no standard length, structure, or mood for a character piece.

> Chopin most often composed short, poetic character pieces for the piano.

> He became a part of Parisian society and had many influential friends.

for nearly ten years, but it was at times a stormy relationship. Dudevant was six years his senior and a somewhat dominating figure: a militant feminist who scandalized polite society by smoking cigars in public and occasionally wearing men's clothes. Her flamboyance seems to have been the opposite of Chopin's quietly charming and somewhat aristocratic personality. The affair ended unhappily about two years before Chopin died of tuberculosis at the age of thirty-nine. Like so many of the romantics, Chopin died young.

He was admired by a number of notable contemporary composers, among them, Liszt, Berlioz, and Robert Schumann, the latter of whom wrote of Chopin in the press, "Hats off, gentlemen, a genius." Indeed he was a genius at pouring so much vital content into short, one-movement forms.

Chopin conveys an emotional message in each of his preludes.

Prelude   Chopin composed the Twenty-four **Preludes,** op. 28 during the years 1836–39. These short pieces traverse a wide emotional range and most successfully deliver the emotional message in a very limited span of time. Prelude no. 1 in C Major consists of little more than two phrases that together last only about forty-five seconds. And yet, despite its brevity, the prelude is a complete and satisfying musical experience. Notice, then, the contrasting qualities of the following preludes: Prelude no. 4 in E Minor (brooding), Prelude no. 7 in A Major (simple and delicate), Prelude no. 20 in C Minor (solemn and majestic), and Prelude no. 21 in B♭ Major (lyrical with a touch of drama near the end).

Chopin turned the Polish polonaise dance into an important type of piano music.

Polonaise   Chopin also reshaped the **polonaise,** a dance of Polish origin, into an elegant and important musical phenomenon. His eleven polonaises were fashioned as character pieces but on a larger scale than his preludes. They are longer and more structurally involved, and they employ internal contrasts of theme and mood. Polonaise in A♭ Major, op. 53 (sometimes called *Heroic*) is an excellent introduction to the genre. It is cast in a large multi-sectional form with the following subdivisions.

Sound and Sense
Polonaise

Title: Polonaise in A♭ Major, op. 53 (Heroic) (1842)
Composer: Chopin
Meter: 3/4
Tempo: Maestoso
Key: A♭ major

A Closer Look

Intro-duction (:29)	A (1:18)		B (1:01)		A' (:40)	C (1:17)		D (1:27)	A' (:38)	Coda (:24)
	a	a'	b	c	a'	c	c'	d	a'	
	(:37)	(:41)	(:41)	(:20)	(:40)	(:37)	(:40)	(1:27)	(:38)	(:24)

Étude   The **étude** (study) was another type of character piece developed by Chopin and Liszt. As well as being superior music, each of the Chopin études presents a specific technical problem for the pianist. The pianist encounters many such problems in his or her effort to master the instrument—difficulties in playing **legato** (smoothly) or **staccato** (playing the notes crisply), in playing extended passages of octaves in the right or left hand, or in moving rapidly from one part of the keyboard to another.

> An étude is a type of character piece written for piano; each usually presents a technical problem for the pianist.

Sound and Sense ♪
Études

Title: Étude, op. 10, no. 5 in G♭ Major (Black Key Étude) *(1829–32)*
Composer: Chopin
Meter: 2/4
Tempo: Vivace
Key: G♭ major

A Closer Look

Chopin said the following about his Twelve Études, op. 10.

> In writing my études I tried to put not only science but also art into them. Since a virtuoso must practice for a long time, he should be given exercises in which he will find proper food for his ears and his soul lest he be bored to death. I am disturbed because there are no beautiful exercises for beginners. A virtuoso has everything open to him; when he is bored by exercises, he can reach out for the most beautiful music. But a poor fellow who cannot play anything except exercises, whose fingers are as though tied, needs beautiful exercises that will save him from becoming disgusted with music. I have tried to write something of this kind, but I haven't been successful, because for the beginner anything is too difficult.

Étude, op. 10, no. 5 in G♭ Major *(Black Key Étude)* addresses the problem of playing rapid triplet figures in the right hand. Its form is: *ABCA*-coda.

Franz Liszt wrote a vast number of character pieces, including three sets of works called *Années de Pèlerinage (Years of Pilgrimage)*. These character pieces are more explicitly programmatic than those by Chopin. Two pieces from the first set are descriptive of water: "Au lac de Wallenstadt" ("By the lake of Wallenstadt"), and "Au bord d'une source" ("By the side of a spring"). In both of these short pieces, Liszt magically captures the rippling effect of water: a dreamy atmosphere for "Wallenstadt" and a playful atmosphere for "By the side of a spring." The form of Wallenstadt is a simple *ABA'*-coda with a rippling figure in the accompaniment throughout the piece. The form of "By the side of a spring" is *A*-bridge-*A'*-bridge-*A''*-bridge-*A'''*-coda, a theme with variations.

Among the best known sets of character pieces is Robert Schumann's *Kinderscenen (Scenes from Childhood)*. Schumann originally composed more than two dozen of these pieces, but he selected only twelve to make up this set, each with a brief descriptive title. Schumann did not intend the *Kinderscenen* for virtuoso pianists, but neither are they for children. The pieces are touching because Schumann has captured the spirit, the innocence, and joy of childhood, not because they detail childish behavior.

It is said of Schumann that he carried something of his childhood with him throughout his life. As we grow into adulthood most of us tend to forget the special joy and wonder of childhood. It is left to an artist such as Schumann to help us remember. That is the real accomplishment of the *Kinderscenen*.

"Traumerei" ("Dreaming"), no. 7 in the set, has sometimes been distorted through overly sentimental arrangements. Nevertheless, in the context of this collection of pieces, it loses none of its appeal when played well.

Listen now to *Kinderscenen*. The pieces are short and should not present any formal problems.

The American composer Edward MacDowell (1861–1908) was also active in the production of character pieces for the piano. Best known among MacDowell's short character pieces for piano is a set of descriptive nature pieces called *Woodland Sketches*.

Liszt's character pieces are more explicitly programmatic than Chopin's.

Schumann's *Kinderscenen* capture the spirit of childhood.

The American MacDowell composed character pieces focusing on nature.

Sound and Sense ♪
Character Piece

Title: Intermezzo, op. 118, no. 2 (1893)
Composer: Brahms
Meter: 3/4
Tempo: Andante
Key: A major

A Closer Look

Brahms composed many works in the vein of characteristic pieces, though his are not overtly programmatic nor do they bear descriptive titles. The Intermezzo, op. 118, no. 2, is an excellent example of Brahms's lyrical, moody, and contrapuntal style of characteristic piece. It is diagramed as follows:

A (1:35)				*B* (1:38)				*A* (1:19)		
a	*a*	*b*	*c*	*d*	*d*	*e*	*f*	*a'*	*b'*	*c*
(:22)	(:23)	(:43)	(:41)	(:22)	(:23)	(:26)	(:32)	(:22)	(:43)	(:42)

Sound and Sense ♪
Character Piece

Title: Andante con moto, *op. 2, no. 2 (1841)*
Composer: Fanny Mendelssohn-Hensel
Meter: 6/8
Tempo: Allegro
Key: B minor

A Closer Look

Several contemporary accounts suggest that the musical gifts of Fanny Mendelssohn-Hensel (1805–47) rivaled those of her younger and more famous brother, Felix. However, her professional career as performer and composer was hindered by the fact that society at that time did not look favorably on such aspirations for women. Nonetheless she was a prolific composer (mostly of songs and character pieces for the piano).

   Andante con moto, op. 2, no. 2, was originally part of a composition called *The Year* containing twelve character pieces, one for each month. In that context *Andante con moto* was called "September by the River." The rippling quality of the accompaniment points to its programmatic basis. The work is diagramed as follows:

A		*B*	*A*		Coda
a	*a'*	*b*	*a'*	*a''*	
(:20)	(:14)	(:39)	(:14)	(:15)	(:18)

The Concerto

Concertos were created during the nineteenth century in response to the public's enchantment with virtuoso pianists. The compositions provided the opportunity for the experts to display their extraordinary talents. Chopin, Liszt, Rachmaninoff, and other composer-pianists often performed their own concertos in public. Mendelssohn, Brahms, Tchaikovsky, and Grieg contributed piano and violin concertos for other virtuosos to perform. The nineteenth century also produced important concertos for viola, cello, clarinet, and other solo instruments, but the greatest and most numerous concertos were written either for piano and orchestra or for violin and orchestra. Of these, the important piano concertos outnumber those for violin.

Robert Schumann

Schumann (1810–56) was in some respects the most romantic and among the most tragic figures of the nineteenth century. In addition to his musical gifts he had a genuine flair for literature and poetry, and like Tchaikovsky, he was trained in the legal profession as a youth. This variety of interests, each holding an equal attraction and demanding an equal commitment, created stress which led to self-abuse. In his zeal to become a concert pianist, Schumann fashioned a leather device to stretch the reach of his fingers. The device left one of his fingers permanently maimed and ended his pursuit of a concert career.

At that time he dedicated himself solely to composition and, in his spare time, to the production of a musical magazine that championed the cause of young, aspiring composers such as Brahms and Chopin. He was an inordinately sensitive person who, by his own admission, could not help being affected by every object, person, and idea around him. To an extraordinary degree his personality was reflected in the songs, piano works, and other pieces he composed.

At the age of twenty he fell in love with Clara Weick, the eleven-year-old daughter of his piano teacher. His interest in her stood the test of time, and ten years later, after many serious quarrels with Mr. Weick, Robert and Clara were married. Despite Robert's mental disturbances, the marriage was a happy one and Clara Schumann became the ultimate interpreter of her husband's piano works.

In his literary works and in his musical scores, Schumann frequently referred to three fictitious persons: Eusebius, the dreamer; Florestan, the fiery revolutionary; and Raro, the knowledgeable arbiter of disputes between Florestan and Eusebius. Florestan and Eusebius conducted their disputes in print, but it is also likely they waged torturous

Piano concertos were composed for performance by virtuoso pianists.

Concertos were written for piano, violin, viola, cello, clarinet, and other solo instruments.

Schumann was zealous in his drive to become a concert pianist.

Eventually he dedicated himself to his compositions and to aiding aspiring young musicians.

warfare in Schumann's mind. His thoughts were torn between those of a dreamer and those of a revolutionary. These conflicting emotions likely influenced Schumann's music and contributed to his ultimate insanity. He died in an asylum in 1856, at the age of forty-six.

Schumann's music reveals the composer's inner conflict.

It is easy and erroneous to go too far in reading these conflicting personalities into some of Schumann's works. On the other hand, it would be a mistake to ignore Florestan and Eusebius altogether, for it seems clear that in a sense they are parts of the unwritten programmatic basis of some of Schumann's music.

Sound and Sense ♪
Piano Concerto

Title: Piano Concerto in A Minor, first movement (1841–45)
Composer: Schumann
Meter: 4/4
Tempo: Allegro affettuoso
Key: A minor

A Closer Look

Schumann's Piano Concerto is cast in the standard three movements: fast-slow-fast. Originally it consisted only of the first movement, but it was later expanded to three movements at the insistence of Schumann's wife, Clara, a well-known keyboard virtuoso.

The first movement is in sonata form (without the double exposition of the eighteenth-century concerto); the second movement is in a large three-part form—*ABA';* the last movement is in sonata form and recalls the *A* theme from the first movement. The first movement is examined here in greater detail.

First Movement

The movement begins with a loud, dramatic cascade of full chords on the piano. (Notice the soloist leads.) This outburst is brief and moves quickly to the orchestra's statement of the *A* theme (in A minor, the principal key of the piece).

The soloist then continues the theme, thus far creating the structure: introduction, *A* in the orchestra, *A* in the piano. An extended bridge passage shared by orchestra and soloist follows, which leads to the key and the location of an expected *B* theme. However, the piano plays the *A* theme, but in the key of C major. In another extended bridge passage, the piano has a dialogue, almost like a conversation, with first the oboe, then the clarinet. Toward the end of the exposition the mood and character of the music change as a marchlike closing theme for the whole orchestra is introduced. This closing theme has the aggressiveness associated with Florestan.

The development section has two parts and is split almost exactly in half. The first half creates an Eusebian dreamlike atmosphere, and the piano and clarinet resume their intimate conversation. But with a crash from Florestan, the dream is interrupted and the remainder of the development, up until the last few measures, is more militant and aggressive.

The recapitulation begins quietly with a statement of *A* in the woodwinds and another statement of *A* in the piano. A little later the mood brightens and the orchestral fire leads to a statement of the *A* theme, this time in the major mode. Once more, piano, clarinet, and oboe resume their private conversation, after which the aggressive closing theme from the exposition reappears and carries the piece to the cadenza. Notice that in the cadenza Schumann makes systematic use of the entire range of the keyboard. The cadenza ends with the conventional trill, after which the coda ends the movement in heroic fashion.

The movement is diagramed as follows:

Exposition

Brief piano introduction, followed by orchestral statement of A	(:26)
A—statement by piano	(:19)
Bridge—orchestra with piano, brief piano solo near midpoint	(1:15)
A (in key of C major)—piano	(:28)
Bridge—orchestra and piano	(1:32)
Marchlike theme	(:34)

Development

First half—Eusebius	(1:35)
Second half—Florestan	(1:44)

Recapitulation

A—orchestra	(:22)
A—piano	(:20)
Bridge—orchestra and piano	(1:12)
A	(:26)
Bridge—orchestra and piano	(1:30)
Marchlike theme	(:15)
Cadenza—piano	(1:46)
Coda—orchestra and piano	(:54)

Edward Grieg's Piano Concerto in A Minor possesses both similarities and contrasts in relation to Schumann's Concerto. The Grieg concerto, like the Schumann, has the standard three-movement format: fast-slow-fast.

Sound and Sense
Concerto

Title: Piano Concerto in A Minor (1868, revised 1906–07)
Composer: Grieg
Recording: P. Entremont/Ormandy, Philadelphia Orchestra
Meter: 4/4
Tempo: Allegro molto moderato
Key: A minor

A Closer Look

The first movement is in the sonata form (without the double exposition) and, like the Schumann Concerto, begins with a dramatic flourish by the pianist.

When listening to this movement, notice that the exposition is rather conventional. It presents two themes of sharply contrasting character: *A* is dramatic, *B* is lyrical. The abbreviated development section features more repetitions of the themes than it does real development of them. These themes, like those in the Tchaikovsky *Pathétique* symphony, are self-contained and are unsuitable for the developmental processes. The recapitulation closely adheres to the order of events in the exposition. The cadenza is a focal point in this movement; it is long, dramatic, and resembles a display of bravura.

A theme

The movement is diagramed here.

Dramatic opening gesture with piano	(:24)
A—orchestra	(:36)
A—piano	(:36)
Bridge—piano and orchestra, playful in character	(:40)
B—cellos	(:19)
B—piano, a lengthy crescendo leads to the development	(1:04)

Development

Concludes with the dramatic opening gesture and leads to the recapitulation	(1:48)

Recapitulation

A—piano and orchestra	(:34)
Bridge—piano and orchestra, playful in character	(:42)
B—orchestra (cellos)	(:18)
B—piano with orchestra	(1:02)
Brief orchestral statement leads to the cadenza	(:13)
Cadenza—pianist ends with a series of trills	(3:00)
Coda	(:37)

The second movement contains two alternating themes: a lyrical one, first introduced by the orchestra, and a more animated one, introduced by the soloist.

The last movement is cast in a very large *ABA'* form, in which there are dramatic differences between *A* and *B*. The opening *A* section has a quick tempo and features a folklike theme played first by the soloist and then elaborated upon by both the orchestra and the soloist. The tempo slows markedly and the texture changes drastically as the *B* section enters. It begins with a lovely flute melody accompanied by strings. The piano then picks up and elaborates on the *B* theme. The *A'* section is marked by the return of the folklike theme from *A,* the original tempo is restored, and the movement concludes with a brilliant, flashy coda.

Art Song

The strong attraction poetry held for many romantic composers led quite naturally to the creation of a significant body of songs in the nineteenth century. In art music, the solo song with piano is usually called art song to distinguish it from popular, folk, or other types of song. Schubert, Robert and Clara Schumann, Brahms, and other German composers were particularly adept at setting German romantic poetry to music. The special name for German art song is **Lied,** pronounced *leed* (plural—Lieder). A Lied is, then, a short lyrical song for solo voice with piano. Sometimes the piano serves as accompaniment, but very often the piano assumes a role nearly equal in importance to that of the voice.

Lieder composers were attracted to many romantic texts and to a bewildering mixture of good as well as poor poetry. Some of the poets whose lines were immortalized by Schubert and other fine Lieder composers would likely be forgotten if their poetry were examined on its own merits.

Franz Peter Schubert

Some classical composers, Mozart and Beethoven for example, wrote isolated examples of Lieder, but the real flowering of the Lied occurred early in the nineteenth century with the first great master of the genre— Franz Schubert (1797–1828).

At a very early age Schubert astonished his teachers by his musical precociousness. One remarked, "He seems to know in advance each new thing I try to instruct him about; I can only sit by in wonder at the child." By the age of seventeen Schubert was producing songs and instrumental music of exceptional quality. He composed *Die Erlkönig* at the age of eighteen, a piece generally regarded as one of the gems of the entire Lieder repertoire.

The art song was a product of the nineteenth-century composer's fascination with poetry.

A Lied is a short lyrical song—based on German poetry—for solo voice with piano.

By the time he was a teenager Schubert was composing songs and instrumental music of high quality.

He spent his entire life, brief though it was, in his native Vienna where he lived as a bohemian (a sort of nineteenth-century precursor of a hippie). He never enjoyed, or perhaps didn't want, steady employment. A circle of intimate friends who recognized his genius often pooled their meager resources to feed and house him. Schubert augmented these resources with occasional teaching jobs (which he detested) and sometimes with the sale of one of his works to a publisher. He spent his days composing and his nights partying—which consisted of conversation, drinking, and the performance of his songs and chamber music.

> Schubert was supported in part by friends who pooled their resources to help him.

Several years before his death he contracted a venereal disease, which caused him to slip into occasional fits of deep depression and which hastened his early death. His death may also be in part attributed to overwork: he was a feverish, nonstop worker, sometimes composing several Lieder in a single day.

> He was a tireless worker, sometimes composing several Lieder in one day.

He lived in the shadow of the much-celebrated Beethoven who preceded him in death by only a year. On Schubert's modest tombstone are inscribed the words: "Music has here buried a rich treasure but still fairer hopes." Not until several decades after his death did the musical public become aware of some of Schubert's most monumental works such as the *Unfinished* Symphony and the *Trout* Quintet.

Some composers created songs from whole sets of poems related to one another by the development of a character or a central theme. Sets of this kind are called **song cycles.** Schubert wrote over 600 Lieder, including two major song cycles—*Die Winterreise (The Winter's Journey)* and *Die schöne Müllerin (The Miller's Beautiful Daughter)*. The examination of only a few of Schubert's many Lieder exposes the range of subject matter, emotional content, and musical content of this composer's work.

> Song cycles are based on sets of poems, all related by character or theme.

An die Musik   Schubert composed music for the following poem by Franz von Schober[2]:

An die Musik	**To Music**

First Strophe

Du holde Kunst, in wieviel grauen Stunden,	O sublime art, in how many gray hours,
Wo mich des Lebens wilder Kreis umstrickt,	when the wild tumult of life ensnared me,
Hast du mein Herz zu warmer Lieb' entzunden,	have you kindled my heart to warm love,
Hast mich in eine bessre Welt entrückt!	have you carried me away to a better world!

2. From Philip L. Miller (editor), *The Rings of Words.* © 1973 Doubleday & Company, Inc., New York, NY. Reprinted by permission.

Goya's *Bobabilicon*—a dark
side of romanticism.

(ca. 1818); Etching and aquatint; 9 9/16″ ×
13 7/8″. The Metropolitan Museum of Art,
Harris Brisbane Dick Fund, 1924

Second Strophe

Oft hat ein Seufzer, deiner Harf' entflossen,	Often a sigh, escaped from your harp,
Ein süsser, heiliger Akkord von dir,	a sweet, solemn chord from you,
Den Himmel bessrer Zeiten mir erschlossen,	has opened the heaven of better times for me—
Du holde Kunst, ich danke dir dafür!	o sublime art, I thank you for it!

Schubert's *An die Musik*
reveals simplicity and
unexpected harmonies.

Schubert set the poem as a simple, strophic Lied, the second strophe beginning with the words "Oft hat ein Seufzer" ("Often a sigh"). When listening to this Lied, notice the marvelous simplicity of the melody. The gently pulsating piano figure established in the two-measure introduction runs uninterrupted throughout the song, and for all of its simplicity it, in conjunction with the gently moving bass line, creates gripping dissonance and unexpected harmony. It is never harsh; rather it is imbued with a dignified and understated strength that underscores the heartfelt, gentle power of the melody and the sentiment of the text.

Schubert's *Erlkönig* conveys
drama and tragedy through
the Lied format.

Erlkönig *Erlkönig,* based on a text by Goethe, is both dramatic and tragic, resulting in a different sort of Lied. The vocalist sings the parts of the four characters who populate this little drama: the narrator, the father, the Erlkönig, and the son.

Goethe's text is derived from the legend of the Erlking (the king of the elves) whose touch is fatal. In *Die Erlkönig,* the victim is the son. Schubert ingeniously differentiates the four characters by creating a tone of voice and harmony that is unique to the individual. The son's fear and anxiety is conveyed by the music he sings while accompanied by a dissonant harmony. The father's voice and music reflect his desire to calm the son. The Erlkönig pleads and tantalizes, and this is also reflected in the music. A rushing triplet figure in the bass line of the piano part appears several times during the course of the song to heighten the tension and drama.

Read the entire text of *Die Erlkönig* before listening to the song. The text is as follows[3]:

Erzähler
Wer reitet so spät durch Nacht und Wind?
Es ist der Vater mit seinem Kind;
Er hat den Knaben wohl in dem Arm,
Er fasst ihn sicher, er hält ihn warm.

Vater
Mein Sohn, was birgst du so bang dein Gesicht?

Sohn
Siehst, Vater, du den Erlkönig nicht?
Den Erlenkönig mit Kron' und Schweif?

Vater
Mein Sohn, es ist ein Nebelstreif.

Erlkönig
Du liebes Kind, komm, geh mit mir!
Gar schöne Spiele spiel' ich mit dir,

Manch bunte Blumen sind an dem Strand,
Meine Mutter hat manch gülden Gewand.

Sohn
Mein Vater, mein Vater, und hörest du nicht,
Was Erlenkönig mir leise verspricht?

Vater
Sei ruhig, bleibe ruhig, mein Kind:
In dürren Blättern säuselt der Wind.

Narrator
Who rides so late through night and wind?
It is the father with his child;
He folds the boy close in his arms,

He clasps him securely, he holds him warmly.

Father
My son, why do you hide your face so anxiously?

Son
Father, don't you see the Erlking?

The Erlking with his crown and train?

Father
My son, it is a streak of mist.

Erlking
Dear child, come, go with me!

I'll play the prettiest games with you.
Many colored flowers grow along the shore;
My mother has many golden garments.

Son
My father, my father, and don't you hear
The Erlking whispering promises to me?

Father
Be quiet, stay quiet, my child;
The wind is rustling in the dead leaves.

3. From Philip L. Miller (editor), *The Rings of Words.* © 1973 Doubleday & Company, Inc., New York, NY. Reprinted by permission.

Erlkönig
Willst, feiner Knabe, du mit mir
gehn?
Meine Töchter sollen dich warten
schön;
Meine Töchter führen den
nächtlichen Reihn
Und wiegen und tanzen und singen
dich ein.
Sohn
Mein Vater, mein Vater, und siehst
du nicht dort
Erlkönigs Töchter am düstern Ort?

Vater
Mein Sohn, mein Sohn, ich seh' es
genau:
Es scheinen die alten Weiden so
grau.
Erlkönig
Ich liebe dich, mich reizt deine
schöne Gestalt;
Und bist du nicht willig, so brauch'
ich Gewalt.
Sohn
Mein Vater, mein Vater, jetzt fasst
er mich an!
Erlkönig hat mir ein Leids gethan!
Erzähler
Dem Vater grauset's, er reitet
geschwind,
Er hält in Armen das ächzende
Kind,
Erreicht den Hof mit Mühe und
Not;
In seinen Armen das Kind war tot.

Erlking
My handsome boy, will you come
with me?
My daughters shall wait upon you;

My daughters lead off in the dance
every night,
And cradle and dance and sing you
to sleep.
Son
My father, my father, don't you see
there
The Erlking's daughters in the
shadows?
Father
My son, my son, I see it clearly;

The old willows look so gray.

Erlking
I love you, your beautiful figure
delights me!
And if you are not willing, then I
shall use force!
Son
My father, my father, now he is
taking hold of me!
The Erlking has hurt me!
Narrator
The father shudders, he rides
swiftly on;
He holds in his arms the groaning
child,
He reaches the courtyard weary
and anxious:
In his arms the child was dead.

Clara Schumann

In contrast to Fanny Mendelssohn-Hensel, Clara Schumann (1819–96)
was groomed by her father to be a professional musician. She succeeded
admirably and for more than half a century she enjoyed an international
career as a concert pianist, often playing works by her husband, Robert.
"Liebst du um Schönheit" ("If You Are in Love with Beauty") is taken
from her collection of *Lieder,* op. 12, (1841). The text is by the famous
German poet Friedrich Rückert. The piece provides a simple, straightforward strophic setting of the poem with a lovely melodic line.

"Liebst du um Schönheit," *Lieder,* op. 12

Friedrich Rückert (1788–1866)

Liebst du um Schönheit, o nicht mich liebe!	If you are in love with beauty, then do not love me!
Liebe die Sonne, sie trägt ein gold'nes Haar!	Give your love to the sun, with its golden tresses!
Liebst du um Jugend, o nicht mich liebe.	If you love youth, then do not love me.
Liebe den Frühling, der jung ist jedees Jahr!	Worship the springtime, which is young every year.
Liebst du um Schätze, o nicht mich liebe!	And if you love riches, do not love me.
Liebe die Meerfrau, sie hat viel Perlen klar.	Adore the mermaid who bears shining pearls.
Liebst du um Liebe, o ja mich liebe!	But if you love for Love's sake, O then love me,
Liebe mich immer, dich lieb' ich immerdar!	for I shall love you for evermore!

Opera

Several different kinds of opera developed in the nineteenth century. These differences are traceable in part to the swelling tide of nationalism which, after midcentury, became an increasingly visible and powerful force in Europe. The Russian group, including Mussorgsky and Glinka, produced operas on a colossal scale utilizing the native tongue as well as subject matter from Russian history and legend.

The greatest of these Russian operas is Mussorgsky's magnificent *Boris Godunoff* (1874). Some sense of its power and of Mussorgsky's earthy musical style and imaginative flair with orchestration is gained from listening to the "Coronation Scene" (scene ii of the Prologue).

Opéra-comique continued to flourish in the nineteenth century. It became increasingly more serious, though, in terms of both subject matter and musical style. It did, however, retain the element of spoken dialogue.

The French developed another opera type at this time called the grand opera. The grand opera (which contained no spoken dialogue) was big and spectacular and usually drew upon historical or epic subject matter for its plots.

But all of the grand operas and opéras-comique were overshadowed by the greatest French opera of the nineteenth century, Georges Bizet's *Carmen* (1875). As it was originally conceived, *Carmen* was technically an opéra-comique since it contained spoken dialogue. These spoken lines were later converted to sung recitative (by another composer) so that *Carmen* could be performed in the grand opera hall. But *Carmen* is not a typical representation of either grand opera or opéra-comique. It is a work unto itself, with subject matter both tragic and "realistic."

The development of opera in the nineteenth century was influenced by nationalism.

Mussorgsky's *Boris Godunoff* is probably the greatest nineteenth-century Russian opera.

In France, as opéra-comique became more serious in subject matter and style, the spectacular grand opera was developed.

The greatest nineteenth-century French opera was *Carmen.*

Verdi dominated Italian opera, while Wagner ignited an operatic revolution in Germany.

In terms of influence, staying power, and widespread public appeal, the Italians and the Germans were the leaders in nineteenth-century opera. The consummate master of the Italian operatic ideal was Giuseppe Verdi, although he did not control the field alone. Early in the nineteenth century Rossini, Donizetti, and Bellini contributed masterpieces such as *Il barbiere di Siviglia (The Barber of Seville)*, *Lucia di Lammermoor*, and *Norma*. And very late in the century, Puccini led the Italian tradition to new areas with masterworks of verismo (the nineteenth-century Italian interpretation of realism) such as *La Bohème*. Despite these composers' monumental work, Verdi remained the central composer of Italian opera.

The German opera and the German operatic ideal were very different from the Italian counterparts, mainly because German music at this time was dominated by one composer: Richard Wagner, who created an operatic revolution in Germany.

Wagner's early operas, such as *Lohengrin* (1846–48) and *Der fliegende Holländer (The Flying Dutchman)* (1841) contained such typical operatic elements as arias, recitatives, and chorus.

The genre created by Wagner is called music drama.

After the mid-1800s, however, Wagner created an entirely new kind of musical-dramatic work. For these works, he dropped the name opera and adopted the new generic title—**music drama.** *Tristan und Isolde* (1857–59) and the *Der Ring des Nibelungen* (1853–74) (which contains four individual works) are music dramas. This music drama is the embodiment of the German operatic ideal of the second half of the nineteenth century.

Italian Opera

Italian and German operas differed from each other in many respects. At the heart of the Italian ideal was the aria—the special song that enraptured audiences. No matter how neatly an aria fits into a story line, it has a tendency to call attention to itself. This tends to stop the flow of the drama, particularly if the aria is followed by thunderous applause from the audience. To the Italians, opera was still a vehicle for singers, and the aria was the singer's focus.

Nineteenth-century Italian opera focused on the singers.

Aside from the overture and other special numbers, the orchestra in an Italian opera functioned essentially as accompaniment to the singers. It rarely called attention to itself and never interfered with or detracted from the singers on the stage. Sometimes the orchestra was so secondary that Wagner was prompted to say that the Italians "treat the orchestra like a big guitar," rather like an ump-chunk-chunk, ump-chunk-chunk accompaniment.

The aria "Quando rapito in estasi," in Donizetti's opera *Lucia di Lammermoor,* demonstrates the memorable quality of melodic line, the virtuosic demands on the singer, and the minimal, accompanimental role of the orchestra. The text to this aria (and the text to the momentary interruption by Alisa) appears below.

Lucia
Quando, rapita in estasi
del più cocente ardore,
col favellar del core
mi giura eterna fe,
in estasi del più cocente ardore, ecc.
gli affanni miei dimentico,
gioia diviene il pianto . . .
Parmi che a lui d'accanto
si schiuda il ciel per me, ecc.

Alisa
Ah! giorni d'amaro pianto
ah! s'apprestano per te!
Si, giorni, ecc.
Ah! Lucia, ah! desisti.

Lucia
Ah! Quando rapito in estasi,
ecc. . . .

Lucia
When, transported in an ecstasy
of most ardent passion,
with heartfelt words
he swears to love me ever,
in an ecstasy of most ardent
passion, etc.
I forget my cares,
tears turn to joy . . .
It seems that at his side
the gates of heaven open to me, etc.

Alisa
Oh, days of bitter weeping
lie in store for you!
Yes, days, etc.
Oh, draw back, Lucia!

Lucia
Ah! When, transported in an
ecstasy, etc. . . .

Arias such as this and small ensemble pieces are called **set numbers.** In the Italian ideal, arias and ensemble numbers are joined by connective recitatives. In opera of this kind, smaller set numbers are joined to create larger structural entities. It becomes obvious when listening to these operas that they are not simply music added to a libretto (text), but that the small sets and larger entities are very carefully and logically constructed. It is only through such skillful control that the music, text, and story can produce maximum impact.

Set numbers are the arias and the small ensemble pieces.

Il barbiere di Siviglia   Rossini's *Il barbiere di Siviglia (The Barber of Seville)* (1816) is among the finest, if not *the* finest, of the comic operas from the nineteenth century, and perhaps of all time. The opening scene of the opera reveals Rossini's musical and comedic gifts and, at the same time, exemplifies the compactness of the overall structure.

Briefly, the dramatic situation of the scene is as follows: Count Almaviva has contracted Fiorello and a group of musicians to help him serenade Rosina, with whom he is secretly in love. They meet just before dawn under her balcony window. When the count realizes that Rosina

Rossini's *The Barber of Seville* may be the finest comic opera of all time.

is not going to appear, he decides to pay off the bumbling musicians and call it a night. A hilarious episode ensues as the musicians, who cannot stop thanking the count for his generosity, do not leave. As they continue to make a racket, the count is beside himself. Finally they do leave and the wonderful character, Figaro—the Barber of Seville, enters.

It would have been easy to dismiss the musicians after their failure to arouse Rosina. Many another composer and dramatist would have done just that. It would be, after all, a convenient and dramatically justifiable thing to do. But Rossini and his librettist took this ordinary situation and transformed it into wonderful slapstick comedy.

Figaro turns out to be an unforgettable character, not so much because of the words he utters, but because of the quality of the vocal line Rossini developed for him. Figaro is something of a braggart and know-it-all, in love with the sound of his own voice. Notice how he holds certain high notes, celebrating the sound of his voice. Despite these human failings, Figaro is still a likable character; the music persuades us to befriend him.

Count Almaviva, however, is depicted as a bumbling fool who seems to have no control over his own destiny, despite the fact that he is a nobleman. Frustrated by his ineffectiveness, he requests Figaro's aid in solving his problems. This can be interpreted as a thinly veiled political statement on Rossini's part: the aristocracy hasn't brains enough to take care of itself.

Rossini's opera carries a political statement.

Here is the text, translation, and formal analysis of the opening part of Act I, scene i. Notice that the three sets are joined by connective recitative.

Act I
Scene i

A Square in Seville.
Set 1

It is daybreak outside Dr. Bartolo's house. Preceded by Fiorello and a band of musicians, Count Almaviva appears.

a

Fiorello	**Fiorello**
Piano, pianissimo,	Softly, softly now,
senza parlar,	without a word,
tutti con me	all of you
venite qua.	come here with me.
Musicians	**Musicians**
Piano, pianissimo,	Quiet as anything,
eccoci qua.	here we are.

Fiorello
Venite qua.

Fiorello
Come here.

Musicians
Eccoci qua.

Musicians
Here we are.

Fiorello
Piano.

Fiorello
Don't make a sound.

Musicians
Piano.

Musicians
Not a sound.

Fiorello
Venite qua.

Fiorello
Come here.

Musicians
Eccoci qua.

Musicians
Here we are.

b

Fiorello
Tutto è silenzio;
nessum qui sta,
che i nostri canti
possa turbar.
Tutto è silenzio, ecc.

Fiorello
All is quiet;
no one's about
to disturb
our serenade.
All is quiet, etc.

Almaviva
Fiorello . . . Olà . . .

Almaviva
Fiorello . . . hey . . .

Fiorello
Signor, son qua.

Fiorello
I'm here, my lord.

Almaviva
Ebben! . . . gli amici?

Almaviva
Well? What about your comrades?

Fiorello
Son pronti già.

Fiorello
They're quite ready.

a'

Almaviva
Bravi, bravissimi,
fate silenzio;
piano, pianissimo,
senza parlar.

Almaviva
Good fellows, splendid!
Hush now,
be very quiet,
don't breathe a word.

Musicians
Piano, . . .
. . . pianissimo, . . .

Musicians
Hush, . . .
. . . hush now, . . .

Fiorello
Senza parlar, . . .

Fiorello
Not a word, . . .

Almaviva
Piano.

Almaviva
Hush.

Musicians, Fiorello
. . . senza parlar

Musicians, Fiorello
(variously)
. . . not a word.

Fiorello
Venite qua.

Almaviva, Musicians, Fiorello

Senza parlar, piano piano, senza
parlar.

Fiorello
Come here.

Almaviva, Musicians, Fiorello
(severally and variously)
Not a word, hush now, not a word.

Set 2

c

Almaviva

Ecco ridente in cielo
spunta la bella aurora,
e tu non sorgi ancora?
E puoi dormir così?
Ah!
Sorgi, mia dolce speme,
vieni, bell'idol mio;
rendi men crudo, oh Dio,
lo stral che mi ferì.

Almaviva
(singing)
Lo, smiling in the heavens
the lovely dawn breaks forth,
whilst you are not yet risen;
how is it you can sleep so?
Ah!
Arise, my sweet content,
come, my pretty adored;
oh Cupid, render less unkind
the arrow that has wounded me.

d

Oh sorte! già veggo
quel caro sembiante:
quest'anima amante
ottene pietà!
Oh istante d'amore!
Felice momento!
Oh dolce contento
che egual, no, non ha! ecc.
Ehi, Fiorello?

Oh, fortune, I see
that dear image now:
grace is vouchsafed
this loving heart!
Oh, moment of love!
Happy moment!
Oh, sweet content
that has no equal! etc.
Hey, Fiorello?

Connective Recitative

Fiorello
Mio signore . . .

Almaviva
Di', la vedi?

Fiorello
Signor no.

Almaviva
Ah, ch'è vana ogni speranza!

Fiorello
My lord . . .

Almaviva
Say, can you see her?

Fiorello
No, my lord.

Almaviva
Oh, how vain are all my hopes!

Set 1'

Fiorello
Signor Conte, il giorno avanza . . .

Fiorello
My lord, day is breaking . . .

Almaviva
A che penso? che farò?

Tutto è vano . . . Buona gente!

Musicians
Mio signor . . .

Almaviva
Avanti, avanti.

Più di suoni, più di canti,
più di suoni
io bisogno ormai non ho.

Fiorello
Buona notte a tutti quanti,
più di voi che far non so.
Buona notte, buona notte, ecc.

Almaviva
What am I thinking of? What shall
I do?

All is in vain . . . Good fellows!

Musicians
My lord . . .

Almaviva
Come here.
*(giving his purse to Fiorello, who
proceeds to pay off the musicians)*

No more playing, no more song;
of music
I have no further need.

Fiorello
Goodnight, one and all,
I've no more use for your services.
Goodnight, goodnight, etc.

Concerted Passage

Musicians
Mille grazie, mio signore, del . . .

. . . favore, dell'onore.

Almaviva
Basta, basta!

Musicians
Mille grazie, . . .

Almaviva
Non parlate, . . .

Musicians
. . . mio signore, . . .

Almaviva
. . . ma non serve, . . .

Musicians
. . . del favore, . . .

Almaviva
. . . non gridate.

Musicians
. . . dell'onore.

Musicians
Ah, di tanta cortesia
obbligati in verità!
Oh, che incontro fortunato!
È un signore di qualità! ecc.

Musicians
A thousand thanks, my lord, for
your . . .
. . . favour and the honour.

Almaviva
That'll do, that'll do!

Musicians
A thousand thanks, . . .

Almaviva
Don't talk, . . .

Musicians
. . . my lord, . . .

Almaviva
. . . it's quite unnecessary, . . .

Musicians
. . . for your favour, . . .

Almaviva
. . . don't shout.

Musicians
. . . and the honour.
*(singing all together, though often
at odds with one another, with
much repetition)*

Musicians
For so much kindness
much obliged, I'm sure!
Oh, what a lucky meeting!
He's a real gent! etc.

Fiorello
Zitti, zitti! che rumore!
Maledetti, via di qua!
Ve', che chiasso indiavolato!
Ah, che rabbia . . .
Oh, che rabbia che mi fa! ecc.

Almaviva
Maledetti! Andate via!
Ah, canaglia! Via di qua!
Tutto quanto il vicinato
questo chiasso sveglierà, sì, ecc.

Almaviva
Basta! basta!

Fiorello
Zitti . . .
. . . zitti!

Musicians
Grazie!

Fiorello
Oh che rabbia che mi fa!

Almaviva
Ah maledetti, andate via,
ah, canaglia, via di qua!

Fiorello
Zitti zitti, ecc.

Almaviva
Maledetti, ecc.

Musicians
Ah, di tanta cortesia, ecc.

Fiorello
Shut up! What a noise!
Curse you! Get out of here!
Look here, what a confounded din!
Oh, what a rage . . .
what a rage they've put me in! etc.

Almaviva
Damned fools! Be off!
What a rabble! Get out of here!
This shindy will raise
the entire neighbourhood, it will!
etc.
(And so on)

Almaviva
That's enough, for heaven's sake!

Fiorello
Shut up, . . .
. . . do shut up!

Musicians
Thanks!

Fiorello
Oh, what a rage they put me in!

Almaviva
You infernal nuisances, be off,
get out, you dogs!

Fiorello
Oh, do shut up, etc.

Almaviva
Damned fools, etc.

Musicians
For so much kindness, etc.
(They continue in the same strain.)

Connective Recitative

Almaviva

Gente indiscreta!

Fiorello
Ah, quasi con quel chiasso
importuno tutto quanto il
quartiere han risvegliato.
Alfin sono partiti!

Almaviva

E non si vede!

Almaviva
*(having at last got rid of the
musicians)*

No sense of discretion . . . the
fools!

Fiorello
With their ill-timed clamour
they've almost woken
the entire neighbourhood.
At last they've gone!

Almaviva
(looking up at the window)

And she hasn't appeared!

Figaro's Voice
La lala lalalalalalala!

Almaviva
Chi è mai quest' importuno?
Lasciamolo passar.

Sotto quegli archi, non veduto,
vedrò quanto bisogna; già l'alba
appare e amor non si vergogna.

Figaro's Voice
La lala lalalalalalala!

Almaviva
Who is it now? Confound it!
Let's wait till he's gone by.
(hiding)
Hidden under these arches,
I'll be able to see all I want;
it's daybreak already and love has
no need to blush.

Set 3

Figaro

La ra la le ra la ra la!
Largo al factotum
della città, largo!
La ran la, ecc.
Presto a bottega,
che l'alba è già, presto!
La ran la, ecc.
Ah che bel vivere,
che bel piacere
per un barbier
di qualità!
Ah bravo, Figaro,
bravo, bravissimo, bravo!
La ran la la, ecc.
Fortunatissimo,
per verità, bravo!
La ran la la, ecc.
Fortunatissimo, ecc.
La ran la la, ecc.
Pronto a far tutto,
la notte il giorno
sempre d'intorno,
in giro sta.
Miglior cuccagna
per un barbiere,
vita più nobile,
no, non si dà.
La la ran la, ecc.
Rasori e pettini,
lancette e forbici,
al mio comando
tutto qui sta.
Lancette e pettini,
lancette e forbici, ecc.
V'è la risorsa,

Figaro
(coming down the street)
la ra la le ra la ra la!
Room for the town's
factotum, make way!
La la la, etc.
Hasten to the shop
for it's morning already, quick!
La la la, etc.
Oh what a fine life!
What fun
for a first-class
barber!
Oh bravo, Figaro,
fine fellow, bravo!
La, la, la, etc.
You're a lucky
man indeed, bravo!
La la la, etc.
You're a lucky, etc.
La la la, etc.
Ready for anything,
day and night
always on the go,
here, there and everywhere.
A better livelihood
for a barber,
a nobler life,
no, there is none!
La la la, etc.
Razors and combs,
lancets and scissors,
ready to hand,
everything's here.
Lancets and combs,
lancets and scissors, etc.
There are the perks

poi, del mestiere	of the job, too,
colla donnetta . . .	with the young ladies . . .
col cavaliere . . .	and with the young gentlemen . . .
colla donnetta, la la la, ecc.	With the young ladies, la la la, etc.
col cavaliere, la la la, ecc.	with the young bloods, la la la, etc.
Ah che bel vivere, ecc.	Oh what a fine life, etc.
Tutti mi chiedono,	Everyone calls for me,
tutti mi vogliono,	everyone wants me,
donne, ragazzi,	ladies, lads,
vecchi, fanciulle.	old men and girls.
Qua la parrucca . . .	Here my wig . . .
Presto la barba . . .	Quick a shave . . .
Qua la sanguigna . . .	I must be bled . . .
Presto il biglietto . . .	Quickly this letter . . .

Italians also became masters of the small vocal ensemble.

Verdi's *Rigoletto* features a masterful quartet.

Small Vocal Ensemble: *Rigoletto*   The Italians also showed a preference for and became the masters of the small vocal ensemble, such as the sextet and the quartet. One of the most memorable of these is found in Act III, scene i, of Verdi's tragic masterpiece *Rigoletto* (1851). The scene begins with some recitative that leads eventually to a strophic aria called "La donna e mobile," then to a duet, and after more recitative, to the spectacular quartet. The text and stage directions that follow will guide you through the action and enable you to envision what is happening and what is on the mind of each of the people in the scene. Gilda has been in love with the Duke, but doesn't know until this scene that the Duke is an evil man, despite her father's, Rigoletto's, warnings.

The Duke and Maddalena, the object of his advances, are inside a run-down road house. Gilda and Rigoletto are able to observe his actions through a hole in one of the walls. Thus, two members of the quartet are inside (Duke and Maddalena), and two are outside (Gilda and Rigoletto).

Notice how Verdi develops each of the characters through song in the quartet. The Duke continues singing in his arrogant and lecherous manner. Maddalena is skittish. Gilda is broken-hearted and her melodic line is full of weeping and wailing. Rigoletto sings in a state of controlled anger.

La sponda destra del Mincio. A sinistra è una casa a due piani, mezzo diroccata, la cui fronte, volta allo spettatore, lascia vedere per una grande arcata l'interno d'una rustica osteria al pian terreno, ed una rozza scala che mette al granaio, entro cui, da un balcone senza imposte, si vede un lettuccio. Nella facciata che guarda la strada è una porta che s'apre per di	The right bank of the Mincio river. Left, a two-storied house, half fallen into ruin. On the ground floor, the interior of a rustic wineshop beyond an arcade. A rough stone staircase leads to a loft above, with a balcony. The outer wall facing the audience is without shutters, and a cot inside is clearly visible. Downstairs, in the wall of the house facing the road, there is a

dentro; il muro poi è sì pieno di fessure, che dal di fuori si può facilmente scorgere quanto avviene nell'interno. Il resto del teatro rappresenta la deserta parte del Mincio, che nel fondo scorre dietro un parapetto in mezza ruina; di là dal fiume è Mantova. È notte. Gilda e Rigoletto inquieto, sono sulla strada. Sparafucile nell'interno dell'osteria, seduto presso una tavola, sta ripulendo il suo cinturone senza nulla intendere di quanto accade al di fuori.

door, opening inward. The wall itself is so full of cracks and holes that whatever takes place within is clearly visible. The rest of the stage represents the deserted fields along the Mincio, which runs behind a ruined parapet in the background. Beyond the river, Mantua. It is night. Gilda is in the road, with Rigoletto, who is obviously tense. Sparafucile, seated at a table in the wineshop, is cleaning his swordbelt. He is unaware of what is taking place outside.

Recitatives

Rigoletto
E l'ami?

Rigoletto
And you love him?

Gilda
Sempre.

Gilda
Even now.

Rigoletto
Pure
Tempo a guarirne t'ho lasciato.

Rigoletto
Yet
I have given you time to forget.

Gilda
Io l'amo.

Gilda
I love him.

Rigoletto
Povero cor di donna! Ah, il vile infame! Ma ne avrai vendetta, o Gilda.

Rigoletto
Poor woman's heart! Ah, the scoundrel! You shall be avenged, o Gilda.

Gilda
Pietà, mio padre—

Gilda
Have pity, my father—

Rigoletto
E se tu certa fossi
Ch'ei ti tradisse, l'ameresti ancora?

Rigoletto
And if you were sure that he is unfaithful, would you still love him?

Gilda
Nol so, ma pur m'adora.

Gilda
I do not know, but he adores me.

Rigoletto
Egli?

Rigoletto
He?

Gilda
Sì.

Gilda
Yes.

Rigoletto
Ebbene, osserva dunque.
(l a conduce presso una delle fessure del muro, ed ella vi guarda.)

Rigoletto
Well, then watch carefully.
(He leads her to an opening in the wall. She looks through into the wineshop.)

Gilda
Un uomo
Vedo

Rigoletto
Per poco attendi.
*(Il Duca, in assisa di semplice
ufficiale di cavalleria, entra nella
sala terrena per una porta a
sinistra.)*

Gilda
(trasalendo)
Ah, padre mio!

Duca
(a Sparafucile)
Due cose e tosto—

Sparafucile
Quali?

Duca
Una stanza e del vino.

Rigoletto
(Son questi i suoi costumi!)

Sparafucile
(Oh, il bel zerbino!)
(Entra nella stanza vicina.)

Gilda
I see
A man.

Rigoletto
Wait a moment.
*(The Duke, wearing the uniform of
a cavalry officer, enters the room
on the ground floor through a
door, left.)*

Gilda
(startled)
Ah, father!

Duke
(to Sparafucile)
Two things—and quickly.

Sparafucile
What things?

Duke
A room and some wine.

Rigoletto
(These are the fellow's habits!)

Sparafucile
(Oh, the gay blade!)
(He goes into an adjoining room.)

Strophic Aria

Duca
La donna è mobile
Qual piuma al vento,
Muta d'accento, e di pensier.

Sempre un amabile
Leggiadro viso,
In pianto o in riso, è menzognero.

La donna è mobile ecc.
E sempre misero
Chi a lei s'affida,
Chi le confida, mal cauto il core!

Pur mai non sentesi
Felice appieno
Chi su quel seno, non liba amore!

La donna è mobile ecc.

Duke
Oh, woman is fickle
As a feather in the wind,
Simple in speech, and simpler of
mind.

Always the lovable,
Sweet, laughing face,
But laughing or crying, a false face,
be sure.

Oh, woman is fickle etc.
Oh, the poor devil
Who gives himself up to her,
And if he trusts her, there goes his
heart!

Yet no man can feel
Quite fully content
Unless, in her arms, he drinks to
Love's health!
Oh, woman is fickle etc.

Sparafucile

(Rientra con una bottiglia di vino e due bicchierl che depone sulla tavola: quindi batte col pomo della sua lunga spada due colpi al soffitto. A quel segnale una ridente giovane, in costume di zingara, scende a salti la scala: il Duca corre per abbracciarla, ma ella gli sfugge. Frattanto Sparafucile, uscito sulla via, dice a parte a Rigoletto:)

È là vostri'uomo? Viver dee o morire?

Rigoletto

Più tardi tornerò l'opra a compire.

(Sparafucile allontana dietro la casa verso il fiume. Gilda e Rigoletto rimangono sulla via, il Duca e Maddalena nel piano terreno.)

Sparafucile

(He returns with a bottle of wine and two glasses, which he puts on the table. Then, with the butt of his sword, he strikes twice against the ceiling. At this signal, a buxom young woman in gypsy costume comes running down the stairs. The Duke tries to greet her with a kiss, but she eludes him. Meanwhile Sparafucile has gone out into the road, he speaks softly to Rigoletto:)

Is that your man? Shall he live or die?

Rigoletto

I'll come back later to conclude our business.

(Sparafucile moves off, around the house to the rear, in the direction of the river. Gilda and Rigoletto remain in the road. The Duke and Maddalena, Sparafucile's sister, are together in the wineshop.)

Duet

Duca

Un di, se ben rammentomi,
O bella, t'incontrai.
Mi piacque di te chiedere
E intesi che qui stai.
Or sappi chi d'allora
Sol te quest'alma adora.

Maddalena

Ah! ah!—e vent'altre appresso

Le scorda forse adesso?
Ha un'aria il signorino
Da vero libertino.

Duca

(per abbracciarla)

Si—un mostro son—

Duke

One day, if I remember rightly,
I met you, pretty girl.
I asked someone about you
And was told you live here.
Let me say that ever since then,
I have abjectly adored you.

Maddalena

Ah! ah! And the twenty more since then,
Do you forget them now?
I think my fine young man
Is a bit of a libertine.

Duke

(trying to kiss her)

Yes—I'm a monster—

Recitative

Maddalena

Lasciatemi,
Stordito.

Maddalena

Leave me alone,
You fool.

Duca
lh, che fracasso!

Maddalena
Stia saggio.

Duca
E tu sii docile,
Non farmi tanto chiasso.
Ogni saggezza chiudesi
Nel gaudio e nell'amore.
(*Le prende la mano.*)
La bella mano candida!

Maddalena
Scherzate, voi signore.

Duca
No, no.

Maddalena
Son brutta.

Duca
Abbracciami.

Maddalena
Ebro!

Duca
D'amore ardente.

Maddalena
Signor, l'indifferente,
Vi piace canzonar?

Duca
No, no, ti vo'sposar.

Maddalena
Ne voglio la parola—

Duca
(*ironico*)
Amabile figliuola!

Rigoletto
(*a Gilda che avrà tutto osservato
ed inteso*)
E non ti basta ancor?

Gilda
Iniquo traditor!

Maddalena
Ne voglio la parola.

Duca
Amabile figliuola!

Rigoletto
E non ti basta ancor?

Duke
Ho, what a hubbub!

Maddalena
Behave yourself!

Duke
And you be sweet.
Don't make such a fuss.
The end of all wisdom lies
In the joy of loving.
(*He takes her hand.*)
Your pretty white hand!

Maddalena
You are joking, sir.

Duke
No, no.

Maddalena
I'm ugly.

Duke
Kiss me.

Maddalena
You're drunk!

Duke
With love.

Maddalena
My cynical friend,
You like to joke, don't you?

Duke
No, no. I want to marry you.

Maddalena
I want your word of honor—

Duke
(*ironic*)
Lovable child!

Rigoletto
(*to Gilda, who has seen and heard
all*)
Haven't you seen enough?

Gilda
Wicked traitor!

Maddalena
I want your word of honor.

Duke
Lovable child!

Rigoletto
Haven't you had enough?

The Quartet

Duca

Bella figlia dell'amore
Schiavo son dei vezzi tuoi;
Con un detto, un detto sol
tu puoi
Le mie pene consolar.
Vieni e senti del mio core
Il frequente palpitar.
Con un detto sol
tu puoi
Le mie pene consolar.

Maddalena

Ah! ah! rido ben di core,
Che tai baie costan poco;
Quanto valga il vostro gioco,
Mel credete, so apprezzar.
Sono avvezza, bel signore,
Ad un simile scherzar.

Gilda

Ah, così parlar d'amore
A me pur l'infame ho udito!
Infelice cor tradito,
Per angoscia non scoppiar.

Rigoletto
(a Gilda)
Taci, il pianger non vale;
Che'ei mentiva or sei sicura.
Taci, e mia sarà la cura
La vendetta d'affrettar.
Pronta fia, sarà fatale;
Io saprollo fulminar.

Duke

Fairest daughter of love,
I am a slave to your charms;
With a word, one word, you have
the power
To quiet all my anguish.
Come, feel the wild beating
Of my lovesick heart.
With one word you have the power

To quiet all my anguish!

Maddalena

Ah! ah! That is really laughable—
How cheap such talk is, really.
What all this stuff is worth,
Believe me, I know exactly.
I am quite used by now, sir,
To foolish jokes like this.

Gilda

Ah, to speak of love in such a way!
The scoundrel spoke so once to me!
O wretched heart, betrayed,
Do not break for sorrow.

Rigoletto
(to Gilda)
Be silent, weeping is useless now.
You are convinced he was lying—
Be silent, and I shall move at once
To hasten our revenge.
It will be quick, it will be deadly,
And I shall know how to strike.

Verdi was not only a great composer, he was also a man of the theater with an uncanny sense of effective drama. The stories of several of his operas are based on works by great literary figures such as Shakespeare and Victor Hugo. Unquestionably, he was well acquainted with fine drama, but ultimately, the power of his operas is derived from the music. To simplify a difficult matter, it can be said that for the Italians, Verdi among them, music was the culmination of expression. The drama and other elements were important, but music was the essence of opera.

The music is the most important element in nineteenth-century Italian opera.

Richard Wagner

To contemplate Richard Wagner (1813–83) is to come face to face with incredible genius, revolutionary innovations, extreme egocentricity, and utter despicableness. He was all these things—the admirable and the deplorable. Let's begin with a brief look at the latter.

Wagner had a talent for making enemies. He also had an insatiable appetite for spending money—other people's money, for he had none of his own. Tens of thousands of dollars were "loaned" to him by friends, acquaintances, and strangers so that he might promote his own works and live in a manner appropriate to an earthly god. More than once he was bailed out of certain trips to debtor's prison by friends who were mesmerized or otherwise coerced by the force of his personality. The money was used to have the walls and ceilings of his living quarters lined with silk, to employ servants to attend to his every need, or on some other extravagance. King Ludwig of Bavaria, a weak-willed young man and one completely under Wagner's spell, handsomely supported the composer and arranged for the construction of a special theater in Bayreuth for the performance of Wagner's operas.

Wagner's first marriage technically lasted for more than thirty years, though it was a stormy relationship marked with numerous separations due to Wagner's frequent infidelities. The most famous of his love affairs involved Cosima von Bulow, wife of Wagner's close friend, Hans von Bulow, and daughter of Franz Liszt. Their liaison began in about 1863 and culminated in their marriage in 1866. Wagner thought nothing of stealing the wife of his good friend and ardent supporter. He seemed to earnestly believe that he was the world's greatest composer, dramatist, and philosopher. As such he was on a higher plane than other mortals and, hence, beyond the mundane morality of society.

But despite all his shortcomings, there is no doubt that he was one of the great artists of the nineteenth century.

German Opera: Wagner's *Gesamtkunstwerk*

Wagner said, "The error in opera lies in the fact that a means of expression, namely music, has been made the object, while the object of expression, namely the drama, has been made the means." In other words, Wagner felt that the ultimate expression of the opera was the drama, and music a means to that end. In his view, the Italians created "the error in opera" with their interpretation.

Given Wagner's bias toward drama, you might expect that his musical interest and abilities were limited. On the contrary, Wagner was not only a gifted musician, but an influential one as well. His ideas about opera and his use of harmony profoundly influenced the course of music in the last half of the nineteenth century and beyond.

Not just opera, but symphonic music as well, was affected by Wagnerian practices.

Wagner theorized about and then put into practice what we now recognize as the ultimate synthesis of the arts—a unification of music, drama, poetry, dance, architecture—to which Wagner gave the German name *Gesamtkunstwerk*. Wagner believed that drama, as a central part of a total art work (or *Gesamtkunstwerk*), revealed the innermost feelings and beliefs of the culture. Wagner was not dealing in terms of a simple comedy or tragedy. The *Gesamtkunstwerk* revealed the thoughts and aspirations of a culture. The most direct and compact mode of drama, Wagner believed, is myth. Wagner's music dramas, then, used myth—Teutonic mythology—as the vehicle for revealing a culture to itself. In his hands the spirit of nationalism was raised to the level of doctrine.

Arias, recitatives, and ensemble numbers were purged from Wagner's music drama because they were too one-dimensional and got in the way of the continuous unfolding of the drama. Wagner opted instead for endless or **infinite melody.** This infinite melody was supported by an ever-active orchestral accompaniment which constantly revealed additional information about a particular character. In fact, there are times in Wagner's music dramas when the orchestra nearly overpowers the singers, making it almost impossible to hear the text. However, when this occurs the emotions and the sense of the text are unequivocally established before the orchestra assumes command. Thus, it really doesn't matter that all of the words are not discernable.

Toward the middle of his career, Wagner discarded the term opera for his stage productions and instead called them music drama. His music dramas incorporated all of the elements just described.

Leitmotifs

Wagner found that his most effective means of unifying these tremendously long music dramas was through the use of leitmotifs. A **leitmotif** is a brief musical gesture that is associated symbolically with a character, object, or idea, so that when the leitmotif is sounded it brings to mind that with which it is symbolically associated. Thus, the character, object or idea need not be present on the stage when the orchestra plays the leitmotif; the audience's attention will be focused on the appropriate character, object, or idea.

A leitmotif may be a melodic phrase, a motive, or even a mere chord. Leitmotifs occur frequently throughout a music drama, and a typical Wagnerian music drama will contain dozens of such leitmotifs. Usually the orchestra plays the leitmotifs, but occasionally they are sung. Once more this points to the very important role of the orchestra in this operatic ideal.

Figure 8.1

1. Storm
2. Storm spell (from Das Rheingold)
3. Siegmund
4. Sieglinde
5. Love

In Wagner's *The Ring of the Nibelungen,* leitmotifs appear throughout the set of four music dramas.

Der Ring des Nibelungen   Wagner's longest work is the set of four music dramas that make up *Der Ring des Nibelungen (The Ring of the Nibelungen)* (1853–74): 1) *Das Rheingold,* 2) *Die Walküre,* 3) *Siegfried,* and 4) *Götterdämmerung.* Each of these music dramas presents its own leitmotifs, and some leitmotifs from earlier sections of the *Ring* are carried over into later ones.

Figure 8.1 presents a set of leitmotifs from the opening scene of *Die Walküre.* You will find numbers at the ends of some lines; these numbers correspond to the list of leitmotifs. For example, at the end of Siegmund's first speech the numbers 3 and 1 appear. This means that during Siegmund's speech, leitmotifs 3 and 1 are heard in the orchestra. Act I begins with an orchestral depiction of a storm that is subsiding. Leitmotif 1 is the "storm" motif. Leitmotif 2 appears a little later in this orchestral introduction, and is called the "storm spell" motif. Leitmotif 2 is carried over from *Das Rheingold* into *Die Walküre.*[4]

4. © 1962 RCA Corporation. Reprinted by permission.

Act i
Scene i

The interior of Hunding's dwelling.
In the middle of the room is a
great ash tree, whose branches
grow through the roof. It is
evening; a thunderstorm is just
subsiding.

Siegmund

Siegmund
(entering hastily and sinking
wearily down beside the fire)

Wess' Herd dies auch sei,
hier muss ich rasten. *(3,1)*

Whose hearth this may be,
here I must rest. *(3,1)*

Sieglinde

Sieglinde
(in the doorway of an inner room)

Ein fremder Mann!
Ihn muss ich fragen.
Wer kam in's Haus
und liegt dort am Herd? *(3)*
Müde liegt er
von Weges Müh'n:
schwanden die Sinne ihm?
wäre er siech? *(4)*

A stranger!
I must question him.
Who is it that came in
and is lying by the hearth? *(3)*
He lies there weary
and travel-worn—
is he unconscious,
is he ill? *(4)*
(looking more closely at Siegmund)

Noch schwillt ihm der Atem;
das Auge nur schloss er;
mutig dünkt mich der Mann,
sank er müd' auch hin.

He is still breathing;
he has fallen asleep.
He looks to me a brave man,
though he is now so exhausted.

Siegmund
Ein Quell! ein Quell!

Siegmund
Drink! Drink!

Sieglinde
Erquickung schaff' ich. *(3,4)*

Sieglinde
I'll bring you refreshment. *(3,4)*
(She fetches a horn filled with
water.) (4)

Labung biet' ich
dem lechzenden Gaumen:
Wasser, wie du gewollt. *(3,5)*

Here is something
for your parched mouth—
the water you called for. *(3,5)*
(Siegmund drinks, and as he gives
her back the horn, he fixes his eyes
on Sieglinde with growing interest.)

Siegmund
Kühlende Labung
gab mir der Quell, *(4)*
des Müden Last
machte er leicht;
Erfrischt ist der Mut,
das Aug' erfreut

Siegmund
The draught has given me
cooling relief, *(4)*
the burden of my weariness
is lightened;
my courage revives,
my eyes enjoy

des Sehens selige Lust: *(4)*
wer ist's, der so mir es labt? *(4)*

Sieglinde
Dies Haus und dies Weib
sind Hundings Eigen;
gastlich gönn' er dir Rast:
harre bis heim er kehrt! *(3)*

Siegmund
Waffenlos bin ich:
dem wunden Gast
wird dein Gatte nicht wehren.

Sieglinde
Die Wunden weise mir schnell! *(3)*

Siegmund
Gering sind sie,
der Rede nicht wert;
noch fügen des Leibes
Glieder sich fest.
Hätten halb so stark wie mein Arm
Schild und Speer mir gehalten,
nimmer floh' ich dem Feind;

doch zerschellten mir Speer und
Schild. *(1)*
Der Feinde Meute
hetzte mich müd',
Gewitter-Brunst
brach meinen Leib;
doch schneller als ich der Meute,
schwand die Müdigkeit mir: *(3)*
sank auf die Lider mir Nacht,
die Sonne lacht mir nun neu. *(4)*

Sieglinde
Des seimigen Metes
süssen Trank
mög'st du mir nicht verschmäh'n.
(4)

Siegmund
Schmecktest du mir ihn zu? *(5)*

Einen Unseligen labtest du—

Unheil wende

the pleasure of sight: *(4)*
who is it that has so restored me?
(4)

Sieglinde
This house and this woman
belong to Hunding;
as a guest he will grant you rest:
wait until he comes home. *(3)*

Siegmund
I am unarmed:
your husband will not rebuff
a wounded guest.

Sieglinde
Quick, show me your wounds! *(3)*

Siegmund
They are but slight,
not worth speaking of;
my limbs are
in good trim.
Had shield and spear but held out
half as well as my arm,
I should never have fled from the
foe;
but spear and shield were shattered.
(1)
The enemy's horde
harried me to exhaustion,
the force of the storm
wore me out;
but quicker than I fled from the
foe,
my weariness has fled from me: *(3)*
night closed on my eyelids,
now the sun smiles on me anew. *(4)*

Sieglinde
Perhaps you will not refuse
a sweet draught
of honeyed mead? *(4)*

Siegmund
Will you taste it first? *(5)*
*(After Sieglinde has sipped the
drink, Siegmund takes a long
draught.) (5,3)*
You have restored an unfortunate
man—
I would avert

der Wunsch von dir! *(4)*
Gerastet hab' ich
und süss geruht:
weiter wend' ich den Schritt.

Sieglinde
Wer verfolgt dich, dass du schon
fliehst?

Siegmund
Misswende folgt mir
wohin ich fliehe;
Misswende naht mir
wo ich mich neige: *(5)*
dir Frau doch bleibe sie fern!
Fort wend' ich Fuss und Blick.

Sieglinde
So bleibe hier!
Nicht bringst du Unheil dahin,
wo Unheil im Hause wohnt! *(6,4,6)*

Siegmund
Wehwalt hiess ich mich selbst:

Hunding will ich erwarten.

misfortune from you! *(4)*
I have enjoyed
a good rest,
now I must wend my way farther.

Sieglinde
Who pursues you, that you must
flee?

Siegmund
Ill-luck follows me
wherever I fly;
ill-luck draws near
wherever I stop: *(5)*
may it stay far from you!
I will turn aside both step and
glance.

Sieglinde
No, stay here!
You cannot bring misfortune
where misfortune dwells already!
(6,4,6)

Siegmund
Wehwalt [Woeful] was what I
named myself:
I will await Hunding.

Summary

Romanticism is the name given to the movement that dominated philosophy and the arts in the nineteenth century. At the core of romanticism was the desire to create a strong, personal bond with nature, and to express the self-discovery and inner peace resulting from that bond. In many cases, this expression demanded a synthesis of several art forms. This synthesis was duly expressed by the gifted romantic composers who were often masters of poetry and literature as well.

The romantic composers adapted classical music genres to the nineteenth-century ideal while also developing genres unique to the times. The symphonies of Mendelssohn and Brahms reveal a classical orientation while the symphonies of Tchaikovsky and Berlioz go beyond the classical form to the program approach. The choral symphony and the tone poem were products of the nineteenth century. Both genres dramatically illustrate the romantic fascination with a synthesis of the arts. Liszt, Borodin, and Strauss were masters of the tone poem.

The piano was very important to the romantic age. Piano music was in great demand and Chopin, Liszt, Robert Schumann, and others filled that need with piano sonatas and character pieces written for piano.

The polonaise and the étude were types of character pieces born in the romantic era. Concertos, too, were composed for piano as well as for violin, viola, and other solo instruments.

The art song resulted when romantic composers set German poetry to music. The German art song is termed "Lied." We considered Lieder composed by Schubert and Clara Schumann.

The opera existed in many forms in the nineteenth century. Italian opera, as characterized by Verdi, focused on the singer, while the German opera, as transformed by Wagner into the music drama, put special emphasis on mythic drama and the role of the orchestra.

Key Terms

choral (dramatic) symphony
tone (symphonic) poem
sonata
character piece

prelude
polonaise
étude
legato
staccato
Lied

song cycle
music drama
set number
Gesamtkunstwerk
infinite melody
leitmotifs

Thinking About It

In the classical era there was a symphonic ideal in which the character, number, and order of movements within the symphony were relatively standardized. Compare the classical symphony to the nineteenth-century symphonies discussed in this chapter. Was there a singular symphonic ideal in the romantic era? Thinking back (or perhaps relistening) to certain examples in this chapter, how would you characterize a tone poem? What could have led the romantics to invent such a thing as the tone poem?

What are some of the differences in the operatic ideal of Wagner and the Italian operatic ideal exemplified by Verdi and Rossini?

Music
in
the
Twentieth
Century

Three Musicians, Pablo Picasso, 1921; Oil on canvas; 80″ × 74″.

Philadelphia Museum of Art: The A. E. Gallatin Collection, Acc. No. 52-61-96

Sounds of the Chapter

Barber
Adagio for Strings ♪

Bartók
Music for strings, percussion and
    celesta
Fourth String Quartet
Out of Doors

Berg
Wozzeck ♪

Berio
Circles

Britten
Serenade for Horn, Tenor, and Strings
A Ceremony of Carols

Cage
*Concerto for Prepared Piano and
    Orchestra*
4' 33''
HPSCHD
Imaginary Landscape no. 4

Carter
Cello Sonata
Piano Concerto
Sonata for Flute, Oboe, Cello, and
    Harpsichord
Three String Quartets

Copland
Appalachian Spring
Music for the Theatre

Crumb
Ancient Voices of Children

Debussy
"Brouillards," *Preludes*, Book II ♪
Danse bohémienne ♪
Images
"La Flute de Pan" ♪
La Mer
"Nuages," *Nocturnes*
Pelléas et Mélisande
Prélude à l' Après-midi d' un faune

George Gershwin
Piano Concerto in F
Porgy and Bess
Rhapsody in Blue

Philip Glass
Einstein on the Beach ♪

Honegger
Jeanne d' Arc au bûcher
Le Roi David
Pacific 231

Ives
"At the River"
Concord Sonata
Fourth Symphony
"General William Booth Enters
    Heaven"
"The Fourth of July," *Holidays*
The Unanswered Question ♪
Universe Symphony
Variations on "America"

Messiaen
Couleurs de la cité céleste

Menotti
Amahl and the Night Visitors

Milhaud
La Création du Monde
Le Boeuf sur le toit ♪

Prokofiev
Third Piano Concerto in C Major,
    op. 26 ♪

Reich
Come Out

Riley
In C

Satie
Desiccated Embryos
Flabby Preludes
Gymnopédie no. 1
Parade
Second to Last Thoughts
Three Pieces in the Form of a Pear

Schönberg
Pierrot Lunaire ♪
Suite for piano, op. 25

Still
Afro-American Symphony

Stockhausen
Gesang der Jünglinge

Stravinsky
Le Sacre du Printemps
Octet
Petrushka
Symphony in C
The Firebird

Varèse
Ionisation ♪

Webern
Five Movements for string quartet

"Columbia the Gem of the Ocean"
"Nearer My God to Thee"
"Shall We Gather at the River?"
"Turkey in the Straw"
"The Volga Boatmen"

Historically, people heard only the music of their own era, but we are exposed to music written in previous eras.

Historically, the listening repertoire of a given audience was limited by time, place, and economics. People listened mainly to the new music of the day: baroque audiences listened to music composed in that era, audiences in the classical era listened to classical music, and so on. Even in the nineteenth century, when there were revivals of earlier kinds of music, the listening public focused on the works of the romantic composers.

However, twentieth-century art music is unique in this respect. We listen to proportionately less art music written in our own century than we do to music written in previous eras. Why is this true? In order to answer this question, we need to focus on technological advancements that have resulted in our diverse musical environment.

The Evolution of Twentieth-Century Art Music

The availability of various types of music is due mainly to technological advancement.

Presently, we have available to us more music, and more kinds of music, than ever has been the case before. We can, if we wish, listen to music of the Renaissance, of the Pygmies of the Ituri Forest, or of J. S. Bach, Vivaldi, Mozart, Beethoven, Mahler; our choices are nearly limitless. We enjoy this diversity of music largely due to the development and refinement of the phonograph, magnetic tape, and other mass communication devices, but there are other reasons.

Tonality was a constant in Western art music until the twentieth century.

From the middle of the seventeenth century to the beginning of this century, functional harmony (tonality) was an identifiable and unchallenged musical reality. Music—virtually *all* music—was written in a key. Thus, despite the idiosyncrasies of individual composers throughout the baroque, classical, and romantic periods, tonality remained a constant in Western art music. It was so deeply ingrained and so much a part of our musical conditioning and expectations that when, in the early twentieth century, some composers began to abandon tonality, the audience was either unable or unwilling to comprehend this new music.

The twentieth century has been a period of musical experimentation.

Although some composers adhered to the structure established in earlier eras, some twentieth-century composers experimented heavily. Composers either remained within the boundaries of tonality (though generally their music became more dissonant), abandoned it temporarily, or discarded it permanently. Some composers continued to write symphonies, string quartets, and piano sonatas, while others created new forms and experimented with previously unexplored instruments and instrumental ensembles. Toward the middle of the twentieth century, some composers began to tap the reservoir of electronically generated sound. Still others explored the visual and spatial parameters of music, suggesting at least a partial redefinition of music. And still other composers explored the outer limits of improvisation and entered the realm of "chance" operation.

Twentieth-century musical activity is analogous to a volcanic eruption where streams of lava shower in all directions. Our century, at least from a contemporary viewpoint, has produced not one broad musical style, but many different styles having few or no apparent interconnections. This situation has made it difficult for audiences to grasp and embrace much of contemporary music. Audiences and serious students of art music sense a fundamental stylistic unity in the music of other eras, but a basic and perplexing disunity exists in twentieth-century music.

> Twentieth-century art music has moved in many directions, producing various styles and disunity.

Despite the fact that, overall, twentieth-century music differs from earlier music in terms of harmony, themes, form, and instrumentation, its diversity is far-reaching. Some works *are* tonal and *do* employ themes and forms that are similar to those of previous eras. Others, as stated earlier, are at the opposite end of the spectrum and are unlike any predecessor. Between these two poles lies a body of music that is less conservative than the former and less radical than the latter.

Musical Trends at the Turn of the Century

Several dominant musical trends and movements are presented in this chapter. These are representative of one of the three "familiarity" categories mentioned in the preceding paragraph. The trend or movement will either correspond directly to one of another era, will be reminiscent of one, or will be totally unique from any musical counterpart.

> Three degrees of familiarity are apparent in twentieth-century art music: direct correspondence with an earlier era; reminiscence of another era; uniqueness.

Impressionism

The early twentieth century was an age of "isms" in the arts. The earliest of these was **impressionism,** a movement that began in painting in the 1870s. Later the term was carried over into the field of music.

The central painters in the impressionist movement were Claude Monet, Pierre Auguste Renoir, and Edgar Degas. Although each had a unique artistic style, they are associated because of their similar treatment of color and light, and also because of their purposeful disregard of photographic reality. Notice in Monet's painting (see fig. 9.1 and colorplate 20) an object that resembles a woman in a pastoral setting. The faithful photographic representation of the scene was not a concern of Monet's; the mix and flow of colors, the play of light upon them, and the urgency to capture the magic and the atmosphere of the moment were his concerns. The reality of the scene is not obliterated, but it is somewhat distorted. This is a purposeful distortion, however, for the painting is not really "about" the woman or the setting; it is more "about" the mood and the atmosphere of the scene.

> Impressionism began in painting with Monet, Renoir, and Degas.

> Impressionist painters recreated the mood and atmosphere of a scene, not the image itself.

Figure 9.1
Impressionist painting: *Woman Seated Under the Willows* by Claude Monet, 1880; canvas; 0.811 cm × 0.600 cm (see colorplate 20).

National Gallery of Art, Washington; Chester Dale Collection.

Impressionist Music—Debussy   It is always risky and not always fruitful to try to draw direct parallels between two different art forms. Nevertheless, some musicians and scholars have found analogies between impressionist painting and certain works by Claude Debussy (1862–1918), and these analogies have some validity. To understand Debussy's music, let's listen to two of his many works for piano. The first, *Danse bohémienne* (1880), is an early work composed several years before Debussy formulated his impressionistic style.

Debussy captured impressionism in music.

Danse bohémienne is a piano piece like countless others written in the late nineteenth century. Despite its charm, the piece alone would not ensure Debussy's position as a master. Notice that *Danse bohémienne* has a very clear-cut *ABA*-coda design, is solidly in a key, and is in 2/4 meter. There is also a clear division of labor between the two hands: the right hand plays the melody (which, you will notice, is singable and memorable) while the left hand plays an accompaniment.

Debussy's Danse bohémienne is characteristic of piano music of the late nineteenth century.

In contrast, listen to Debussy's "Brouillards" from *Preludes,* second book (1910–13). What is the form of this piece? Does it sound as if it is definitely in a key? What meter is it in, and can you sing a melody? In terms of texture, is there an unmistakable division of labor between the right and the left hand?

"Brouillards" is impressionistic—its key, the meter, and texture are not readily apparent.

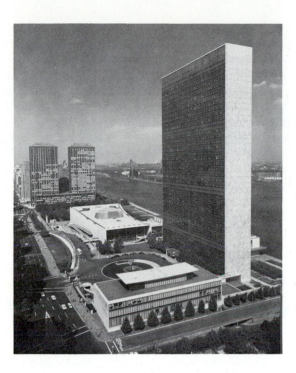

A twentieth-century image.
Courtesy, The United Nations

The formal structure of *Danse bohémienne* is predictable and conventional. For example, the return of the *A* section is not surprising. But practically nothing about the structure of "Brouillards" is predictable: the events in the piece do not seem to connect with one another, but merely succeed one another. It is evident only after repeated listenings that this order of events is purposeful, not accidental. A clear sense of tonic and dominant does not emerge from the harmony. The chords are not extremely dissonant, yet the key is not well defined. The key is not obliterated, but it is veiled.

The piece is in 4/8 meter, but this is not immediately apparent when listening to the work. In the place of melody, fragments of thematic material are presented, yet these don't constitute a theme in the conventional sense. The fragments materialize and then disappear in the texture. The texture is not divided into melody and accompaniment; rather, the right hand and the left are interwoven in such a way that each plays an equal role. Thus, in form, rhythm, harmony, melody, and texture, Debussy departed from the norms of his immediate background. Debussy's music reflects the dawning of a new era—the era of twentieth-century music.

Every so often a composer comes along who has a special touch with orchestration. Debussy was such a composer. His major orchestral works—*La Mer, Prélude a l'Après-midi d' un faune, (Prelude to the Afternoon of a Faun), Images,* and the three *Nocturnes*—all possess a touch of magic.

Claude Debussy
(1862–1918)
The New York Public Library

Debussy's impressionist music reflects the experimentation of the twentieth century.

Debussy's wonderfully atmospheric piece, "Nuages," was introduced in chapter 4. Listen to the piece again, this time concentrating on a different perspective and taking into consideration the context of twentieth-century musical practice. "Brouillards" suggests the possibility of an unconventional formal structure in Debussy's works. For instance, Debussy's works can be analyzed in terms of sections, but a major difference exists between his sectional forms and the sectional forms of earlier composers. Some of Debussy's content, for example from section *A,* is likely to appear in some guise in section *B*. This shared content creates a situation where there are no sharply defined differences between the various sections of the same piece; the lines between the sections are blurred. Debussy was also fond of repeating sections, but at the same time introducing new material in the repetitions. This practice creates both old and new sections simultaneously.

In diagraming forms in baroque, classical, and romantic works, the symbol *A'* has been used to indicate a nonliteral repetition of *A*. In Debussy's music, the *A'* is either inaccurate, or at best, incomplete. In his music those repeated sections having new and significant material are better designated *A+*.

Listen to the piece just to take in its sound and mood before proceeding to the Sound and Sense. Once you have heard the piece, study the formal diagram, and with it in hand, listen to "Nuages" once again.

> Debussy's atmosphere pieces are unconventional; he combined standard musical practices with twentieth-century innovations.

> The symbol *A+* designates a nonliteral repetition of a section plus the introduction of new material.

Sound and Sense
Twentieth-Century Sectional Form

Title: "Nuages" from Three Nocturnes (1893–99)
Composer: Debussy
Recording: Andre Previn, London Symphony
Meter: 6/4
Tempo: Moderato
Key: Modal on B

A Closer Look

A—Introduces a gently floating figure played on   (2:23)
    clarinets and bassoons, followed by a mysterious figure
    played on the English horn (this is a terse,
    fragmentary figure so typical of Debussy). The
    floating figure is repeated, this time by the string
    section, and the English horn fragment is stated twice
    more

Floating figure

Mysterious figure

> B—Begins with a dark, slow, ascending figure stated by   (:43)
> the lower woodwinds. Behind this figure, the strings
> restate the floating figure from A—this is an instance
> of shared content mentioned earlier
>
> A+—Repeats the English horn fragment two more   (1:32)
> times. The floating figure is stated by the strings; this
> time, however, the violas and cellos add a soft plucking
> backdrop. Toward the close of this section, a solo viola
> introduces a new theme-fragment, thus creating the
> need for an A+ rather than a simple A'
>
> C—A new theme is introduced by flute and harp.   (1:11)
> Although this theme seems to have no conventional
> sense of direction, it is long and shapely enough to be
> a genuine melody
>
> Coda—Is introduced by the English horn figure. The   (2:00)
> piece ends slowly and very quietly

The success of this piece owes a great deal to Debussy's masterful orchestration. It would be a very different piece, and far less successful, if it were to be played on a piano instead of by an orchestra. Debussy employed a large orchestra that never rises to full voice; in fact, there is only one measure marked *f* (the last measure of the *B* section). The remainder of the piece is marked *mp* or softer. The size and potential power of the orchestra is not disguised, but Debussy subtly restrains this coiled power.

Through orchestration, Debussy created the illusion of space and distance. Just at the close of the first English horn statement in the *A* section, listen carefully for the low, rumbling tympani (marked *ppp*) and the simultaneously sounding violins far, far above. The same illusion of space is evident later in the *A* section as the English horn figure is restated under the floating figure in the violins. The French horns add another spatial dimension, for they seem to be sounding from a distance. With this illusion of space, listen again to the entire *C* section.

Symbolism

A literary movement called **symbolism** (another early twentieth-century "ism") developed in Paris shortly after impressionism. The symbolist poets and playwrights were fascinated by the raw materials of language—words—and the sonorous qualities of them. Their poetry often consisted of words that were carefully selected and strung together because of the way they sounded, rather than because they made syntactical sense. The symbolist poets were willing to distort syntax in order to expose the sheer beauty of words and the symbolic references evoked by them.

Symbolist poets and playwrights focused on words rather than meaning.

Art Nouveau: Tiffany lamp
(see colorplate 21).
© Ron Cooper/EKM-Nepenthe

Debussy's music shows the influence of symbolism.

Symbolist poetry is subtle, mysterious, erotic, and carries an unspoken element of danger and fear.

Debussy set symbolist poetry to music.

Debussy was attracted to the ideas and aesthetics of the symbolists, several of whom were his close friends. His only opera, *Pelléas et Mélisande,* is based on a text by symbolist Maurice Maeterlinck, and *Prélude a l' Après-midi d' un faune (Prelude to the Afternoon of a Faun)* was inspired by a text by another symbolist, Stéphane Mallarmé.

Symbolist poetry was especially attractive to Debussy. This is a suggestive art, one that hints and suggests rather than one dealing with concrete descriptions of things and ideas. Typical ingredients of symbolist poetry include a sense of mystery, veiled eroticism, potential danger, and fear. There are also frequent evocations of an ancient decaying world—often the world of classical antiquity. The poetry is subtle and refined, but rarely is it dramatic or heroic.

Some of these qualities of symbolist poetry are evident in the poem "La Flute de Pan" by Pierre Louÿs, another friend of Debussy's. Debussy set this strange, enigmatic poem to music. When listening to the song, notice how perfectly Debussy's vocal line and piano part fit the mysterious mood of the text, shown here.

"La Flute de Pan"

Pour le jour des Hyacinthies,
I m'a donné une syrinx faite
De roseaux bien taillés,
Unis avec la blanche cire
Qui est douce à mes lèvres comme
    le miel.

"The Flute of Pan"

On this day of Hyacynthus,
He has given me a pipe made
Of well-cut reeds,
Joined together with white wax
That is as sweet as honey on my
    lips.

Il m'apprend à jouer, assise sur ses genoux;	He teaches me to play while I sit on his knees;
Mais je suis un peu tremblante.	But I tremble just a little.
Il en joue après moi, si doucement	He plays it after me so softly
Que je l'entends à peine.	That I can hardly hear him.
Nous n'avons rien à nous dire,	We have nothing to say,
Tant nous sommes près l'un de l'autre;	So close are we to one another;
Mais nos chansons veulent se répondre,	But our songs want to harmonize,
Et tour à tour nos bouches	And gradually our lips
S'unissent sur la flûte.	Are united on the flute.
Il est tard;	It is late;
Voici le chant des grenouilles vertes	Here is the chant of the green frogs
Qui commence avec la nuit.	That begins with the night.
Ma mère ne croira jamais	My mother will never believe
Que je suis restée si longtemps	That I stayed out so long
A chercher ma ceinture perdue.	In search of my lost belt.

A great deal is suggested in this poem, but little that is concrete is divulged; the whole episode is bathed in mystery. The poem is also vaguely erotic, and the words "I tremble just a little," hint at some undefined fear. Pan, the half-man, half-beast creature from classical antiquity, is in modern times associated with music (his flute), but in mythology he is also supposed to have had the power to incite irrational fear in others (our word *pan*ic is derived from this side of Pan's personality). Thus, Louÿs aptly introduced this element of fear in his poem.

As mentioned earlier, there was a school of impressionist painters united by similar ideas about painting. At the same time, a circle of symbolist authors evolved because they, too, felt a kinship in literary convictions. These two groups of artists found a common aesthetic ground. The impressionist artists distorted photographic reality; the symbolist authors distorted syntactical reality. The impressionist painters were fascinated by the raw materials of painting—color and light; the symbolists were enthralled by the raw material of literature—words.

Unlike these artistic areas, no similar circle or school of music was established in Paris. Debussy was the sole musical representative of the impressionist/symbolist faction, and most of his closest friends were painters or poets, not composers. But Debussy's musical style had a profound influence on younger, contemporary composers and on composers of succeeding generations. Principal among these were the Frenchman Maurice Ravel (1875–1937), the American composer Charles Griffes (1884–1920), and the Englishman Frederick Delius (1862–1934). Some aspects of Debussy's harmonic practices and his orchestration impressed many other composers and even affected American popular music, especially movie music beginning in the 1940s.

"La Flute de Pan" exhibits the characteristics of symbolist poetry.

Impressionist painters and symbolist poets came together on common aesthetic ground.

Though no school of impressionist/symbolist musicians evolved, Debussy had a profound influence on many twentieth-century composers.

Expressionism

The chaotic, mean, and ugly state of the world during the opening years of the twentieth century was partly responsible for the emergence of an artistic movement called **expressionism.** Expressionist writers such as Franz Kafka (1883–1924) described the horrifying destruction of European civilization in their publications. These works were capable of exposing raw nerves, and expressing the horror, emotionalism, terror, pain, and agony felt by humanity. Expressionism survived into the mid-twenties, reacting against the horror and inhumanity of World War I.

Expressionism revealed the unpleasant truth of human existence—a reflection of the horror of World War I and its aftermath.

Expressionism, whether in literature, painting, or music, did not attempt to create beauty. It strove rather to express the unvarnished and terrible truth of human existence. Where impressionism viewed the world objectively and covered it with a beautiful, sensuous surface, expressionism looked at the world subjectively from the inside out.

The three principal exponents of musical expressionism were Austrians.

Schönberg   The principal exponents of musical expressionism were Arnold Schönberg (1874–1951) and two other Austrian composers who were once his students: Alban Berg (1885–1935) and Anton Webern (1883–1945).

Schönberg's expressionist music evolved over time.

The fertile, innovative mind of Arnold Schönberg led his style through several evolutionary stages. As a young man his style showed the influence of Brahms and Wagner. But in the first and second decades of the twentieth century, he produced a number of atonal expressionistic works. And in the 1920s Schönberg developed—literally invented—a new method of organizing pitches: the twelve-tone system. This system, and expansions of it, have had far-reaching implications on twentieth-century music. Its principles and methodology have been adopted, in varying degrees, by hundreds of European and American composers since World War II.

In the early twenties Schönberg invented the twelve-tone system.

Schönberg's *Pierrot Lunaire* (1912) is a quintessential expressionist work. Based on twenty-one poems by Albert Giraud, the work is scored for a small instrumental ensemble and voice. The activity of the voice in this work has become a trademark of musical expressionism. Schönberg wrote this part not to be sung in the conventional manner of singing, nor to be spoken as in dramatic recitation, but to partake of both singing and speaking. This type of vocal utterance is called ***Sprechtstimme.*** *Sprechtstimme* is not as lovely as singing nor as dramatic as speech can be, but its position between the two endows it with a peculiarly evocative and highly charged emotionalism. The text to the first poem of *Pierrot Lunaire* appears here.

Arnold Schönberg
(1874–1951).
The New York Public Library

Mondestrunken	Moondrunk
Den Wein, den man mit Augen trinkt,	The wine that only eyes may drink
Giesst Nachts der Mond in Wogen nieder,	Pours from the moon in waves at nightfall,
Und eine Springflut überschwemmt Den stillen Horizont.	And like a springflood overwhelms The still horizon rim.
Gelüste, schauerlich und süss,	Desires, shivering and sweet,
Durchschwimmen ohne Zahl die Fluten!	Are swimming without number through the flood waters!
Den Wein, den man mit Augen trinkt,	The wine that only eyes may drink
Giesst Nachts der Mond in Wogen nieder.	Pours from the moon in waves at nightfall.
Der Dichter, den die Andacht treibt,	The poet, by his ardor driven,
Berauscht sich an dem heiligen Tranke,	Grown drunken with the holy drink—
Den Himmel wendet er verzückt	To heaven he rapturously lifts
Das Haupt und taumelnd saugt und schlürft es	His head and reeling slips and swallows
Den Wein, den man mit Augen trinkt.	The wine that only eyes may drink.

Much of the music composed by Schönberg and his two students during the early decades of the century is marked by extreme dissonance and by feverish emotionalism. Tonality (functional harmony) was abandoned in this music, so it is often referred to as **atonal**.

Expressionist music exhibits extreme dissonance, emotionalism, and atonality.

Webern   Webern's *Five Movements* for string quartet (1909) is an excellent introduction to his stylistic traits as well as to the realm of musical expressionism. The five movements are extremely brief: movements two and four are each only thirteen measures long, but each presents an extraordinary amount of emotional intensity and range of emotions. Every phrase, every motive, almost every note creates an emotional impact, so condensed are these emotions. When listening to movement one, notice how quickly and drastically the moods change. On a higher structural level, notice the radical difference in mood and atmosphere as movement one progresses into movement two.

Webern's music is charged with emotional intensity and mood change.

Berg's *Wozzeck*   Alban Berg's *Wozzeck* (1921) is a monumental work of the later stages of musical expressionism and ranks among the greatest and most powerful operas of the twentieth century. It consists of three acts, each having five scenes, in which the grisly story of Wozzeck unfolds, a man in the process of a complete mental, moral, and spiritual disintegration. Wozzeck, an underling in the army, is hounded and abused

*Berg composed an expressionist opera—*Wozzeck,* the story of one man's tragic existence.*

The Holy Face, Rouault (see colorplate 23).

Musee National D'Art Moderne, Centre Georges Pompidou, Paris

by his superiors. He is humiliated by his common-law wife, Marie, whom he murders at the peak of his insanity. In his madness Wozzeck returns to the rural lake that is the scene of his crime. He wanders out into the lake, which he believes has turned to blood, and drowns.

The small child of Wozzeck and Marie is left behind to find his own tragic way in the world. In the final scene of the opera, Wozzeck's orphan is playing on a homemade stick horse. His playmates rush to him and say: "Hey, you . . . your mother is dead." In one of the classic understatements in the history of opera, the scene ends—or perhaps we should say it disappears quietly, almost sweetly.

The complete text to act III, scenes ii and v, is shown here. Ideally you should listen to the entire opera with text in hand. If, however, time is limited, these two scenes at least introduce you to the work and to the vocal, harmonic, and orchestral practices of Berg at this stage in his career.

Act III
Scene ii

(Waldweg am Teich. Es dunkelt. Marie kommt mit Wozzeck von rechts.)

Marie
Dort links geht's in die Stadt. 's ist noch weit. Komm schneller!

Wozzeck
Du sollst dableiben, Marie. Komm, setz' Dich.

Marie
Aber ich muss fort.

Wozzeck
Komm. *(sie setzen sich)* Bist weit gegangen, Marie. Sollst Dir die Füsse nicht mehr wund laufen. 's ist still hier! Und so dunkel.—Weisst noch, Marie, wie lang' es jetzt ist, dass wir uns kennen?

Marie
Zu Pfingsten drei Jahre.

Wozzeck
Und was meinst, wie lang' es noch dauern wird?

Marie
(springt auf)
Ich muss fort.

(Forest path by a pool. Dusk is falling. Marie enters with Wozzeck, from the right.)

Marie
The town lies over there. It's still far. Let's hurry!

Wozzeck
You must stay awhile, Marie. Come, sit here.

Marie
But it's getting late.

Wozzeck
Come! *(They sit down)* So far you've wandered, Marie. You must not make your feet so sore, walking. It's still, here in the darkness.—Tell me, Marie, how long has it been since our first meeting?

Marie
At Whitsun, three years.

Wozzeck
And how long, how long will it still go on?

Marie
(jumping up)
I must go!

Wozzeck

Fürchst Dich, Marie? Und bist doch fromm? *(lacht)* Und gut! Und treu! *(zieht sich wieder auf den Sitz; neigt sich, wieder ernst, zu Marie)* Was Du für süsse Lippen hast, Marie! *(küsst sie)* Den Himmel gäb' ich drum und die Seligkeit, wenn ich Dich noch oft so küssen dürft! Aber ich darf nicht! Was zitterst?

Marie

Der Nachttau fällt.

Wozzeck

(flustert vor sich hin)

Wer kalt ist, den friert nicht mehr! Dich wird beim Morgentau nicht frieren.

Marie

Was sagst Du da?

Wozzeck

Nix.

(Langes Schweigen. Der Mond geht auf.)

Marie

Wie der Mond rot aufgeht!

Wozzeck

(zieht ein Messer)

Wie ein blutig Eisen!

Marie

Was zitterst? *(springt auf)* Was willst?

Wozzeck

Ich nicht, Marie! Und kein Andrer auch nicht!

(packt sie an und stösst ihr das Messer in den Hals)

Marie

Hilfe!

(sinkt nieder. Wozzeck beugt sich über sie. Marie stirbt.)

Wozzeck

Tot!

(richtet sich scheu auf und stürzt geräuschlos davon)

Wozzeck

Trembling, Marie? But you are good? *(laughing)* and kind! and true! *(He pulls her down again on the seat; he bends over her, in deadly earnest)* Ah! How your lips are sweet to touch, Marie! *(kisses her)* All Heaven I would give, and eternal bliss, if I still could somtimes kiss you so! But yet I dare not! You shiver?

Marie

The night dew falls.

Wozzeck

(whispering to himself)

Who cold is, you who shiver, will freeze no more in cold morning dew.

Marie

What are you saying?

Wozzeck

Nought!

(A long silence. The moon rises.)

Marie

How the moon rises red!

Wozzeck

(He draws a knife)

Like a blood-red iron!

Marie

You shiver? *(She jumps up)* What now?

Wozzeck

No-one, Marie! If not me, then no-one!

(He seizes her and plunges the knife into her throat)

Marie

Help!

(She sinks down. Wozzeck bends over her. She dies.)

Wozzeck

Dead!

(He rises to his feet anxiously, and then rushes silently away)

Funfte Szene
Scene Five

♪ *(Strasse vor Mariens Tür. Heller Morgen. Sonnenschein. Kinder spielen und lärmen. Mariens Knabe auf einem Steckenpferd reitend.)*

(In front of Marie's door. Bright morning. Sunshine. Children are playing and shouting. Marie's child is riding a hobbyhorse.)

Die Spielenden Kinder
Ringel, Ringel, Rosenkranz, Ringelreih'n!
Ringel, Ringel, Rosenkranz Rin . . .
(unterbrechen Gesang und Spiel, andere Kinder sturmen herein)

Children
Ring-a-ring-a-roses, all fall down!

Ring-a-ring-a-roses, all . . .

(They stop, and other children come rushing on)

Eins Von Ihnen
Du Käthe! . . . Die Marie . . .

One of These
Katie! . . . Marie . . .

Zweites Kind
Was is?

Second Child
What is it?

Erstes Kind
Weisst' es nit? Sie sind schon Alle 'naus.

First Child
Don't you know? They've all gone out there.

Drittes Kind
(zu Mariens Knaben)
Du! Dein Mutter ist tot!

Third Child
(to Marie's child)
Hey! Your mother is dead.

Mariens Knabe
(immer reitend)
Hopp, hopp! Hopp, hopp! Hopp, hopp!

Marie's Child
(still riding his horse)
Hop, hop! Hop, hop! Hop, hop!

Zweites Kind
Wo is sie denn?

Second Child
Where is she now?

Erstes Kind
Draus' leigt sie, am Weg, neben dem Teich.

First Child
Out there, on the path by the pool.

Drittes Kind
Kommt, anschaun!
(Alle Kinder laufen davon.)

Third Child
Let's go and look!
(All the children run off.)

Mariens Knabe
(reitet)
Hopp, hopp! Hopp, hopp! Hopp, hopp!
(zögert einen Augenblick und reitet dann den anderen Kindern nach.)

Marie's Child
(continues to ride)
Hop, hop! Hop, hop! Hop, hop!

(hesitates a moment, and rides off after the other children.)

Stravinsky's Early Works

Igor Stravinsky (1882–1971) is among the most honored and celebrated composers of the twentieth century. His works have all been recorded and have been performed all over the world. Countless articles, books, and special studies have been written about him, his life, and his music. He is unquestionably one of the giant figures in twentieth-century art music, and his influence on other composers is incalculable.

In the course of his long, productive career, Stravinsky's personal style continuously evolved and changed. This evolution can be categorized into three distinct style periods: the early works, up to about 1917; the middle, or "neoclassic" period, up to about 1951; and the late works, created during the last twenty years of his life. On the surface, each of the three styles sounds unique. However, one aspect of Stravinsky's creativity is obvious in all three. Each has the same uniquely powerful rhythm. This rhythm is especially effective in dance pieces, as evidenced by the popularity of Stravinsky's work in this musical genre.

Petrushka   Stravinsky burst upon the Parisian musical scene with the production of three ballets that established him as a luminary in the musical world: *The Firebird* (1910), *Petrushka* (1911), and *Le Sacre du Printemps (The Rite of Spring)* (1913). All three are scored for a very large orchestra, all have story lines based on Russian folklore, and all employ Russian folk melody.

Igor Stravinsky (1882–1971).
The New York Public Library

Stravinsky is a major twentieth-century composer.

Stravinsky's art music shows three distinct styles, all of which have powerful rhythm.

Stravinsky's early ballets are based upon Russian folklore and feature Russian folk melodies.

Sound and Sense
Ballet

Title: Petrushka *(1911)*
Composer: Stravinsky
Recording: Steinberg, Pittsburgh Symphony

A Closer Look

The setting of *Petrushka* is a fair, and the time framework is a single day. The ballet is divided into four scenes. In the first scene, a showman appears with his three puppets—Petrushka (a clown), a beautiful ballerina, and the evil but fascinating Moor. The showman charms his puppets to life with his flute. To the astonishment of a gathering crowd, the puppets jump down from the stage and begin to dance.

In the second scene, Petrushka, who has become the most human of the puppets, is in his cell. Here, the audience is made aware of Petrushka's humanlike emotions: he bitterly resents the showman, but falls in love with the ballerina. The scene ends as Petrushka, in frustration, hurls himself at a portrait of the showman.

Scene three takes place in the Moor's cell. A love scene between the ballerina and the Moor is interrupted by Petrushka's arrival. Petrushka is beaten and thrown out.

The final scene occurs in the evening at the end of the day's festivities. Petrushka is killed by the Moor, and his corpse lies in the street as it begins to snow. But Petrushka's ghost appears above the stage, threatening and thumbing his nose at the showman.

The following is a listening guide for the first scene:

A—The atmosphere of the fair is conveyed—sparkling,   (:49)
shimmering orchestration. A leaping motive in the flute
enters periodically and sails over the rest of the texture

B—The full orchestra plays (homophonically) a bright,   (:26)
energetic Russian tune that has the rhythm

This accompanies the performance of a group of slightly drunk, prancing merrymakers.

C—A stroke on the timpani announces the arrival of the   (:18)
showman. A few bars later, the leaping motive from *A*
reappears

D—A few bars after the *A* repetition, the tempo slows and   (:39)
two twittering flutes call attention to an organ grinder
and a street dancer. The organ grinder plays on

E—The street dancer plays a triangle and dances to a   (2:53)
   popular tune played by flutes and clarinets. The tune
   disappears briefly and then returns. Intermittently, the
   leaping motive from *A* returns. Then there are varied
   repetitions of *CABAA,* culminating in a big climax that is
   followed immediately by a long roll on the drums. This
   completes the first large section of this scene. It runs
   directly into the concluding portion
F—After a brief introduction, a playful flute solo is   (1:50)
   heard—this is the showman playing his flute. After a
   short but brilliantly orchestrated episode, the flute, with
   three little strokes, brings the puppets to life
G—A fast Russian dance is played by the full orchestra.   (2:36)
   The tune has the rhythm

Notice that the piano is an active member of the orchestra, and although it
plays a solo later in this section, it is not treated as a soloist with orchestra,
but rather as a legitimate member of the orchestra. This was a new role for
the piano, one that held great attraction for later composers.

At the beginning of the second scene, after an introduction of a
few measures, two clarinets play a theme-fragment. Notice that something sounds peculiar. This peculiarity stems from the fact that the clarinets are playing in two different keys at the same time. The first clarinet
plays the theme-fragment (which has come to be known as Petrushka's
theme) in the key of C, while the second clarinet plays it in the key of
F♯. This type of music, performed simultaneously in two different keys,
is called **bitonality.** (Music written in three or more simultaneously
sounding keys is called **polytonality.**) In the history of music there are
isolated examples of bitonality and polytonality, but these practices were
not widely used until the early twentieth century. Thus, they are considered harmonic innovations of our century.

*Bitonality is music performed
simultaneously in two different
keys; polytonality is music
played in more than two keys
at the same time.*

Bartók

Béla Bartók (1881–1945) had several musical careers: he was a pianist,
a teacher, and an important folk music collector of his native Hungary
as well as elsewhere. He was also active in music education and was one
of the giant composers of the twentieth century.

Collecting and studying folk music was not a hobby for Bartók; it
was a scholarly and musical passion. Many of his compositions reflect
this passion, for they abound with Hungarian folk melodies and rhythms.

*Bartók's diverse types of
compositions reflect his
scholarly interest in Hungarian
folk music.*

Bartók's string quartets are considered among the greatest of the twentieth century.

Bartók's music did not enjoy widespread popularity during his lifetime, but since the end of World War II, his popularity has grown dramatically. His six string quartets, composed from 1909–39, are now regarded as among the greatest written during the twentieth century. They are popular the world over and are frequently recorded by various string quartet groups.

The Fourth String Quartet (1928) is in some respects not a typical string quartet, for it has five movements rather than the customary four. The work does, however, present some features that are typical of Bartók's style. The harmonic language is at times extremely dissonant, but it generates excitement and interest rather than repulsion. The thematic materials are either drawn directly from folk sources or are newly composed by Bartók and resemble folk song. Many of his themes are compact and limited to a narrow range; they revolve around relatively few pitches and intervals. The sense of color is very pronounced in his work. Color refers to the harmony and special effects Bartók draws from the instruments. Notice that in the fourth movement of this quartet, there are several types of pizzicatos, including one in which the fingernail causes the string to snap against the wooden neck of the instrument, producing a percussive sound. Bartók also requires the players to strum their instruments like guitars.

Bartók's style includes: dissonance, folk themes, colorful harmony, pizzicatos, and unique rhythms.

Bartók's Rhythm   Bartók's rhythms are as individual and unique as Stravinsky's. The peculiar yet fresh flow of many of Bartók's rhythms are also derived from Hungarian folk music. The meters in this type of music are different from the regular meters of Western European music. For example, the 9/8 meter is normally beat and felt in three beats of three eighth notes each:

But in Bartók's music, the accents are likely to produce different groupings of eighth notes, and hence an entirely different feel for the 9/8 meter:

Bartók's Structure   Bartók is one of the most ingenious and innovative twentieth-century composers in terms of musical structure. The large-scale structure of the Fourth String Quartet is as follows:

Movement	1	2	3	4	5
Thematic content	A	B	cdc	B′	A′

The diagram reveals the symmetrical shape of the five-movement piece. The outer movements (one and five) are similar because they share variations of the same material. The central movement (three) is not linked to another, but notice that it, too, has the symmetrical shape *cdc*.

Be aware that the outer movements of this work are contrapuntal—counterpoint is a central ingredient in Bartók's music. The inner movements, two and four, have the character of the scherzo. In terms of texture, they are opposites of each other: the second movement is muted and legato (smooth, connected playing), while the fourth movement presents a wide variety of pizzicato playing. Both of these movements proceed at a breathtaking pace. The central movement, on the other hand, is very slow and mysterious. Its *c* sections feature cello solos with obvious folk or gypsy music roots. These solos are played against a soft, dissonant background of long-held notes on the other three instruments. The *d* section is a night music episode for which Bartók is famous. (Remember the movement called "The Night's Music" from Bartók's *Out of Doors* suite we met in chapter 4?) The chirping of birds and the zinging and twittering of insects are given full and magical voice in this *d* section.

Music for Strings, Percussion and Celesta   Bartók's *Music for Strings, Percussion and Celesta* (1937) has found a permanent place in the repertoire of many major symphony orchestras. It is one of the earliest major works to feature and realize the potential of the percussion family. Concertgoers who are turned off by "dissonant music" are attracted to this work, even though it abounds with dissonance. There is much in the work that is fascinating, haunting, and compelling.

In this work, two string orchestras are played against a third body of instruments consisting of celesta, xylophone, harp, timpani, other percussion instruments, and piano, which is used mainly for its percussive effects in a manner similar to Stravinsky's use of the piano in *Petrushka*. There are four movements in the piece, each of which develops a different mood. However, there are some general similarities between movements one and three and between two and four. The structure of interrelationships is very complex, such that a detailed explanation of them at this point would be less useful than broad comments about some of the salient features of the work. With the following comments in mind, listen to the piece several times.

**Béla Bartók
(1881–1945).**

Symmetry is common in Bartók's movements.

Counterpoint is central to Bartók's music.

Bartók is famous for his night music episodes.

Bartók's *Music for Strings, Percussion and Celesta* is one of the first major works to feature the percussion instruments.

Bartók uses the piano for percussive effect.

Figure 9.2

Celesta enters

The first movement is a fugue, the subject of which is long and full of short chromatic twists and turns. It is confined to the range of a perfect fifth and is thus very compact. There are twelve successive statements of the subject, each one beginning on a different pitch. The arrival of the twelfth entry marks the climax of the movement. Having arrived at that point, Bartók inverted the theme (turned it upside down), and in another series of staggered entries, returned it to the original starting pitch, *A*. At that point, the celesta enters for the first time. The plan of this movement is diagrammed in figure 9.2.

The mood of the second movement is entirely different in character. Some of the featured thematic material is reminiscent of folk music, but it is treated in a saucy, playful manner and moves in and out of passages of extreme dissonance. Notice that the piano is used in a percussive, barbarous way and that there are extended solo passages for the timpani. The movement is in a sonata form, although this may not be immediately obvious. The exposition presents the energetic *A* theme on the piano. Later, a loud strike on the timpani ushers in the skittish *B* theme in the violins. The development section, the longest part, introduces a new theme that becomes the basis for another fugue. An extended passage for timpani signals the recapitulation, which is considerably different from the exposition.

In the third movement, the night music atmosphere returns. Special features of the movement include timpani **glissandos** (sliding from one pitch to another), another gypsylike theme in the low strings, an extended passage in which the celesta creates an atmosphere rather like a gauze of pure color, without the benefit of anything resembling a real theme. The whole movement is, in fact, given over to washes of color and the atmosphere of the nighttime. The movement ends as it began—quietly and mysteriously.

Folk song elements are present in the last movement. There are also exact repetitions of the fugue subject of the opening movement. Again, the piano is used in a percussive manner. Near the end of this final movement, the music quiets down momentarily and then concludes with a furious rush.

The Music of Ives

The music of American Charles Ives (1874–1954) was virtually ignored until shortly before his death. However, in recent years, a widespread enthusiasm for it has developed and has resulted in numerous performances and recordings of his works. Ives was a rugged individualist who stubbornly clung to his musical-philosophical beliefs and refused to conform in the ways that might have gained him popularity. He was a man who was truly ahead of his time; thus it took the musical public about half a century to catch up with and recognize the nature and the quality of his music.

Charles Ives (1874–1954).
The New York Public Library

Ives, in the spirit of Thoreau, was a rugged individualist.

The Individualist   Among Ives' heroes was Henry David Thoreau, the American transcendentalist writer, who was himself a rugged individualist. A few lines from Thoreau's *Walden* aptly describe Ives:

> Why should we be in such desperate haste to succeed and in such desperate enterprises? If a man does not keep pace with his companions, perhaps it is because he hears a different drummer. Let him step to the music which he hears, however measured or far away.

Ives believed that, because he would be forced to conform or compromise in order to "succeed" in music, his creative powers would suffer if he were to make music his career. Instead, he elected to pursue a career in life insurance and proved to be very successful at it. He composed in the evenings and on weekends, working at an upright piano in the attic of his home in Danbury, Connecticut. In the seclusion of this environment, Ives exercised his freedom to create many kinds of music: tonal, atonal, sacred, secular, and music for voices and various instrumental ensembles. Ives was also an experimenter: he wrote bitonal and polytonal works; he retuned a piano in quarter tones (that is, intervals smaller than the minor second); and he used tone clusters that are batches of adjacent pitches. He envisioned, but purposely did not complete, a gigantic work called the *Universe Symphony* (conceived in 1910). The three sections of the symphony were to represent the "formation of the waters and mountains"; the "earth, evolution in nature and humanity"; and "heaven, the rise of all to the spiritual." The work was to have been performed by a number of choruses and orchestras spread out over various mountains and valleys. Such was the incomparable imagination of this gentle New England man at the turn of the century.

Ives composed many kinds of music and experimented with bitonality and polytonality.

Ives conceived of a major work entitled *Universe Symphony.*

Ives was a patriotic American and a deeply religious person, though not in any orthodox sense. This may account for the fact that many of his works quote patriotic songs, hymn tunes, and other songs native to America. These quotations are sometimes misunderstood by those not familiar with Ives' character and philosophy and so appear humorous. Ives did have a very active sense of humor, but generally the quotations from well-known tunes were not employed for their comedic value.

Ives' patriotism and religious zeal are reflected in his compositions.

The tunes and the fresh environments Ives created for them were important to the substance of his music. Ives said that in music it is not so much what happens, but the way it happens. You can expect to hear "Turkey in the Straw," "Nearer My God to Thee," "Columbia the Gem of the Ocean" (one of Ives' particular favorites, used in several different pieces), and many other tunes as you acquaint yourself with his music. But keep in mind the importance of the way these tunes occur, not simply that they do occur.

"The Fourth of July"   "The Fourth of July" is the first movement of a larger piece called *Holidays* symphony. As a young boy, Ives had been thrilled by two marching bands, each playing a different piece, coming toward each other from opposite directions. The young Ives was situated at the point where the two bands converged, and the clash of the two was pure excitement to him. Again, it was not so much what happened, but the way it happened.

"The Fourth of July" is a musical recollection of that experience. After a quiet beginning, the piece develops into a free fantasy on "Columbia the Gem of the Ocean" and some other tunes. Toward the close of the movement there is a passage of tremendous excitement, clashing rhythms, and roaring dissonance. This passage ends as abruptly as it began and the soft murmuring strings carry us off into the evening on a Fourth of July many years ago.

Included among his other major works are the *Concord* Sonata (for piano), Fourth Symphony (for which Ives suggests using two conductors), *The Unanswered Question* (heard in chapter 4), *Variations on "America"* (for organ), and over a hundred songs. His output was not prolific, but failing health and perhaps lack of recognition contributed to the fact that in the later years of his life he composed very little.

Of Ives' collection of songs, the most dramatic is "General William Booth Enters Heaven." One of the most charming is "At the River," Ives' unique adaption of the old hymn "Shall We Gather at the River?"

Music between the Wars

Dadaism

> Honor can be bought and sold like the arse. The arse represents life itself like potato-chips, and all you who are serious-minded will smell like cow's dung. Dada alone does not smell: it is nothing, nothing, nothing. It is like your hopes: nothing.

This quotation is from one of the numerous "Manifestos" published by various dadaist groups early in the twentieth century.

Is it a joke? If so, it's not particularly funny—strange maybe, but not humorous. Is it serious? If so, it is a grim, nihilistic view of life. That

Many familiar tunes were woven by Ives into new musical fabrics.

Ives' "The Fourth of July" was inspired by a childhood experience involving two marching bands.

The dissonance is reminiscent of the two bands coming together, each playing a different march.

is the most enigmatic thing about the curious movement called dada: we can never be sure whether it was intended to be funny or serious or perhaps both.

In the years surrounding World War I, several strange, short-lived movements developed that were partly artistic and partly political in nature. The horror, slaughter, and scope of World War I shook European civilization to its very roots. Because of this war, there was reason to believe that humankind had become a race of mad dogs. Out of revulsion, and as a reaction against this state of affairs, these movements were spawned.

After World War I, many movements were spawned in Europe.

Some of the movements, futurism, for example, preached violence, anarchy, the overthrow of all institutions and conventions, and the establishment of an entirely new civilization based on action and the adoration of machines. The movement called for a music created from the sound of machines, rattles, scrapers, and other noisemakers.

Futurism advocated the overthrow of the present establishment and its replacement with a machine civilization.

Dadaism, too, grew out of the ashes of World War I, but it was a less violent and more productive movement than futurism. This movement espoused the philosophy that it is better to laugh at the world than to further destroy or lament it; it is better to admit and reflect the insanity of humankind than to pretend that all is at last well. Dada is the French term for hobbyhorse, a purposeless name appropriate for the outrageous antics of the dadaist movement members.

Dadaists reflected the insanity of humankind rather than advocated further destruction.

Erik Satie   A body of dadaist music as such is nonexistent, but some music does develop the dadaist spirit of fun. Although he was not an official member of the dadaist movement in Paris, some of the music, as well as the mannerisms, of Erik Satie (1866–1925) captures the spirit of dada.

Satie, an eccentric, captured the dadaist spirit in his compositions.

Erik Satie's behavior has earned him the label "eccentric." He appended his signature with "gentle, medieval musician," and it is said that he wore nothing but gray suits, and that he ate nothing but white foods. His sense of humor, too, was offbeat. He said of himself:

> Ask anyone, and he will also tell you that I am no musician. This is quite true. Since the beginning of my career, I have been a phono-metrographist . . . I measure sound. Phono-meter in hand, I blithely weigh all of Beethoven . . . all of Verdi, etc. The very first time I used a phono-scope I examined a medium-sized E♭. I assure you in all sincerity that I have yet to see anything quite as repulsive! . . . On my phono-scale, a common F♯ attained the weight of ninety-three kilograms! (It came from a very fat tenor.) Have you ever heard of the science of cleaning sound? It's filthy, you know.

Even the titles of some of his works are imbued with dadaist nonsensical humor: *Three Pieces in the Form of a Pear, Second to Last Thoughts, Flabby Preludes,* and *Desiccated Embryos,* all composed for

Twittering Machine by Paul
Klee, 1922; watercolor, pen
and ink; 16¼″ × 12″.

Collection, The Museum of Modern Art, New
York. Purchase

Satie's ballet, *Parade,* caused a
scandal.

Satie's revolution was caused
by bringing the sounds of the
street into the concert hall.

piano. The production of his ballet, *Parade,* in 1917, caused a scandal
in Paris because of its unorthodox content and presentation. Satie composed the music, Jean Cocteau wrote the scenario, and Pablo Picasso
designed the cubist-style sets and costumes. The score calls for a standard orchestra as well as a revolver, roulette wheel, and typewriter.

Given all of this as a background, what can we expect the music
to be like? The most astonishing aspect of *Parade's* music is its tame-
ness. Like all of Satie's music, it is essentially simple and consonant.
Cocteau said, "We want to create art with an axe." Despite this an-
nounced goal, Satie's music is gentle and at times even melancholy. Some
of his themes even border on banality and his orchestration is modeled
on music-hall sound rather than elegant, polished orchestral sound characteristic of many of his contemporaries. In effect, Satie brought the
sounds of the street into the concert hall, a most shocking and revolutionary concept in music. To an audience accustomed to the music of
Brahms and Tchaikovsky, Satie's music was shocking, not because it was
trenchantly dissonant or wild, but because it struck them as disgustingly
and arrogantly cheap.

Sound and Sense
Dadaist Style

Title: Parade *(1917)*
Composer: Satie

A Closer Look

Listen to the first few minutes of *Parade*—until the sounds of the gunshots. This will serve as an introduction to Satie's dadaist style. This brief encounter includes the following:

A homophonic statement in the brass, in the form of a slow fanfare
A serene, repetitious tune
A fugue
Another repetitious tune played first by the clarinet, then picked up by other members of the orchestra building to a full statement
A vaguely Oriental-sounding section
Ragtime, music hall section
Typewriter solo
The gunshots

Not all of Satie's music can be called dadaist. For example, his most famous piece, *Gymnopédie* no. 1, is not. Originally written for piano, the piece was later orchestrated by Debussy, and in more recent times has been incorporated into a work by the rock group Blood, Sweat, and Tears. Listen to the original (piano) version first. It may not be profound, but it is delicate and charming, and it creates a unique mood.

Satie's popularity, though never monumental, has increased with time even though his output was limited. Those elements of his music that were considered banal and cheap by audiences during his lifetime are fresh and touching to contemporary audiences. There was a revival of interest in Satie's music during the late 1960s with the rise of a movement called neo-dadaism. But even before that time, Satie's influence was evident in the works of some young composers known as **Les Six** (the French Six).

*Satie's most famous work—*Gymnopédie *no. 1—is not dadaist.*

Satie's music has been more popular recently than it was with his contemporaries.

Young composers influenced by Satie formed a group called "Les Six."

The French Six

Only three of the six members of this group had an impact on twentieth-century music: Darius Milhaud (1892–1974), Francis Poulenc (1889–1963), and Arthur Honegger (1892–1955). The other members of the group were Germaine Tailleferre (1892–1983), Louis Durey (1888–1979), and Georges Auric (1899–1983). None of them ever studied with Satie, but each profited from his encouragement and guidance. Milhaud, early in his career, and Poulenc, to a lesser degree, were influenced by some of Satie's music and by his irreverent attitude toward art music. Honegger, a very capable composer, was less radical in his views and was less directly influenced by Satie.

The French Six, or perhaps more accurately the French Three, produced a handful of sturdy, enduring works that are still performed frequently. Some of their music, however, borders on the trivial.

Honegger's best known works are his two dramatic oratorios, *Le Roi David (King David)* (1923), and *Jeanne d' Arc au bûcher (Joan of Arc at the Stake)* (1938), as well as the tone poem *Pacific 231* (1923).

Pacific 231 is the name of a French train. In using a train for the subject, Honegger strayed from the nineteenth-century programmatic basis of a tone poem of either a person, an idea, or a scene drawn from nature. Honegger's choice of a train for this purpose is a distinctly twentieth-century idea. The short work is a marvel of musical realism, for it effectively captures the sounds, motion, and speed of the train using a conventional orchestra.

The piece begins with the train in the station, huffing and puffing, slowly gathering the steam necessary to get the enormous machine into motion. We can actually sense the buildup of power. It slowly moves from the station and gradually picks up tempo until it reaches its full speed dashing across the countryside. Then the opposite process begins: the slowing of the train. Finally it reaches its destination—the station at the other end of the line.

Notice the new "sound effects" Honegger creates with the orchestra. These are essential to the success of the composition. Notice, too, that although there is, by nineteenth-century standards, considerable dissonance, the piece does not greatly deviate from the sense of being in a key.

Milhaud   Milhaud was one of the most prolific of contemporary composers. He composed in all the major genres and incorporated into his own style elements of several kinds of music, including jazz and Latin American rhythms. His most experimental works (and many people believe, his best works) date from his early career. At that time Milhaud was particularly fond of polytonality, especially evident in his *Le Boeuf sur le toit (The Bull on the Roof)* (1919). Milhaud assembled several popular melodies, mostly of Brazilian origin, and separated them from one another by a recurring rondo theme, which also begins the piece.

These three men produced music that is still performed today.

Honegger's tone poem Pacific 231 is an example of twentieth-century musical realism.

Sound effects created by the orchestra are essential to the success of the piece.

Polytonality is evident in Milhaud's early works.

Toward the end of the rondo theme, a flute produces a fragment in one key, followed by a clarinet echoing the fragment in another key. The first Brazilian melody occurs next, the initial phrase of which is solidly in key. When this phrase is repeated, however, the harmony becomes discordant, as though someone were playing the wrong notes. The notes are, in fact, correct, but they are also in several different keys. The music-hall sound of the brass and the popular atmosphere of this work suggest that Milhaud was here influenced by Satie.

A somewhat more serious but no less experimental work is Milhaud's ballet, *La Création du Monde, (The Creation of the World)* (1924). In the 1920s several art music composers became fascinated with American jazz and tried to incorporate some of its spirit into their concert works. Milhaud did this in several of his works, but primarily in this ballet. *La Création du Monde* is also one of the earliest art music works to extensively use the saxophone.

Milhaud incorporated American jazz into his ballet, *The Creation of the World.*

Neoclassicism

Stravinsky's New Style   Igor Stravinsky's tremendous success in the early years of the century is attributable to the three ballets mentioned earlier. These, as was explained, relied heavily on Russian folk music, pounding rhythms, and a huge, colorful orchestra. However, at the close of World War I Stravinsky began changing his style dramatically, thus confusing the musical world. He abandoned the large orchestra in favor of small instrumental ensembles, and the thicker, many-toned chords in favor of leaner harmonies. He also worked more with tonality and began writing works that were in a key. In the 1920s, 1930s, and 1940s Stravinsky composed sonatas, a violin concerto, a piano concerto, symphonies, and even concerti grossi. In other words, he reverted to the genres, textures, and tonality of the classical era and, in some instances, to the baroque era.

After World War I, Stravinsky reverted to the genres, textures, and tonality of the classical era and the baroque.

Stravinsky succeeded in bringing a new freshness to these traditional forms and practices. Other composers emulated him, creating what amounted to a movement. In time, the movement acquired a label—another twentieth-century "ism"—**neoclassicism.** But the influence of the baroque on this movement is just as great as the influence of classicism. Thus the movement could just as easily have been labeled neobaroque.

The movement that formed around Stravinsky and his emulators is called neoclassicism, but because of the importance of baroque elements to this music, it could have been termed neobaroque.

Sound and Sense
Neoclassic (Neobaroque) Stravinsky

Title: Octet *(1923, revised 1952)*
Composer: Stravinsky

A Closer Look

Stravinsky's *Octet* is a piece in which both classical and baroque elements are welded to create a new musical amalgam. Its unorthodox instrumentation includes flute, clarinet, two bassoons, two trumpets, and two trombones. The work is in three movements and is prefaced by a slow introduction called "Sinfonia." It is in a key, though, as we shall see, it is liberally peppered with unexpected and brittle dissonances. Stravinsky professed an "emotional detachment" in this work; he referred to it as "an object." It is not an emotive piece, but rather it is a carefully ordered collection of acoustic and temporal phenomena.

The Slow Introduction

The Sinfonia serves the same purpose as the slow introductions Haydn used in many of his late symphonies. It also sets the stage for what is to follow by briefly acquainting the listener with the unusual sonorities produced by this odd grouping of instruments.

First Movement

Two themes are deployed in this movement in allegro moderato tempo. The first is wide ranging and staccato:

The second theme, which is narrower in range and is marked by syncopation, first appears about 30 seconds into the movement:

The first theme then reappears to close out the movement. These themes are obviously different in character from the folksy themes of *Petrushka*. The chords and texture are much leaner in *Octet* than in *Petrushka,* but the generating force of rhythm with its Stravinskian eccentricities is the same in both works. Notice, for example, in measure 6 of theme one that the anticipated flow of four even eighth notes per bar receives a jolt—measure 6 has five eighth notes instead of the expected four.

Second Movement

Stravinsky took the concept of theme with variations, a form favored in both the baroque and classical eras, and reshaped it to his own needs. The theme section is, of course, stated first. This is followed by the first variation that

Plate 13
Solid geometric shapes and the sense of serenity are important features of this
Renaissance painting.

Madonna with Child and Saints; Giorgione; Cathedral (Duomo) of Castelfranco Veneto.

Plate 14
Action and drama speak in this painting from the baroque.

Rape of the Daughters of Leucippus; Rubens; Scala/The Art Resource, New York.

Plate 15

An example of the fanciful, decorative rococo style (see chapter 6).

Hofkirche; © Jeff Smith/EKM-Nepenthe.

Plate 16
A rococo scene (see chapter 6)—notice how the muted colors and the slender
figures contrast with those in the baroque painting in plate 14.

A Party in the Open Air; Watteau; Bildarchiv preussischer Kulturbesitz.

Plate 17
The romantic fascination with nature is evident in this nineteenth-century landscape painting (see chapter 8).

A View near Volterra; Jean-Baptiste-Camille Corot; Date: 1838; canvas; 0.695 cm × 0.951 cm; National Gallery of Art, Washington, Chester Dale Collection.

Plate 18
The dual romantic themes of freedom and heroism are expressed in this
nineteenth-century painting (see chapter 8).

Liberty Leading the People; Delacroix; Alinari/The Art Resource, New York.

Plate 19

Once more, the romantic fascination with nature is evident in this landscape.

Forest of Fountainbleau, Jean-Baptiste-Camille Corot; Date: ca. 1830; canvas; 1.756 cm × 2.426 cm; National Gallery of Art, Washington, Chester Dale Collection.

Plate 20
Notice how the blurred outlines distort photographic reality, analogous to
Debussy's distortion of tonality (see chapter 9).

Woman Seated Under the Willows; Claude Monet; 1880; canvas; 0.811 cm × 0.600 cm; National Gallery of Art,
Washington, Chester Dale Collection.

Plate 21
Tiffany Lamp, an example of Art Nouveau style (see chapter 9).

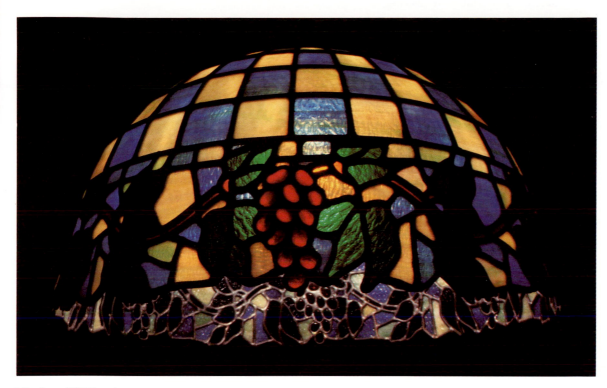

Plate 22
A new vision and a reshaping of elements are analogous to new forms and the
dissolution of tonality as discussed in chapter 9.

Three Musicians; Pablo Picasso; 1921; oil on canvas; 80″ × 74″; Philadelphia Museum of Art, The A. E. Gallatin
Collection ACQ# 52-61-96.

Plate 23
The thick texture, dark colors, and haunted eyes are typical of expressionistic paintings. This vision is analogous to the expressionistic music of Schönberg and Berg (see chapter 9).

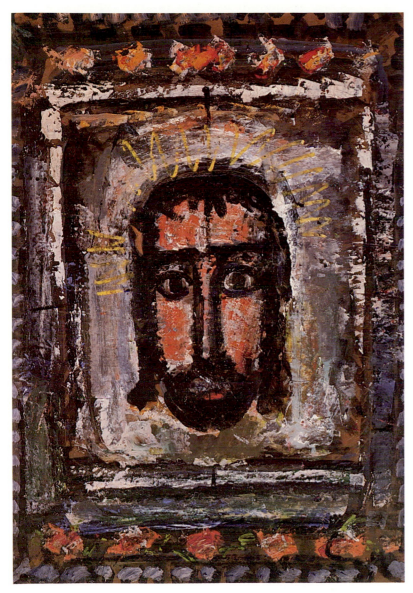

The Holy Face; Roualt; Musee National D'Art Moderne, Centre Georges Pompidou, Paris.

Plate 24
This is a different sort of expressionistic painting, lighter in texture and color
than the Roualt in plate 23. Still, it exemplifies the pent-up raw emotion that
we find in the music of Anton Webern (see chapter 9).

Twittering Machine; Paul Klee; 1922 watercolor; pen and ink; 16¼″ × 12″; The Museum of Modern Art, New
York, Purchase.

features, among other things, running passages for the bassoons. Then the second variation is introduced, which is marchlike in character. The first variation then returns, which is a departure from baroque and classical norms. A third and fourth variation are followed by another repetition of the first variation. The movement concludes with a fifth variation that contrasts sharply with the others in terms of tempo and mood.

Third Movement (Finale)

The finale follows without pause and has a modified rondo form: *ABAC*-coda. In a classical rondo the form would have concluded with another statement of *A;* Stravinsky omits this and moves directly to a heavily syncopated coda.

Stravinsky's Symphony in C (1940) (which deliberately alerts us to the fact that the work is in a key) is a prototypical neoclassic work. Based directly on the model of the late eighteenth-century symphony, this one has the standard four movements: fast-slow-dance (scherzo)-slow/fast. The slow portion of the last movement is the only structural departure from the classical norm.

Your knowledge of Haydn and Mozart symphonies should help you recognize the sonata-allegro form of the first movement. There is even a similarity between Stravinsky's *A* theme and the *A* theme (first movement) of Mozart's well-known Symphony no. 40 in G Minor.

While Stravinsky was an early and important advocate of neoclassicism, it is inaccurate to name him its inventor. Many composers from the 1920s to the present have produced works that to varying degrees are neoclassic. This does not mean, however, that the music of all these composers sounds alike. Each was attracted to one or more aspect of neoclassicism: tonality, the genres, themes, forms, or instrumentation. Thus, Stravinsky and Prokofiev could each write a neoclassic piece, but the Stravinsky piece would sound uniquely like Stravinsky, while the Prokofiev work would sound only like Prokofiev.

Prokofiev Russian Sergei Prokofiev (1891–1953) was another important composer during the years between the wars. Many of his compositions fall into the neoclassical category. In his autobiography (1941), Prokofiev outlined three basic aesthetic/stylistic lines in his music: (1) a lyrical line that is peppered by the lively spirit of the scherzo; (2) a classical line that is a reflection of his love for the music of Beethoven, Haydn, Mozart, and others; and (3) a motor line, referring to his frequent use of perpetual motion rhythms. These attributes are obvious in Prokofiev's music. They are, for example, clearly evident in his Third Piano Concerto in C Major, op. 26.

Stravinsky's Symphony in C is based directly upon the eighteenth-century symphony.

Compare Stravinsky's symphony to Mozart's Symphony no. 40 in G Minor.

Many twentieth-century composers were attracted to neoclassicism, though their works do not sound alike.

Prokofiev identified three basic aesthetic/stylistic lines in his music.

Sound and Sense ♪
Neoclassic Piano Concerto

Title: Third Piano Concerto in C Major, op. 26 (1921)
Composer: Prokofiev
Recording: Gary Graffman/Szell, Cleveland Orchestra
Meter: 4/4
Tempo: Andante-allegro
Key: C major

A Closer Look

The premier performance of this work was well received in Chicago in December of 1921, but weeks later it was roundly panned at a performance in New York. The work may well have been ahead of its time, for it has since become a staple of the modern repertoire and is frequently programmed and recorded. The work has the classical three movement format: fast-slow-fast. The first movement lacks a cadenza and is in sonata-allegro form. The theme of the introduction is reminiscent of the Russian folk song "The Volga Boatmen."

First Movement

Andante (introduction), allegro (sonata-allegro form)

Introduction
    Begins with a lyrical theme in the clarinet, is joined by   (:38)
        strings and leads to *A* in the new tempo
    A—this vigorous theme is stated first by the piano and   (:19)
        then by the orchestra with piano
    Bridge—near the end of the bridge the piano plays some   (1:10)
        thunderous chords which slow the tempo and lead to *B*
    B—played first by an oboe with pizzicato strings, then   (:43)
        picked up by piano and orchestra
    B'—the piano plays a kind of caricature of the *B* theme   (:13)
    Bridge—   (1:05)

Development
    Introduction theme and *A* and *B* are developed   (2:01)

Recapitulation
    A—   (:18)
    Bridge—   (1:08)
    B—   (:45)
    Coda—(derived from *A*)   (:23)

Second Movement

The second movement, a theme with five variations and coda, presents a theme that is heavily laden with a lyrical scherzo quality. Notice that just as the theme begins to turn sweet, Prokofiev introduces sour dissonance.
    The form of the second movement is as follows:

Theme—mainly in woodwinds   (1:00)
First variation—stated by the piano   (1:08)

Second variation—piano with orchestra, perpetual motion	(:48)
Third variation—full chords, very energetic	(1:10)
Fourth variation—slow, lyrical, almost dreamlike	(2:21)
Fifth variation—faster	(1:26)
Coda—the theme is restated in ornamented form and is filled with driving energy. However, the movement ends abruptly and quietly.	(1:27)

Third Movement

The third movement begins with a theme in the bassoons that is then extended and developed. Then follows a sarcastic theme played by the piano in alternation with strings and woodwinds. It, too, is expanded and developed. Suddenly and quite unexpectedly a long, lyrical section, dominated by two subthemes, enters. This builds to a romantic climax reminiscent of Rachmaninoff's works. The movement and the piece conclude with a brilliant extended coda in which the first theme of this movement is prominently featured.

The Americana Composers

During the years between World War I and World War II, several talented young American composers emerged as significant musical figures. This group includes Aaron Copland (b. 1900), Samuel Barber (1910–1981), Walter Piston (1894–1976), Roger Sessions (1896–1985), Virgil Thomson (b. 1896), and George Gershwin (1898–1937), the composer who bridged the gap between art and popular music. These composers were born at the turn of the century, and so they are considered children of the twentieth century. Several of them eventually held teaching positions at prestigious American universities and became prominent figures in art music circles in this country. More than a few studied composition in Paris with the legendary composition teacher, Nadia Boulanger (1887–1980), truly one of the great women in the history of Western art music.

Important American composers emerged between the wars.

A number of American women were also active in the field of composition at the time, though they generally did not receive the recognition and public support they deserved. This group includes Amy Beach (1867–1944), Ruth Crawford Seeger (1901–53), Miriam Gideon (b. 1906), and Louise Talma (b. 1906).

Until early in this century, the United States labored under an artistic inferiority complex that made it difficult for American composers to be accepted as serious artists. But this situation began to change with the emergence of this group of young Americans. Their composition skills and artistic sensitivities demanded attention.

Not until the twentieth century were American composers accepted as serious artists.

Copland's compositions incorporated distinctly American music and themes.

The music was consciously composed to have broad appeal.

In time, these composers became a source of national pride. Some of them, most notably Copland, began to experiment with indigenous music and subject matter. Their works incorporated American jazz and folk music, along with distinctly American themes. This experimentation was reflected in the songs, operas, ballets, orchestral music, and movie music these composers created.

Copland, Barber, and several others consciously crafted and tailored their musical styles to appeal to a larger audience. Each in a highly individual way created music that was lyrical and energetic without being abrasive.

Sound and Sense

Americana Style

Title: Music for the Theatre *(1925)*

Composer: Copland

A Closer Look

Copland's *Music for the Theatre* is composed of a set of five short pieces ranging in length from three to five minutes, and it is scored for a small orchestra. The pieces are all tonal though there are many effective, pungent dissonant sonorities. This music is not designed to frighten an audience out of its wits with prolonged dissonance and complex counterpoint, but it is tastefully designed to appeal to a broad audience. It is intended to sound familiar to an audience that has relatively little acquaintance with art music. The music is "comfortable," yet it does not stoop to cheap musical tricks or to oversimplification. It is possible to detect the influence of 1920s jazz, and some thematic material is reminiscent of folk song.

The first piece, called "Prologue," presents an *A* theme played by the trumpet. The strings enter quietly and provide a cushion for the lyrical *B* theme, played by an oboe. A faster, heavily syncopated and jazzy development section follows, at the conclusion of which the *A* and *B* themes are recapitulated, ending the piece quietly.

The second piece, "Dance," again displays the influence of jazz. Bassoon and percussion play a saucy *A* theme. Muted trumpet and then clarinet pick up a *B* theme to the thumping background of the piano playing an ostinato. *A* and *B* are repeated, and a brief, abrupt coda ends the piece.

"Interlude," the third piece in the set, is the most folklike in quality. The English horn plays an extended melancholy theme that resembles music from an epic western movie. Gradually the strings, the piano, and percussion emerge to form a background as the clarinet picks up the theme and adds to it some blue notes. One by one, other solo instruments enter against the soft, velvety string background. The English horn restates its original solo to end the piece quietly.

"Burlesque," the fourth in the set, sharply contrasts with the preceding piece. It has the form *ABAB*. The *B* theme features a jazzy trumpet that plays against the background of a lazily bouncing accompaniment.

The last piece in the set, "Epilogue," restates themes from "Prologue" and "Interlude." The clarinet begins by stating the trumpet theme from "Prologue," though here the mood is very different. The piece and the set end quietly.

Another notable Copland work is *Appalachian Spring* (1944), a ballet he composed for dancer Martha Graham. The story presented in the ballet is very simple, detailing life in an American pioneer community in the early nineteenth century. The most famous excerpt from *Appalachian Spring* is a set of variations Copland wrote on the folk hymn "Simple Gifts." The work is still performed as a ballet, but the orchestral arrangement is even more popular today.

Copland's ballet *Appalachian Spring* features an American theme and an American folk hymn.

Sound and Sense ♪
The American School

Title: Adagio for Strings *(1938)*
Composer: Barber
Meter: 4/2
Tempo: Adagio
Key: B♭ minor

A Closer Look

Another example of music from the American school is Samuel Barber's *Adagio for Strings*. It is a seven-minute work built on a single theme. This softly undulating theme is long, slow, and haunting. It winds around a few notes, then leaps upward with complete naturalness and effortlessness. The work contains a great deal of counterpoint, but it is never fussy or intricate. It, too, seems to evolve and roll with ease. The harmonic language is tonal and soft, though not without sad and touching dissonances. Many listeners will recognize this work as the background music for *Platoon* (1987), a powerful film about the war in Vietnam.

The theme or variations of it is stated five times before reaching an impressive climax in the high strings. A coda that includes a final shortened statement of the theme then follows. In all but one case there is a clear break between the end of one statement of the theme and the start of the next. Graphically illustrated, the structure looks like this:

A	A'	A''	A'''	A''''	Climax	Coda
Theme in violins (:48)	Theme in violins (1:07)	Theme in violas (:59)	Theme in cellos (:44)	Theme in cellos (1:40)		(2:15)

Gershwin

George Gershwin (1898–1937) occupies a unique position in the history of American music. In his brief career most of his energies were devoted to creating popular songs for Broadway shows. Dozens of these songs are still performed today, decades after they were written—a testament to his remarkable achievement.

Gershwin was not a jazz musician, but he had a keen ear for certain rhythmic and harmonic elements found in jazz of the 1920s and 1930s. These became ingredients of his own style and, for the masses who were unacquainted with real jazz, Gershwin's music epitomized the style. He was thus a preeminent composer of popular songs which had the added dimension of the flavor of jazz.

His interests and ambition exceeded the bounds of popular music, however, and led him to create a small group of works cast in genres from the realm of art music: opera (*Porgy and Bess,* 1935), symphonic poem (*Rhapsody in Blue,* 1924), concerto (Piano Concerto in F, 1925), and a few others. It has sometimes been suggested that in works such as these Gershwin "bridged the gap" between popular and art music. An examination of the Piano Concerto in F reveals that that is true only in a general sense.

As we have seen, the piano concerto in the eighteenth and nineteenth centuries normally consisted of three movements—fast-slow-fast—and featured the piano both in concert with the orchestra and alone in solo passages such as cadenzas. The first movement usually presented thematic materials in the exposition section which were then developed in various ways in the development section. This presentation and development of musical materials is central to art music, but except in

Gershwin focused his energies on composing for Broadway shows, but he imbued many of his songs with a jazz style.

Because Gershwin also composed in art music genres, it is said that he bridged the gap between popular and art music.

isolated instances, the process is foreign to popular music. And it is absent from Gershwin's Piano Concerto in F. Instead, the first movement presents a series of self-contained melodies, of which some are repeated and others are not. What results is not an organically unified whole, but rather a string of memorable tunes loosely tied together by short bridge passages.

The Piano Concerto in F lacks a number of characteristics of art music.

Sound and Sense

An Offshoot of American Art Music

Title: Piano Concerto in F (1925)
Composer: George Gershwin
Recording: St. Louis Symphony Orchestra,
Leonard Slatkin, Jeffrey Siegel, Pianist

A Closer Look

Two brief flourishes by timpani and high woodwinds lead to:

A—in low woodwinds and low strings	(1:18)
A—the tail of which is repeated and expanded, leading to:	(1:18)
B—solo piano, slower tempo	(1:06)
B—piano with orchestra, dissolving into solo piano, a bridge to	(1:00)
C—a faster, more energetic theme in strings, then full orchestra. The theme is extended and leads to	(:45)
B'—piano with orchestra. There is a brief piano cadenza	(1:00)
D—mainly in woodwinds, growing to full orchestra with piano taking command of the bouncy theme. The passage is extended and leads to	(1:54)
E—a more lyrical theme in the strings. This is extended and leads to	(1:36)
F—a vigorous theme with a repetitive bass part in the piano. At the end of this section the solo piano leads to	(1:23)
E'—in woodwinds and strings with piano filigree. A big buildup leads to	(1:00)
B'—loud and full	(:52)
D'—orchestra with piano	(1:35)

The Twelve-Tone System

In 1925 Arnold Schönberg produced the first piece of music composed entirely in accordance with the principles of the **twelve-tone system.** He had been formulating the system for some years and had composed a partial twelve-tone work as early as 1923, but the system was not fully formulated until 1925.

What is the twelve-tone system? Simply stated, it is a means of organizing pitches to create musical coherence and consistency. As mentioned previously, there are twelve different pitches normally employed in the music of the Western world:

C C♯(D♭)D D♯(E♭)E F F♯(G♭)G G♯(A♭)A A♯(B♭) B
1 2   3 4   5 6 7   8 9   10 11   12

Schönberg's idea was to relate these pitches only to one another rather than to have them relate to and be subservient to a few pitches and chords. In tonality, pitches and chords are arranged so that they all relate to tonic, dominant, and subdominant, and all ultimately resolve into and relate to the tonic. In a real sense, Schönberg's system released all pitches of their obligations to the tonic and allowed them to become free agents related only to one another. The system is a careful, logical means of avoiding tonality.

One of the principles of this system is that no single pitch is repeated until all of the other eleven pitches have been sounded. Thus, if the first pitch in a given piece is C, it will not reoccur until C♯, D, D♯, E, F, F♯, G, G♯, A, A♯, and B have been sounded. These pitches can be sounded one at at time, as in melody, or they can be sounded in clusters, that is, chords. Another principle is that melodies and chords that sound similar to melodies and chords found in tonality are avoided.

The basic building blocks of the twelve-tone system are the **tone row** and versions of it. The tone row is a series of twelve different pitches and their attendant intervals. The row is the basic thematic and harmonic material out of which the music is made. Figure 9.3 shows the row from Schönberg's *Suite* for piano, op. 25 (1925).

A group of pitches such as in this row has an intrinsic relationship to certain versions of itself. Such a relationship exists (1) in the upside-down version of the row, (2) in the backwards version, and (3) in the upside down and backwards version. In the twelve-tone system the upside-down version of the row is called the **inversion;** the backwards version is called the **retrograde;** and the upside-down and backwards version is called the **retrograde inversion.** These versions of the row are illustrated in figure 9.4.

In figure 9.4 the row is referred to as the "original" or simply "O"; it is the original row from which the other versions spring. Notice that this original begins by moving up a half step and then up a whole step, and so on. The inversion begins by moving *down* a half step and then *down* a whole step, and so on. In other words, when the original moves up by a specific interval size, the inversion moves down by that same specific interval size. When the original moves down, the inversion moves up. The retrograde is simply the mirror version of the original: it starts

Schönberg's twelve-tone system is a careful, logical method of organizing pitches to avoid tonality.

No pitch will reoccur until the other eleven have been sounded.

The tone row is a series of twelve different pitches and their attendant intervals.

An upside-down row is the inversion, a backwards row is the retrograde, and an upside-down and backwards row is the retrograde inversion.

Figure 9.3

Figure 9.4

with the last pitch of the row and follows the series backwards to the first pitch of the row. As its name implies, the retrograde inversion is the retrograde in upside-down form.

Any of these four versions can be transposed (moved up or down) to begin on any other pitch. Eleven transpositions are possible for each of the versions. There are, then, 4 × 12 or 48 possible versions of the row, the total available pitch material for a given twelve-tone composition.

In twelve-tone composition, there are forty-eight possible versions of the row.

Listen now to Schönberg's *Suite* for piano. It is composed in the manner of a baroque keyboard suite with the following movements: prelude, gavotte, musette, intermezzo, minuet and trio, and gigue.

Schönberg's system ordered pitches in serial fashion—hence the name **serial music.** His student, Webern, expanded the system by serializing rhythms, dynamics, and timbres, and he also developed a rhythmic language that was startlingly new and different. Webern's approach to pitch and rhythm was highly intellectual, mathematical, esoteric, and above all, musical. His music and ideas had an enormous impact on post-World War II serialist composers.

Webern expanded upon Schönberg's system.

Music after World War II

Since about 1950 a flood of new ideas has emerged and many different events have taken place in the world of music, both popular music and art music.

In trying to assess the major developments in art music over the past several decades, four trends command our attention: (1) the rise of electronic music; (2) the exploration of chance operations and multimedia possibilities; (3) the emergence of minimalism; and (4) the adaption and expansion of more conventional practices. These trends are not necessarily mutually exclusive—many composers have successfully blended several of these elements and techniques.

The Rise of Electronic Music

Just after the end of World War II several types of electronic equipment were either invented or refined. The ensuing decades saw an increase in such inventions and refinements, so that today we have a fund of highly sophisticated and versatile electronic instruments that are being put to a variety of uses.

Musique concrète, the earliest type of electronic music, manipulated natural or conventional sounds.

The earliest form of electronic music is called ***musique concrète.*** It was developed in France in the late 1940s by Pierre Schaeffer and Pierre Henry. It consisted of tape-recorded music whose sounds were produced by thunder, airplanes, traffic, factory whistles, other environmental noises, or by conventional musical instruments and voices. The taped sounds could then be manipulated in various ways: accelerated or slowed, overdubbed, imbued with reverberation, spliced, etc. The character of a given *musique concrète* work is thus determined by the qualities of the captured sounds, their manipulation, and the imagination of the composer.

Pure electronic music does not use altered natural sounds but rather includes sounds created by electronic devices.

A slightly later development resulted in the creation of "pure" **electronic music,** that is, music whose recorded sounds are not natural but rather are generated by electronic devices that produce various basic sound wave forms. These forms can be altered by means of modulators, a device that takes two differing sounds and mixes them to produce a new sound. Other devices, such as filters, are used to change the quality of a given sound.

The first electronic music studio was established in Cologne, Germany, in 1951. In the remaining years of that decade electronic studios were established at numerous locations in Europe and the United States.

Synthesizers are now standard "instruments" for many composers and musicians.

This mixing, splicing, and manipulating were rather cumbersome and time consuming for the composer of electronic music, but these processes were dramatically enhanced with the introduction of the synthesizer in the next decade. A **synthesizer** is an electronic instrument capable of both producing sounds and modifying them in a variety of ways. The RCA electronic music synthesizer was established at the Columbia-Princeton Music Center in 1959 where Milton Babbitt has long been a central composer. From the 1960s through the 1980s synthesizers of various types have become well established in many universities and among a wide range of rock groups.

The electronic music composer is free to employ any or all of the infinite variety of sounds that can be produced by a sophisticated synthesizer, as well as any ordinary pitches and sounds of conventional instruments. If he or she has the right equipment, sounds can be altered or distorted in limitless ways, and different kinds of sounds can be combined in equally limitless ways.

The smallest standard interval commonly employed in Western music is, as stated in chapter 2, the minor second: c to c♯ for example. But with the proper electronic equipment, forty to fifty individual pitches between c and c♯ can be obtained by the simple rotation of a dial.

Electronic music is no less revolutionary in terms of rhythm. Nonelectronic music measures musical time in terms of beats, meters, and tempos. Electronic music measures time in terms of inches per second of tape, so beat and meter are eliminated. Thus, an infinite number of durational values and mind-boggling rhythmic complexities are available in electronic music, and the composer is not at the mercy of human performers to accurately deliver them.

Detroit Industry; 1932–33, Diego M. Rivera, Mexican, 1886–1957; Fresco.

© The Detroit Institute of Arts, Founders Society. Purchase, Edsel B. Ford Fund and Gift of Edsel B. Ford, Acc. No. 33.10N

The composer of electronic music has access to an unlimited number of pitches and rhythms.

Sound synthesizer.
© Maher/EKM-Nepenthe

In pure electronic music, nothing is left to chance.

Electronic music cannot be analyzed in terms of beat, meter, rhythm, and other traditional elements.

Stockhausen's *Song of the Youths* is a landmark in electronic music.

Some composers, Babbitt among them, celebrate the idea of having absolute control over every aspect of their compositions, including the performance of them. Electronic instruments ensure the composer that his or her works will remain intact, as they were conceived, without the risk of human error during performance. In pure electronic music nothing is left to chance: no one will sing or play out of tune, no one will assume the wrong tempo or fail to properly execute the most intricate rhythms. This may seem cold and impersonal, and there is no denying that in some respects pure electronic music is depersonalized; yet unfailing precision in performance has definite merit.

As has been seen, pure electronic music differs from all other music in fundamental ways. Therefore, it cannot be interpreted or analyzed according to traditional methods. If we attempt to force electronic music into preconceived musical pigeonholes we will only be frustrated and disappointed.

Karlheinz Stockhausen

Karlheinz Stockhausen (b. 1928) has emerged as a central figure in the field of electronic music. He has written pure electronic works, nonelectronic pieces, and a now-famous composition for voice and electronic instruments called *Gesang der Jünglinge (Song of the Youths)*. This work is generally considered a landmark in the development of electronic music. Listening to the work and understanding its construction leads to the conclusion that it is, among other things, a technological wonder.

Gesang der Jünglinge sounds incredibly complicated, yet the sound materials from which it is constructed are relatively simple: one human voice and eleven different electronically generated sounds. All of the sounds can be filtered, mixed, and dubbed (recorded over the original sound at different pitches and speeds). Stockhausen began by recording the voice of a youthful choirboy singing and sometimes speaking the following text:

This piece combines one human voice and eleven different electronically generated sounds.

Preiset den Herrn, ihr Werke alle des Herrn;

O all ye works of the Lord, bless ye the Lord:

lobt ihn und über alles erhebt ihn in Ewigkeit. . . .

Praise Him and magnify Him for ever. . . .

Preiset den Herrn, Sonne und Mond;

O ye Sun, and Moon, bless ye the Lord;

preiset den Herrn, des Himmels Sterne.

O ye Stars of Heaven, bless ye the Lord.

Preiset den Herrn, aller Regen und Tau;

O ye Showers, and Dew, bless ye the Lord;

preiset den Herrn, alle Winde.

O ye Winds of God, bless ye the Lord.

Preiset den Herrn, Feuer und Sommersglut;

O ye Fire, and Heat of Summer, bless ye the Lord;

preiset den Herrn, Kälte und starrer Winter. . . .

O ye Cold, and icy Winter, bless ye the Lord. . . .

Stockhausen was less interested in the text being sung in a "meaningful" way than he was in the sounds produced by the boy's voice. These individual sounds, which he calls "phones" (from phonetics), are blended into the electronic sounds of the work, and some are electronically altered. By means of multiple dubbings, the single voice is made to sound like several voices singing simultaneously. Thus, from one voice comes many different sounds, rhythms, and timbres.

Similarly, the handful of basic electronic sounds are manipulated to yield a rainbow of sounds and timbres.

Sound and Sense
Electronic Music

Title: Gesang der Jünglinge (Song of the Youths)
Composer: Stockhausen

A Closer Look

In this composition as in any music, it is critical that we get our bearings—that is, that we have some idea of structure and of activities that take place. With repeated listenings, the differences between the various activities should be apparent. The description and order of these activities is listed below. Notice that in most cases one section of activities is set off from the next by silence. Thus, silence is a unifying factor in this piece.

The piece begins with a fanfare made of electronic gurgles, squeaks, pops, and grunts. It ends softly.

Silence

The boy's voice enters next. In the background is a soft accompaniment of new electronic sounds. The activity swells to a chord; there is a soft ending.

Silence (very brief)

Multiple voices in counterpoint are heard behind a solo voice. The electronic sounds are now more numerous and active. Later, speech develops into singing but then returns to the multiple-voice background. The section ends with a long-held note.

Silence

This is a longer section than the others, containing speech, *Sprechtstimme,* and singing. The electronic sounds create some violent periodic outbursts and some hitherto unexplored low notes.

Silence

This section begins with electronic screeches and bird calls. There are snatches of solo and of multiple voices, followed by more bird calls and swarming sounds.

Multiple voices are reduced to a solo voice having echo effects. In the background there are rattling sounds. Then a solo voice sings against a background of silence. Soon the rattling sounds reoccur. Throughout the remainder of this long section, listen for thumping sounds that resemble low drums playing an almost recognizable tune. A chorus fades in and out and there are patches of speech. The section ends quietly.

Silence

Voices are heard far in the distance behind a solo voice and a very animated electronic accompaniment.

Silence

A low hum gradually swells and builds to a chorus of humming voices.

Silence

A quick, jerky flourish ends the piece without warning.

Chance Music

The composer of chance music gives up most of the control over the performance of the piece.

The composer who seeks absolute control over all aspects of his or her composition is at the opposite end of the aesthetic pole from the composer of **chance,** or **aleatory, music.** The composer of chance music willfully abdicates some or most of the control over what happens in a given composition. For example, instead of indicating specific notes, rhythms, or dynamics to the performers of the piece, the composer might say to them, "Here are some notes and rhythms. Please play them in any order, at any speed, but play them all very, very softly." Thus the composer's work is part composition in the usual sense of the word, and it is part suggestion. When the performers follow the specific directions and the nebulous suggestions, they create a piece of music that happens by chance. The chances are that the piece will never be the same in any subsequent performances. For the composer, the performers, and perhaps even the audience, this is the desired situation.

A piece of chance music will never sound exactly the same at any two performances.

Some composers of chance music have resorted to completely random processes for selecting the materials included in their compositions. The composer collects numbers, forms, and other kinds of information from rolling dice, flipping cards, or throwing darts at tables of numbers. The gathered information then suggests to the composer chords, rhythms, instrumentation, and other elements of the composition.

There are, though, degrees of chance. Some composers use chance in a restricted way, reserving chance for only certain portions of a given composition. Others try to build into the composition as much chance as is possible without a chaotic result.

Some people who are active in the field of chance music state that there is no purpose in this type of music. Others attempt an explanation of chance music in philosophical terms, or in vague terms about freeing music from the shackles that have imprisoned it for centuries. Exactly how it is being freed, and precisely how music will improve with this "freedom" are questions that have not yet been adequately answered.

Composers of chance music differ over the philosophy behind it.

But to give chance or aleatory music its due, it should be said that there are composers in the movement who are honestly and skillfully exploring the outer limits of music. Some venture beyond these limits and into a realm beyond music as we know it, but may find they have to retrace their steps. It is also possible that these explorers may succeed in expanding the limits of music as it now exists.

Many composers of chance music are experimenting beyond the realm of music as we know it.

Cage   The spiritual leader of chance music is John Cage (b. 1912), who first legitimized the use of chance operations in musical composition. In 1951 he wrote (or designed) a piece called *Imaginary Landscape no. 4*. The work requires twenty-four performers and twelve radios; for each radio, one performer rotates the station dial and another performer operates the volume dial. All performers read from written parts and are directed by a conductor.

Obviously *Imaginary Landscape no. 4* can never sound the same twice. The content of the piece is determined by which radio stations are picked up by the twelve different radios during the performance of the piece. The time of day and the geographical location also affect the content. At any performance no one, including Cage himself, can determine the final outcome.

The outcome of a chance music performance can not be predicted.

Four years later, in 1954, Cage "composed" a piece called *4' 33''*. In this piece a person with a watch sits at a piano playing nothing at all for four minutes and thirty-three seconds. The noises of the audience as well as all other audible sounds during the performance are the sound material of the piece. Clearly, it is impossible for *4' 33''* to sound the same way twice.

(To my knowledge there are no recordings of these pieces. In fact, recording a piece that is supposed to be different each time it is performed would be pointless and would counter the philosophy on which it rests.)

Other works by Cage use chance operations, but in a more restricted sense. Among the most elaborate of these is *HPSCHD* (1971), which he wrote with Lejaren Hiller, a composer who specializes in computer-generated music. *HPSCHD* consists of fifty-one electronic sound tapes, seven solo compositions for harpsichords, and elaborate slide shows and other visuals. Unlike *4' 33''*, recordings of *HPSCHD* are available. Music is thus blended with visual images to create what has come to be known as a mixed media event or "happening."

Some composers have become involved in **theater music** by enlarging the sound resources of conventional instruments and voices while at the same time exploiting the visual or "theatrical" aspects of live performances. Beginning in the 1960s, composers sometimes required the unorthodox of their performers: a trombonist was asked to take the instrument apart and play on only a part of it; an oboist was required to gently stroke the instrument with a felt mallet; a flutist was instructed to run the fingers rapidly over the keys without blowing into the instrument; a singer was asked to gurgle and scream instead of sing; a pianist was required to manually strum the strings of the piano. As early as the mid-1940s John Cage wrote music for prepared piano, which is a piano having bits of metal, glass, rubber, plastic, or other articles placed in its strings. At its worst the prepared piano is cheap and gimmicky, but when prepared and performed with taste and skill, the instrument can offer a thrilling array of new sounds. Cage's *Concerto for Prepared Piano and Orchestra* (1951) reveals the prepared piano at its most beautiful.

Minimalism

As its name suggests, **minimalist** music, in its purest form, is created from a limited fund of materials: simple, diatonic melodies; ostinatos; uncomplicated and static harmonies; and drones (long sustained notes). It is music that focuses on sounds per se and is concerned with what sounds are (in terms of tone color) rather than what they do (in a functional sense). Typically, melodic motives and repetitive rhythmic figures change slowly, almost imperceptibly, in the course of a piece of minimalist music. Steve Reich (b. 1936), one of the foremost minimalist composers, has exhibited a fascination with "phasing," a process in which several performers begin playing the same melodic-rhythmic pattern together and then gradually fall out of phase with one another as, one by

Cage's compositions are innovations in the field of music.

Composers of theatrical music often asked the unorthodox of their performers.

Prepared piano can offer an exciting new array of sounds.

Minimalist music focuses on the tone color of sounds instead of their function.

one, the voices speed ahead or fall behind the others. His *Come Out* (1966) is exemplary of this process (though the work is made from one speaking voice which engages in phasing through a series of tape loops).

Terry Riley's (b. 1935) *In C* (1964), a ninety-minute work (minimalist works tend to be quite protracted), is prototypical of the style. In its slow, deliberate, repetitive way it is almost trance-like and has an affinity with certain kinds of electronic rock music from the 1970s and 1980s.

Philip Glass (b. 1937), like most minimalists, performs with his own group and is thus a composer-performer of his own music. The opera *Einstein on the Beach* (1975) is exemplary of Glass's engaging and hypnotic minimalist style. It consists of four acts and five connecting "Knee Plays." There are three recurring themes and images: Trains, Trials, and Spaceship. An excerpt from Train One (act one) will introduce you to the nature of minimalist music.

Sound and Sense ♪
Minimalist Music

Title: Einstein on the Beach *(1975) (excerpt from Train One)*
Composer: Philip Glass

A Closer Look

The performing forces include flute, soprano and alto saxes, electric organ and other keyboards, solo voice, and small chorus. Train One begins with a brief repetitive figure played by the saxes; the saxes are then joined by other members of the ensemble that introduce further repetitive figures. The character and length of these figures begin to change periodically and almost imperceptibly.

A danger in grouping these composers under a single stylistic label is that one might assume that their music all sounds alike—and it does not. While they all partake of some of the same ideas and procedures, each has a distinctly personal style.

In addition, there are other composers who are not usually thought of as minimalists but who, from time to time, employ certain minimalist techniques. Morton Feldman (1926–87) shared the minimalist's fascination with sound and tone color, and much of his music, oddly enough, is directed to be played at a low volume, which forces the listener to listen very carefully. Varèse's *Ionisation* (see chapter 2) celebrates the tone colors of percussion instruments and focuses our attention on them rather than on melody and harmony. ♪

Each minimalist composer had a unique style.

Adaptions and Expansions

Many contemporary composers have found that their musical needs are best served by following paths blazed by composers from earlier in this century, regardless of the type of music—tonal, atonal, serial, or experimental. Today, these men and women are successfully adapting and expanding upon the music of their predecessors. Much of the music of Stravinsky, Bartók, Ives, Schönberg, and others, which was once so controversial, has come to be regarded as traditional. Some has even been assured a permanent place in the repertoire of Western art music. These early twentieth-century traditions, and those from several other eras, are a dominant force in the art music scene today.

A reader should not conclude, however, that the composers discussed under this heading are somehow lacking in originality. Rather, each of them used a particular style or process as a point of departure and adapted or expanded the tradition to create a fresh, personal style.

A wealth of art music has been created across the globe by composers in the later decades of the twentieth century. Though it is impossible to include all the important names and works in this chapter, a selective overview can acquaint us with some of them and can help us appreciate the marvelous diversity of music in our time.

Some composers found their musical voices in terms of tonality or expanded versions of tonality. The great representative of British music in this time frame was Benjamin Britten (1913–76) who, in works such as *Serenade for Horn, Tenor, and Strings* and *A Ceremony of Carols,* combined a somewhat dissonant tonality with memorable vocal lines and the distinct flavor of nationalism. The German Paul Hindemith (1895–1963) devised his own form of expanded tonality and combined it with intricate counterpoint, reminiscent of earlier German master contrapuntists such as J. S. Bach. Gian Carlo Menotti (b. 1911) also remained within the realm of tonality as evidenced by his several popular operas, including the immensely successful *Amahl and the Night Visitors.* In a real sense Menotti is the modern extension of the Italian opera tradition, the successor to Verdi and Puccini. Manuel de Falla (1876–1946) infused his essentially tonal style with the sounds and rhythms of his native Spain. Heitor Villa-Lobos (1887–1959), somewhat more daring harmonically, did the same for his Brazilian heritage. William Grant Still (1895–1978) blended his tonal style with the sounds of the black American blues and jazz—especially in his *Afro-American Symphony* (1933).

Many composers born in the 1920s and 1930s began their careers as serialists. Some, like Luciano Berio (b. 1925) and George Crumb (b. 1929) moved in other directions, however. Berio's *Circles* (1962) incorporates some elements of chance and theater; the singer, accompanied by harp and a battery of percussion instruments, moves about the stage and is called upon to produce vocal sounds not normally associated with traditional singing. In works such as *Ancient Voices of Children*

Composers often "borrow" a previous style or type of music and use it as a point of departure to create a new sound.

Tonality was embraced by a number of influential composers.

Other composers successfully blended music of their native lands into their compositions.

Serialism, chance music, theater music, symbolism, and mysticism have all played a role in the music of the 1920s and 1930s.

(1970) Crumb creates some of the same atmosphere, but with a mystical and symbolistic bent.

The mystic and the exotic are nowhere more forcefully set forth than in some of the works of Oliver Messiaen (b. 1908). In *Couleurs de la cité céleste* (*Colors of the Celestial City,* 1963), he combines quotations from Gregorian chants (see chapter 10), rhythms derived from classical Indian music, bird calls, and his own set of "modes."

Many regard Elliott Carter (b. 1908) as the true successor to Charles Ives and among the greatest American composers of this century. At various times he studied briefly with several different teachers, including Nadia Boulanger in Paris, but he is essentially self-taught. His music is outside the sphere of tonality and at times is quite dissonant, but beyond that his music is difficult to describe and account for. He belongs to none of the schools or spheres of influence outlined in this chapter; his is a musical style unto itself. Like some of the music of Charles Ives, Carter's textures are often dense and multilayered, and yet each part emerges from the texture with marvelous clarity. Each part also has a "personality" much like a character in a drama. This is similar to the layers of texture—woodwinds, strings, and solo trumpet—in Ives's *The Unanswered Question.*

Carter, with his unique style, is considered the successor of Ives and a great American composer.

Carter's fascination with rhythm led him to develop a procedure known as **metrical modulation**—a precise and systematic transition from one metrical speed to another rather than an abrupt change of tempo. His Cello Sonata (1948) was the first piece to employ this procedure, and it is used in many of his large-scale works after 1948: Piano Concerto (1963–65); Three String Quartets (1951, 1960, 1971); and the Sonata for Flute, Oboe, Cello, and Harpsichord (1952–53).

Metrical modulation offers an alternative to an abrupt change of tempo.

Summary

From the beginning of the seventeenth century until the twentieth century, functional harmony was the musical constant unifying the compositions of the baroque, classical, and romantic eras. Some twentieth-century composers, however, abandoned tonality in favor of experimentation with other musical possibilities. The result was expressionism, the twelve-tone system, electronic music, and chance music. Other composers remained faithful to functional harmony while expressing themselves through impressionism, polytonality, and neoclassicism. Students of twentieth-century art music have concluded that the century has produced no one fundamental, stylistic unity, but instead has offered a basic and perplexing diversity.

At the turn of the century, the impressionist movement was dominant in both art and music. Painters such as Monet, Renoir, and Degas created art with the purpose of reproducing a mood rather than an image. Debussy's impressionist music offered undefined illusion as in "Nuages."

Early in the twentieth century, symbolism focused on the beauty of words. Symbolist poets wrote of mystery, eroticism, danger, and fear. Debussy set some of this poetry to music. "La Flute de Pan" is an example. Schools of music did not grow up around these two movements, but Debussy reflected their philosophies in his music and influenced other twentieth-century composers through his harmonic practices and his orchestration.

Expressionism was a direct statement about the decline of European civilization in the early decades of the twentieth century. Literary men and women, painters and musicians, used their media to express repulsion at the state of human existence. The atonal music of expressionism was born in Austria at the hands of Schönberg. Atonal music, fueled by dissonance and emotionalism, is exemplified by Schönberg's *Pierrot Lunaire* and Berg's *Wozzeck*.

Many of Stravinsky's works are masterpieces of twentieth-century music. Typical of his early pieces is the ballet *Petrushka* scored for a large orchestra and based upon Russian folklore. *Petrushka* features bitonality and polytonality—both within the functional harmony system.

Bela Bartók, like Stravinsky, utilized folk themes and melodies. Counterpoint is central to Bartók's music, but he also features compact themes, unique rhythms, unusual accent patterns, and ingenious structures. His *Music for Strings, Percussion and Celesta* is a complex piece featuring the percussion family.

American composer Charles Ives experimented in both tonal and atonal music. He, like Bartók and Stravinsky, focused on native folk tunes, but his use of the tunes is unique. The inclusion of folk music and popular songs and hymns is central to his compositions.

The music and movements that emerged between the wars were diverse. The twenties witnessed the development of artistic activity in reaction to the horror and destruction that had just engulfed the world. Dadaism presented a nihilistic view of life while futurism preached violence and anarchy. Many of Erik Satie's works represent dadaism in music through simple consonance and banality. Satie's influence is seen in the experimental compositions of Milhaud, Poulenc, and Honegger.

The inclination of Stravinsky, Prokofiev, and other composers of the twenties was to turn to the past for inspiration. In their compositions, neoclassicism flourished, rich with concertos and symphonies. This music actually combined characteristics of the classical and the baroque eras, as in Stravinsky's *Octet*.

It was between the wars that some American composers gained recognition. Copland, Barber, Piston, Sessions, and Thomson—all children of the twentieth century—created a distinctly American art music. Copland in particular featured American folk music and American themes in his works.

At the same time, a musical revolution occurred in Europe with the introduction in 1925 of Schönberg's twelve-tone system. Composers who preferred atonal music were given a means of systematic organization of pitches. No longer would atonal pieces be the work of a few expressionist composers. The tone row is the building block of the twelve-tone system, and forty-four variations of each row are possible. Schönberg's student, Webern, expanded this system and created a collection of serial music.

Post-World War II composers have experimented with the twelve-tone system, serial music, and unique methods of creating sound from traditional instruments, such as the prepared piano. Electronic music has moved to the forefront in the past decades, offering an infinite number of durational values and rhythmic complexities.

An appreciation for chance music has also arisen since World War II. The composer suggests musical activities that can never be duplicated in any two performances. The field of chance music offers a realm of future exploration.

In more recent times the synthesizer has become an important musical resource. Musical styles as diverse as those of Milton Babbitt (with its enormous complexity) and the minimalism of Philip Glass employ the instrument. Synthesizers have also become a part of the rock music scene and have been used in the making of background music for movies and television programs.

Key Terms

impressionism

symbolism

expressionism

Sprechtstimme

atonal

bitonality

polytonality

glissandos

dadaism

Les Six

neoclassicism

twelve-tone system

tone row

inversion

retrograde

retrograde
 inversion

serial music

musique concrète

electronic music

synthesizer

chance (aleatory)
 music

theater music

minimalist music

metrical
 modulation

Thinking About It

Several different musical/aesthetic "isms" have been discussed in this chapter. What are some basic differences between them? For example, how are the goals and achievements of impressionism different from those of expressionism? From neoclassicism? From dadaism? Which specific pieces of music support your answers?

Compile a list of twentieth-century works that are either tonal or have a close relationship with tonality. Construct a second list of works that are clearly not tonal.

CHAPTER

10

Music
in
the
Middle
Ages

Gothic architecture, West Portals Cathedral, Reims
Print and Picture Dept., Free Library of Philadelphia

Sounds of the Chapter

Machaut
Je puis trop bien
Ma fin est ma commencement
Messe de Notre Dame
S' il estoit nulz

Victimae paschali laudes

Historians have called the
period from the dawn of
Christianity to about 1450 the
Middle Ages.

The period comes between
classical antiquity and the
Renaissance.

The church of the Middle
Ages was the center of
intellectual activity.

The vast majority of people
were illiterate.

In A.D. 312, Emperor
Constantine legitimized
Christianity.

The Roman Catholic liturgy
included texts, chants, and
ceremony.

The Middle Ages, or medieval era, is a label applied to the period from the dawn of Christianity to about 1450. This long period of time has been further subdivided by historians into the "Dark Ages" (the first eight centuries A.D.), the "Age of Charlemagne" (ninth and tenth centuries), the "Gothic Age" (twelfth and thirteenth centuries), and the "Ars Nova" (fourteenth century). All of this vast expanse of time is called the Middle Ages.

But what was it in the middle of? The label "Middle Ages" suggests that it was somehow a less cultivated period than those that preceded (the Graeco-Roman classical period) and followed (the Renaissance). The term further implies that during the Middle Ages, Western civilization either stood still or marked time—a mere valley between the mountaintops of classical antiquity and the Renaissance.

In certain respects the early Middle Ages was a "dark" era. Warfare, barbarous invasions, devastated economic and political systems, and the appalling decline in learning and scholarship nearly extinguished the light of civilization. Nearly, but not quite.

The church of the Middle Ages was the center of scholarship, not just for ecclesiastical matters, but in all fields of knowledge. Most of what is known about life in the Middle Ages has been preserved for us in handwritten manuscripts that were painstakingly prepared by monks and other clergy. Printing was unknown; and books would have been useless except to the literate minority.

Nearly all music up to the twelfth century (of which we have documentation) was sacred music. Musicians of the early Middle Ages undoubtedly composed secular music also, but there are no manuscripts that confirm its existence. Since the church was the center of literacy and learning, it was the only institution in a position to record (write down) music, musical practices, and theory. Naturally, the clergy recorded only those elements that applied to sacred music.

The Formation of the Gregorian Chant

In A.D. 312 Emperor Constantine, who had recently converted to Christianity, issued the Edict of Toleration, legalizing the Christian religion. Since Christianity was no longer an underground movement, its membership and influence grew quickly over a large geographical area.

At about this time the Christian church in Rome—the Roman Catholic church—began to organize its worship services. These services included texts (both scriptural and nonscriptural), melodies called **chants,** and various ceremonies that were sanctioned for use in the church. Broadly speaking, all of this was called the **liturgy** of the church, and each sanctioned text, chant, and ceremony was called a **liturgical item.**

In the fourth, fifth, and sixth centuries, the number of these liturgical items grew rapidly. Eventually the number of liturgical items exceeded practicality; there were hundreds or perhaps thousands of designated chants, for example.

Popes and other high officials in the Roman Catholic church decided that a more uniform set of beliefs and practices was needed, and this required a massive reduction and codification of the liturgy. This was accomplished during the papacy of Gregory I, who served from 590–604. In gratitude for his enormous contribution, the melodies of the Roman church have since that time been called **Gregorian chants.** Let us first examine the nature of this music and then see how it was used in the various services of the Roman Catholic church.

Pope Gregory I codified the liturgical items.

The Nature of the Gregorian Chant

The Gregorian chants were entirely monophonic (one line melodies), and were always associated with a text. Church leaders believed that the text was somehow more memorable and meaningful when sung rather than merely spoken.

Gregorian chants are monophonic and associated with a text.

There are two basic kinds of Gregorian melodies. The first is **static,** with many repeated notes and few melodic leaps (see fig. 10.1). The other type of Gregorian melody is similar to our contemporary ideas of melody. Notice in figure 10.2 that the melody has more of a shape and uses several kinds of melodic intervals.

Gregorian melodies typically are restricted to a fairly narrow range; many are contained within an octave. They usually proceed by half steps and whole steps, with some larger melodic intervals.

Scholars are still not sure exactly how these melodies operated rhythmically. However, they probably were not metrical according to our understanding of meters. The pitches of the melodies may have been sung in even-note values, they may have been sung in groups of twos and threes, or another method might have been used. Today these melodies are usually notated as even-note values without stems, but manuscripts show that a very different kind of notation was used in the Middle Ages. Figure 10.3 shows a page from an eleventh-century manuscript. The figures above the text are the notation of the melody.

Gregorian melodies were not metrical.

Today, we notate Gregorian melodies as even-note values without stems.

Church Modes   Since the mid-seventeenth century the Western world has organized its music according to tonality—music is in a key and in either the major or minor mode. Music in the Middle Ages and the Renaissance, however, was organized somewhat differently: it was modal rather than tonal. In this context, **mode** does not mean simply being in the major or minor mode. Modal music is not in a key but is in one or

Music from the Middle Ages is in a church mode rather than in a key.

Figure 10.1

Figure 10.2

another of the church modes. This modal music sounds somewhat different; it seems to lack a sense of progression and direction that emerges from melodies that are in a key. But, as noted earlier, modal scales are employed in much of today's rock music and jazz.

Each of the eight church modes used in the Middle Ages has a different interval structure, and each has a Greek name—Dorian mode, Phrygian mode, Lydian mode, Mixolydian mode, and so on. In its purest form each mode has only seven different pitches. One of these is called the **finalis,** the pitch on which the melody usually ends, which is similar to the tonic pitch in tonal music. Another common pitch in modal music is called the **reciting tone,** which is similar to the dominant pitch in tonal music.

In summary, Gregorian music is vocal, monophonic, modal, limited in range, and moves in a freely flowing rhythm.

In the church modes the finalis is similar to our modern tonic pitch, while the reciting tone acts as does our dominant pitch.

The Integration of the Gregorian Chant with the Mass

During the first several hundred years of its existence the church developed two major types of worship: the Mass and the Canonical or Office Hours. Here we will examine the Mass.

The **Mass** was a worship service celebrated by priests, bishops and other clergy. Bishops often presided at the Mass in a cathedral, while a priest celebrated Mass for the common people in a parish or neighborhood church. The Mass in the smaller parish church was much less elaborate than those in the cathedral, and so it had much less music. Eventually, the cathedrals were opened to congregations, thus exposing more to the music performed there. Since the Gregorian chant in itself comprised the whole of church music in the Middle Ages, it would be difficult to exaggerate its importance at that time.

Masses celebrated in cathedrals included more music than those offered in parish churches.

Ordinary and Proper   Today the Mass consists of elements that were gradually incorporated over a period of about 1,000 years. The individual parts of the Mass belong to one of two categories: the **Ordinary** or the **Proper.** The Ordinary, as these parts are called collectively, are

The Mass comprises two types of text—the Ordinary (which does not change) and the Proper (which varies according to the church calendar).

Figure 10.3
Music manuscript from the
late Middle Ages.
© The Bettmann Archive

chanted or spoken at every Mass and their texts never change. For example, the first Ordinary, the Kyrie, is heard near the beginning of every Mass. The Kyrie is recited, and its text is always:

Kyrie eleison (Lord have mercy)
Christe eleison (Christ have mercy)
Kyrie eleison (Lord have mercy)

A Proper item, on the other hand, is so called because its text is appropriately or properly performed only at a specific time of the church year, or on one specific day of the year. For example, certain Proper texts are appropriate only during the Easter or the Christmas season. Text or prayers in honor of a given saint are proper to and read only on that saint's day.

Today the five major Ordinary items of the Mass are, in order: the Kyrie, Gloria, Credo, Sanctus, and Agnus Dei. Interspersed within the Ordinary are a number of Proper items. The outline below lists most of the items of the Roman Catholic Mass as it was structured around A.D. 1000. Only those items in lowercase letters were spoken. All other items were sung by the priests or the choir. Notice how important music was in the Mass.

Elements from both the Ordinary and the Proper were set to music.

The Order of the Mass

Ringing of the bells to welcome the priest(s)	
INTROIT (entrance music for the priest[s])	Proper
KYRIE ELEISON	Ordinary
GLORIA (Glory to God in the highest . . .)	Ordinary
Collect (a reading of various prayers)	Proper
A reading from the Bible	Proper
ALLELUIA	Proper
SEQUENCE (only used at certain times of year)	Proper
A reading from the Gospel	Proper
Homily (Sermon. Frequently omitted, but when included it was an amplification of the Biblical readings of the day.)	
CREDO (We believe in one God . . .)	Ordinary
OFFERTORY (the collection of the offering)	Proper
Prayers over the Eucharist (the bread and wine)	Proper
SANCTUS (Holy, Holy, Holy, Lord . . .)	Ordinary
Other special prayers and sayings	Ordinary
Pater Noster (Our Father)	Ordinary
AGNUS DEI (Lamb of God)	Ordinary
Eucharist (Distribution of communion)	Proper
Other closing prayers	
ITE MISSA EST (the Mass is ended, go in peace)	Ordinary

The Gregorian chant (with translation below) in figure 10.4 dates from about the year 1000. It is a **sequence**—a liturgical chant proper to the Easter season—and is called *Victimae paschali laudes* (let Christians dedicate their praises to the Easter victim). *Victimae paschali laudes* is one of the most famous and among the most beautiful Gregorian chants. The order of the Mass list indicates where the sequence appeared in the Mass. (There are several recordings of the chant, including the one in the *Norton Anthology of Western Music* (album I, side 2, band 1).

The sequence Victimae paschali laudes is a beautiful example of Gregorian chant.

Figure 10.4

Copyright 1946, 1949 by the President and
Fellows of Harvard College, © renewed 1974,
1977 by Alice D. Humez and Willi Apel.

Let Christians dedicate their praises to the Easter victim.
The lamb has redeemed the sheep; the innocent Christ has reconciled the
    sinners with the Father.
Death and life have fought in wondrous conflict; after death the leader of life,
    living reigns.
Tell us oh, Mary what thou sawest upon the way?
I have seen the sepulchre of the living Christ, and the glory of the rising Christ.
The angelic witnesses, the veil and the garments.
Christ, my hope, has arisen, he goes before his own into Galilee.
We know in truth that Christ has arisen from the dead: be merciful unto us, O
    victorious king: Amen.

The Beginnings of Harmony

Manuscripts from the ninth century provide the earliest documentation
of harmony. These manuscripts describe a two-part harmony called **organum,** which consists of a melody in the lower voice and a duplication
of this melody in the upper voice, usually a perfect fifth above the lower
line. The two parts generally move parallel to one another.

     Historians believe that the anonymous authors of these manu-
scripts did not invent harmony, but rather they described an existing
musical practice.

The earliest documentation of
harmony—organum, or two-
part harmony—comes from
the ninth century.

Figure 10.5

The invention of harmony is one of the most significant developments in the entire history of music. It created a cataclysmic change in the nature of Western music. From its crude beginnings in the Middle Ages, harmony developed, was ordered in different ways, and has dominated Western music.

Figure 10.5 shows an example of this earliest form of harmony—organum—moving in parallel, note against note in both voices.

Harmony changed the nature of Western music.

The Emergence of Polyphony

Gradually, composers drifted from the dogged parallelism of early organum and developed a freer, more fluid type of harmony. Other kinds of intervals were used, and the two parts of the texture began to move at different speeds, rather than in a note-for-note fashion.

By the twelfth century, organum had expanded into three parts: the lowest part called **tenor** (meaning "held," not to be confused with the male voice classification called tenor); a voice above this called **duplum;** and a higher voice called **triplum.** The music was still modal but was now polyphonic rather than monophonic.

Lengthy compositions from the twelfth century exist and, in some cases, the names of the composers are known. Prior to this era, composers rarely signed their compositions, so nearly all earlier music is anonymous. But in the Gothic era—the twelfth and thirteenth centuries—there is evidence of a gradual secularization, a new awareness that the artistic and creative powers of humans were a source of pride. This sense of self-recognition increased until the Renaissance, in the fifteenth century, when it flourished.

As secular music emerged, composers gained recognition for their pieces and began signing them.

A highly regarded school of polyphonic composition was based at the cathedral of Notre Dame in Paris, where composers such as Léonin and later Pérotin greatly expanded the horizons of harmony. With their contemporaries, they composed a great body of sacred polyphonic music, including a durable and expressive form called the **motet,** the foremost genre of the thirteenth century.

The typical thirteenth-century motet had three voices, with the lowest voice usually holding longer note values than the upper two. The upper two voices, consequently, seemed to be moving faster than the lowest voice. Oddly, each voice sang a different text, and it was not unusual for the tenor to have a Latin text while the upper voices had two different French texts. The thirteenth-century motet illustrated in figure 10.6 reveals its polytextual and bilingual features, and a recording of it is found in *Masterpieces of Music Before 1750* (vol. 1, side 1, band 10).

The thirteenth-century motet featured three voices, each singing a different text.

Figure 10.6

[continued]

Figure 10.6
Continued

The stable, consonant intervals of this harmonic language were the octave, the perfect fifth, and the perfect fourth. Other intervals, such as thirds and sixths, were perceived as dissonances that required resolution. (In the tonal system familiar to us, however, the thirds and sixths are consonants.) If this motet's harmony sounds archaic, it is because of the presence of so many octaves, fifths, and fourths. Although they may not sound dissonant, they do seem rather incomplete.

Consonant intervals were considered to be the octave, the perfect fifth, and the perfect fourth.

The Ars Nova: Period of Change

War ravaged France and England throughout the fourteenth century. An economic depression developed early in the century, severely affecting the middle and lower classes with wartime taxes and the loss of lives. Riots and revolts against authority became almost commonplace.

Moreover, the Roman Catholic church, for centuries the undisputed authority in both religious and civil dealings, was in jeopardy. The French popes refused to move to Rome, the traditional seat of the papacy, and began to reside at Avignon instead. Toward the end of the century the church was put in the ludicrous position of having to recognize two popes, one in Rome and one in Avignon.

Another factor that contributed to the turmoil in Europe was the bubonic plague. It spread from Italy to France, Spain, England, and elsewhere in the mid-fourteenth century. Some countries lost as much as one-third of the population to the horrors of the black death.

Universities, the arts, the church, and society in general survived the troubles of the fourteenth century, but all were profoundly affected. The stranglehold of the church was broken, and a more secular society was created. Indeed, this was the first truly secular era since the birth of Christianity.

One result of the secularism of the Ars Nova was the interest in honoring people of accomplishment. The notion of "the arts" and the "artist" as understood today were products of the turbulent fourteenth century. Prior to this the artist, who was viewed as a craftsman rather than as creator, was content to work anonymously. This work, whether musical, architectural, or other, was done for the glorification of God, not for the self-fulfillment of the craftsman. Broadly speaking, the people of the medieval era viewed themselves as sinful, wicked creatures, wholly unworthy of praise for their crude work.

However, this medieval attitude began to change in the Ars Nova, and by the dawn of the Renaissance, the conversion to the appreciation of art and artist was complete.

Music of the Ars Nova

A single-voice texture was the norm in the Dark Ages, while a two-voice texture was used during the Age of Charlemagne and into the Gothic era. In the Ars Nova, however, a three-voice texture became the norm. Often the lower voice, and sometimes the two lower voices in the texture, were played by various instruments, while the upper voice alone carried the text (similar to an instrumentally accompanied solo song).

Harmony began to change too. There was a definite shift to the full triad (root, third, and fifth) and a more liberal use of thirds and sixths as harmonic intervals. Though these were still considered dissonant, the fourteenth century audiences began to take delight in these

The term applied to the fourteenth century in France and England is Ars Nova.

Revolts against authority threw the Roman Catholic church into upheaval, while wars and plague severely diminished the European population.

The turbulent fourteenth century broke the dominance of the church and provided support for a secular society.

The concept of the artist as creator was born during Ars Nova.

During the span of the Middle Ages the one-, two-, and finally three-voice texture was developed.

Figure 10.7
Illuminated manuscript of the
fourteenth century.
© The Bettmann Archive

Church modes were altered by
chromatic pitches.

sounds. Many chromatic pitches were introduced, and the integrity of
the church modes began to erode. Music was still modal, but the use of
modality decreased until, by the seventeenth century, it was superseded
by tonality.

Rhythm became more flexible and complex, and a greater variety
of note values was introduced. Musical notation underwent dramatic
changes—an improvement over eleventh-century notation shown in figure
10.3. Figure 10.7 shows a page from a fourteenth-century manuscript.

Machaut

The most celebrated composer of the Ars Nova was the Frenchman Guillaume de Machaut (ca. 1300–1377). Machaut was a visible figure in the fourteenth century, not only as a composer of sacred and secular music, but also as a trouvère and priest. **Trouvères** were groups of scholar-musicians, many of whom were priests, some of them migrants, who wrote a considerable amount of poetry and accompanying music. Some of this secular music has been preserved in manuscript form. Fourteenth-century manuscripts from many parts of Europe contain works by Machaut, and he was held in such high regard that a drawing of his face appears in manuscripts along with his music. Clearly he was not anonymous; he was an honored and celebrated musician.

Machaut, a priest, a trouvère, and an Ars Nova composer, was celebrated in his own time.

Machaut is known for introducing some of the most advanced harmonic, rhythmic, and formal musical practices of the Ars Nova. His works exhibit most of the major musical trends of the time.

Nonimitative counterpoint was plentiful in the three-voice texture, but occasionally Machaut and other composers employed imitative counterpoint, which came to dominate music of the Renaissance.

Also characteristic of the Ars Nova were the manipulation of pitches and rhythms in patterns, and the fascination with musical and textual puzzles. This fascination is evident in the use of **isorhythm,** in which patterns of note values are repeated. Figure 10.8 shows (in modern notation) the isorhythmic tenor part from a three-voice motet by Machaut, *S' il estoit nulz.* The repetitions of the pattern of note values are set off by double-bar lines. A recording of the isorhythmic motet is available in the anthology *Historical Anthology of Music in Performance* (vol. 1, no. 44).

Isorhythm was a feature of some music from the Ars Nova.

Machaut displayed his interest in musical puzzles and his technical prowess in a work called *Ma fin est ma commencement (My End is My Beginning).* In this work, the upper voice of the texture is the exact retrograde of the middle voice, and the second half of the lowest part is the retrograde of its first half. Whether or not this is actually heard in the piece is unimportant. It is, however, the kind of masterful pitch manipulation in which a twentieth-century serialist composer would take pride. This work is available in *The History of Music in Sound* (vol. 3, side 1, band 5).

Messe de Notre Dame   The *Messe de Notre Dame* is Machaut's most important sacred work. It is the first polyphonic setting for the Ordinary of the Mass written by a single composer, and it sets the precedent for this type of composition in the Renaissance.

Machaut composed the first polyphonic setting for Mass Ordinary.

Figure 10.8

Trouvères' music featured fixed
forms such as the ballade.

Ballade   Despite Machaut's renown as a composer of sacred music, he
devoted more time to secular music. The trouvères developed a number
of fixed forms—specific poetic and musical structures. These fixed forms
developed, over the course of time, into rigid poetic-musical structures,
such as rondeau, ballade, and virelai—each with a prescribed number
of lines and sections.

For example, the **ballade** has the following poetic-musical structure:

Music	*A*	*A*	*B*
text	first verse	second verse	third verse

A good example of the ballade is found in *Historical Anthology
of Music* (vol. 1, no. 45); it is Machaut's *Je puis trop bien*. The translation follows:

(1) I can all too well compare my lady
     To the image which Pygmalion made.
(2) It was of ivory, so beautiful, without peer,
     That he loved it more than Jason did Medea.
(3) Out of his senses, he prayed to it unceasingly,
     But the image answered him not.
     Thus does she treat me who makes my heart melt,
     For I pray her ever, and she answers me not.

Notice as you listen that the music is the same for verses 1 and 2,
while the music for verse 3 is different.

Summary

In this chapter we considered the forces that shaped the Middle Ages. In this period the dominance of the Roman Catholic church tells the story. The majority of the European population was illiterate. Scholarship and intellectual activity was carried on by the clergy. It is in the church that we find the music and the composers.

After Emperor Constantine legitimized the practice of Christianity in A.D. 312, the Roman Catholic worship service, the liturgy, evolved. By the sixth century such a massive number of liturgical items had been created that Pope Gregory I called for their codification. Out of gratitude to him, church leaders named the chants of the church "Gregorian" chants.

A Gregorian chant was entirely monophonic and associated with a text. There were two forms: static and melodic. These melodies occurred within a narrow range. Church modes, rather than tonal keys, were the elements of organization.

Medieval composers created music for the elements of the Proper and the Ordinary of the Mass. These pieces were shared with the congregation. Our example was the sequence entitled, *Victimae paschali laudes,* an Easter-time Proper.

The invention of harmony in the ninth century caused a major change in Western music. A school of polyphonic composition was located at the Notre Dame cathedral in Paris. This school devised the motet, a three-voice piece with a narrow range of consonance that dominated music in the thirteenth century.

During the fourteenth century, the Ars Nova, the European world experienced a change in focus. Revolts against authority brought an end to the total dominance of the Catholic church and laid the foundation for a new secular society. It was at this time that composers were first viewed as creators motivated by self-fulfillment, rather than as craftsmen in the service of God.

The most celebrated composer of the Ars Nova was Machaut—a trouvère and priest. Machaut composed for the church and for the emerging secular society. He was part of the movement toward more modern forms of harmony and new standards of consonance and dissonance.

The flexible rhythms, the sophistication of musical notation and the emergence of nonimitative counterpoint in the fourteenth century lead us directly to our next discussion—the music and flavor of the Renaissance.

Key Terms

chant	reciting tone	duplum
liturgy	Mass	triplum
liturgical item	Ordinary	motet
Gregorian chant	Proper	trouvères
static	sequence	isorhythm
mode	organum	ballade
finalis	tenor	

Thinking About It

Reflect on the history of musical texture from the dawn of Christianity through the Ars Nova. How would you describe this history, and what sorts of musical examples would you use to illuminate the points you make?

Again, using the entire era of the Middle Ages, how would you summarize the issue of sacred versus secular?

11

Music
in
the
Renaissance

Madonna of the Rose Garden, Stefan Lochner.
Wallraf-Richartz Museum, Cologne, Germany

Sounds of the Chapter

Byrd
Christ Rising Again ♪

Farnaby
Loth to Depart

Gabrieli
Gloria in Excelsis Deo ♪

Gibbons
Pavane Lord Salisbury

Josquin des Prez
Ave Maria ♪
Mass: *Pange Lingua*

Luther
Ein' feste Burg ist unser Gott

Marenzio
S'io parto, i' moro ♪

Morley
Now Is the Month of Maying ♪

Palestrina
Mass: *Aeterna Christi munera*

Mass: *L'homme armé*

Nineteenth-century historians termed the fifteenth and sixteenth centuries the "Renaissance," a French term meaning rebirth.

Renaissance is a French word meaning rebirth, but is also widely used as a cultural and stylistic label for the fifteenth and sixteenth centuries. The label was applied by nineteenth-century historians who concluded that the fifteenth and sixteenth centuries, like classical antiquity, was a peak period of great and noble accomplishments in Western civilization—a veritable mountaintop.

It may be true that these same historians perceived their own age, the nineteenth century, as a cultural and artistic mountaintop, and thus felt an affinity with the Renaissance. The people of the nineteenth century were probably more fully aware of the achievements of the Renaissance than those who actually experienced the Renaissance. Still, there can be little doubt that these people—especially the educated minority—knew that they were living in an extraordinary time, a time of intellectual and artistic magnificence, and that things were changing so dramatically that the world appeared new in many ways. The Renaissance was, after all, the age of Shakespeare, Botticelli, Da Vinci, Michelangelo, Raphael, Titian, Copernicus, Palestrina, and Columbus.

Those educated in the Renaissance were aware of the period's enormous intellectual and artistic accomplishments.

Humanism Reborn

A spirit of humanism was reborn.

If the age was really a renaissance, what was reborn? More than anything else a spirit, known as **humanism,** was reborn in the Western world. The main thrust of the humanistic movement was humanity's pride in itself. This spirit had largely been absent since the collapse of the Graeco-Roman classical civilization. Humanism allowed humankind to celebrate the great thinkers, artists, scientists, and explorers of the period without losing their religious moorings.

In many respects the Renaissance was a secularized era, especially when compared to the God-centered Middle Ages. Still, the abundance of sacred music, religious painting, and the Protestant Reformation dispel the idea that the people of the Renaissance turned their backs on God. However, the so-called Renaissance man—one knowledgeable in many fields—was not submissive, viewing himself as a mere creature. On the contrary, he was a self-confident person who took great pride in his ability to think, reason, and create. This was a positive atmosphere for creative artists and thinkers. Moreover, the presence of an adventuresome spirit in the Renaissance made it possible for humankind to discover literally a "new world."

Though the church was not abandoned during this period, the Renaissance man valued thought, reason, and creativity.

The invention of printing caused a revolution in the world of communication.

The invention of printing in the fifteenth century opened up another kind of world. Printed material was much less expensive than handwritten manuscripts, which resulted in the wide dissemination of all kinds of learning and information. The printed page that is taken for granted today was new in the Renaissance, and can be credited with a dramatic increase in learning and the exchange of information.

General Characteristics of Renaissance Music

Harmony

Music in the Renaissance was still governed by modality rather than tonality, but there was an increased interest in the expressive power of chords. Whereas harmony in the Middle Ages was for the most part an accident of the horizontal lines of the texture sounding simultaneously, harmony in the Renaissance was a conscious attempt to focus on the sheer beauty and emotional force of vertical sonorities (chords).

Counterpoint

Despite the increased interest in vertical sonorities, Renaissance composers were the consummate masters of imitative counterpoint. The duality of beautiful harmony and ingenious counterpoint is a hallmark of Renaissance music.

Texture

The standard four-voice texture of the era was similar to modern four-part choral texture: soprano, alto, tenor, and bass. There are many examples of textures with more and fewer than four parts, but the four-part choral texture became a norm in the Renaissance.

Rhythm

Renaissance rhythm resembles the modern concept of meter, though in some ways the rhythm of Renaissance music seems more pliant and supple. Perhaps this is due to fewer heavy downbeats and strong accents in Renaissance music.

Sacred Music

In the Renaissance it also became necessary to make a distinction between two types of music based on religious affiliation: Protestant and Catholic music.

Music of the Protestant Reformation

Most widespread religious movements, early in their history, develop a body of music that is used as an adjunct to worship. As we have seen, this was true of the Roman Catholic church at the dawn of the Christian era, when the Gregorian chant was developed for this purpose. The Protestant sects that emerged from the Reformation followed this pattern,

Renaissance composers integrated into their works harmony, imitative counterpoint, the four-voice texture, and rhythm that seems to us quite modern.

Sacred music of the Renaissance is either Catholic or Protestant.

The Protestant denominations that emerged from the Reformation created music for their worship services.

too. Various Protestant denominations in the Renaissance—Lutheran, Calvinistic, and Anglican—each produced distinctive musical genres: chorales, metrical psalms, and anthems. Let us now take a closer look at these types of sacred music.

Lutheranism

The Lutheran worship service that developed closely resembled the Catholic Mass, and many parts were sung. As a result, a body of texts and melodies, called **chorales,** was assembled. The texts of some of these chorales were Biblical, but many were newly composed religious verses written in German, rather than the Catholic Latin.

Chorales (text and melody) were written for Lutheran services.

The chorale melodies came from various sources. Some melodies were borrowed from the fund of Gregorian chant. Martin Luther was a priest in the Roman Catholic church prior to the Reformation, so it was quite natural that he used some familiar music for the Lutheran church. Other chorale melodies were appropriated from secular sources, while still others were newly composed by Martin Luther (who was also a trained musician) and by several of his churchmen.

Luther strongly encouraged lay involvement in church music.

Monophonic chorales were well-suited for congregational singing.

Through the Middle Ages and Renaissance, music in the Catholic church was performed more and more by priests and professional choirs of men and boys. The church congregation had little if any opportunity to participate in the performance of music. Martin Luther felt very strongly that the congregation, the lay people, should be actively involved in the new church's music. A simple music was necessary for this purpose since something as complex as a Renaissance motet would have been far beyond the musical capabilities of any congregation. But monophonic chorales were not beyond their means, and these chorales proved to be a powerful and personal means of worship. In time many of the Lutheran chorales were harmonized in four parts—soprano, alto, tenor, and bass—and resembled contemporary hymns.

A Mighty Fortress Is Our God, like many other German chorales, has an *AAB* form.

The most famous chorale is *Ein' feste Burg ist unser Gott (A Mighty Fortress Is Our God)*. This melody was composed by Luther himself. Recall that the text of this chorale was discussed in chapter 5 as the basis for a chorale cantata by J. S. Bach. The musical structure of *Ein' feste Burg* is simple: three long phrases with the shape *AAB*. Many German chorales have this form.

Calvinism

The Frenchman John Calvin was another very important figure in the Protestant Reformation of the early sixteenth century. While Martin Luther's doctrines led to the establishment of a single Protestant sect, Lutheranism, the doctrines and ideas of Calvin were disseminated to several Protestant sects, principally Presbyterianism.

Calvin was not trained in music and, unlike Luther, his interest in music as an adjunct to worship was limited. He believed that music should be simple and unemotional. Further, the only texts set to music should be scriptural texts, namely the 150 Psalms of David. The Psalms were translated from the original Hebrew into French, cast in poetic meters, and set to melodies. These are called **metrical psalms** or **psalmody.**

At the urging of some of his advisors, Calvin eventually relaxed his stance on music and allowed the previously monophonic metrical psalms to be composed for four-part harmony. Thus, both Lutheran and Presbyterian churches developed the practice of congregational singing.

Because Calvin's preference was for simple, unemotional music, psalmody was popularized by the Calvinist sects.

Anglicanism

The Anglican church or the Church of England also retained much of the service and ceremony of the Roman Catholic church, including the Mass. From a musical viewpoint, the most significant contribution of the Anglican church was the development of the **anthem.** The anthem was a choral work with an English text performed with or without accompaniment. Typically, the anthem was more complex than a simple four-part chorale, psalm, or hymn, and it was designed for a trained choir rather than for congregational singing. It was similar to the Catholic motet in both substance and function. Some anthems used a chorus and one or more soloists. An anthem that included a solo was called a **verse anthem.**

Anglican church anthems were choral works designed for trained choirs rather than congregational singing.

Verse anthems featured solo work.

William Byrd   England's greatest composer of the late Renaissance was William Byrd (1543–1623). Although Byrd, a Catholic, wrote a considerable amount of music for the Roman church, he ironically was the acknowledged master of the verse anthem that was composed for use in the Anglican church.

In Byrd's verse anthem, *Christ Rising Again,* two soprano soloists ♪ alternate with a full chorus, accompanied by a group of string instruments. The text and the layout of this verse anthem are listed below:

The Catholic William Byrd was the greatest composer of Anglican Renaissance music.

> *Soloists:* Christ rising again from the dead, now dieth not.
> *Choir and soloists:* Death from henceforth hath no power upon Him. For in that He died He died but once to put away sin.
> *Soloists:* But in that He liveth He liveth unto God.
> *Choir and soloists:* And so likewise count yourselves dead unto sin, but living unto God.
> *Soloists:* In Christ Jesus our Lord.
> *Choir and soloists:* In Christ Jesus our Lord.

Leda, by the Renaissance. master, Leonardo da Vinci.
Royal Library, Windsor Castle

Music of the Catholic Church

The Mass

The schism in the Catholic church was healed early in the fifteenth century, and at that time certain composers, particularly in the Netherlands, began to set the Ordinary of the Mass to music. This group of composers included Guillaume Dufay (ca. 1400–1474), Joannes Okeghem (ca. 1430–95), and the Englishman John Dunstable (ca. 1370–1453). Composers from all parts of Europe continued to expand and develop Mass composition in the fifteenth and sixteenth centuries, creating a vast repertoire of magnificent music for the Ordinary of the Mass.

One of the most important musical/technical advances of the Renaissance was the perfection of imitative counterpoint. This was balanced by the enrichment of chordal harmony, mentioned earlier. Thus, Renaissance music—especially the music written for the Mass—features textures rich with counterpoint and chordal homophony.

Renaissance liturgical music is rich with counterpoint and chordal harmony.

Many Masses from the Renaissance are based in part on some preexistent melody, all or part of which is usually found in each movement of the Mass. For example, a Mass entitled *L'homme armé (The Armed Man)* is one that had incorporated the popular melody of the same name. Many of the Renaissance composers used this particular melody as a structural building block in composing Masses. Early in the Renaissance Dufay borrowed from it, as did Okeghem. Later, Josquin des Prez used it, and, at the end of the Renaissance, Palestrina. However, *L'homme armé* was but one of many melodies that were used by various composers as building blocks for their mass compositions.

Many Renaissance Masses feature popular melodies as building blocks.

Palestrina's Mass *Aeterna Christi munera* is based on an old Gregorian melody of the same name. The "Sanctus" from this Mass adheres to the pitches of the old Gregorian melody while simultaneously incorporating Renaissance imitative counterpoint. The Latin text and the English translation appear below:

Gregorian melodies often appear in Renaissance Masses.

Sanctus, sanctus, sanctus,	Holy, holy, holy
Dominus Deus Sabaoth.	Lord God of hosts.
Pleni sunt coeli et terra gloria tua,	Heaven and earth are full of Thy glory;
Hosanna in excelsis.	Hosanna in the highest.

Notice that Palestrina has divided the Sanctus into four sections, reflecting the four lines of the text. There is a clear break between the first and second sections, but the other sections overlap. Each of the four sections begins with an individual motive which is then imitated in each of the other voices in the texture. For example, the first section, which is built on the words "Sanctus, sanctus, sanctus," starts with a rising motive in the sopranos. This motive is then imitated in the altos, then in the tenors, and a little later, in the basses. (Recorded in *History of Music in Sound,* vol. IV.)

Josquin des Prez

Josquin des Prez (ca. 1450–1521), known by contemporaries as "The Prince of Music," is generally regarded as the greatest composer of the Renaissance. His Mass *Pange Lingua* is one of his major works. The Gloria from this Mass exemplifies the full range of musical/technical processes that were perfected in Renaissance choral music.

Among the greatest Renaissance composers was Josquin des Prez.

Sound and Sense

Renaissance Choral Music

Title: "Gloria" from the Mass Pange Lingua
Composer: Josquin des Prez

A Closer Look

This movement has four-part imitation, along with sections in which Josquin separates the four parts into two pairs. In these pairs the alto line imitates the soprano's theme, while the basses imitate a different theme sung by the tenors. Thus, two pairs of voices simultaneously present and imitate two different themes—a complex process, but one that Josquin handles with apparent ease. There are also homophonic patches that contrast the heavily contrapuntal sections.

Josquin also varies the texture using one, two, three, or four voices. In this way the texture never becomes monotonous. On the contrary, it is complemented with variety.

Josquin's mastery is more fully appreciated by listening to this movement while studying the following outline. Notice that the piece is divided into several sections, each devoted to a portion of the text.

Text	Activity
Section I	
(Gloria in excelcis Deo)	(Four voices in imitative
Et in terra pax bonae volumtatis.	counterpoint. The voices enter as follows: tenor, bass, soprano, alto.)
Section II	
Laudamus te,	(Tenor and bass in imitation.)
Benedicimus te,	(Soprano and alto imitate each other. Bass and tenor imitate each other.)
Adoramus te,	(Tenor and bass imitate each other. Soprano and alto imitate each other.)
Glorificamus te,	(Soprano and alto imitate each other. Tenor and bass imitate each other.)
Gratius agimus tibi	(Soprano and tenor imitate each other. Alto and bass imitate each other.)

Propter magnam gloriam.   (Tenor and bass imitate each other.
                                       Soprano and alto imitate each
                                       other.)

Section III

Domine Deus, Rex coelistis, Deus   (Soprano and alto alone.)
  Pater omnipotens.
Domine Fili unigenite Jesu Christe.   (Bass and tenor in imitation.
  Domine Deus, Agnus Dei, Filius   Soprano and alto free, i.e., not in
  Patris   imitation.)

Section IV

Qui tollis peccata mundi,   (Four voices in imitative
                                       counterpoint, entering as follows:
                                       soprano, alto, tenor, bass.)

Miserere nobis.   (Four voices in chordal
                                       homophony.)

Qui tollis peccata mundi,   (Tenor and bass only in
                                       homophony.)

Suscipe deprecationem nostram.   (Four voices in chordal
                                       homophony.)

Section V

Qui sedes ad dextreram Patris,   (Soprano and tenor in imitation.)
Miserere nobis quoniam.   (Soprano and tenor, then soprano
                                       and alto.)

Section VI

Quoniam   (Tenor and bass alone.)
Tu solus sanctus.   (Four-voice imitation.)
Tu solus Dominus.
Tu solus Altimus,
Jesu Christe.

Section VII

Cum sancto spiritu in gloria   (Soprano and bass in imitation.
Dei Patris. Amen.   Tenor and alto in imitation.)

The English translation of the Gloria: (Glory to God in the highest) And
peace to His people on earth. We praise Thee, we bless Thee, we worship
Thee, we glorify Thee. We give thanks to Thee for Thy great glory. O, Lord
God, heavenly King, God the Father almighty. O, Lord, the only begotten son,
Jesus Christ. O, Lord God, Lamb of God who takes away the sins of the
world, have mercy on us. Thou who takes away the sins of the world, receive
our prayer. Thou that sittest at the right hand of the Father, have mercy on
us. For Thou alone art holy; Thou alone art the Lord. Thou only art most
high, Jesus Christ. With the Holy Spirit in the glory of God the Father.
Amen.

The Renaissance Motet

The motet, which became secularized in the late Middle Ages, was refashioned and reunited with the Catholic church in the Renaissance. In the hands of Josquin and many others, the **Renaissance motet** became a serious, large-scale work with a sacred Latin text. Many of the features of the Renaissance Mass are also found in the "classic" Renaissance motet: the sections of imitative counterpoint, the homophonic patches, and some diversity in texture. There are also many examples of Renaissance motets based on a borrowed preexisting melody.

> The Renaissance motet shows imitative counterpoint, homophonic patches, and diversified texture.

All of these features are found in Josquin's motet, *Ave Maria.* Follow the several sections of imitation by consulting the Sound and Sense when listening.

Sound and Sense ♪
Classic Renaissance Motet

Title: Ave Maria
Composer: Josquin des Prez

A Closer Look

Notice that in addition to these several sections there are three larger divisions of the work: the first part is in the equivalent of duple meter, the second in triple, and the third part returning to duple.

Duple Meter
    Section I: Ave Maria gratia pleve.
    Section II: Dominus tecum.
    Section III: Benedicta tu in mulieribus.
    Section IV: Et benedictus fructrus ventris tui, Jesus Christus Filius Dei vivi.

Triple Meter
    Section V: Et benedicta sint beata ubera tua quae lactaverunt regem regum.

Duple Meter
    Section VI: Et Dominum Deum nominum Deum nostrum.

Secular Music in the Renaissance

The Madrigal

The dominant form of sixteenth-century secular vocal music was the madrigal, which was composed for four to six male and female voices.

The Italian and the English, or Elizabethan, madrigals were the dominant forms of secular vocal music in the sixteenth century. A **madrigal,** whether Italian or English, is a composition for four to six (occasionally eight) voices, built on a secular text. The most favored subjects of madrigal texts were love, in all its forms, and pastoral settings. Text settings tended to be colorful and graphic; descriptive imitation or "word painting" (discussed in chapter 4) was often utilized. Most madrigals were composed for and performed by men and women of the upper classes. Madrigals were intended for the entertainment and edification of these people.

Italian madrigals were dramatic and emotional; English madrigals were generally lighthearted.

Italian Madrigal   Generally speaking, **Italian madrigals** were more dramatic and emotional than the more lighthearted English madrigal, though there are many exceptions. The expressive and dramatic powers of harmony were utilized in both Italian and English madrigals, and both types used sections of imitative counterpoint.

Marenzio's Italian madrigal *S'io parto, i'moro* is a good example of this genre.

A fine example of the dramatic Italian style is *S'io parto, i'moro (This parting kills me),* composed by one of the masters of the genre, Luca Marenzio (ca. 1560–99). The text is as follows:

S'io parto i' moro,	This parting now kills me,
E pur partir conviene,	And yet I still must leave thee,
Morrò dunque il mio bene,	I shall die then, my dearest,
E questa mia partita	And this my sad departing
Che mi ti toglie,	That takes me from thee,
Mi torrà la vita.	Takes from me my being.
Dolorosa partita che m'ucci di,	Ah, this cruel departing doth slay me,
Quei che congiuns' Amor	For those whom love hath joined,
Perche divi di?	Ah, how divide them?

Notice the expressive use of dissonance on the word "kills" (first line), and again on "ah" (third-to-last line). A clever and subtle use of descriptions (see chapter 4) occurs on the word "divide" (last line), where the steady pulse of the quarter note is suddenly divided into eighth notes. Notice the melancholy feeling in the song—though the text deals with love, it is a tragic, unrequited love. This text is typical of many Italian madrigals.

Elizabeth I supported the development of the arts in England.

Elizabethan Madrigal   The arts in general and music in particular flourished during the reign of Elizabeth I (reigned 1558–1603). In fact, her prominent role in the cultural life of England resulted in the label "The Elizabethan Age."

The **Elizabethan madrigal** was based on the Italian madrigal model, but it quickly developed a British personality. Though the Elizabethan madrigals displayed a wide range of subject matter and mood, the most famous type was the lighthearted pastoral variety. Among the most famous of all Elizabethan madrigals is *Now Is the Month of Maying* by Thomas Morley (1557–1603), a pupil of William Byrd. The use of a refrain consisting of nonsense syllables is typical of this kind of Elizabethan madrigal.

Elizabethan madrigals were popularized by composer Thomas Morley.

This pastoral madrigal is essentially homophonic; the only bits of imitation occur on the refrain "Fa-la-la." The text is:

Now is the month of Maying,
When merry lads are playing,
Fa la la.
Each with his bonny lass,
Upon the greeny grass,
Fa la la.
The Spring clad all in gladness
Doth laugh at Winter's sadness,
Fa la la.
And to the Bagpipes sound,
The Nymphs tread out their
  ground,
Fa la la.
Fie then, why sit we musing,
Youth's sweet delight refusing?
Fa la la.
Say dainty Nymphs and speak,
Shall we play barley break?
Fa la la.

William Shakespeare.
Free Library of Philadelphia

Recently there has been a renewed interest in the sixteenth-century madrigal, and a number of professional and amateur groups have been formed for the purpose of performing this music. In addition, newly discovered madrigals and madrigal composers have come to light in recent years. Included in this group are at least two women: Maddalena Casulana (ca. 1540–90), an Italian noblewoman, and the ill-fated Anne Boleyn (1507–36), the second wife of King Henry VIII of England.

Interest in Elizabethan madrigals has increased recently.

Keyboard and Instrumental Music

During the Renaissance, the harpsichord emerged as an important keyboard instrument, though the full realization of its possibilities did not occur until later, in the baroque era. Many of the English madrigal composers were also active in producing music for the harpsichord or its English equivalent, the virginal. Included in the group of English virginalist composers are William Byrd (ca. 1540–1623), Thomas Morley,

The harpsichord rose in importance during the Renaissance.

Orlando Gibbons (1583–1625), Giles Farnaby (ca. 1560–1600), and John Bull (ca. 1563–1628). The majority of their compositions were sets of variations and Renaissance dances arranged for the keyboard.

Sets of variations and Renaissance dances were arranged for keyboard.

An example of variations for virginal is Giles Farnaby's *Loth to Depart,* a popular sixteenth-century melody. A recording of it is found in *Masterpieces of Music Before 1750,* no. 29. The *Historical Anthology of Music,* no. 179 offers a pair of dances, a pavane and a galliard, in the piece for virginal called *Pavane Lord Salisbury* by Orlando Gibbons.

Renaissance composers wrote pieces for the viols.

Various composers also wrote music for viols, which are stringed instruments of various sizes. (Viols were used to accompany the verse anthem by Byrd, *Christ Rising Again.*) Many genteel English homes had, as a matter of course, a set of viols that were kept in a specially built chest and used for family entertainment and other social occasions. The viols are the ancestors of the modern string quartet instruments.

Other instruments used in the Renaissance include recorders, shawms, regals, sackbuts, small portable organs, and various drums and hand-held percussion instruments. Most instrumental music was written for dances, and most had the *AABB* structure—the immediate forerunners of the baroque dance suite.

Most Renaissance dance music had the AABB structure.

Working in Venice, the famed organist and composer Andrea Gabrieli (ca. 1510–86), along with his equally famous nephew, Giovanni Gabrieli (1557–1612), developed a distinctive, colorful, and expressive style in the late Renaissance. These monumental works, complemented at the time by the spectacular acoustics of Venice's St. Mark's Cathedral, where they were originally performed, often utilized two or more choirs of voices, one or more organs, and an ensemble of brass instruments.

In Venice, pieces were composed specifically for the acoustics of St. Mark's Cathedral.

Let us close this chapter on music in the Renaissance by listening to Andrea Gabrieli's *Gloria in Excelsis Deo,* written for four choirs of voices, viols, organs, trumpets, and trombones.

Summary

The Renaissance celebrated the rebirth of humanism. In humanistic style, this period of fifteenth- and sixteenth-century European history produced writers, scientists, artists, and composers who altered the course of Western civilization.

The secular world of the Renaissance accommodated the Church and its music. Both sacred and secular music characteristically included these elements: chordal harmony, imitative counterpoint, four-voice texture, and modernized rhythm.

The religious sects that emerged from the Reformation had a profound effect on the sacred music of the period. Martin Luther's emphasis on congregational singing was the impetus for the creation of chorales. The sects based in John Calvin's doctrines developed metrical psalms/psalmody—biblical texts set to simple music. The Anglicans preferred complex choral pieces designed for trained choirs. William Byrd composed many of these anthems. Roman Catholics continued to set the Ordinary of the Mass to music. Renaissance Masses featured various quotations of popular melodies, Gregorian melodies enriched with imitative counterpoint, and a refashioned motet form. Josquin des Prez's Masses are very famous.

The dominant form of secular music in the sixteenth century was the madrigal, a composition for four to six male and female voices featuring expressive harmony and imitative counterpoint. Italian madrigals, popularized by Luca Marenzio, were dramatic and emotional, and they typically focused on tragic, unrequited love. Elizabethan madrigals were lighthearted, pastoral pieces. One of the most famous composers of this genre was Thomas Morley.

Keyboard and instrumental music were also important in the Renaissance. Variations and dances were composed for harpsichord by madrigal composers while music for organs, trumpets, trombones, and viols was composed for performance in St. Mark's Cathedral, Venice, and in many other places. Renaissance dance music, with *AABB* structure, was played on popular period instruments such as the recorder, shawms, regals, sackbuts, and small portable organs.

We have sampled just a bit of the music of the Renaissance, but I hope that the importance of this period has been reinforced in your mind.

Key Terms

humanism	anthem	madrigal
chorale	verse anthem	Italian madrigal
metrical psalms (psalmody)	Renaissance motet	Elizabethan madrigal

Thinking About It

One way to help you understand important advances in Renaissance music is to contrast it with your understanding of medieval music. Even when done in general terms, this can help bring some important differences into focus. For example, contrast the thirteenth-century motet discussed in chapter 10 with the Josquin motet discussed in this chapter. What are the differences in harmony? In the number and kind of voices? In textural activity?

Outside the Sphere of Western Art Music

12

American Popular Music to 1950

Jukebox.
© Ron Cooper/EKM-Nepenthe

Sounds of the Chapter

Arlen
Hooray for What?

Harry Armstrong
"Sweet Adeline"

Barnet
"Cherokee"

Basie
"One O'Clock Jump"

Berlin
As Thousands Cheer
"Easter Parade"
"God Bless America"

Crosby
"Learn to Croon" ♪

Dorsey
"Boogie Woogie"
"Marie"
"Opus One"

Durante
"Can Broadway Do without Me?" ♪

Ellington
"Caravan"
"Take the A Train"

Evans
"In the Good Old Summertime"

Fitzgerald
"A Tisket-a-Tasket"

Foster
"Beautiful Dreamer"
"Camptown Races"
"Come Where My Love Lies
   Dreaming"
"Jeanie with the Light Brown Hair" ♪
"Laura Lee"
"Massa's in the Cold, Cold Ground"
"My Old Kentucky Home"
"Oh, Susanna"
"Old Black Joe"
"Old Folks at Home"
"Ring, Ring the Banjo"
"Way Down Upon the Swannee River"

Gershwin
"I Got Rhythm"
Of Thee I Sing

Goodman
"Don't Be That Way"
"Sing, Sing, Sing"
"Well Get It"

Herman
"Woodchopper's Ball"

James
"Ciribiribin"

Lombardo
"Auld Lang Syne" ♪

Miles/Sterling
"Meet Me in St. Louis, Louis"

Miller
"In the Mood"
"Little Brown Jug"

Porter
"I've Got You under My Skin"
"Night and Day"

Shaw
"Begin the Beguine"

Thornton
"On the Banks of the Wabash"

Woodworth
"The Old Oaken Bucket"

Work
"Come Home, Father"
"A Foggy Day in London Town"
"And the Angels Sing"
"April in Paris"
"As Time Goes By"
"Brother Can You Spare a Dime?"
"By the Light of the Silvery Moon"
"Daily Bread"
"Dancing on the Ceiling"
"Darkness on the Delta"

"Don't Blame Me"
"Halleluia I'm a Bum"
"Heading for the Last Roundup"
"I Wouldn't Trade the Silver in My
   Mother's Hair"
"If I Ever Get a Job Again"
"I'm in the Mood for Love" ♪
"In the Shade of the Old Apple Tree"
"Isle of Capri"
"It Happened in Monterey"
"It's Only a Paper Moon"
"I've Got My Love to Keep Me Warm"
"Let Me Wah-hoo, Wah-hoo, Wah-hoo"
" 'Leven Pounds of Heaven"
"Little Sir Echo"
"Lord Randall"
"The Lord's Prayer"
"Love Walked In"
"The Merry-Go-Round Broke Down"
"Midnight in Paris"
"Moon Coming over the Mountain"
"Moon of Spain"
"The Mother Song"
The Music Man
My Fair Lady
"My Mom"
"My Sweetheart's the Man in the
   Moon"
"Over the Rainbow"
"Pennies from Heaven"
"Please Don't Talk about Me When
   I'm Gone" ♪
"Red Sails in the Sunset"
"Shine on Harvest Moon"
"Song of India"
"Stay as Sweet as You Are" ♪
"Stormy Weather" ♪
"Sweet Adeline"
"Three Little Words" ♪
"What Are Little Girls Made Of?"
"Where Have You Been, Billy Boy?"
"You Call It Madness, But I Call It
   Love"
"You! You're Driving Me Crazy"

The changes in American popular music have reflected the changes in the nation itself.

Three distinct styles emerged between 1850 and 1950.

American popular music is often erroneously viewed as a static phenomenon, a music that has remained stylistically constant, exhibiting only minimal change. On the contrary, American popular music has undergone some significant changes that have reflected changes in the culture at large.

From the 1850s through the early 1950s, no fewer than three styles of popular music are evident. The songs of Stephen Foster exemplify the first of these styles, the genteel tradition of the mid-nineteenth century. Later in the century, popular music changed with the rise of the Tin Pan Alley era around the 1890s. And a third dramatic stylistic change occurred around 1930 with the emergence of swing.

The Dissemination of American Popular Music

Music in some form or other has always been an important part of the American tradition. Evidence suggests that the earliest music brought to America was predominantly sacred—mostly psalms and hymns. However, this by no means precludes the probability that the migrating Europeans also brought secular music with them when they immigrated. They must surely have found this secular music enjoyable and must have appreciated it for its nostalgic value.

The first American songs were kept alive by oral tradition.

Many early American songs were composed anonymously, disseminated and kept alive through the process of oral tradition. Frequently these songs changed from generation to generation or from location to location, with the changes reflecting the personalities and experiences of the groups who used the songs.

Such songs were actually more legendary than popular. Strictly speaking, they were personal rather than standardized, and they were not commercially oriented. They were, in fact, recomposed as they migrated from place to place, always adapting the personal statement of the bearer of the song. Thus, the anonymous (seventeenth-century?) composer of the ballad "Lord Randall" provided the basis for the anonymous nineteenth-century composer who rewrote the material into the song "Where Have You Been, Billy Boy?".

Nineteenth-century sheet music cover.
© EKM-Nepenthe

The Rise of the Sheet Music Industry

The commercial sheet music business, as well as the Protestant sacred music business, blossomed in America in the early nineteenth century. Publishing houses, catering to the regional tastes of their prospective customers, emerged in larger cities from the East (Boston, New York, Philadelphia, and Baltimore) to the Midwest (St. Louis, Chicago, Cincinnati, and Milwaukee).

Although printed music had been available for several hundred years, it was not until the middle of the nineteenth century that a large body of printed music existed—sheet music, freshly composed, intended for commercial purposes, and distributed widely to the American public. Many of the songs by Stephen Foster, Dan Emmett (1815–1904), Henry Russell (1812–1900), and others from the mid-nineteenth century achieved commercial success, largely because of the sale of sheet music. Despite these successes, the sheet music *industry* did not develop until later in the century, in the late 1880s and 1890s. At that time many song publishers from around the country converged in a district of New York City that came to be known as Tin Pan Alley.

Some American songwriters achieved commercial success in the mid-nineteenth century.

The sheet music industry did not emerge in the United States until late in the nineteenth century.

With the rise of Tin Pan Alley many regional publishing houses began to devote more resources to the sheet music industry. The switch was not entirely geographical, for there was a concomitant switch from the diversity of regional song types to an increasingly homogeneous song style.

The sheet music industry flourished during the period from 1890 to the 1920s, when it was superseded by other, faster modes of dissemination. It was soon clear that the sheet music industry would have to take a back seat to the other media. The radio, the phonograph, and the sound motion picture are all products of the early twentieth century, and by 1930 all three were commercial successes.

The radio, the phonograph, and the motion picture gave Americans, from coast to coast, a common music.

Because of these new media, the term popular assumed a magnitude theretofore unknown and perhaps not even dreamed of. Consider, for example, that a song popular in Boston in 1850 or even 1890 may never have been heard by someone living in San Francisco, Denver, or Houston. But a song beamed over the airwaves in 1927 could be heard over all of the 27,850,000 home-owned radio sets in the country. Since the population of the United States in 1927 was only 119,000,000, it was possible, then, for one in four Americans to listen to a given song at the same time.

Audience Participation

Audience participation was important during the Tin Pan Alley era, as it was prior to that time. Printed music was purchased for performance at home around the family piano. But with the advent of the new media, audiences assumed a largely passive role. The audience heard popular music over the radio and in the movies, and bought recordings of their favorite popular songs. There was a movement away from active participation in the performance of music toward a passive acceptance of it. The notable exception to this was in the field of dance, a type of participation that has been a constant in American music.

The new media decreased the importance of participation.

However, Americans did actively participate in popular music through dance, spawning the creation of dance bands.

Dance   Indeed, as the audience became passive in terms of actual performance, interest in dance increased. This interest was manifest in the various dance crazes of the 1920s, such as the Charleston and the Black Bottom, and in the foxtrotting and jitterbugging of the 1930s and 1940s. By the 1930s the traveling dance bands became an important factor in popular music. By the late 1930s, the big band era was in full bloom, and in cities across the country the big name bands played before large and enthusiastic crowds of dancers.

The movie musical became popular in the twenties and thirties.

Film   The movie musical, an infant in the late 1920s, grew to adulthood at a dizzying pace in the 1930s, and by the close of that decade many of the recognized landmarks of the genre had been produced, attracting millions of viewers.

Musical Comedy   The American musical comedy also came of age in the 1930s. By the late 1920s the operetta (and other European forms of musical theater) had begun to decline on Broadway, relinquishing its popularity to the musical comedy. The Broadway audience, typically more affluent and snobbish than the movie and radio audiences, responded to the music of George Gershwin, Cole Porter, Irving Berlin, Richard Rodgers, and Jerome Kern, at the expense of the Europeans— Johann Strauss, Franz Lehar, Victor Herbert, and Gilbert and Sullivan.

Broadway music appealed to the higher socio-economic classes in the 1930s.

The Genteel Tradition

The genteel tradition describes the life style of middle class Americans in the early nineteenth century.

In the early decades of the nineteenth century, middle-class Americans prided themselves on honest labor, comfortable surroundings, and the cultivation of good manners and taste. This has been appropriately dubbed the **genteel tradition.** A particular kind of popular music was a part of this tradition.

The so-called **parlor song** was performed both in public and at home with the family around the piano in the parlor. Typically, the parlor song consisted of simple, diatonic harmonies that supported equally unpretentious melodies, frequently marked by fermatas on high notes or textually dramatic points. In general, the texts were overly emotional or nostalgic, with such subjects as the homeless, afflicted children, and lost love. There were also many moralizing texts.

Parlor songs featured overly emotional texts.

Notice the sentimentality in these examples.

The text of Samuel Woodworth's "The Old Oaken Bucket" is typical of the sentimental parlor song:

> How dear to this heart are the scenes of my childhood,
> When fond recollection presents them to view,
> The orchard, the meadow, the deep tangled wildwood,
> And ev'ry lov'd spot which my infancy knew.
> The widespreading stream, the mill that stood near it,

The bridge and the rock where the cataract fell;
The cot of my father, the dairy house by it,
And e'en the rude bucket that hung in the well.

The old oaken bucket, the iron bound bucket,
The moss covered bucket that hung in the well.

Henry C. Work was among the most popular composers of the era. He won fame with texts such as "Come Home, Father":

Father, dear father, come home with me now!
The clock in the steeple strikes one.
You said you were coming right home from the shop,
As soon as your day's work was done.
Our fire has gone out, our house is all dark,
And mother's been watching since tea,
With poor brother Benny so sick in her arms,
And no one to help her but me.

Come home! come home! come home!
Please, father, dear father, come home.
Hear the sweet voice of the child
Which the night winds repeat as they roam.
Oh, who could resist this most plaintive of prayers?
"Please, father, dear father, come home."[1]

Today this may seem to be the most banal and tacky kind of sentimentality, but it was precisely that which tugged at the heartstrings of the audience of the day. It is vintage genteel tradition.

This music was a part of the genteel tradition.

Stephen Foster

Stephen Foster (1826–64) was born into this tradition, and many of his songs are closely related to it. "Beautiful Dreamer" (1864), "Come Where My Love Lies Dreaming" (1855), and "Jeanie with the Light Brown Hair" (1854) are all songs about departed or unattainable love. "My Old Kentucky Home" (1853), "Way Down Upon the Swannee River," and "Old Folks at Home" (1851) are filled with a nostalgic longing for the past. The other basic type of song that Foster wrote belongs to the minstrel show tradition. "Oh! Susanna" (1848) and "Camptown Races" (1850) are examples of this type.

Despite the melancholy nature of many of Foster's songs, all of his compositions are in major keys. His nostalgic songs and his songs of lost or unrequited love are cast in slow or moderate tempos. The subject of love is never treated in a lighthearted or playful manner. "Jeanie with the Light Brown Hair," "Beautiful Dreamer," and "Come Where My Love Lies Dreaming" move at a dignified pace.

Stephen Foster (1826–64).
© The Bettmann Archive

Most of Foster's compositions are melancholy or nostalgic.

1. Source: Margaret Bradford Boni, *Songs of the Guilded Age,* Western Publishing Company, Inc., 1960, pp. 131–32, 16–18.

Love is earnest and the loved one beautiful: "borne like a vapor on the summer air." She is sweet: "Why has the happy dream blended with thee, Passed like a fleeting beam, sweet Laura Lee?" She is idealized: "Starlight and dewdrops are waiting for thee. Beautiful dreamer, queen of my song, list while I woo thee with soft melody." Anachronistic expressions such as "borne," "thee/thy," "o'er," "e'een," "'tis," and "list" are typical of the genteel tradition.

Most of Foster's songs are diatonic to the extreme; the harmony is generally restricted to the primary chords of the key (tonic, subdominant and dominant). "Camptown Races" (1850), for instance, is built entirely on the tonic and dominant chords, save for one measure of subdominant harmony on the words "Gwine to run all day." "Massa's in the Cold, Cold Ground" (1852) uses only tonic, dominant, and subdominant, and "Old Black Joe" (1860) is limited to those three chords except for one chromatic chord just before the close of the second phrase of the song. "My Old Kentucky Home" uses a chromatic chord near the end of phrases one and three but the rest of the harmony is limited to the primary chords. "Jeanie with the Light Brown Hair" and "Beautiful Dreamer" are only slightly more harmonically adventurous.

The melodic style of these songs also bears the mark of simplicity: diatonic whole and half steps comprise most of the melodic intervals. Like the chords that support them, the melodies are amazingly free of chromatic intervals. Some of his most famous tunes are flavored with pentatonicism: "Oh! Susanna" and "Camptown Races" are completely pentatonic; "Ring, Ring the Banjo" (1851) and "Laura Lee" (1851) are mostly pentatonic; and only the middle section of "Old Folks at Home" (1851) is nonpentatonic. The tunes are almost folklike in their simplicity and in their frequent use of pentatonicism.

Foster's true gift was in the realm of melody. For all of their simplicity, these melodies have a beauty that render them memorable to this day.

In retrospect, it seems clear that when Foster died near the end of the Civil War, a whole tradition of American popular music passed away. Shortly thereafter, a new, more brazen style emerged to replace it.

The Tin Pan Alley Era

Foster's songs contrast sharply with the songs that were popular in the Gay 90s—the **Tin Pan Alley** era. Many of these songs were as chromatic as Foster's were diatonic, their harmonic language abounds with chromatically altered chords, quick modulations, and slithering inner parts. The "close harmonies" of these songs were, in contrast to those of Foster, very dissonant and raucous. They were easily adaptable to the barbershop quartet format that was so popular in America near the turn of the

---

Margin notes:

Foster's loved one is always idealized, often using quaint expressions.

Foster's harmony is often restricted to the primary chords of the key.

Simple melody characterizes Foster's songs.

The genteel tradition seems to have died with Foster in the 1860s.

The popular barbershop quartet sound typifies the music of Tin Pan Alley, or the Gay 90s.

Singing around player piano.
© Jane Kramer/EKM-Nepenthe

century. It is difficult to think of "Sweet Adeline" (1903, Harry Armstrong) without conjuring up the sound and the image of the musta-
chioed, straw-hatted male quartet. The same is true of "On the Banks
of the Wabash" (1898, James Thornton), "In the Good Old Summertime" (1902, George Evans), "Shine on Harvest Moon" (1904), and
dozens of others. Listen now to a barbershop rendition of "Please Don't
Talk about Me When I'm Gone."

The restlessness of the harmony in these songs may reflect the national economic, industrial, and geographic expansion that was occur-
ring at that time. As has been seen, even the popular music business
expanded into an industry during those years. The placid harmonies of
Foster's songs belonged to an earlier, more genteel and static time that
was disrupted by the Civil War.

The restlessness found in
popular music reflects the
economic upheaval of the
period.

Songs from the Tin Pan Alley era also differed from the genteel
era in terms of subject matter, idioms, and specific words.

Verse and Refrain

In the gay 90s, popular songs adhered to the format of **verse and refrain.**
The refrain was roughly analogous to an aria, and the verse was analogous to a recitative that preceded the aria. The function of the verse
was to establish the plot and then lead into the more melodious and

The verse and refrain format
was characteristic of American
popular music in the 1890s.

The verse told the story, but often only the refrain is remembered.

memorable refrain. With most of these songs it was the verse, not the refrain, that actually told the story of the song. Today when these songs are performed the verse is almost always omitted. Thus, the general public often misinterprets the true nature of many of these songs.

For example, "Meet Me in St. Louis, Louis" (1904, Kerry Miles and Andrew Sterling) is actually a very roguish song, a fact evident not in the refrain that many people know but in the verse that one rarely hears. The refrain reads as follows:

> Meet me in St. Louis, Louis, meet me at the fair,
> Don't tell me the lights are shining anyplace but there.
> We will dance the Hoochee Koochee,
> I will be your tootsie wootsie
> If you will meet me in St. Louis, Louis,
> Meet me at the fair.[2]

In the verses we learn that the singer of the song is actually a woman who has just left her husband:

> When Louis came home to the flat
> He hung up his coat and his hat,
> He gazed all around, but no wifey he found,
> So he said, "Where can Flossie be at?"
> A note on the table he spied,
> He read it just once, then he cried.
> It ran, "Louis dear, it's too slow for me here,
> So I think I will go for a ride."
> (Refrain)
> The dresses that hung in the hall
> Were gone, she had taken them all.
> She took all his rings and the rest of his things;
> The pictures he missed from the wall.
> "What! Moving?" the janitor said,
> "Your rent is paid three months ahead."
> "What good is the flat?" said poor Louis, "read that."
> And the janitor smiled as he read.
> (Refrain)[3]

The true nature of the song is revealed in the verse.

Similarly, the verse to "In the Shade of the Old Apple Tree" clarifies the meaning of the song, not evident from merely listening to the refrain. The song is, in fact, a tragedy—the loved one of the person singing the song is buried under the old apple tree. Similarly, the verse to "Sweet Adeline" tells us something that the refrain barely suggests, namely, that the song is about unrequited love.

2. Ibid.
3. Ibid.

The lyrics from "In the Good Old Summertime" (1902, Ron Shields and George Evans) are just as saucy as those from "Meet Me in St. Louis, Louis." "You hold her hand, and she holds yours, and that's a very good sign, that she's your tootsie-wootsie in the good old summertime." The tootsie-wootsie is a far cry from the beautiful dreamer. To speak of the loved one as a tootsie-wootsie during the genteel era would have been scandalous. On the other hand, to suggest that the tootsie-wootsie who dances the Hoochee Koochee could ever have been "borne like a vapor on the summer air" would have been laughable in the Gay 90s.

Gay 90s musical language is not the refined language of the genteel tradition.

The many "moon" songs of the Gay 90s introduced a number of slang words to the vocabulary of love texts, words such as spoon, swoon, and croon, were used primarily because they rhyme with moon. Such songs as "By the Light of the Silvery Moon" "Shine on Harvest Moon," and "My Sweetheart's the Man in the Moon" replace the dignity and sentimentality of Foster's love songs with a brassiness, even vulgarity. The refrain of "My Sweetheart's the Man in the Moon" is as follows:

Songs of the Tin Pan Alley introduced slang words into the American vocabulary.

> My sweetheart's the man in the moon, I'm going to marry him soon.
> 'Twould fill me with bliss, just to give him one kiss,
> But I know that a dozen I never would miss.
> I'll go up in a great big balloon, And see my sweetheart in the moon.
> Then behind some dark cloud where no one is allowed,
> I'll make love to the man in the moon.

> *Second verse:*
> Last night when the stars brightly shone, he told me through love's telephone,
> That when we were wed, he'd go early to bed,
> And never stay out with the boys, so he said.
> We are going to marry next June, the wedding takes place in the moon.
> A sweet little Venus, we'll fondle between us,
> When I wed my old man in the moon.

Popular music has always been secular music, but with some of the outrageous songs from the 1890s, it appeared even more so. The harmony of these songs, with their self-conscious, almost defiant chromaticism, and the naughty, rebellious quality of their lyrics, evoked indignation from those who had grown up in the genteel tradition. At this time the dress and appearance of young people also began to change. This may have been the first of several generation gaps that have occurred in American culture, and popular music was definitely a contributing factor.

Popular music increased the gap between Americans reared in the genteel tradition and the youth of the 1890s.

Popular Music in the 1930s

Popular music is certainly perishable; most of it is hastily produced, quickly consumed, and soon forgotten. The audience for popular music in the 1930s had a voracious appetite for songs and a remarkably fickle attitude toward them. The smash hit of a given day usually became tomorrow's nonentity.

To satisfy this insatiable appetite, hundreds of composers and lyricists combined to create about 10,000 published songs during the years 1930–39. That averaged nearly three songs every day, or one song every eight hours, or, to carry the breakdown to an extreme, the thirties witnessed the production of roughly four measures of popular music every sixty minutes—a phrase an hour.

The perishability of these songs is demonstrated by their short life span—very few have survived the thirties to become what are commonly known as **standards,** or songs that have continued to be performed to the present day. "Night and Day" (1932, Cole Porter), "Easter Parade" (1933, Irving Berlin), and "I Got Rhythm" (1930, George and Ira Gershwin) are examples of standards.

Composers and lyricists in the thirties continued to supply the recitativelike verses mentioned earlier, but for the most part performers, and hence audiences, tended to ignore the verse. (One exception is Broadway shows, where the verse had a necessary dramatic function.) For most audiences the refrain was the golden moment; it was the memorable part of the song, and the verse was forgotten. The era of the story-telling song was over, and it became increasingly clear that the verse was dispensable.

Song Forms

Most popular songs from the thirties contain four- and eight-bar phrases in regular patterns. These songs usually fall into three categories: (1) *AABA,* in which each of the four sections contains eight measures for a total of thirty-two measures. The eight-bar *B* section is usually referred to as the "release." Most of the songs from the decade have this *AABA* design. (2) *AA* or *AA',* in which each section contains sixteen bars, again with a total of thirty-two bars. These are the one-idea songs that operate without benefit of a contrasting *B* section. Only about one quarter of the decade's songs are of this type. (3) Songs that encompass a variety of formal designs, ranging from more extended forms such as *AABACA,* to an occasional twelve-bar blues. This category, which is more or less a catch-all for rare formal types, comprises many of the instrumental numbers from the big band era and very few other compositions.

It is obvious, then, that almost all of the songs written in the thirties have either the *AABA* or *AA* form. However, some of the most memorable and popular songs have utilized unconventional forms. For

Cole Porter (1893–1964).

example, many of the songs of Cole Porter, one of the most successful composers in American popular music history, have atypical formal structures: "Night and Day" (1932), or "I've Got You under My Skin" (1936). Duke Ellington's "Caravan" (1937) has a seldom-used structure but it, too, has become a standard.

Cole Porter composed in unconventional forms.

Of course, most of the successful songs used the more common *AABA* format:

"Dancing on the Ceiling" (1930)
"As Time Goes By" (1931)
"Don't Blame Me" (1932)
"Easter Parade" (1933)
"It's Only a Paper Moon" (1934)
"I'm in the Mood for Love" (1935)
"Stormy Weather" (1933)
"Red Sails in the Sunset" (1935)
"Pennies from Heaven" (1936)
"I've Got My Love to Keep Me Warm" (1937)
"Love Walked In" (1938)
"Over the Rainbow" (1939)

AABA form is common to these standard pieces from the thirties.

The longevity of these songs is impressive—each has been recorded numerous times over the decades. However, the vast majority of 1930s songs written in the *AABA* design were permanently discarded by the public very shortly after they were written.

George Gershwin
(1898–1937).

Lyrics in the thirties touched
on a wide range of topics.

Love songs remained popular
throughout the decade.

Lyrics

The lyrics of thirties songs dealt with a fairly diversified range of subject matter. Love, nostalgia, fads, the exotic, the family, and the depression were all topics that sparked the creativity of songwriters.

Love   Although this diversity of subject matter exists, more than half of the songs from the thirties deal with the subject of love. In general, these songs fall into three categories:

♪
1. Love ballads in which the subject of love is treated in a romantic and positive way, as in "I'm in the Mood for Love":

    I'm in the mood for love, simply because you're near me.
    Funny, but when you're near me, I'm in the mood for love.[4]

♪
2. Lighthearted love lyrics—that treat the subject in a more flippant way, as in "Three Little Words":

    Three little words, eight little letters
    Which simply mean I love you.[5]

3. Lyrics dealing with lost or unattainable love, as in "Stormy Weather":

Can't go on, everything I had is gone
Stormy weather, since my man and I ain't together
Keeps raining all the time.[6]

Certain images from many love ballads of the thirties point unmistakably to escapism. In addition, a number of love lyrics suggest whimsical fancy, in which the adored one (who is quite literally adored) is frequently pictured as an angel. Such is the case with "And the Angels Sing (1939), in which the mere sound of the loved one's voice is enough to produce heavenly choirs:

You speak, and the angels sing
The angels sing the sweetest song I ever heard.[7]

The subject of love was treated in diverse ways.

Romantic love was sometimes envisioned as a state of euphoria that borders on sweet madness, as in the song "You Call It Madness, But I Call It Love" (1931). "You! You're Driving Me Crazy" (1930) is more lighthearted but no less mad.

One also finds romantic love likened to a state of alcoholic haziness in "You Go to My Head":

You go to my head and you linger like a haunting refrain.
I find you spinning round in my brain, like the bubbles in a glass
    of champagne.[8]

Nostalgia   As with the genteel tradition, nostalgia often figured in songs from the 1930s. Several hundred songs were composed that were little more than reminiscences of the peaceful, happy atmosphere of days gone by. These songs focused on a longing to return to the old homestead in the south, a sentimentality about the tranquility of the mountains, and memories of the old west with its wide open spaces and big sky.

Nostalgia was a popular subject for songs in the thirties.

Oddly enough, many of these nostalgic songs idealizing the deep South or the Southwest were partially influenced by the popularity of cowboy movies throughout the decade. Many of these songs were written by people who lived in New York City or Hollywood, and few had any firsthand knowledge of the settings and people about whom they rhapsodized. Similarly, the audiences who popularized the songs lacked this firsthand knowledge of the subject. Most of the popular music audience

The South and Southwest were idealized in song.

6. STORMY WEATHER (KEEPS RAININ' ALL THE TIME) by Ted Koehler & Harold Arlen © 1933 MILLS MUSIC, INC. © Renewed 1961 ARKO MUSIC CORP. International Copyright Secured. All Rights Reserved. Used by permission.
7. AND THE ANGELS SING © 1939 by Bregman, Vocco and Conn, Inc. Copyright renewed 1966 by Bregman, Vocco and Conn, Inc. and Twentieth Century Music Corp. International Copyright Secured. All Rights Reserved.
8. YOU GO TO MY HEAD © 1938 (Renewed) Warner Bros. Inc. All Rights Reserved. Used by permission.

did not live in the South or the Southwest. In fact, those two areas of the country stubbornly clung to their own regional music and shunned mainstream popular music for the most part.

Sentimental lyrics also abounded—songs about old rocking chairs, the little church in the valley, an empty saddle, old spinning wheels and wagon wheels, a cabin in the pines, and homes in Georgia, Texas, and the Carolinas.

The past was also remembered with longing.

All of these nostalgic and sentimental songs spoke of a sweetly remembered, but safely irretrievable, past. They were lyrical messages to a confused society that was moving ever more swiftly toward urbanization and industrialization. Little exoticism and no nostalgia were attached to a cement factory, a conveyor belt, or a typewriter. But the "Darkness on the Delta," the "Moon Coming over the Mountain," or "Heading for the Last Roundup" were grist for the romantic mill.

Novelty Songs **Novelty songs** represent a relatively small portion of the total songs from the decade. Of all the types of popular songs, novelty songs tend to have the shortest life span. As the fads and crazes that precipitate such lyrics fade and are replaced by new fads, the novelty songs and the fads that spawned them evaporate.

Novelty songs depend upon fads for their existence.

With few exceptions novelty songs were products of Tin Pan Alley. This was one type of song that the sheet music industry could still claim as its own success. The novelty song was supposed to burst on the scene with great force, make its sales in a rush, and then disappear in the wake of the next novelty song. Songwriters and publishers surely recognized that novelty songs were not destined to become big money-makers over a long period of time. In a sense, the novelty song was like a joke—it is funniest and most impressive on first hearing, but after that interest wanes.

The repetition of nonsense syllables is important in novelty songs.

Notable among the novelty songs of the thirties were "Let Me Wah-hoo, Wah-hoo, Wah-hoo" (1936), "The Merry-Go-Round Broke Down" (1937), and "Little Sir Echo" (1939). The success of these songs is based in part on a very puerile ingredient: the repetition of nonsense syllables such as wah-hoo, oom-pa-pa, or yoo-hoo—the sorts of nonsense words that amuse children.

The silly things that attract the attention of the public are unpredictable, which means what may have amused the public in the 1930s would likely get little or no reaction from audiences of both earlier and later decades.

Exotic songs were popular in the thirties.

Exotic Another important and fairly large body of songs from the 1930s may be categorized as "exotic." Some of these songs could also be included in the category of love songs, a few could be classified as novelty songs, but all of these exotic songs catered to the American fascination with mysterious, distant lands. In fact, most of these songs are identified by a specific location, as noted in the following:

"Moon of Spain" (1930)
"It Happened in Monterey" (1930)
"Song of India" (1932)
"April in Paris" (1932)
"Isle of Capri" (1934)
"Midnight in Paris" (1935)
"A Foggy Day in London Town" (1937)

An examination of the collection of exotic songs from the thirties reveals that the audience and the songwriters were most interested in Hawaii (and by extension, the South Seas), and in Latin America. These two locales seemed to epitomize the idea of the exotic in the mind of the American popular music audience.

Family   There were few devotional songs and songs about family life during the decade. The thirties might be considered an era endowed with artificiality, but this artificiality never encroached on the private domain of family life. Personal family matters, such as a wayward son or daughter, or a father given to gambling or drinking, were not discussed. One finds no "birds in gilded cages" or young women who are "more to be pitied than censured." There were no songs dealing with children begging, "Come home, father," for dirty linen was not aired in public. These were private matters, and either good taste or fear of humiliation prevented discussion of them.

Since there were few songs that discussed such problems, there were also few songs that offered advice, criticism, or admonition—no didacticism from the soap box.

Very few songs dealt with maternal or deistic subjects, and of those that did, most came across as flat statements, not as exhortations. "The Mother Song" ("M is for the million things she gave me") (1930), "I Wouldn't Trade the Silver in My Mother's Hair" (1932), "Daily Bread" (1931), "My Mom" (1932), "The Lord's Prayer" (1935), " 'Leven Pounds of Heaven" (1931), and "What Are Little Girls Made Of?" (1933) typify and nearly exhaust this repertoire.

Patriotism   The thirties did produce one very popular patriotic song: Irving Berlin's "God Bless America" (1938). This song seemed to give expression to the nation's latent spirit of patriotism, and during the war years this song became the rallying cry of servicemen and civilians alike.

Margin notes:

A distant land was often the subject of an exotic song.

Hawaii and Latin America were considered especially intriguing.

Personal and family issues were not appropriate song topics for the thirties.

One patriotic song of the thirties did gain widespread popularity—"God Bless America."

The powerful downbeats of its metrical scheme place all the right textual syllables in positions of unmistakable strength:

> *"God"* . . . A-*"Mer"*-ica . . . *"Love"* . . . *"Home."*

The spirit of the song, as well as its important nationalistic flavor, lent itself to the patriotism of the time.

The Depression   Ironically, very few songs of the time dealt with an obvious, though somber, subject—the Great Depression. "Brother Can You Spare a Dime?" (1932) was the quintessential song dealing with the depression. "Halleluia I'm a Bum" (1932) flippantly spoke of the desperation of the situation, as did "If I Ever Get a Job Again" (1932). George Gershwin's Broadway musical *Of Thee I Sing* (1931), Berlin's *As Thousands Cheer,* and Harold Arlen's *Hooray for What?* are filled with political barbery, but the vast majority of the songs from the decade make no mention of the depression and its many social and economic problems.

Very few songs faced the economic reality of the depression.

Defining Swing

The thirties witnessed a major change in the manner of playing and singing popular music, and during the decade a style of performance developed that remained in vogue until after the end of World War II. Not all of the bands from the era were swing bands, nor were all of the male singers crooners, but swinging and crooning were important developments.

Swing was popularized in the 1930s.

"Swing" and "the swing era" are terms that have been in general use since the 1930s, but some people erroneously assume that swing and the swing era are one and the same thing—that swing flourished exclusively during the swing era.

The term **"swing,"** however, has a substantial history: it was a verb used by some of the earliest jazz musicians. Jellyroll Morton described swing as a rhythmic and phraseological action that takes place in jazz. In words and in musical demonstration, Morton eloquently described the process of swing and insisted that without it, jazz was inconceivable.

Swing, an integral part of jazz, describes the performance of jazz music.

In simplest terms, swing can be described as a performance practice unique to jazz; more than any other factor, it is the performer's swinging that causes the performance to be labeled "jazzy." Swing is largely a temporal phenomenon, but it also involves a particular kind of musical ambiance. To swing the rhythm of a given tune is to play it with a deliberate disregard for its indicated note values, and to play it with certain accents and inflections that run counter to the direction of its notation.

Benny Goodman (clarinet) and band: *sax*—Arthur Rollins, Hymine Shertzen, George Koenig; *trumpet*—Chris Griffin, Harry James, Ziggy Elman; *trombones*—Murray MacEachern, Red Ballard; *drums*—Gene Krupa.
© AP/Wide World Photos, Inc.

The Big Band Era

Because swing has always been a part of jazz the phrase **"swing era"** is misleading; it is too limiting. The swing era embraces the years from about 1932 to 1945, but even as a label for that time period the phrase is not accurate, if considered literally. These were the years during which the big dance bands were a vital part of the American popular music scene, but only some of the bands played swing. For example, the band of Benny Goodman (b. 1909), the "King of Swing," predominantly played swing, while Guy Lombardo (1902–77) played "the sweetest music this side of heaven," a type of music devoid of swing and having no connection with jazz. There were dozens of big dance bands operating during the swing era, and depending upon the type of music played, they can be separated into swing bands and sweet bands, or into the vast gray area between the two.

The Big Band Era embraced the years 1932–45.

Not all the big bands featured swing music.

Swing Bands

Some of the best known white swing bands were formed during the mid-to-late 1930s as Benny Goodman, Tommy Dorsey, Glenn Miller, Jimmy Dorsey, and Artie Shaw organized their groups.

The white swing bands performed primarily at dances, but the biggest names among them sometimes had lucrative contracts with radio networks, movies, and of course, the recording industry. Their audiences were usually young (teen and college age), white, and middle- or upper-income. To make themselves marketable, many of these bands (such as those headed by Benny Goodman, Tommy Dorsey (1905–56), Glenn Miller, and Artie Shaw (b.1910)) played a mixture of instrumental swing and popular ballads, though the ballads usually outnumbered the pure swing instrumentals.

White swing bands usually played a mixture of instrumental swing and popular ballads.

This was not true of the black swing bands, such as the one led by Fletcher Henderson. Their audiences feasted on a diet much richer in jazz and blues; ballads were of secondary importance.

Black swing bands offered more jazz and blues.

Count Basie   In the late 1920s Count Basie (1904–84) was a member of the Kansas City-based Bennie Moten band, one of the hottest swing bands of the era. When Basie formed his own band in the mid-thirties, it was built along the same lines as the Moten band. The Basie band played with real drive and energy. Its repertoire included fewer ballads, leaning more heavily on swing blues and riff tunes. One of the most famous arrangements from the entire swing era, and the archetypal riff tune piece, is Basie's "One O'Clock Jump" (1937). This recording became a jukebox favorite during the big band era and resulted in nationwide popularity for the Basie band.

The Count Basie band focused on swing blues and riff tunes.

Glenn Miller   The most celebrated name to emerge from the big band era is that of Glenn Miller (1904–44). His tragic and mysterious disappearance on a military flight from England to mainland Europe during 1944, the appeal of his music to the young at heart and to the innocent jitterbuggers of the World War II generation, and the utterly distinctive style and "sound" of his band have contributed to his posthumous image as the grand master of the swing era. For many, Miller's "In the Mood" is alone sufficient to describe, indeed, epitomize an era of American popular music.

Glenn Miller was probably the favorite band leader of the period.

Although many popular music forms have emerged since the demise of the big band era, the abiding popularity of the Miller band clearly demonstrates that an audience of significant number still exists for this music. Miller remains a popular figure, and his music is still a paying proposition.

Miller's music has retained its popularity.

The Success of Swing Bands   Some of this success must be attributed to the nostalgia of men and women who were attached to this music in the thirties and forties, and who continue to appreciate the musical comfort and stability of the Miller band. The current boon in nostalgia and the curiosity seekers among younger people are, doubtless, also a part of the reason for the continuing success of the Miller band. As happens with every generation of music lovers, the fans of swing-era music have clung to "their" music because it is a point of stability for them. As their generation returned from the war to pick up the threads of civilian life, they discovered that popular music was one of many things that had changed or was beginning to change. The sentimental ballads and the big band swing arrangements so familiar during the thirties and early forties were being pushed aside by a younger generation who wanted something else, something that was foreign. The emergence of bebop and progressive jazz (see chapter 13) in the mid-to-late forties also left them shaking their heads—they could make no sense of it.

As this generation attempted to build careers in the affluent postwar years and tried to adapt to swiftly changing social patterns and mores, comfort was found in the musical stability represented by the Miller band (and in the many things this kind of music symbolized and represented). Though the world was moving and changing at a rapid pace, Glenn Miller's music was stable, memory-laden, and still interesting.

This phenomenon, however, is not unique to the generation that enjoyed swing music. The musical genre of a particular era will continue to appeal to its audience long after its popularity has waned. Its sound will inspire the memory of youthful confidence and security, of familiarity and consistency in an ever-changing world.

Swing Sells Although only fifteen records sold more than 500,000 copies during the thirties, the recording business did very well, largely due to the popularity of the jukebox. Some of the decade's best-sellers were swing arrangements that were at the time, and have been ever since, associated with one specific band/or singer: Tommy Dorsey's "Marie" (1937), Ella Fitzgerald's "A Tisket-a-Tasket" (1938), Artie Shaw's "Begin the Beguine" (1938), Harry James' "Ciribiribin" (1939), and Glenn Miller's "In the Mood" and "Little Brown Jug" (both from 1939). Similarly, "Well Get It," "Don't Be That Way," and "Down South Camp Meeting," belong to the Benny Goodman band; "Opus One" and "Boogie Woogie" belong to Tommy Dorsey; "Take the A Train" belongs to Duke Ellington; "One O'Clock Jump" to Count Basie; "Cherokee" to Charlie Barnet, and "Woodchopper's Ball" to Woody Herman.

Songs popularized by a particular big band were the major sellers in the thirties.

Sweet Dance Bands

At the opposite end of the spectrum from the true swing bands are those that are unmistakably sweet. This sweet sound was dominated by white bands. Black sweet bands with national reputations were practically nonexistent in the 1930s; there was no call for them by black audiences, and no effective means for them to compete with the white bands for the attention of white society.

White sweet bands offered an alternative to the swing bands of the thirties.

Guy Lombardo   One of the most commercially successful dance bands ever was that led by Guy Lombardo. His repertoire, style, and arrangements are prototypical of the hotel-style, **sweet dance bands** of the thirties and later. Guy Lombardo's band catered to the fairly affluent, nonswing stratum of society. The band had a sound of its own, characterized by a monochromaticism that never approached raucous or loud. The rhythm section was rather bouncy and metronomic, and the tempos were kept unerringly steady for the dancers. Lombardo's often-heard rendition of "Auld Lang Syne" exemplifies this style.

The Guy Lombardo band was in the enviable position of having a profitable home base while enjoying nationwide exposure. Dance crowds and ballroom managers were eager to have them perform. Lombardo's enormous popularity bears witness to the fact that swing bands were not the only kind of instrumental ensemble that had an impact on audiences in the 1930s—the popularity of sweet dance music has endured, also.

Singing in the Thirties

Music audiences develop ideals and standards for singers. To some extent audiences dictate how singing should sound and the types of emotional and vocal ingredients that should enter into the singing style. In large measure, audiences are influenced by some particularly electric or novel singer. As the audience changes, as from one generation to the next, the standards and notions about singing often change. A new or different kind of music is usually accompanied by a change in singing styles.

There were three distinct singing styles in American popular music of the 1930s: the tenor or "clean" style; the stage or "talking" style; and the crooning or "dirty" style. The tenor and stage styles were vocal traditions from the nineteenth century. Crooning, on the other hand, was a product of the 1930s. During that decade, crooning, which at first appeared to be a mere fad, developed into a genuine tradition and became the dominant style of the time. Its supremacy in popular music remained intact until the mid-1950s with the emergence of rock and roll, when a new style of singing took over.

Tenor or "Clean" Style

The roots of the **tenor style** can be traced to several sources, one being the Irish tenor who sang in a clear, high, and often melodramatic way. This style was exceedingly popular in this country.

The purity or "cleanliness" of vocal quality in the tenor style was usually matched by "clean" lyrics. Typically, the tenor style singer avoided lyrics that dealt with controversial or morally questionable subject matter, such as criticism of traditional values, or drinking and gambling.

Guy Lombardo's band typified the sweet band sound, which also appealed to dancers.

The national popularity of Guy Lombardo lasted several decades.

Audience standards for singing tend to change as the style of popular music changes.

Singers in the thirties offered three styles: tenor, talking, and crooning.

Tenor style, which was clean in quality and subject matter, reminded listeners of the genteel tradition.

The tenor style of singing was particularly popular with middle and older age groups in the thirties—a throwback to the genteel tradition of the early nineteenth century. To the older age groups, this style seemed healthy and wholesome, a buffer against a creeping moral decay that they sensed in the country, and in some types of music. The world was in the process of change and so was the style of American popular music. For many, the tenor style symbolized a return of the good old days, and was a comfort to those who decried or resisted change. Typical of the style is "Stay as Sweet as You Are."

Tenor style was considered sophisticated.

The style also appealed to those who expected to hear evidence of legitimate voice training from their singers. And, unlike the other popular singing styles, the tenor style could claim a filial relationship to "high brow" music, which was also desirable to many.

Talking Style

The stage or **talking style** was a product of the vaudeville stage and nightclub circuit, both of which were rougher, much less sophisticated forms of theater. The singers from these forms of musical theater were actually more comedians or song and dance men than legitimate vocalists. Since their audiences were often noisy and rowdy, these performers developed voices that had the capacity to "bark" their songs in a somewhat abrasive fashion. It was not their intention to produce beautiful sounds—quite the contrary. Their ranges were limited, their vocal quality was husky, and their delivery was a mixture of genuine singing and rhythmic talking. They set the standard for more recent musical comedy roles such as Harold Hill in *The Music Man* and Henry Higgins in *My Fair Lady*.

The talking style was an abrasive, nightclub style of singing.

The stage or talking style singer also depended on visual effects, such as soft shoe routines. These visual effects added another dimension to the singers' performances and helped to compensate for a lack of vocal prowess.

Talking style was often combined with visual effects.

A good example is "Can Broadway Do without Me?" by Jimmy Durante, who was among the most amusing and successful of the talking style performers.

Crooning or "Dirty" Style

From the birth of the recording industry in the 1870s until the mid-1920s, all songs were recorded through an acoustical process. The performer—Enrico Caruso was an early favorite—had neither microphone nor amplification, but played or sang directly into a recording horn, which activated a stylus that cut the pattern of the sound waves into tinfoil (in the case of cylinder recording) or into wax (in the case of early disc recording). By today's standards the acoustic process obviously is

From the 1870s until the 1920s singers recorded their songs through recording horns.

primitive. This unsophisticated process is incapable of capturing nuances, soft sounds, a wide range of frequencies and many standard timbral combinations. It was best equipped to record the full-bodied voice, such as Caruso's.

In the 1920s the microphone and amplifier revolutionized the recording process.

The microphone was introduced to the recording industry in the early 1920s. After 1925, the electric recording with microphone and amplifier replaced the acoustic process, became standardized, and has remained in use to the present day.

The breathy quality of crooning demanded amplification for the singer under most circumstances.

Crooning was a term applied to a particular singing style. The crooner typically sang with half a voice and produced a breathier sound than that of a trained full-voiced singer. Thus, unless the crooner were singing in intimate surroundings, he or she needed amplification in order to be heard. The microphone became the solution to this dilemma.

An incident reported in *Variety Magazine* in 1931 suggests the extent to which the new term "crooner" was used by the public. Under the headline "Pair of Crooners Crooning Ballads Got Hostess Sore," the report described two men arrested for crooning outside of a young woman's house:

> "They came to my house and remained outside the apartment door. They crooned and crooned . . ." she said.
>   "I was in no humor to be crooned for. I was tired and I begged them to leave, but they insisted upon crooning.
>   "I then called the cop," stated the hostess.

The crooning style sounded uniquely American.

To identify with crooning was to be with it, or up-to-date. Undoubtedly, the crooner was a symbol of newness, and the sleekness and intimacy of his style clashed with the singing tradition that had dominated the American popular scene for many decades. The crooning style sounded fresh and uniquely American.

Critics of crooning predicted its early demise.

Often in the history of popular music a newly emerging style or manner of performance is greeted by critics and experts as nothing more than a momentary fad. The advent of crooning in the 1930s was greeted with just such a prediction, since it was a dramatic break with previous popular music practices. The predictions of its early demise, however, did not materialize.

Rudy Vallee was the first well-known crooner, but Bing Crosby epitomized the style.

Rudy Vallee (1901–83) was the first well-known singer who was nominally considered a crooner. Vallee was associated with the kind of syncopated orchestra fashionable with New York society in the early decades of this century, and his vocal delivery never overstepped the polite boundaries of that particular style. The blues, which was being brought to the attention of a sizable white audience in the 1920s, had no effect on his singing style, nor was he tempted to swing or "jazz up" his delivery.

Bing Crosby with Shirley Ross
in *Waikiki Wedding*, 1937.
© Springer/Bettmann Film Archive

Bing Crosby   Bing Crosby (1904–77) did not invent crooning, but his
voice became the standard against which all other crooners would be
measured. Crosby, unlike Vallee, could make a legitimate claim to a jazz
background. The performance practices of the many jazz musicians
whom he knew and with whom he worked had a profound impact on his
singing style.

As you listen to Crosby's version of "Learn to Croon," note that
his style closely resembled that of the swing musician. The effortlessness
and nonchalance of his delivery, his penchant for imitating jazz instruments (sometimes with modest improvisational lines and figures), and
his ability to swing, imply that his ear was attuned to musicians such as
Jack Teagarden, Louis Armstrong, and Bix Beiderbecke.

Moreover, Crosby had a unique quality—humor. Crosby's humor
was infectious, but not self-conscious. Though he had the ability to move
his audience to tears with a slow, sad ballad, he could put the same audience in good humor with his up-tempo pieces. He often accomplished
this by caricaturing himself, poking fun at the crooner with all those
"Boo boo boo boos."

The Demise of the Swing Era

The big bands disappeared after World War II.

To paraphrase an important title from the 1930s, the swing era was "gone with the war." The big bands fell on hard times after the war and soon disappeared entirely. The ghost of the big band era was occasionally visible in revivals of the Glenn Miller band and other bands, and in some cases these bands managed to keep their grip on at least a small audience. A significant number of swing musicians either went into studio work, or evolved new styles that were in touch with the changing face of jazz. A few, like Ellington and Basie, somehow managed to keep their bands together. Others left. But for the most part, an era in the history of American popular music was over.

Summary

Our study of American popular music has revealed that the period from the mid-nineteenth century through the 1940s was one of great change. During these years American popular music moved through three distinct stages: the genteel tradition, Tin Pan Alley, and swing.

From the colonial days music played a role in the American tradition. It was not until the middle of the nineteenth century, however, when sheet music was commercially distributed, that Americans across the country began listening to the same music. It is at this time that we can begin to identify an American popular music style.

The life-style of the middle-class American in mid-nineteenth century is termed the genteel tradition. Popular music in the form of the parlor song was a part of this tradition. The songs offered simple, diatonic harmony, unpretentious melodies, and nostalgic, sentimental texts. These songs were typically played at home on the family piano. Stephen Foster's music epitomizes this style.

In the Gay 90s the mood called for a more dissonant, raucous music—that of Tin Pan Alley. These restless songs featuring saucy verses reflected the economic, social, and political upheaval of the times.

The popular music of the 1930s featured primarily *AABA* and *AA* form. Few songs offered unconventional form. From 1930 to 1939, approximately 10,000 songs were published, ranging in topic from love to nostalgia to the exotic.

"Swing" describes the way much of the thirties music was played. It was popularized by many of the big dance bands such as those of Tommy Dorsey and Glenn Miller. Other bands, including Guy Lombardo's, however, played a "sweet" music that did not swing.

Plate 25
An image from the Great Depression years: gentle and melancholy. Compare it to the mood of Samuel Barber's *Adagio for String Orchestra* (chapter 9).

Nighthawks; Edward Hopper; 1942; oil on canvas; 76.2 cm × 144 cm; Friends of American Art Collection, 1942.51

Plate 26
The clean lines, sharply defined shapes, and general sense of precision and
balance suggest neoclassicism. See chapter 9 for the discussion of
neoclassicism in twentieth-century music.

Composition in White, Black, and Red; Piet Mondrian; 1936; oil on canvas; 40¼″ × 41″. The Museum of Modern
Art, New York, Gift of the Advisory Committee.

Plate 27
A seemingly random pattern of color creates a painting with great energy and density. See the discussions of electronic music and chance music in chapter 9.

Number 1; Jackson Pollock; 1948; oil on canvas; 68″ × 8′8″; The Museum of Modern Art, New York, Purchase.

Plate 28
The pop art movement of the 1960s has some connection to the dadist
movement from the early twentieth century (see chapter 9).

Green Coca-Cola Bottles; Andy Warhol; 1962; oil on canvas; 82½'' × 57''; collection of Whitney Museum of
American Art, New York. Purchase, with funds from the friends of Whitney Museum of American Art 68.25.

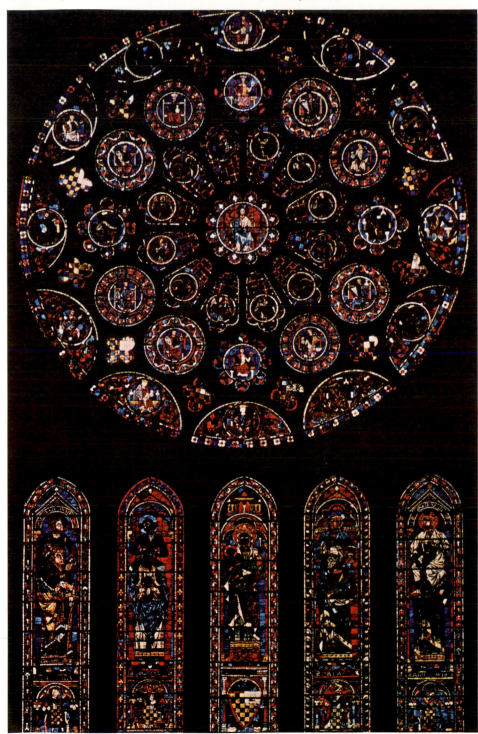

South Rose Window and Lancets; Chartres Cathedral; Scala/The Art Resource, New York.

Plate 30
A serene, intelligent visage from the Renaissance (see chapter 11).

Ginevra de'Benci; Leonardo da Vinci; Date: ca. 1474; wood; 0.388 × 0.367, reverse: 0.382 cm × 0.367 cm; National Gallery of Art; Washington, Ailsa Mellon Bruce Fund.

Plate 31
A masterwork by Michelangelo, a luminary of the humanistic Renaissance.

Creation; Michelangelo; Sistine Chapel Ceiling; Scala/The Art Resource, New York.

Plate 32
An American family in the nineteenth century (see chapter 12).

The Sargent Family; American School; Date: 1800; canvas; 0.974 cm × 1.280 cm; National Gallery of Art;
Washington; Gift of Edgar William and Bernice Chrysler Garbish, 1953.

Plate 33
A jukebox from the late 1930s or early 1940s (see chapter 12).

Plate 34
The Beatles (see chapter 13).

Plate 35
African musicians.

Plate 36
A Balinese gamelan orchestra.

The most popular singing style of the period was crooning. Singers Rudy Vallee and Bing Crosby popularized a breathy style that appealed to audiences across the country. Also popular were the clear tenor style reminiscent of the genteel tradition and the talking style that had developed on the vaudeville stage and in the night club. This style was the abrasive, husky sounding form popularized by Jimmy Durante.

The swing era, which encompassed the musical traditions of the period from 1930 through 1945, died soon after the conclusion of World War II. American popular music would soon after be termed "rock."

Key Terms

genteel tradition	novelty song	tenor (clean) style
parlor song	swing	talking (stage)
Tin Pan Alley	swing era	style
verse and refrain	sweet dance bands	crooning
standard		

Thinking About It

It is difficult to single out only a few of the quality compositions from this era because of the vast and diverse collection that exists. Thus, instead of specific Sound and Sense examples, the following list of works from the three major genres is provided. These recordings remain popular enough that locating them should not present a problem. You are encouraged, then, to listen to as many recordings as possible.

From the Genteel Tradition

Songs by Stephen Foster	Nonesuch H 71268 Stereo
Gregg Smith Singers: Songs of S. Foster	Turnabout 34609
An Evening with Henry Russell	Nonesuch H 71338
Songs by Henry Clay Work	Nonesuch H 71317

From the Tin Pan Alley Era

Come Josephine in My Flying Machine	New World Records NW 233
Barber Shop Quartet Favorites	Coral 20012

From the Swing Era

Benny Goodman—Giants of Swing Treasure Chest (3 vols.)	MGM E3788, 89, 90
Duke Ellington: Greatest Hits	Reprise 6234
Brother Can You Spare a Dime?	New World Records NW 270
Rudy Vallee: Heigh Ho, Everybody	Olympic Records OL-7128
The Music Goes Round and Round	New World Records NW 248
Singing Troubadors on the Air	Star-Tone Records ST-206
The Great Big Band Vocalists	Columbia Special; Products CSS 1507
The Original Big Band Hits	RCA R 212227

There are also collections of hits from the thirties and forties by Bing Crosby and by many of the big bands.

CHAPTER

13

Jazz

Duke Ellington (1899–1974).
© AP/Wide World Photos, Inc.

Sounds of the Chapter

Armstrong
"Hotter Than That" ♪
"West End Blues" ♪

Broonzy
"Baby Please Don't Go"
"I Got Up in the Mornin' Blues"

Brubeck
"Take Five" ♪

Coleman
"Happy House" ♪

Coletrane
"Alabama"

Ellington
"Caravan"
"Mood Indigo"
"Solitude"
"Sophisticated Lady"

Gershwin
Rhapsody in Blue

Goodman
"Down South Camp Meeting" ♪

Hooker
"Blues before Sunrise"

Joplin
"Maple Leaf Rag" ♪

King Oliver
"Dippermouth Blues" ♪

Leadbelly
"The Bourgeois Blues"
"The Gallis Pole"

Morton
"Maple Leaf Rag" ♪

Parker
"Groovin' High"
"Ornithology" ♪
"White Christmas" ♪

Spaan
"Worried Life Blues"

Trumbauer
"Riverboat Shuffle" ♪

Waller
"Numb Fumblin' " ♪
"Whispering"

The Nature of Jazz

Jazz did not develop as an isolated musical form. It is similar to other kinds of music, but in some important respects jazz is different from classical, popular, and folk music, so it is dealt with individually. In this chapter we will find out how and in what ways jazz differs from other kinds of music.

Pure jazz emerged sometime in the early years of the twentieth century. Jazz was born in the South and its parents were black Americans. Its emergence was the result of the confluence of several different musical streams. Each of these streams—swing, improvisation, blues, rag, and the European tradition in instrumentation and harmony—has a history that is much older than jazz itself.

Like other music studied thus far, jazz continued to evolve, and it developed into several different styles: early New Orleans jazz, 1920s hot jazz, swing in the 1930s and 1940s, bop and cool jazz in the 1940s and 1950s, and new jazz since the 1960s.

With the emergence of each of these styles jazz changed superficially, yet a permanent inner core has remained. At the heart of this core are swing and improvisation.

Swing

Though swing was briefly discussed in chapter 12, a more detailed investigation is now necessary. **Swing** is largely a temporal phenomenon. It is a manner of performing rhythm that is unique to jazz. Swing is the element most vital to jazz: without it, the music wouldn't sound like jazz. Swing musicians deliberately deviate from the true note values of a given melody. For example, a jazz musician confronted with this group of eighth notes:

will usually not play them thus. Instead, he or she might swing the even eighth notes like this:

or this:

Jazz emerged in the American South in the early twentieth century.

Several styles of jazz have evolved.

Swing, a uniquely jazz rhythm, and improvisation are the core of jazz.

True note values are deliberately avoided.

Some notes are held for longer or shorter periods than their notated values, some beats or fractions of beats are unexpectedly accented, and some pitches may be added to the notated melody, filling the gaps between the specified pitches of the melody. One of the striking things about swing is that it sounds so nonchalant, almost careless, but in fact it is very precisely controlled. One doesn't have to be born with the sense of swing—it can be learned—but many classical and rock musicians are unable to capture the rhythm, partly because swing cannot be precisely notated.

Swing cannot be precisely notated.

For instance, listen to the well-known song "White Christmas" to hear what happens to its rhythm when Charlie Parker swings it on his alto sax. Listen as the melody is presented with relatively few alterations. Then compare Parker's swinging version with the way the song is usually sung by popular singers. Can you feel the difference?

The swing with which Parker plays is present in all true jazz. Swing is one of the core ingredients of jazz that transcends all stylistic boundaries.

Improvisation

Whereas swing has to do with *how* things are played in jazz, **improvisation** has to do with *what* is played in jazz. Simply stated, improvisation is a process in which musical ideas are created and played almost simultaneously. Improvisation is not something read off of a page or merely memorized; it is spontaneous rather than studied.

Improvisation is spontaneous, but structured.

On the other hand, improvisation does not happen by accident. The improviser creates music within the bounds of a predetermined formal and harmonic structure. The improviser does not just play anything that comes to mind. To illustrate this let's return to Parker's recording of "White Christmas."

First, sing "White Christmas" to yourself. You should be able to detect that the song is in 4/4 meter and that it has four sections, each of which is eight bars long: *A* (eight bars), *B* (eight bars), *A* (eight bars), *B'* (eight bars). This thirty-two-bar pattern is called a **chorus.** Listen to the first chorus again. Notice that it is a full chorus of thirty-two bars. Now listen to the next chorus played by Parker. This second chorus is thirty-two bars long and it uses the same harmony as the first chorus, but there is a very noticeable difference between the two. The difference is improvisation in the second chorus. Parker plays an improvisation of great complexity and beauty, swinging the rhythm all the while. The melodic line of "White Christmas" all but disappears in this improvisation, but the song's formal structure and harmony are kept rigidly intact. The freedom of the improvisation is anchored to the preexistent harmony and form of the song. In a sense, freedom develops from control.

Each thirty-two bar pattern in "White Christmas" is called a chorus.

In improvisation the melodic line almost disappears, while formal structure and harmony remain intact.

Now listen to the next chorus played by Parker. In it is heard a new and different improvisation, but once more, the form and the harmony remain unchanged. Try singing the song softly to yourself as Parker plays these two choruses. If you maintain the tempo you will notice that in every case you and Parker come to the ends of phrases and sections simultaneously.

The recording continues with two thirty-two-bar choruses for trumpet. This is followed by a concluding chorus in which sax and trumpet repeat the melody of the opening chorus.

Though swing and improvisation were probably the most important precursors of jazz, now consider the other musical styles that led to its development.

Early Jazz

New Orleans' divergent culture contributed to the makeup of jazz.

The earliest jazz is associated with the city of New Orleans. In the nineteenth century New Orleans experienced an influx of a variety of people, customs, and music. The Spanish, French, African, Cajun, and Creole heritage of New Orleans was, and is, clearly visible and audible even to the casual observer. These various cultures contributed to the musical style we now recognize as jazz.

Blues

The blues scale is the major and minor third above tonic and the minor seventh above tonic.

Worried notes typify blues music.

In the late nineteeth and early twentieth centuries black country **blues** singers generally sang solo or accompanied themselves on the guitar. In either case, the vocal quality they produced was rooted in African rather than European musical traditions. The blues singer's delivery included various vocal scoops, groans, falsetto, and other ornaments. The melodic lines of blues often featured both the major and the minor third above tonic, and also the minor rather than the customary major seventh above tonic (this constitutes the blues scale). The blues singer's delivery also included **worried notes**—notes performed with a vocal shake or quiver, noticeably out of tune, sometimes, with European scales (some pitches smaller than the minor second).

These qualities can be heard in all of the following songs from the anthology *The Best of the Blues,* vol. 1: "The Bourgeois Blues" and "The Gallis Pole" by Leadbelly; "Blues before Sunrise" by John Lee Hooker; "Baby Please Don't Go" and "I Got Up in the Mornin' Blues" by Big Bill Broonzy; "Worried Life Blues" by Otis Spaan, and "I'm a Stranger Here" by Sonny and Brownie.

The twelve-bar blues was the most popular blues form.

Blues came in many sizes and shapes in the early twentieth century, but the twelve-bar blues, with which you are familiar, emerged as the most frequently used and the most influential pattern. The twelve-bar blues became the norm not only for singers, but also for jazz instrumentalists who adopted the form.

For the country blues singer the guitar was the required accompanying instrument since pianos were rare or nonexistent, especially for blacks, in the rural south. But urban blues singers, generally somewhat more sophisticated than rural musicians, began to use the piano for accompaniment. Eventually this led to the development of a whole school of blues/jazz piano players, among whom Ferdinand "Jelly Roll" Morton was a central figure.

Rag

In the St. Louis and Kansas City area, another brand of piano music developed in the 1890s: **ragtime,** or **rag.** Rag was a more cultivated style. It didn't swing, but syncopations dominated the right hand with space provided for improvisation.

An excellent demonstration of the stylistic difference between pure rag and early New Orleans jazz is Scott Joplin playing his composition, "Maple Leaf Rag." Next listen to Jelly Roll Morton playing the same piece but adding swing. The Joplin version, with its almost classical purity and stiffness, is clearly not jazz, but the Morton version definitely is, demonstrating a basic difference between New Orleans jazz and ragtime.

Rag music was an ingredient in the formation of jazz, though it was not as important as swing, improvisation, and blues.

Harmony and Instruments

With some exceptions, all rag pieces composed from 1890 to 1910 (when the craze for rags subsided) were written for the piano—a European, not an African, instrument. Thus, while ragtime and early jazz were essentially the products of black genius, European instruments and harmonies were important in the development of rag and jazz. In essence rag and jazz were the union of the two musical traditions—West African and European.

Jazz: A European-African Combination

Marching bands were very popular in New Orleans before the turn of the century, and these bands utilized European harmony and instruments: trumpets, trombones, tubas, clarinets, drums, and others. However, the musicians were usually blacks who retained some of their West African musical traditions. The rhythm of tribal music is much more intricate and complex than that of Western art and folk music. **Polyrhythms** (two or more different, simultaneously operating rhythms) are common yet so different from the European heritage that the Europeans of the early 1900s generally considered African rhythm to be chaotic.

Improvisation is an ingredient of ragtime.

Scott Joplin (1868–1917).
© The Bettmann Archive

The majority of rags were composed for piano.

Ragtime and jazz combine elements of African and European musical traditions.

Blacks brought African music tradition to the American marching band.

African polyrhythms were considered by many to be chaotic.

The black musicians blended their musical heritage with the musical heritage of the Europeans, which resulted in a unique sound that helped to set the stage for the birth of jazz.

Jazz resulted from the blend of European technique and African delivery.

European musical traditions, then, provided the techniques (instruments) and theory (harmony), but African traditions influenced the delivery of the music—its soul.

In summary, the blending of swing, improvisation, blues, rag, and the fusion of West African and European musical traditions resulted in New Orleans jazz.

New Orleans Bands

New Orleans jazz bands consisted of: piano, bass fiddle, drums, clarinet, trumpet, trombone, and sometimes a guitar or banjo.

Early New Orleans jazz bands were small, normally consisting of piano, bass fiddle, drums, clarinet, trumpet, trombone, and sometimes guitar or banjo. Piano, bass, drums, and guitar or banjo formed the rhythm section, while clarinet, trumpet, and trombone were called "front line" instruments. Each of the front line instruments played solos, yet all three were also joined in ensemble, with the trumpet playing the main melody, the clarinet weaving improvisational embroidery above, and the trombone creating a line below.

The repertoire of these bands consisted of instrumental blues (sometimes with vocals), rags, and other short structures such as stomps and breakdowns. Usually a performance consisted of the following:

One or two choruses for the ensemble
Solo chorus(es) for trumpet
Solo chorus(es) for clarinet
Solo chorus(es) for trombone
Closing chorus for the ensemble

Group improvisation is more important than the solo in New Orleans jazz.

Despite the importance of solos in New Orleans style jazz, group improvisation is valued above all else. The importance of group improvisation is obvious in many of the recordings of King Oliver's Creole Jazz Band. King Oliver (1885–1938) was one of the early legendary jazz trumpet and cornet players. Listen to his recording of "Dippermouth Blues." (Oliver plays first cornet and the young Louis Armstrong plays second cornet in this recording.)

Sound and Sense ♪
New Orleans Style Jazz

Title: "Dippermouth Blues"
Composer: King Oliver

A Closer Look

"Dippermouth Blues" has the following structure:

Brief introduction by the ensemble
Chorus for ensemble—group improvisation
Chorus for ensemble—group improvisation
Chorus for clarinet
Chorus for clarinet
Chorus for ensemble—group improvisation
Chorus for cornet
Chorus for cornet
Two more choruses for ensemble
Brief coda

Notice that even during the solo choruses the other instruments remain active, particularly at the ends of phrases. Though each instrument improvises, there is a sense of group creation, unified by the common harmonies and the twelve-bar blues form they all share.

1920s Hot Jazz

Jazz flourished in New Orleans, particularly in a section of the city known as Storeyville. Storeyville was a place of excitement and vice, with rough bars and brothels. In 1917 city officials closed Storeyville, and many jazz musicians found themselves out of work. As a result, New Orleans jazz went on the road.

Prior to this, other centers of jazz had been developing in Chicago, Kansas City, New York, and other places. In the late twenties blues and jazz recordings became more popular in America. Some of the great New Orleans jazz musicians, such as Louis Armstrong, moved to Chicago in the early twenties.

The expansion of jazz in Chicago was partly the result of economics. Jazz musicians from New Orleans and elsewhere in the South came searching for steady work in Chicago and other parts of the more affluent north during the Roaring Twenties. Many speakeasies (bars

In 1917 New Orleans jazz was forced out of its element in Storeyville.

Jazz spread across America in the 1920s.

A taste for jazz in northern cities created a demand for jazz musicians.

where liquor was sold illegally during Prohibition), restaurants, and clubs in Chicago catered to a white clientele that developed a taste for jazz, thus creating a demand for jazz musicians.

Armstrong had a tremendous impact upon jazz musicians there, but he began to deviate from the New Orleans jazz tradition, creating a kind of jazz that emphasized soloists. A sample of Armstrong's music at that time is found in his recording of "West End Blues."

Louis Armstrong put the focus on the jazz soloist.

Louis Armstrong (1900–1971).
© The Bettmann Archive

Sound and Sense ♩
Jazz Soloists

Title: "West End Blues"
Composer: Louis Armstrong

A Closer Look
A flashy, cadenzalike solo introduces "West End Blues."

Chorus for ensemble (note the twelve-bar blues structure)
Chorus for trombone
Chorus for clarinet with vocal interjections
Chorus for piano
Final chorus for ensemble

Hot jazz was Armstrong's style.

The hot side of Armstrong's jazz can be heard in "Hotter Than That." This is the kind of solo performance that set the Chicago and New York musicians on their ear. "Hotter Than That" is a thirty-two-bar structure that is prefaced by an eight-bar introduction. There is a chorus for ensemble, one for clarinet, and a half chorus for trombone, the other half for the ensemble. A spectacular chorus follows, with Armstrong singing instead of playing the trumpet. The piece ends abruptly with a clever duet with voice and guitar.

New Elements in Twenties Jazz

The jazz of the twenties changed in several ways as illustrated in "Riverboat Shuffle" played by Frankie Trumbauer and his orchestra. The group comprised white musicians, whereas jazz had formerly been played almost exclusively by blacks. Beginning in the twenties many white musicians became fascinated with and very adept at playing jazz. (This was the incubation period for white musicians who would become the leaders of many of the swing bands in the thirties and forties.)

The white jazz musicians who began playing in jazz bands in the twenties became the leaders of swing bands in the thirties and forties.

Chicago style jazz featured the soloist.

"Riverboat Shuffle" has the drive of New Orleans style jazz and some of its group improvisation, but clearly the central feature of this Chicago style piece is the solo work of Bix Beiderbecke (1903–31), the legendary white trumpet player who became a sort of jazz hero. While Chicago style is hot and bouncy, Beiderbecke's personal style is more lyric and not as raucous as Armstrong's forceful playing. Armstrong's solo improvisation, however, was assimilated by and became an important part of Chicago style jazz.

The saxophone became a prominent instrument for the first time with jazz. This piece features Trumbauer's instrument, the C-melody sax, which quickly gave way to alto, tenor, and baritone saxes in jazz. Whereas early jazz did not normally incorporate the sax, it became increasingly important in the twenties and in Chicago style jazz. Saxophones thus found a home in jazz, and before long a whole school of alto sax players and a school of tenor sax players blossomed.

Twenties jazz brought the sax to prominence.

"Riverboat Shuffle" also contains several short **breaks,** which are brief passages played by a soloist while the remainder of the group, including the entire rhythm section, remains silent. This type of break temporarily halts the steady flow of the beat. The break is as old as jazz itself and was an integral part of blues and of New Orleans jazz. The break was not new in Chicago jazz, but the interesting harmony of the breaks in pieces like this one was innovative. The chord vocabulary of jazz was expanding to include new and more dissonant and complex harmonies.

During a jazz "break" the soloist plays while the rest of the band is quiet.

The first breaks in "Riverboat" occur near the beginning of the piece with five in the guitar. This is followed by a short piano break. Listen for the dissonance of these breaks. Later in the piece there is a clarinet break, two in the trumpet, three in the trombone, then one each in clarinet, trumpet, sax, and guitar, and sax.

The standard size of a New Orleans band was five to seven players. Many groups in the twenties maintained that number, but groups of eight to ten or more became increasingly common and laid the groundwork for the big swing bands of the thirties. Trumbauer's group featured eight players and ten different instruments.

Toward the end of the 1920s jazz bands grew in size.

Thus "Riverboat Shuffle" exemplifies several new trends in twenties jazz: the inclusion of white performers, the focus on solo improvisation, the rise of the sax, the expansion of the harmonic language, and the move toward larger bands.

Stride Piano

The twenties also saw the rise of new styles of piano playing: boogie woogie (discussed in chapter 14) and **stride piano.** Broadly speaking, stride style established three things: (1) left-hand patterns that activated beats two and four in the 4/4 meter, resulting in a definite four-beat rather than a two-beat feeling; (2) right-hand improvisations that often assumed the character of solo lines played by a trumpet or another single

New styles of piano playing emerged in the 1920s.

Stride style established new left- and right-hand patterns.

line instrument; and (3) an expansion of the harmonic language of jazz to include ninth and eleventh chords, and other complex chords and dissonances.

The examples of early jazz heard up to this point are in 4/4 meter, but they have the feeling of only two major beats to the bar (except in slow blues). Confirm this by listening to the examples again.

With stride piano, however, the left hand produces four distinct beats to the bar. A variety of patterns can be used to create this feeling: syncopation coupled with nonsyncopation, full chords on all four beats, melodic fillers on beats two and four, or extended countermelodies in the left hand.

By listening to the left-hand activity and by sensing the number of beats in the bar, the evolution from ragtime piano to New Orleans jazz piano to stride can be traced. With this in mind listen once more to the Joplin version of "Maple Leaf Rag," then to the Jelly Roll Morton (1890–1941) version, and then to an example by the great stride pianist, Fats Waller (1904–43): "Numb Fumblin'."

In Waller's stride style, notice the flexibility of the rhythm and beat, the intricacy of the improvisational lines, and the fullness of the harmonic language.

In stride piano, the left hand plays four beats to the bar.

Swing in the Thirties and Forties

Whereas New Orleans jazz leaned heavily on group improvisation and twenties jazz emphasized solo improvisation, the big swing bands featured both ensemble playing and solo improvisation. During this era popular songs were jazzed and thus became staples of the swing jazz repertoire.

Big swing bands combined ensemble playing and solo improvisation.

The face of jazz changed with the emergence of the big bands. The size of the group was doubled as the solo clarinet, trumpet, and trombone swelled to four reeds, three trumpets, and two trombones. With a group of this size, it became necessary to indicate to the players specifically what they were to play and when to play it. Without this information, musical chaos would undoubtedly result. Either by notation or by rote each player had to learn and play his own part of the arrangement. The arranger thus became very much like a composer, writing out the ensemble sections and at least some of the underscore sections that supported the improvisational solos in the work.

The swing band of the 1930s was larger than the jazz band had been, and each member was assigned a specific part to play.

Jazz Players

Paul Whiteman (1890–1967), called "the King of Jazz," was definitely not the reigning jazz musician. His inclination was to water down jazz, to popularize aspects of it, and to make it palatable to the general public. In his hands, jazz was neither created nor very well served, but after the success of his famous Carnegie Hall concert of 1924 in which Gershwin's *Rhapsody in Blue* was featured, Whiteman began, increasingly, to feature real jazz players as soloists with his orchestra. Among them were Bix Beiderbecke, Bunny Berigan, Red Nichols, Jimmy and Tommy Dorsey, and, in the early thirties, Bing Crosby and the Rhythm Boys. When the jazz players left or sat out, Whiteman's orchestra deteriorated into pure corn. But when they played, these musicians offered most white Americans their first taste of jazz.

Soloists in Paul Whiteman's orchestra became well-known jazz players.

Black and White Jazz

Black and white swing bands played jazz differently as is noticeable in recorded performances. The black bands played swing first, played proportionately more of it than white swing musicians, and played for audiences who reveled in their performances. They played with an intensity, abandon, and drive unmatched by most of the white swing bands. The fire with which the best black bands played did not result, however, in ensemble sloppiness or imprecision, and the great sidemen (soloists) achieved a level of technical skill and creative inventiveness envied by all musicians.

Black swing bands were famous for intensity, drive, and creative inventiveness.

The white bands, several of which were excellent performing groups, tended to play with more restraint. Not only was the volume more subdued, but all aspects of the rendition were presented without excess or extravagance.

White swing bands were more subdued.

January 16, 1938, marked the first-known occasion of black and white jazz musicians publicly playing together. Teddy Wilson and Lionel Hampton joined forces with Benny Goodman (and others) in a legendary concert at Carnegie Hall. They broke the "color line" in jazz, just as nine years later Jackie Robinson and the Brooklyn Dodgers did in the world of professional baseball.

In 1938 the "color line" in jazz was broken as black and white musicians played together at Carnegie Hall.

Certainly black and white musicians were aware of one another's work prior to this time, and it is a fact that some of the best of the black musicians had a profound influence on the development of many white jazz musicians; Goodman himself profited greatly from the exposure to certain black players.

As important as this Carnegie Hall concert was, it was in essence only the first step in a long journey. It did not tear down the walls between black and white performers on a wholesale scale and it had little immediate impact on the divisions between black and white popular music and jazz audiences. From the beginning until the end of the swing era there remained differences between the tastes of the audiences, and these differences were reflected in the repertoires and performances of black and white swing bands.

The repertoires of black and white swing bands reveal the differences in their audiences' tastes.

The Genius of Ellington

Jazz, like any other type of music, occasionally produces a musician of genius, one who clearly stands apart from his contemporaries and profoundly affects and influences others. Edward Kennedy "Duke" Ellington (1899–1974) was such a figure. Ellington was an extremely prolific composer of diverse works, many of which have become standards: "Mood Indigo" (1931), "Sophisticated Lady" (1933), "Solitude" (1935), "Caravan" (1937), and others. He also composed hundreds of original jazz works, a number of more extended concert works, and some large-scale sacred works. His accomplishments are all the more impressive inasmuch as his schedule was jammed with performances almost throughout his entire career. It is astonishing that the man found the time to write as much as he did. Even under the constraint of this hectic schedule, Ellington's body of works contains little that is repetitious. Rather, it contains a seemingly endless flow of fresh and arresting musical ideas.

Duke Ellington is respected as both a jazz musician and a jazz composer.

Ellington's abundant, original jazz compositions contain fresh and innovative musical ideas.

Bop and Cool

After the swing era, the next significant developments in jazz came with the emergence of **bebop,** or **bop,** in the late forties, and **cool jazz** shortly thereafter. Bop and cool dominated jazz music through the fifties and into the sixties. Both styles have many similar characteristics. Each were reactions to the big swing bands and the style of jazz they played. The normal size of a bop group or cool group was five to seven players—three rhythm, and two, three, or four front line instruments. This was a drastic reduction from the size of a typical swing band.

The swing bands played a kind of jazz that was designed for dance, so they were really dance bands. Bop and cool jazz, on the other hand, were more intellectual forms of jazz. Bop—with its complex rhythms and frantic tempos—was designed for listening rather than dancing. And many cool jazz musicians were well-educated, so cool jazz soon became infused with the harmonic language, counterpoint, and formal structure of classical music. It was at this time that some began to speak of jazz as an "art form."

Bop was a hot kind of jazz principally centered in the East (mainly in New York City). As its name implies, cool jazz was cooler and more detached. It flourished primarily in the Los Angeles area.

Swing bands were actually dance bands, whereas bop and cool jazz were intended for listening.

Cool jazz was considered an art form when performed by the well-educated jazz musicians of the 1950s.

Bop was a hot, New York City-centered jazz style.

Characteristics of Bop

Bop is characterized by a frantic, almost angry quality noticeable in both the frenzied tempo and in the aggression with which the players performed. The complexity of the expanded chord vocabulary is another bop characteristic. The new chords and chord progressions struck some

Bop is frantic and frenzied.

Charlie Parker (1920–55).
© The Bettmann Archive

older musicians as wild to the point of being chaotic. But probably the most startling thing about bop is its rhythm: the bop drummer creates a fresh variety of polyrhythms, and the front line improvisers weave long and complicated lines filled with unexpected accents and sections of rapidly-played notes. The sound of the bop sax or trumpet is normally very tight and brittle in both fast and slow numbers. Lushness of tone is discarded in favor of a more aggressive sound.

Many musicians were responsible for the formation of bop, but two in particular—Charlie Parker (1920–55) and trumpeter Dizzy Gillespie (b. 1917)—emerged as giant figures in the movement. Both are heard, together with Max Roach (b. 1924), one of the best bop drummers, in "Ornithology."

"Ornithology" is based on a thirty-two-bar theme that is first stated by the ensemble, followed by several thirty-two-bar improvisational choruses by Parker and Gillespie, and concluded with a restatement of the first chorus played by the ensemble. Notice that the theme sounds almost like an improvisation and is more complicated than that of a standard pop song. And though the solo choruses may sound complex, they have the same harmony and formal structure as that of the theme.

Max Roach keeps a relentless and furious pulse with brush on cymbal, while simultaneously creating an intricate web of polyrhythms and oddly distributed accents. The rhythm of bop takes the standard 4/4 meter and divides it into eight pulses, unlike New Orleans jazz (two major pulses) and swing (four pulses).

Aggressive rhythm is characteristic of bop.

Charlie Parker and Dizzy Gillespie were major figures in bop.

Notice the complex theme in "Ornithology."

New Orleans jazz exhibited two major pulses: swing exhibited four, and bop exhibited eight.

Each of the four quarter notes in bop is divided into a pair of eighth notes, and any one of these can be accented.

The bass keeps the beat while the piano provides the harmony.

The bass player maintains the steady beat, playing either four or eight beats to the bar. The piano cooperates with the bass, supplying the harmonic underpinning but also adding accents at various locations within the bar.

The format of Charlie Parker's "Groovin' High" is very similar. It is based on an old popular song, "Whispering." "Whispering" is a thirty-two-bar structure—*A* (sixteen bars) and *A'* (sixteen bars). Once more, all of the solo choruses are based on the structure and chords of this song.

Characteristics of Cool Jazz

Cool jazz improvisation is gentle and smooth.

Since cool jazz uses many of the elements of bop, some musicians were active in both cool and bop at various stages in their careers. Cool, however, is characterized by a softer approach in general. The cool soloist's tone is softer and smoother than the brittle sound of bop. The improvisatory lines contain fewer notes and are gentle, rather than savage. The harmonic language is similar to that in bop, but where the bop musician can make a series of chords sound almost atonal, the cool musician makes the same chords sound much calmer. The cool drummer rides with brush on cymbal, but with a much gentler touch than the bop drummer, and

The cool jazz musician approaches the music with restraint and aloofness.

the division of the 4/4 bar into eight pulses is less obvious in cool jazz. Where the bop musician plays aggressively, the cool musician plays with restraint and assumes a sort of aloofness.

Some of these qualities are evident in "Take Five," played by Dave Brubeck (b. 1920) (piano) and Paul Desmond (1924–77) (alto sax), two legendary cool musicians.

This piece is in the rare 5/4 meter.

New Jazz

Since the 1960s jazz has become segmented, with each branch adopting names such as "the new thing," "funk," or "third stream." Many musicians have made significant contributions to the **new jazz,** but two particularly prominent figures are Ornette Coleman (b. 1930) and John Coltrane (1926–67).

Though Coleman's jazz may sound different at first, it is based in part on the old New Orleans group improvisation. Coleman attempted to free jazz from predetermined themes and chord progressions, allowing musicians greater freedom in improvisation. In Coleman's "Happy House," each of the players is given a notated musical fragment on which

John Coltrane (1926–67).
© AP/Wide World Photos, Inc.

Modern jazz quartette—
proponents of cool jazz.
© Historical Pictures Service, Inc., Chicago

to base his improvisation; chords and themes are freely invented by the performer on the spot. Complex counterpoint and pungent dissonances emerge from this musical tapestry, but notice that, through it all, the music swings just as any jazz does.

John Coltrane's "Alabama" commemorates the tragedy of local schoolchildren killed in a bombing. "Alabama" fluctuates between several different moods, reflective of Coltrane's multiple reactions to the event. The influence of blues, swing, and improvisation are evident in this composition.

Coltrane's "Alabama" exhibits the influence of blues, swing, and improvisation.

Summary

As we began our study of jazz, we pictured it as having an ever-changing outer surface and a permanent inner core. This core contains the two elements basic to all jazz music—swing and improvisation. Swing describes how the unique rhythm of jazz is played. Improvisation describes the process through which spontaneous jazz music is created.

The history of jazz began with the influx of diverse elements in the city of New Orleans in the nineteenth century. This complex culture created musical forms that produced the earliest jazz.

Black country blues emerged from this culture in the late nineteenth century. The vocal quality of this music was rooted in African tradition. While country blues singers played the popular twelve-bar blues on the guitar, urban blues singers adapted the form to piano.

Piano playing took a different turn in the North where ragtime developed in the 1890s. Rag, unlike pure jazz, does not swing.

The marching band, popular in New Orleans during this period, blended the black musicians' West African musical traditions and polyrhythmic style with European harmony and instruments, to produce a unique sound that set the stage for jazz.

True jazz was first produced by small New Orleans bands. These jazz bands were made up of a piano, bass fiddle, drums, clarinet, trumpet, trombone, and sometimes a guitar and banjo. Group improvisation was the key element in the performance.

In the 1920s jazz moved north from New Orleans to become "hot" in the hands of famous composer/musician Louis Armstrong and others. Hot jazz was a central feature of the "Roaring Twenties."

1920s jazz showed these new elements: white performers, solo improvisation, a dominant sax, expansion of harmony, and larger band size. The twenties also witnessed the rise of two new piano styles—boogie and stride.

The swing bands that rose to prominence in the 1930s and 1940s were larger than the jazz bands of New Orleans and featured both ensemble playing and solo improvisation. Group improvisation lost some of its spontaneity when performed by these large bands. Black swing musicians reveled in intensity while white swing bands played jazz with more restraint.

Following on the heels of the swing era came the period of bop and cool. These forms dominated jazz in the fifties and early sixties. While the large swing bands played dance music, the small bop and cool bands appealed more to intellectuals.

Bop was a hot jazz style characterized by a frantic tempo, polyrhythms, and complex improvisation. The music of Charlie Parker and Dizzy Gillespie exemplifies this style. Cool jazz performs the characteristics of bop in a smoother, more gentle style.

The post-1960s jazz has exhibited a less formal structure and a diversity of melodic types.

Based upon our knowledge of jazz structure and our understanding of jazz history, we can predict that the jazz of the future will continue to swing and improvise while evolving in form.

Key Terms

swing	rag (ragtime)	stride piano
improvisation	polyrhythms	bop (bebop)
chorus	hot jazz	cool jazz
blues	break	new jazz
worried notes		

Thinking About It

Now that you have some understanding of various styles of jazz, you should listen to several examples of each of the styles to reinforce the connection between what has been said about these styles and the actual performances of them. There are many fine recorded anthologies of jazz that should be available to you.

C H A P T E R

14

Rock Music

Michael Jackson being honored for his successful "Thriller" album.

Sounds of the Chapter

Laverne Baker
"Jim Dandy"

The Band
"Like a Rolling Stone"

The Beach Boys
"Fun, Fun, Fun"
"Little Deuce Coupe"
"Surfin' U.S.A."

The Beatles
"A Day in the Life"
"A Little Help from My Friends"
"Being for the Benefit of Mr. Kite!"
"Come Together"
"Eleanor Rigby"
"Fixing a Hole"
"Getting Better"
"Good Morning"
"Lovely Rita"
"Love Me Do"
"Lucy in the Sky with Diamonds"
"Polythene Pam"
"Sgt. Pepper's Lonely Hearts Club Band"
"She's Leaving Home"
"Taxman"
"When I'm Sixty-Four"
"Within You, Without You"
"Yesterday"

Chuck Berry
"Roll over Beethoven"
"School Days"

Black Sabbath
"A National Acrobat"

Pat Boone
"Ain't That a Shame"
"I Almost Lost My Mind"
"Love Letters in the Sand"

David Bowie
"Fame"

James Brown
"Good, Good Lovin' "
"Please, Please, Please"

Chubby Checker
"The Twist"

Eric Clapton
"Lay Down Sally"

Bill Doggett
"Honky Tonk"

Fats Domino
"I'm Walkin' "

The Doors
"Break on Through"
"Light My Fire"

The Drifters
"Fools Fall in Love"
"Searchin' "

Bob Dylan
"Like a Rolling Stone"
"The Times They Are A-Changin' "

Aretha Franklin
"Satisfaction"
"You Make Me Feel (Like a Natural Woman)"

Bill Haley
"Rock around the Clock"

Oscar Hammerstein
"You Are Too Beautiful"

Jimi Hendrix
"Manic Depression"
"Purple Haze"
"The Star Spangled Banner"

Buddy Holly
"Peggy Sue"

Jefferson Airplane
"White Rabbit"

Elton John
"Benny and the Jets"

Janis Joplin
"Get It While You Can"
"Me and Bobby McGee"
"Piece of My Heart"

The Kingston Trio
"Tom Dooley"

Led Zeppelin
"Stairway to Heaven"

Meade Lux Lewis
"Honky Tonk Train"

Little Richard
"Good Golly Miss Molly"
"Lucille"
"Tutti Frutti"

Clyde McPhatter
"Long Lonely Nights"
"Money Honey"
"The Treasure of Love"

Elvis Presley
"Heartbreak Hotel"
"Hound Dog"
"I'm All Shook Up"

Otis Redding
"I've Been Loving You Too Long"
"Try a Little Tenderness"

The Rolling Stones
"Satisfaction"

The Supremes
"Run, Run, Run"
"You Can't Hurry Love"

The Talking Heads
"Burning Down the House"
"Once in a Lifetime"

Ernest Tubb
"I'm Walkin' the Floor over You"

Joe Turner
"Shake, Rattle and Roll"

U2
Joshua Tree

Chuck Willis
"C. C. Rider"
"Mashed Potatoes"
"The Pony"
"Popeye"
"The Slop"
"Work with Me Annie"

Rock has been America's
popular music since the 1950s.

Rock has assumed several
styles over the years.

Rock is both an era and a style
in American music.

No one musician is responsible
for the birth of rock.

Little Richard (b. 1932).
© AP/Wide World Photos, Inc.

For music that was so often labeled "a passing, obnoxious fad," rock has endured a long time. As public music, one with wide public acceptance and unprecedented commercial success, its life has already exceeded the bounds of an entire generation, and nearly forty years after its first public splash, its demise is nowhere in sight. Rock music in one form or another has, since the mid-fifties, become the new American popular music.

But rock has not stood still all this time, merely repeating itself; instead it has consistently evolved into new and different forms. Thus we cannot speak of *a* rock music, but must instead examine and account for several different branches of rock. Some music mentioned in this chapter has little apparent relationship to what we might call the core of rock—for example, rhythm and blues, country music, and commercial folk music. We must remember, however, that rock not only replaced the kind of American popular music discussed in chapter 12, but it was also responsible for freeing the previously rigid boundaries of what Americans accepted as popular music. In this sense rock should be understood both as a style (with many substyles) and as an era in popular music—an era in which a diversity of musical types have flourished. It is important to be aware of this double significance of rock.

It is impossible to determine who invented rock and when: there is no single inventor and no specific date of birth. However, several musicians and events are associated with rock's early years.

A movie called *Blackboard Jungle* featuring Bill Haley (1925--81) and the Comets appeared in 1955 and included a song called "Rock Around the Clock." Haley was a benign, baby-faced, almost middle-aged man with a background in country swing music.

In that same year Little Richard's "Tutti Frutti" was released. Little Richard (b. 1932) was a wild young man from Macon, Georgia with a background in gospel music and rhythm and blues.

In 1956 Elvis Presley's million-seller "Heartbreak Hotel" was released. Presley (1935–77) was a surly-looking young southerner with a background in country music and white gospel music. His looks, clothes, accent, and attitude were aggressively, even arrogantly, different from his contemporary popular musicians.

Rock was not born during the years 1955–56, nor was it invented by Bill Haley, Little Richard, or Elvis Presley. But *Blackboard Jungle,* "Tutti Frutti," and "Heartbreak Hotel" revealed to the public that a musical, aesthetic, and attitudinal change was taking place. These were the first announcements on a public scale that the attitudes of youths were changing and that the musical impulses to which they responded were very different from those of previous generations. The success of this music with teenagers in the mid-to-late fifties was staggering.

Elvis Presley (1935–77).
© AP/Wide World Photos, Inc.

The Roots of Rock

The terms **"rocking and rolling"** and **"rocking and reeling"** are found in black cultural history as early as the first decades of the twentieth century. At that time the terms had both a sacred and a secular connotation. They were used as a kind of exultation in black gospel music, and they were used to describe sexual activity. In both instances the terms seemed to suggest energy, joy, and passion.

"Rocking and rolling" carry black sacred and secular connotations dating to the early twentieth century.

R & B

Sometimes the terms "rock" and "rockin' " appear in the lyrics of a type of black music that emerged in the thirties and forties called **rhythm and blues.** Rhythm and blues (or R & B) is the most immediate and direct ancestor of rock and roll music of the fifties.

    In the thirties and forties the mass white audience listened to the popular songs discussed earlier, and to the music of the big bands. This was their popular music. During that same time period, many blacks listened to this music, too, but they also listened to more hard-line jazz, gospel music, blues, and R & B. All of these genres were their music,

R & B emerged in the 1930s and 1940s.

Black audiences favored diversified musical genres during the thirties and forties.

but R & B was created by black musicians and designed for black audiences. R & B was distinctly different from white popular music.

For example, the lyrics of R & B songs were earthier and more temporal in nature than the standard white ballad of the same time period. This is evident in a comparative study of the text of the popular song for white audiences written below and the R & B text that follows it. Both are love lyrics.

"White" Popular Song

"You Are Too Beautiful" (lyrics by Oscar Hammerstein)
You are too beautiful my dear, to be true,
And I am a fool for beauty.
Fooled by a feeling that because I found you,
I could have bound you, too . . .
Love does not stand sharing,
Not if one cares.
Have you been comparing my every kiss with theirs?
If on the other hand, I'm faithful to you,
It's not through a sense of duty;
You are too beautiful and I am a fool for beauty.[1]

R & B Song

"Work with Me Annie"
Work with me Annie, work with me Annie,
Work with me Annie, work with me Annie,
Work with me Annie.
Let's get it while the gettin' is good
So good, so good, so good, so good.
Annie please don't cheat,
Give me all my meat,
Ah oo oo oo oo oo,
So good to me
Work with me Annie,
Let's get it while the gettin' is good.[2]

The difference between the two is obvious. Now, not all R & B texts are as graphic as this, but generally speaking, R & B texts are simpler than white popular song texts, and less ladened with quasi-poetic imagery. The language is definitely down to earth.

As discussed in chapter 12, very few popular songs from the thirties and forties have the form and harmony of the twelve-bar blues. However, the majority of R & B vocal and instrumental numbers are cast in the twelve-bar blues format.

1. © 1932 (Renewed) Rodart Music Corp. All Rights Reserved. Used by Permission.

2. "Work With Me Annie" (Hank Ballard) © 1954—Armo Music Publishing Company. Copyright renewed and assigned to FORT KNOX MUSIC INC. and TRIO MUSIC CO., INC. Used by permission. All rights reserved.

Compare the R & B lyrics to the lyrics of a contemporary song written for white audiences.

Most R & B is in twelve-bar blues format.

The basic beat of R & B was also very different from white popular songs. R & B developed a special accent pattern within the 4/4 meter that is characteristic of the style. In this back beat pattern, the downbeat is accented, beats two and four are heavily accented, and beat three has no accent at all. Graphically illustrated the pattern looks like this:

Beat	1	2	3	4	1	2	3	4
4/4	x	X	o	X	x	X	o	X

The following recorded examples illustrate this pattern. Notice that the drummer consistently emphasizes beats two and four.

> "C. C. Rider" by Chuck Willis (*History of Rhythm and Blues,*
>   vol. 3, side 2, band 5)
> "Jim Dandy" by LaVern Baker (ibid., vol. 3, side 1, band 7)
> "Shake, Rattle and Roll" by Joe Turner (ibid., vol. 2, side 1,
>   band 6)
> "Honky Tonk (part II)" by Bill Doggett (*Great Hits of R & B,*
>   side 1, band 1)

Having detected the beat pattern, listen to these same examples again. You will discover that they are all in the twelve-bar blues form. Present as well in these examples is a phenomenon known as a **riff**—a type of ostinato. A riff is a short melodic fragment, usually either two or four bars in length, that repeats obstinately throughout a song or a large section of a song.

The instrumentation of R & B was distinct from that of white popular music. It usually consisted of piano (or electric organ), drums, one or two guitars, and often a honking tenor sax. The sax and the lead guitar were the principal solo instruments.

Hard-core R & B singers often sang with rather raspy voices, and their delivery was often punctuated by a variety of whoops and yells. The backup vocal groups sang repetitive phrases and words, sometimes repeating nonsense syllables, or sometimes singing ooos or humms. This is evident in "Searchin' " by the Drifters (*History of Rhythm & Blues,* vol. 3, side 2, band 2).

In terms of lyrics, formal (and) harmonic structure, beat, instrumentation, and vocal style, R & B contrasted sharply with white popular music of the forties. But one of the major differences is less audible, and has to do with a basic attitude toward music; indeed toward life itself. Whereas white popular music was lush, polite, and dreamy, R & B was basic, sometimes brutally frank, and imbued with a carefree spirit. It was this spirit that took hold of the rock and roll audiences that emerged in the fifties.

The back beat accent pattern characterizes R & B.

The R & B group featured a piano, drums, guitars, and tenor sax.

R & B lead singers were backed up by vocal groups.

Country

Country music was also different from white popular music in terms of lyrics, instrumentation, and vocal style. The lyrics of country music songs were simple, down-to-earth, and free of poetic artificiality and dreams. The instrumentation of country music was very similar to that of R & B except that a raucous and wiry fiddle took the place of the honking tenor sax. The country singer sang very differently than the crooner or the big band singer. The country music singer produced a nasal quality that was punctuated by a variety of whoops (yodels) and groans. In addition, the beat of forties country music often resembled that of R & B. All of these qualities, including the beat, can be heard in the country hit of the late forties "I'm Walkin' the Floor over You" by Ernest Tubb. (You should be able to find this recording in one of the several anthologies of country hits presently available.)

The attitude of the country singer bordered on arrogance; he or she was not ashamed of being different from mainstream popular singers. These people thoroughly enjoyed their music the way it was. Moreover, they didn't give a hang if not a single slick Yankee liked it or them.

Strange as it seems, white country music and black R & B had more in common with each other than either had with white popular music. They were both southern and both unimportant as far as the New York music industry was concerned.

Rock and roll, the first kind of rock music, is essentially an extension of R & B, though it also resembles country music. Considering the racial climate of the time and the disinterest of large audiences in country music, rock and roll definitely needed white performers in order to succeed commercially. It is therefore not surprising that the first giant of rock and roll was Elvis Presley, a white, southern singer and guitarist with a background in country music.

Rock and Roll

Although rock and roll was essentially an extension of R & B, there were some differences between the two. For one thing, the language of R & B had to be cleaned up and purged of its too obvious sexual overtones. By law, radio stations could not broadcast such language as is found in "Work with Me Annie." So the language was scrubbed up in rock and roll and made legal for the general listening public. Many in the adult audience still didn't approve of the simple-minded language and the uncouth vocal style, and though they may have felt the music was immoral, they could not argue that it was illegal.

The texts of rock and roll songs were mainly about teenage puppy love, high school dances, cars, and similar topics. Songs dealing with love were free of the sentimentality and artificiality found in love songs from

Country music replaced the R & B sax with a fiddle.

Country singers were proud of their music and their audience.

Elvis Presley brought his country music background to rock and roll.

Rock and roll grew out of R & B.

Rock and roll lyrics were written to appeal to teenagers.

the thirties and forties. Elvis Presley's "I'm All Shook Up" (1957), Buddy Holly's (1938–59) "Peggy Sue" (1957), and the Drifters' "Fools Fall in Love" (1957) are typical. In much the same vein is a fine rock and roll song, "I'm Walkin'" (1957) by Fats Domino (b. 1928), a former R & B singer who had some success in the tamer and more broadly based world of rock and roll.

Some songs were part celebration of rock and roll and part anti-establishment. This is true of Chuck Berry's (b. 1926)"School Days" (1957) (hail, hail rock and roll) and his famous "Roll over Beethoven" (1956).

Apart from the thrill of the music itself, the self-ostracism of this music appealed greatly to a mass teenage audience looking for a means to express its own rebelliousness and anxious to assert its independence from the values of its elders. The music brought this motley, diverse audience together and became its rallying point. The music was theirs and theirs alone. No one else wanted it. With this music, northern and southern teenager, culturally different in so many ways, were united. Even more impressive, black and white youths found some common and mutually enjoyable ground in rock and roll, while race relations in the adult world were still in a deplorable state.

The older generation took a very dim view of rock and roll music and the effect it seemed to have on teenagers. They called it illiterate, mindless, filthy, the devil's own music, and void of any musical or poetic value. Rock concerts in the late fifties and early sixties were banned in some places, broken up in some places, and heavily policed in general. There were instances of riotous behavior by some teen rockers and alleged brutality by some officers of the law. This was partially caused by the enthusiasm and excitement of the music itself, and partially caused by a broadly based misunderstanding between parents and teenagers, something that came to be called the "generation gap."

The parents of these teenagers had recently suffered through a war and had a real sense of how grim and serious life can be. The sentimentality of the popular songs of their generation offered them solace. However, the grimness, seriousness, and sentimentality were lost on the younger generation. They rebelled against it. The more parents tried to forbid it, the more attractive rock and roll became to teenagers.

Rock and Roll Beat

Rock and roll took over the beat of R & B. Often in rock and roll this beat was underscored by a thumping, relentless pattern of quarter notes divided into eighth notes or into eighth note triplets. The two types are superimposed on the R & B beat illustrated in figure 14.1. In both cases the rhythm of rock and roll radiated vitality and the lure of dance.

Some rock and roll was deliberately anti-establishment—a way for teenagers to express their rebellion.

Rock and roll served as a common bond uniting all American teenagers.

Rock and roll music contributed in part to the generation gap.

Rock and roll imposed a new rhythm on the R & B beat.

Figure 14.1

Rock and roll's "eight to the bar" was borrowed from boogie woogie, a piano style form popularized in the 1930s and 1940s.

The eighth note division is called "eight to the bar" and was borrowed from **boogie woogie,** a piano style that appeared in the thirties and forties but may be much older than that. A boogie takes the shape and harmony of the twelve-bar blues and, within that framework, the left hand plays a steady succession of eight eighth notes per 4/4 measure while the right hand plays figures and improvisations against it. (Pianist Meade Lux Lewis was an important boogie woogie player and can be heard in "Honky Tonk Train" [*Smithsonian Collection of Classical Jazz,* record 4, band 2].) Little Richard and several other rock and roll piano players adopted the "eight to the bar" pattern. You can hear it in two of Little Richard's biggest hits: "Lucille" (1957) and "Good Golly Miss Molly" (1958). The pattern is found also in several of Elvis Presley's early hits, including "Hound Dog" (1956).

Rock and Roll Instrumentation

The instrumentation of rock and roll is similar to that of R & B.

The instrumentation of rock and roll is very similar to that of R & B. In the case of Little Richard and Jerry Lee Lewis (b. 1935), the piano is more prominent because they were piano players themselves. For others (Presley, for example) the guitar is the featured solo instrument.

Rock and roll was big business by the late fifties.

By the late fifties it was clear to those in the New York music industry that there was a vast teenage rock and roll audience. The general affluence of the postwar years put money into the hands of this audience. Rock and roll record sales soared, and, little by little, radio stations across the country began to convert to a steady diet of rock and roll. This music was big business.

Soft Rock and Roll

A softer rock and roll emerged in the late fifties and early sixties.

In the late fifties and early sixties, a brand of **soft rock and roll** emerged. It was textually less abrasive, the rock beat was muffled (but not always extinguished), and the background instrumentation sometimes included soft violins. The singer shied away from the harsh sounds of hard-core rock and roll and took a position closer to old-style crooning.

One of the most successful singers of soft rock and roll was Pat Boone (b. 1934). From his toothy grin to his white buckskin shoes, he seemed somehow clean and gentlemanly; even the teenager's parents could accept him. Among his biggest hits were "Ain't That a Shame" (1955) (actually a slow R & B song by Fats Domino), "I Almost Lost My Mind" (1956) (a country song disguised in soft rock and roll), and "Love Letters in the Sand" (1957) (a popular song from the thirties).

Other young solo singers, such as Frankie Avalon, Fabian, Paul Anka, and Ricky Nelson were also successful with soft rock and roll. Clyde McPhatter, who sometimes sang with the Drifters, was a black singer who was successful in both hard-core rock and roll ("Money Honey") and soft rock and roll ("The Treasure of Love," "Long Lonely Nights").

From Fifties Rock and Roll to Sixties Rock

Rock music began to change in the 1960s. American youth began to view the fun-loving, hard-driving rock and roll and the soft, syrupy kind of rock and roll as kid's stuff. The audience, who had recently reveled in rock and roll, began to look upon it as mindless and juvenile. Consequently, the "roll" gradually disappeared, leaving the term "rock" to stand alone. Rock and roll was high school music, but the rock of the sixties was college music. Sixties audiences were ready for more sophisticated things: lyrics that did more than simply rhyme, instrumentalists who played more than three chords and who played with considerable skill, themes and harmonies that were thought provoking, and singers who had studied the great blues and jazz singers of the past, and were discontent with "doo-wat-da-doo-da-wah."

Motown

But the changeover was neither complete nor universal. The echoes of rock and roll, somewhat altered, lingered in the sixties. Groups such as the Temptations and the Supremes (later Diana Ross and the Supremes) from Detroit produced music that was essentially an extension of rock and roll, though their lyrics were more high-toned and the Supremes were certainly sophisticated in manner and dress. The elegance of their singing and stage presence came to epitomize the Motown (motor town, or Detroit) style. They sang such rock and roll songs as "You Can't Hurry Love" (1966) and "Run, Run, Run" (1964), but also songs by Rodgers and Hart. They recorded an album of Christmas songs and appeared at posh dinner clubs. Whereas their counterparts in R & B and rock and roll were raucous, even raunchy, the Supremes were beautiful and very ladylike. They personified Motown elegance.

Pat Boone exemplified this soft rock and roll.

Other male singers contributed to the popularity of soft rock and roll.

In the sixties a new rock for the college audience emerged.

The sixties rock audience sought more sophistication and complexity than rock and roll could offer.

The Supremes personified Motown in the sixties.

The Twist

The big dance craze of the early sixties was the twist, popularized by Chubby Checker (b. 1941) (a play on the name Fats Domino) with the song "The Twist" (1960). Jet-setters and the rich were among those attracted to the fun of the twist. High society and teenyboppers who could afford the admission to the Peppermint Lounge, the national twist headquarters in Manhattan, danced to the "Mashed Potatoes," "The Slop," "The Pony," "Popeye," and of course "The Twist." Twist music was little more than rock and roll in the form of a game, providing a chance for the bored wealthy to go musically slumming. When the game was over, the twist died a quick death.

Surf

The high school aura of old-fashioned rock and roll carried over to a new type of music from southern California called surf rock, popularized by the Beach Boys and their good-natured songs about surfing, sun, cars, and Californians. The Beach Boys found a large audience for such songs as "Surfin' U.S.A." (1963), "Little Deuce Coupe" (1963), and "Fun, Fun, Fun" (1964). (Surf music enjoyed a mild comeback in the early 1980s.)

Dolled-up rock and roll, the twist, and surf music were popular for a time, but they were peripheral to the major thrust of rock music in the 1960s. Many groups with serious musical and poetic intentions began to appear. The field of rock widened and deepened considerably in the sixties.

The Beatles

Though rock music was born and bred in the United States, it has not been limited to these shores. Since the sixties, rock has become an internationally cherished music, particularly among the young. Building upon the models of American blues, R & B, and rock and roll, a number of British groups created their own exciting brands of rock. One of these, the Beatles, from Liverpool, England, is regarded by many as the most successful, inventive, and influential group in the entire history of rock.

Not only their music, but also their hairstyle caused a revolution among young males: long hair for males became popular for the first time since the nineteenth century. The long hair, beards, and moustaches were visible symbols of commitment to the new rock generation. By the end of the sixties, beads, necklaces, army fatigues, and blue jeans with multiple patches fleshed out the symbolism. The looks, attitudes, values, and most importantly, the music of the Beatles stood at the center of an

The Beatles in 1964.
© AP/Wide World Photos, Inc.

international revolution of youths angry about the war in Vietnam, the alarming depersonalization of society, and the questionable values of their elders.

The four Beatles were endowed with ordinary musical skills, but with work and with careful listening to their precursors such as Little Richard, Chuck Berry, Buddy Holly, and Elvis, the Beatles became a very accomplished and sophisticated musical group.

Their early and late recordings are separated by a wide musical gulf. Compare, for example, "Love Me Do" (1964) with "Come Together" (1969). The Beatles, as musicians and as songwriters, were constantly growing and changing, setting the style for new trends in rock. The real strength of the Beatles, however, lay in the melodic and poetic talents of John Lennon (1940–80) and Paul McCartney (b. 1942), who wrote many unforgettable songs. These songs ranged from the poignant "Eleanor Rigby (1966)" and "Yesterday" (1965), to the clever, as in "Polythene Pam (1966)" and "Taxman" (1967), to the philosophical, as in "A Day in the Life" (1967).

With time, the Beatles developed a sophisticated musical style.

The poetic and musical talents of Paul McCartney and John Lennon gave the Beatles' music an unusual poignancy and cleverness.

Sgt. Pepper

The songs in the *Sgt. Pepper's Lonely Hearts Club Band* album work together to develop a theme of human need.

The Beatles' masterpiece is the album *Sgt. Pepper's Lonely Hearts Club Band* (1967). This album consists of twelve songs, and while each is interesting and enjoyable in its own right, they form a collective unity not unlike that of a nineteenth-century song cycle. The songs are part of a larger whole and develop a central theme.

This theme is people in need: some are in desperate need; some don't even know they're in need. All of them need to be loved and some seek philosophical answers, such as the reason for their existence.

The album begins with the title song, which is repeated as the second to last song in the set. In this song, the Beatles act as storytellers, recounting the lives of people in need. This glimpse of the contemporary human condition is presented as a variety show having numerous acts, evident in the lines from the opening song, "We hope you will enjoy the show" . . . "Sit back and let the evening go."

In the second song, "A Little Help from My Friends," a question is put to the individual: "Do you need anybody?" The reply is, "I need somebody to love." What will happen if you don't find such a somebody? "I'll get by with a little help from my friends," even "get high . . ."—a reference to the escapism of drugs.

Song 3: "Lucy in the Sky with Diamonds." Composer Lennon maintained that this song has nothing to do with drugs. The fact remains, however, that the song speaks of someone's need to escape an unwanted reality.

Song 4: "Getting Better." This song is about a person who is grudgingly optimistic about love and life. Things are improving because the individual's needs have been fulfilled by another.

Song 5: "Fixing a Hole." The song deals with a person who wants to be alone; he fears intervention by other people or ideas that might somehow pose a threat to his familiar life-style.

Song 6: "She's Leaving Home." The teenager runs away from home, hoping to fulfill "something inside that was always denied for so many years." The deserted parents are confused and hurt, with needs of their own.

Song 7: "Being for the Benefit of Mr. Kite!" The circus is being performed "for the benefit of Mr. Kite," again suggesting the fulfillment of needs.

Song 8: "Within You, Without You." George Harrison's song, with its Eastern musical and philosophical overtones, is a desperate plea to see beyond one's self—to hurdle the illusions and snatch the truth. It is the only song in the cycle that directly points a finger at the listener. The songs asks, "Are you one of them?"

Song 9: "When I'm Sixty-Four." This is a nice replica of an old-fashioned British music hall song, but within the context of this song cycle the question, "Will you still need me?" is not as casual as it seems on its flippant surface.

Song 10: "Lovely Rita." Anyone, even the most casual acquaintance, might fill Rita's need for intimacy.

Song 11: "Good Morning." This is a song about a most ordinary bloke who is oblivious to the shallowness of his life: "I've got nothing to say, but it's O.K."

Song 12: "A Day in the Life." This song looks at a man who is frustrated by what he perceives around him—death and callousness.

The Beatles conclude the album on an optimistic note, suggesting that there are answers and ways to fill our needs, and offering to "turn you on" to them.

Sgt. Pepper's Lonely Hearts Club Band made generous use of brass and strings, something unheard of in earlier rock music. They also experimented with a variety of electronic techniques including playing tapes backwards. The Beatles were clearly a long way from rock and roll musically, poetically, and conceptually.

The Rolling Stones

One of the most famous and influential rock groups of the sixties was the Rolling Stones. The name of the group reflects their musical career for, like the Beatles, the Stones have never stood still stylistically for very long. In their evolution they have touched nearly all rock bases, from early R & B to hard-core blues, hard rock, protest music, and a touch of jazz.

The Stones' image and personality differed from that of the Beatles. The Stones were raunchier and more aggressively antiestablishment (on and off stage). Their music, too, was meaner and closer to the spirit of R & B. Lead singer Mick Jagger offered a stage presence much more erotic and sinister than that of the Beatles.

The Stones' success began in the mid-sixties with their most famous composition, "Satisfaction" (1965), and at that time their popularity rivaled that of the Beatles. For more than twenty years they continued to play to packed houses around the world.

Soul

The Beatles and Rolling Stones hit with such force that the collective attention was temporarily diverted from the activities of American rock performers. Though they were momentarily eclipsed, they were not inactive: the Americans—men, women, black, white, soloists, and groups—

While the Beatles and Rolling Stones occupied the forefront of rock, other musicians were changing the makeup of the music.

continued to create and change the makeup of rock. In the sixties, rock received a major infusion of new blood with the emergence of soul music.

The roots of this music can be traced to rural southern black religious music—a type called **gospel music.** The subject matter and texts of gospel music are religious in nature, but the singing style is almost indistinguishable from blues singing, a secular music. Drums, guitars, and piano are frequently used in gospel music as accompanying instruments. These are the same instruments used in blues, R & B, and early rock and roll.

White congregations were accustomed to and expected one kind of vocal style in church (nice, clean, and proper) and a different vocal style in popular music. They were also accustomed to the organ in church, not drums and guitars. The whites, then, made a definite distinction between sacred and secular music, and to allow any secular sound to enter the music of the church was to flirt with sacrilege. This is one of the reasons why some whites looked upon sacred and secular black music as "primitive," "childlike," or even "paganistic." They didn't understand that singing about Jesus with fire, passion, and pain in the voice was not sacrilegious but was born of very deep religious convictions. Moreover, these were people whose singing style reflected the real, personal sufferings of black people at that time.

When this passionate singing style—part blues, part religious ecstasy—was applied to secular texts, it acquired the name **soul** music. In the mid-sixties Aretha Franklin (b. 1942) emerged as the Queen of Soul. Many of her albums are readily available, but you should listen in particular to the songs "You Make Me Feel (Like a Natural Woman)" (1967) and "Satisfaction" (1968). James Brown (b. 1932) and Otis Redding (1941–68), both from Macon, Georgia, are vintage soul singers. Listen to Brown's "Please, Please, Please" (1964) and "Good, Good Lovin' " (1966) and to Otis Redding's "I've Been Loving You Too Long" (1965) and "Try a Little Tenderness" (1966).

Other Sixties Rock

Folk Rock

The most popular song in this country in 1959 was "Tom Dooley" by the Kingston Trio. The song told a story—a story abut a man condemned to die for the murder of his sweetheart; it was sung in three-part harmony to the accompaniment of an acoustic (nonelectric) guitar and bass. Thus, in terms of subject matter and sound it was radically different from rock and roll. The popularity of the Kingston Trio helped set the stage for the success of **folk rock** in the sixties and early seventies.

Towering above all folk rock singers in the sixties was Bob Dylan (real name Robert Zimmerman, b. 1941). Dylan came from a true folk background, and in the early sixties he produced such prophetic songs

---

Most white Americans did not understand or appreciate black gospel music.

When the passionate gospel style was brought to secular music, the result was soul.

Aretha Franklin's, James Brown's, and Otis Redding's sixties songs are vintage soul.

Bob Dylan was the most famous of the folk rock musicians of the 1960s.

as "The Times They Are A-Changin' " (1963). But beginning in the mid-sixties he abandoned his acoustic guitar in favor of an electric guitar (a rock instrument) and joined forces with a group that eventually took the name The Band. Together they recorded a number of fine songs, including "Like a Rolling Stone" (1965). In this and other songs Dylan managed to fuse elements of folk music with the rock sound.

The folk branch of rock music continued to flourish into the seventies with artists such as Arlo Guthrie, Joni Mitchell, Peter, Paul, and Mary, Joan Baez, and Simon and Garfunkel.

West Coast Rock and Acid Rock

Looking back, it seems certain that the mid-to-late 1960s was, among other things, a crazy time. The war in Vietnam, the explosion in drug use, and the relaxation of certain rules of social conduct contributed to the atmosphere. Rock music changed dramatically: like the "real" world, rock music (or some of it) became violent, revolutionary, and drug oriented. The onstage gestures that some rock singers made and the lyrics they sang became far more explicit than R & B at its raunchiest.

Rock changed dramatically in the 1960s, becoming more violent, revolutionary, and drug oriented.

Increasingly the new sixties rock became a part of life, if not a way of life, for hippies, yippies, flower children, militant underground movements, and also for many "straights." A number of nonscientific surveys revealed that a surprisingly high percentage of American youths made some use or claimed to have made some use of pot (marijuana) or acid (LSD), a mind altering drug with unpredictable and sometimes tragic consequences for the user. A new branch of rock—**acid rock**—became an integral part of this scene.

Sixties rock even became a way of life for some young people.

Several groups from San Francisco and other parts of the west coast created a music that blended into, and in fact reflected the mores of this psychedelic subculture. Some of this music was heavily electronic and loud to the point of ear-shattering. Jefferson Airplane was one of the most successful of the San Francisco bands, and their popularity quickly spread nationwide. Such songs as their "White Rabbit" (1967) left no doubt about their drug orientation.

Acid rock clearly reflects the drug and psychedelic culture.

The Doors was a group with a similar and more violent orientation. "Break on Through" (1967) and "Light My Fire" (1967) were two of their songs that ranked high on the national charts. The leader of the group, Jim Morrison (1944–71)—the epitome of the acid rock performer—more than once found himself in trouble with drug and indecent exposure charges.

The sixties also produced some important solo performers. Jimi Hendrix (1943–70), a young man from the Northwest, was an amazing guitarist (left handed at that!), whose playing bordered on true virtuosity when he chose to allow it. He used controlled feedback as the central part of many of his songs, such as "The Star Spangled Banner" (1968) and "Manic Depression" (1968).

The guitar playing of Jimi Hendrix bordered on virtuosity.

Janis Joplin (1943–70).
© AP/Wide World Photos, Inc.

Janis Joplin was a talented
blues singer who gave
spellbinding performances.

Acid rock was a means of
expressing frustration with the
values of an older generation.

In the 1970s and 1980s no one
type of rock was dominant.

The influence of the blues is
evident when listening to Eric
Clapton or the Allman
Brothers.

Hendrix had a wild, nihilistic stage act in which, drenched with sweat and full of contortions, he set his guitar on fire while the volume was turned up to full gain. It was as if the agonizing death screams of the electric instrument were being heard. Hendrix's "Purple Haze" is among the best known songs of the late sixties. Tragically, Hendrix died much too young.

Janis Joplin (1943–70) was another very talented singer whose career was also cut short by an early death. Joplin, from Texas, was the lead singer in Big Brother and the Holding Company, a San Francisco band. She was a very gifted singer of the blues and, in her own way, was as much a virtuoso performer as was Jimi Hendrix. Part of her stage appeal was based on sex, though not in the explicit manner of Hendrix or Morrison. She was at her best singing the blues in a husky, full throttle voice, though she sang other songs with tenderness and poignancy. Her audiences were spellbound by her performances. Among her best known recordings are "Get It While You Can" (1971), "Piece of My Heart" (1970), and "Me and Bobby McGee" (1971).

Many acid rock performers and even more in their audiences were seething with anger and were vociferously antiestablishment. To be accurate, this anger was born not of madness, but was born out of a deep-rooted and bitter frustration with a culture that seemed to them to have lost its moral and ethical marbles.

More Recent Rock

Throughout the 1970s and 1980s rock has been characterized by a profusion of diverse styles. In fact, so many different styles have emerged, and rock audiences have become so fragmented, that it is impossible to identify one branch of rock music as dominant. Some of the more influential branches of this period are examined here.

Blues Rock

In the late sixties and early seventies some groups, both British and American, began to listen in earnest, perhaps for the first time, to some of the legendary blues performers such as Big Bill Broonzy and Bessie Smith (both of whom are widely recorded, so you should seek out and listen to some of their records). The vocal and guitar styles of some of these legendary figures were important influences on the music of the **blues rock** musicians.

Years before Eric Clapton (b. 1945) had a song on the top forty charts he was the guitar player in a British blues-oriented group called Cream. Clapton is a fine rock guitarist on whom the influence of country blues is unmistakable—even in his less artistic but more commercially successful numbers, such as "Lay Down Sally" (1978).

Much the same influence is apparent in several prominent American rock groups. Some of the best of these groups were from the South, like the Allman Brothers band of Macon, Georgia. An incredible number of singers from the American North and Midwest, and singers from England, have developed southern or black southern accents, but the Allman Brothers were the real southern article, and the very sounds of their voices remind us anew of the southern ancestry of rock music.

Heavy Metal

Heavy metal rock emerged in the U.S. and in England in the early 1970s. Among its principal exponents are the American groups Led Zeppelin and Aerosmith and the British group Black Sabbath. Its immediate ancestor is the acid rock of the sixties, though heavy metal bands tend to be louder, use more electronically distorted sounds, and employ endless short riffs. Black Sabbath's "A National Acrobat" (1973) is typical of the style. Depending upon one's point of view, the lyrics are either mystical or meaningless. Led Zeppelin's "Stairway to Heaven" (1970) is also typical of the style, but more subdued. It is a long work (true of many heavy metal pieces) that begins almost sweetly, but toward the end it becomes increasingly loud and violent.

Heavy metal has its roots in acid rock.

Glitter Rock

Two British performers, David Bowie (b. 1947) and Elton John (b. 1947), epitomize a brand of music that has come to be known as **glitter rock.** Elaborate stage sets and costumes (jump suits, leather boots, makeup, ostrich feathers, etc.) are important ingredients of this style. The visual impact is almost on equal footing with the music and lyrics. Bowie often employs sophisticated recording techniques, including the judicious use of electronically distorted sound, as in "Fame" (1970). Elton John, a classically trained pianist, uses more conventional techniques and instruments including, obviously, the piano. He has written and performed a number of memorable songs; "Benny and the Jets" (1974) was very popular in this country.

In glitter rock and punk rock, the performer's visual impact is as important as the music.

The performances of David Bowie and Elton John (in the 1970s) exemplify the glitter rock style.

Punk Rock

The 1970s also saw the emergence of **punk rock,** which began in England and traveled to America. Like the late sixties' American rock music, punk rock was antiestablishment to the point of being offensive not only to the economic-governmental establishment, but also to great numbers of young people from the rock audience. The punkers' message to their young followers, particularly in Great Britain, was: "You are disenfranchised. The establishment calls you weird, so celebrate your weirdness—

Punk rock was as antiestablishment as the rock of the late sixties.

dye your hair green, wear a safety pin through your nose and a swastika around your neck." The Sex Pistols and other punk rock groups rebelled against both the commercial and the artistic success of much sixties' rock, and they called for a simpler, stripped down rock music generated only by raw energy.

Although some of the attitudes and antics of the punk rock movement are still in evidence, hard-core punk rock music had pretty much vanished by the late 1970s. Groups such as the B52s, the Violent Femmes, and others appear to have sprung originally from punk rock but have since gone off in other directions. There are other groups from the late 1970s that fall under the broad umbrella of an ill-defined label, New Wave.

Punk rockers had no regard for commercial success; their music was one generated by raw energy.

Singers/Songwriters

The 1970s and 1980s produced a wealth of fine singers, some of whom were also songwriters. But again, their styles and the subjects about which they sing are as diverse as the rest of the rock field. Though many could be mentioned, among the most prominent and successful are Billy Joel, Boz Skaggs, Carly Simon, Barry Manilow, Whitney Houston, Prince, Stevie Wonder, Madonna, Bruce Springsteen, Cindy Lauper, and John Cougar Mellencamp.

Jazz Rock

Jazz rock combines traditional jazz and rock instruments.

The beat, the guitar, and the lyrics of mainstream rock, when fused with the swing, chord progressions, horns, and saxophones of jazz, create a branch called **jazz rock.** For a long time the typical rock group consisted of a basic quartet of players—keyboard, drums, bass guitar, and lead guitar, while one or more of the players handled the vocals. Groups such as Chicago, Blood, Sweat and Tears, and others added to this basic rock quartet nonrock instruments: alto sax, trumpet, trombone. Other groups and individuals who have worked with this hybrid form include Electric Flag, Santana, pianist Chick Correa, and trumpeter Miles Davis.

Art Rock

Art music instruments and thematic materials have also found a niche in rock.

Other groups from the seventies and eighties blended rock rhythms with instruments normally associated with art music, such as violins and cellos and/or thematic materials borrowed from art music. Prominent among the **art rock** groups are Electric Light Orchestra, Mahavishnu Orchestra, Emerson, Lake and Palmer, Genesis, Kansas, and others.

Rock in the Late 1980s

Increasingly, over the last decade or so, sophisticated synthesizers and drum machines have become commonplace in the rock world and are employed by groups from virtually every corner of the globe. This is important because the synthesizer and allied electronic techniques have become to recent rock what the electric guitar was to rock and roll. Perhaps more importantly, rock has become a global music—a kind of universal musical language.

In addition, several recent groups have adapted minimalist techniques (see chapter 9): the Englishman Brian Eno, the German groups Kraftwerk and Tangerine Dream, the British group Police, and the American Laurie Anderson, among others. No single stylistic label could hope to cover rock music from the 1980s for, while much of this music partakes of a singular pool of resources, there is great diversity among and between the various groups and soloists. Similarly, no single group can be cited as the "voice of the age." But two groups from among many can be cited as particularly inventive and fascinating: the Irish group U2 (listen especially to their album *Joshua Tree,* 1988) and the American group The Talking Heads with songs such as "Burning Down the House" (1984) and "Once in a Lifetime" (1984).

Rock has found universal acceptance.

No single style of rock prevailed in the 1980s.

Summary

Rock music, whatever the specific style, attempts to capture some element of the spirit of its time, and to give voice and focus to it. Our appreciation of each style can be enhanced by an understanding of the spirit of the times that produced rock music.

In the mid-to-late fifties musicians such as Elvis Presley, Bill Haley, and Little Richard notified the older generation of an approaching musical revolution that represented the widening "generation gap." The revolution came in the form of rock and roll.

The roots of rock and roll are found in rhythm and blues and in country music. R & B was black music created for black audiences in the thirties and forties. The twelve-bar blues form, a unique accent pattern, and explicit lyrics were characteristic of R & B. The R & B instrumentation consisted of a piano, drums, a guitar, and a tenor sax, playing with a free spirit that attracted the attention of the young.

Country music, on the other hand, offered simple lyrics and instrumentation similar to that of R & B, except that a fiddle replaced the sax. The accented second and fourth beat of the four-beat pattern also resembled the R & B flavor.

Rock and roll in the fifties directed its appeal to teenagers with its songs of puppy love, dances, and cars. It offered a means of expressing rebellion against the older generation and acted as a force unifying teenagers of diverse geographic and socio-economic backgrounds. Rock and roll's "eight to the bar" pattern and guitar sound radiated an unmistakable new music. By the end of the decade, the music was also big business.

In the late fifties a softer rock and roll was popularized by Pat Boone, but this brand was quickly overshadowed by the sophisticated sixties rock of Motown musicians, exemplified by the Supremes and the Temptations.

The symbol of the new rock generation was the Beatles. These musicians created a musical revolution and set the style for the decade.

While the Beatles were in the spotlight, another genre of music was emerging in the background. Aretha Franklin, James Brown, and Otis Redding took black gospel music, added blues, and produced soul music.

Rock music continued to reflect the spirit of the times. The acid rock of the sixties was an integral element of the worldwide drug culture. Performers such as the Doors and Jimi Hendrix were at the center of this scene.

The folk rock of Bob Dylan, Joan Baez, and others offered a rebellious generation music ripe with nontraditional political statement.

Rock in the seventies appeared in the diverse forms of blues rock, jazz rock, heavy metal rock, glitter rock, punk rock, and art rock. Though music in the 1980s was no less diverse, fewer specific styles were evident. Some performers adopted minimalist techniques while others defied categorization.

The constant in rock has been the guitar. The rock of the 1990s will most likely continue to reflect the changing times through this instrument.

Key Terms

rocking and reeling
  (rocking and
  rolling)
rhythm and blues
  (R & B)
riff
country music

boogie woogie
soft rock and roll
gospel music
soul
folk rock
acid rock

blues rock
heavy metal
glitter rock
punk rock
jazz rock
art rock

Thinking About It

Examine the rock music of today—songs by recent performers and groups
not mentioned in this chapter, plus the music of performers who have
endured for years, such as Diana Ross, Grace Slick, the Stones or Crosby,
Stills, and Nash. Analyze these songs in terms of musical and textual
content and see to what extent each of these types of music owes something to early styles of rock.

Music
in
the
Non-Western
World

Chinese school girls play string instruments at a performance in Nanking in the Yhang Su Province.
© AP Wide World Photos, Inc.

There are those who contend that something that has no price has no value. Music however, is an exception, for as stated in the first chapter, music is important in the most remote corners of civilization and in the deepest reaches of history, and though it is for all peoples a treasure that has great value, it has no price.

Music is a priceless treasure around the world.

Music is universal, but there are differences between the music of one culture and that of another. Sometimes the differences are so pronounced that a person from one culture cannot automatically find enjoyment and satisfaction in the music of another culture. This happens because that person tries to interpret the foreign music in terms of his or her own understanding of music. Frustration and even annoyance set in when the foreign music doesn't correspond to preconceived ideas about music. But the frustration and annoyance can be minimized as ideas about what music can be are broadened. Although great satisfaction in a given foreign music is not guaranteed, if it is understood it can be appreciated. It may still seem a little strange to us, but at least we can appreciate it as someone's music, and thus as a thing of value. The intelligent pursuit of this understanding is a worthy enterprise in and of itself, but given a world in which there is increased interdependence among cultures, this pursuit of understanding is even more important.

Characteristics of satisfying and enjoyable music also vary from culture to culture.

As technology makes the world "smaller," an understanding of foreign culture is essential.

This chapter will deal with selected examples drawn from musical traditions of the non-Western world—cultures outside of Europe and North America. All musics of the world use time and sound, and all have form and meaning. In this chapter we will explore how the measurement of time, the quality of sound, the dimensions of form, and the meaning or function of music change from culture to culture.

381

Africa

The vast continent of Africa, the second largest continent on earth, is home to more than 500 million people living in more than fifty countries. The continent is enriched by scores of different languages, dialects, religions, forms of government, economies, customs, and ethnic groups.

North Africa

The great Sahara Desert forms a natural border between North Africa and sub-Saharan Africa (see fig. 15.1). Beginning in the seventh century A.D. most of North Africa adopted the Islamic religion from the Near East. Arabic was considered the scholarly language and in time became the semi-official language of much of the region. So, at least in terms of religion and language, North Africa is unified. But it is important to recognize that throughout the region there is much cultural and racial diversity. In this context we can speak only in general terms about the music of North Africa.

In terms of religion and language, North Africa is somewhat unified.

In the past century Western music and musical practices have influenced and been influenced by music from cultures around the globe. And while musical tastes are changing in North Africa, the following comments deal with traditional North African music, not with music in which the influence of West is apparent.

Historically, there has been a preponderance of solo vocal music (monophony) or vocal music with instrumental accompaniment. Favored musical instruments in the region include the duff (tambourine), ud (lute), tabl (drum), jank (harp), and nay (reed pipe). Even in purely instrumental music, monophonic or heterophonic textures are dominant and improvisation is an important element.

North African music, which is highly improvisational, includes monophonic or heterophonic textures.

Melodies are improvised on the pitches of varius scales which are called maqamat. A **maqam** might, for example, contain 24 pitches to the octave. Given that our Western scale contains but 12 pitches with the minor second as the smallest available interval, it is clear that a maqam will contain pitches smaller than our minor second. It is for this reason that the music may sound "out of tune" to our Western ears.

A useful introduction to some of this music, vocal and instrumental, is found in the recording *Arabic and Druse Music,* Ethnic Folkways Library, FE 4480.

Sub-Saharan Africa

In the space provided here it is impossible to examine even a handful of the many musics in sub-Saharan Africa, nor is it possible to cite a "typical" African music. There is simply too much diversity, but some general characteristics of the music will be outlined.

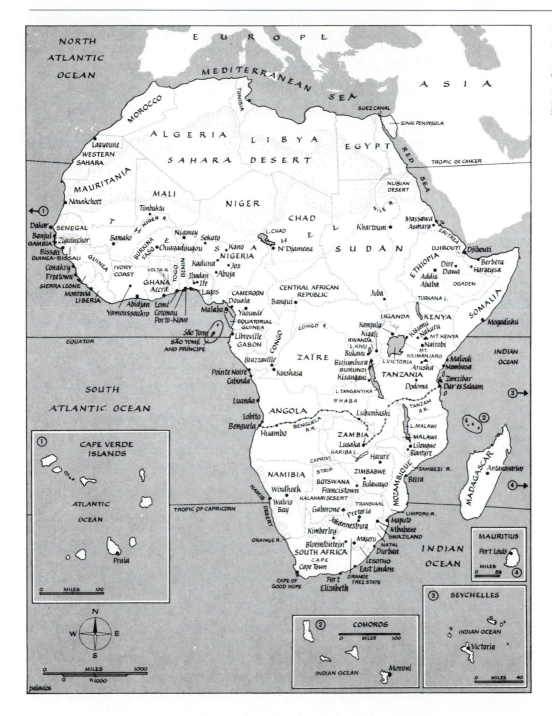

**Figure 15.1
Africa**

From *Africa*. Copyright
© 1978, 1979, 1981,
1983, 1985 by Sanford J.
Ungar. Reprinted by
permission of Simon &
Schuster, Inc.

Music is not viewed as sacred or secular; rather, it is an integral part of everyday life.

Some cultures from this part of Africa have art music and popular music, and some have sacred and secular music, but generally Africans do not make these distinctions. Music is not viewed as an art in the Western sense, nor as a phenomenon that is separate from the everyday functions of life. Rather, music is inextricably tied to life itself.

Another important distinction is the absence of designated musicians in many of the sub-Saharan cultures. In the Western world, the term "musician" applies to a select few whose musical talent and dedication set them apart from the average person. In many central and southern African cultures all children learn at an early age how to make music. In a real sense all people from this region are musicians, for music is an integral part of African life.

In many sub-Saharan cultures all children learn how to make music—it is not a function left to a small group of musicians.

For example, the tribe that depends upon catching wild animals for food would not undertake the hunt without performing the prescribed music associated with the hunt. The music is as important as the spear or poison dart that fells the hunted animal. There can be no doubt that such music has meaning, not only in an aesthetic sense, but in a spiritual and even practical sense.

Rhythm, which is a central force in sub-Saharan music, sounds complex to Western ears.

In much of the music from this region, rhythm is the central force. Melody and (in some cultures) harmony are important, but less so than rhythm. The music is driven by rhythm, often a very complex rhythm to our ears. Rhythm suggests movement, and indeed a great deal of African music involves dance. Drums of various sizes and shapes, scrapers, rattles, xylophones, and many other percussion instruments are prevalent.

The voice is second only to percussion instruments in importance.

In addition to percussion instruments, flutelike instruments, whistles, animal horns, and certain kinds of stringed instruments are employed. The dominant instrument (apart from percussion instruments), however, is the human voice, with or without text.

The Ba-Benzélé Pygmies   The Ba-Benzélé (or the Babinga) is one of several different tribes of Pygmies that live in the jungle regions of central Africa. For centuries the Pygmies have been private, nomadic peoples, but in recent times, the Pygmies have settled in private camps for more prolonged lengths of time.

Their communities are loosely organized but democratic. The nomadic life dictates as a practical matter that there are few permanent possessions—possessions are too burdensome to carry. As a general rule, then, the Ba-Benzélé and other Pygmy groups do not carry musical instruments with them, except for whistles and small drums. As a result, their music is predominantly vocal. But the Pygmies traditionally have been very adept at using instruments fashioned by other tribes with whom they come into contact on their many journeys.

Pygmy music is primarily vocal.

For centuries the Pygmies' reputation as master musicians was legendary. It is reported that even the Pharoahs of ancient Egypt included Pygmy musicians in their courts.

Their music, like that of most sub-Saharan cultures, uses many of the same intervals and some of the harmonies used in the Western world, but they also employ pitches that sound out of tune to Western ears. There is widespread use of pentatonic structures and some use of modes similar to those of the medieval (Western) church.

Very little of sub-Saharan music is notated. The music is learned through oral transmission, and improvisation is such a central part of the music that notation would be of limited value.

The music of many African cultures is included in *An Anthology of African Music,* Barenreiter Musicaphon-Unesco Collection—a multirecord set.

Asia

Asia, our largest continent, comprises about 30 percent of the world's land area and includes India, China, Japan, Indonesia, vast stretches of Siberia, North and South Korea, and numerous other countries (see fig. 15.2). In the 1970s, the population of this immense region was estimated to be in excess of 2 billion. But the population is unevenly distributed: India is the most densely populated country on earth, while parts of Siberia average ten people per square mile.

Nearly all of the world's major religions flourish in one or more parts of Asia. Racial and linguistic diversity is greater in Asia than in any other part of the world.

Once more, space limitations will allow for commentary on only a few of the many musics that thrive in Asia.

Indonesia

The Republic of Indonesia comprises the largest collection of islands in the world. There are about 6,000 individual islands, many of them quite small, and about half are populated (see fig. 15.3). There is considerable ethnic and linguistic diversity in Indonesia, though not to the extent that exists in Africa. The earliest cultural influences in Indonesia came from ancient China and India, but since about the thirteenth century the dominant religion has been a modified form of Near Eastern Islam. Coupled with this Islamic tradition in Indonesia is a mystical worship of nature and ancestors.

The Pygmies' reputation as master musicians is legendary.

The Pygmies use pentatonic structures and modes that are similar to those in medieval music.

Indonesian music reveals a diverse ethnic and religious tradition.

Figure 15.2
Asia.

Reprinted with
permission of The Free
Press, a Division of
Macmillan, Inc. from
*The Widening Gulf:
Asian Nationalism and
American Policy* by Selig
S. Harrison. Copyright
© 1978 by The Free
Press.

Figure 15.3
The Republic of
Indonesia.

From Bernard Dahm,
*History of Indonesia in
the Twentieth Century*
(Praeger Publishers, New
York, 1971), pp. x & xi.
Copyright © 1971 by
Praeger Publishers.
Reprinted with
permission.

Gamelan musicians from Bali.
© Eugene Gordon/Photo Researchers, Inc.

Balinese music is primarily
instrumental, performed by a
gamelan.

Bali   The music of Bali contrasts sharply with the previously examined
African music. For one thing, although solo and choral singing can be
found in the culture, traditional Balinese music is primarily instrumental. Several kinds of instruments are combined to form an orchestra
called a **gamelan.** In Bali and in neighboring Java, all cities, and even
tiny rural villages, have at least one gamelan. Some of this orchestral
music is intended for pleasure only, some of it is used to accompany native
dances and pantomime dramas, but much of it is performed in conjunction with the religious ceremonies that are central to the Balinese culture.

Much Balinese music is tied to
religious ceremony.

A full-scale gamelan employs twenty-five to forty players and the
following instruments:

> Gongs of several sizes and pitches
> Sarons—instruments with a series of bronze keys that are struck
>   with a wooden mallet
> Wooden xylophones
> Hand-struck drums
> Sulings—flutelike instruments
> Rebab—a two-string fiddle

A nuclear melody is at the core
of every gamelan composition.

Each instrument has a specific role to play in the gamelan. At the
core of a gamelan composition is the **nuclear melody.** This is a composed
and frequently notated melody that is often quite old. It is thought that

Figure 15.4
Balinese music.

there are between three and four thousand nuclear melodies in the Balinese gamelan repertoire. In a performance some instruments play a nuclear melody, others play essentially the same melody but in longer note values, and still other instruments play an elaboration of the nuclear melody, but add many faster notes to it. This texture produces a layered effect that adds a shimmering quality to the music. An example of Balinese gamelan music appears in figure 15.4, as transcribed into Western notation.

The texture of gamelan music gives it a layered effect.

Drums provide rhythmic continuity and color. Gongs are used to indicate various parts of the formal structure: some mark the ends of phrases, some mark the ends of subsections, and others mark the formal divisions of the music. In many cases, pairs of gongs are used, one gong pitched slightly higher than the other, which adds to the shimmering effect of the music.

Drums provide the rhythm while gongs indicate the structure.

Much of this music at first seems out of tune to Western ears since many of the intervals and the whole tuning system are different than Western music. Once these differences are accepted as norms for this music, however, the beauty of gamelan music is better appreciated.

Gamelan music does not sound like the Western music with which we are familiar.

An introduction to this music is provided in the recording *Musical Traditions in Asia,* from Archive.

India

Two separate but closely related traditions dominate the art music of India: the north Indian or Hindustan tradition, and the south Indian or Karnatic tradition. Both are ancient traditions and both use essentially the same instruments, sounds, time measurement, formal structures, and performance practices, though the terminology may differ. The south Indian or Karnatic tradition is discussed here, but some of the techniques and principles are applicable to the Hindustan tradition as well.

India has two distinct music traditions.

Figure 15.5
Adi tala.

India's classical music tradition is free from Western influence.

Although modern Indian music has been influenced by the West, India's classical music tradition is free of this influence. Some of the classical music—instrumental, vocal, and dance/dramatic—is designed for sacred purposes, some for entertainment, and some for both.

The temporal side of Indian music is governed by repetitive time cycles called **talas.** A tala consists of a collection of beats grouped into various units within the cycle. A beat is called an **akshara,** a unit is called an **anga.** In modern practice there are dozens of different talas, and each has a specific name that has some extra-musical connotation. Illustrated in figure 15.5 is **adi tala.**

Each tala has a name and an extra-musical connotation.

The adi tala contains eight aksharas that are grouped into three angas. Notice that the angas are not all the same length: the first has four beats, the second has two beats, and the third two beats—4 + 2 + 2. The Western notion of downbeat and upbeat does not exist in this kind of rhythm.

The bounds of improvisation are set by the tala.

For the performer, a tala is the rhythmic foundation from which further rhythmic improvisation springs. The performer's expertise is measured by this ability to improvise rhythmically within the structured bounds of the tala.

The Indian raga has some characteristics of the Western scale.

The sonorous aspect of Indian music is tied to the **raga.** A raga is somewhat like a scale in Western music yet is more complex. A raga is like a scale in that it contains a set number of pitches arranged in some ascending and descending order. But whereas our chromatic scales have twelve pitches and our diatonic scales have seven, some Indian ragas have seven or fewer pitches, some have twelve or more, and many contain pitches not found in Western music. In other words, every raga has a set number of pitches, but they don't all have the same number of pitches. In addition, a raga and a Western scale differ in the order in which various pitches are introduced. For example, instead of playing:

Not all ragas have the same number of pitches.

```
1 2 3 4 5 6 7
c d e f g a b
```

a raga might introduce its pitches this way:

```
1 4 2 7 3 5 6
c f d b e g a
```

Vina player.
© D. Chawda/Photo Researchers, Inc.

and the descending version of the raga may introduce the pitches in still another order.

But a raga is more than a collection of pitches. A given raga is associated with certain melodic bits that belong only to that raga. And certain pitches of a given raga may require a specific kind of ornamentation. For example, the pitch "C" may be ornamented in one raga but not in another.

There are several dozen ragas in modern usage and all have extramusical names that may be associated with a certain mood or even a specific time of day. Thus, a raga has a kind of emotional, even a spiritual, quality.

The raga determines the emotional and spiritual quality of the piece.

Memorizing and mastering the many talas and ragas, and developing the enormous improvisational skill necessary to breathe musical life into them, is a full-time occupation requiring years of dedication and hard work. It is not surprising then that the Indian culture, unlike the Ba-Benzélé culture, has a specific class of musicians. The true masters of this class are called **gurus.**

Indian master musician/ teachers are called "gurus."

In south India the principal musical instrument of the guru is the vina, a relative of the harp family. The vina has four melody strings and three drone strings.

Classical music for the vina is essentially soloistic music, though in concert a drum called a mridanga and a violin (held in front rather than under the chin) are sometimes used as accompaniment.

In classical music, the vina often plays solo.

Japan

Since the late nineteenth century Western art music has been a fact of life in Japan; it is broadcast over Japanese radio stations, while opera houses, ballet theaters, and concert halls are firmly established institutions in many large cities. Some of the most famous conductors and instrumentalists with worldwide reputations are Japanese.

Traditional Japanese music is kept alive by professional musicians.

But this music coexists with several types of traditional Japanese music, some of which have long histories. Traditional music is kept alive by skilled, professional musicians who take pride in the musical tastes of their ancestors.

Buddhism, one of the world's major religions, was formed in India in the fifth century B.C. It quickly spread throughout much of Asia and became the dominant religion in Japan in about A.D. 500. Much of Japan's traditional music is therefore associated with various religious ceremonies and the chanting of Buddhist monks.

Much of Japan's sacred music is associated with Buddhism and much of its secular music is associated with a form of drama called Noh drama.

In the secular realm the Noh drama is one of the dominant genres and among the most ancient, having originated in the fourteenth century A.D. The **Noh drama** is a sort of play with dialogue, songs, and choruses accompanied by a small instrumental ensemble. The dialogues are delivered in recitative style; the songs are more melodious. Melodies in the Noh drama fall into two categories—yowagin (lyrical) and tsuyogin (strong)—which differ in terms of placement and range of the basic tones of the scale. The scales are essentially pentatonic with other pitches clustered around the basic ones. Attention is lavished on the smallest nuances and vocal inflections. The singer painstakingly commits them to memory. Here and in other forms of Japanese traditional music, improvisation plays almost no role—a sharp contrast to some other types of music we have discussed. One of the central goals of this and other traditional music is to create as much tonal diversity as possible out of a severely limited fund of materials.

Performers must memorize the smallest nuances and vocal inflections.

There is very little improvisation in Japanese music; the emphasis is on tonal diversity.

The instrumental ensemble, known as **hayashi,** usually consists of a flutelike instrument called a nokan, two drums with hourglass shapes, and a third drum which is set on a stand.

The koto, which is like a zither, is used as a solo instrument or as part of an ensemble.

The most popular Japanese instrument, however, is the **koto,** a zitherlike instrument with thirteen strings. The koto, which rests on the floor as the performer sits or kneels to play it, is used as a solo instrument and as a member of an instrumental ensemble.

The music cited above as well as other types of traditional Japanese music is found on the recording *Japan,* Unesco Collection, a Musical Anthology of the Orient.

The West Indies—The Reggae Music of Jamaica

Reggae is a style of popular music that originated in Jamaica in the 1960s. In it are blended elements of Afro-Jamaican and North American rhythm and blues music. Its rhythm is characterized by a pattern that accents the afterbeats of a 4/4 meter:

Beat			
1	2	3	4
ta-ta-TUM	ta-ta-TUM	ta-ta-TUM	ta-ta-TUM

Melodies are simple and usually confined to a narrow range. Chord changes are few and simple. Lead voices are often backed by other voices in simple three-part harmony. Electric bass lines are prominent, but other instruments employed include electric guitar, organ, drums, and one or more horns (sax, trumpet, trombone). The guitar is played in an unusual manner that can be described as **slashing** in which the player forcefully strums the strings creating a somewhat percussive sound.

The roots of reggae are in ska and rock-steady, Jamaican music that is similar to R & B.

The ancestry of reggae includes two other types of Jamaican popular music: ska and rock-steady. There are some differences between ska and rock-steady, but in their separate ways they imitated the R & B and early rock and roll of the 1950s. The imitations were imperfect, owing doubtless to the inherent musical proclivities of the young Jamaican blacks who attempted the imitations. What resulted was a fresh, new music with a personality of its own.

Reggae is considered by some to be the unofficial music of the religious cult known as Rastafarianism. This is a messianic cult that maintains that Adam and Jesus were black and that stories of the scriptures have been corrupted by white missionaries for political and economic reasons. The Jamaican Rastafarians also revere the late emperor of Ethiopia, Haile Selassie (also known as Ras Tafari), as a son of God who will one day lead poor black Jamaicans back to their rightful homeland in Africa and deliver them from white domination. There are, then, religious overtones to much of reggae music. Texts dealing with protests and threats to white supremacists are couched in mystical terms and jargon not understood by whites.

Reggae is also associated with Rastafarianism, so the music has religious overtones.

Reggae has had little success among the black audience in the United States and only marginal success in the white mainstream market. Bob Marley (1945–1981) and the Wailers emerged as cult heros among the Rastafarians in Jamaica and had one song on the pop charts in this country in 1976: "Roots, Rock, Reggae." In addition, there was a mild craze for reggae among white college students in the late 1970s and early 1980s.

The fate of reggae in Great Britain has been very different: it found an enthusiastic audience among the large West Indian population of London, and in the followers and some of the performers of punk rock. The punkers felt a kinship with the message of reggae lyrics and with the outlaw cultishness of the reggae phenomenon.

Summary

Our look at non-Western music focused on music of North and South Africa, several Asian cultures, and one type of music from Latin America. In each of these cultures music plays a major role.

An appreciation of these non-Western music traditions can stem only from an understanding of how the musical components of time, sound, form, and function work together.

Although the continent of Africa is as diverse as it is large, we can generalize to a degree about its musical heritage. Music is an integral part of the African's daily life. For that reason, no class of musicians exists—rather, all people are musicians. African music is primarily a vocal music with a dominant rhythm that sounds complex to us. Because improvisation is such a central part of the music, notation is of little use.

The music of Bali is primarily instrumental and designed to be performed by an orchestra—the gamelan. This gamelan music is composed around a nuclear melody, producing a layered effect. In Balinese music, drums provide the rhythm and gongs articulate the structure.

Karnatic Indian music is organized by beats (aksharas), collections of beats (talas) and units (angas). The tala provides the rhythmic structure from which improvisation flows. The raga determines the emotional and spiritual quality of the music. Because of the skill necessary to work within the Karnatic musical boundaries, a class of musicians, gurus, developed within the culture.

The Japanese Noh drama uses singers and a small instrumental ensemble as its performing forces. This is a very subtle music in which attention to minute details of vocal and instrumental utterances is paramount. In contrast to some other kinds of music examined in this chapter, the Noh drama makes little use of improvisation.

Reggae music, developed only recently, blends elements of Afro-Jamaican music and rock and roll. Reggae melodies and harmonies are, generally, not complicated. For some, reggae is the music of the religious cult known as Rastafarianism.

We have had only a glimpse at non-Western music. The understanding and appreciation developed here, however, will serve you well as you explore other "foreign" musics.

Key Terms

maqam	anga	hayashi
gamelan	adi tala	koto
nuclear melody	raga	reggae
tala	guru	slashing
akshara	Noh drama	

Thinking About It

If you wish to gain some understanding of non-Western music it is critical that you listen to the examples cited in this chapter or to other similar recordings that may be available in your library. As you listen, answer these basic questions about what you hear:

Describe the texture of this piece.

Does the piece seem to have beats and meter or is rhythm measured in some other way?

Identify any musical instruments by family-type: string, woodwind, brass, percussion.

In your own words, describe the vocal quality of the singers.

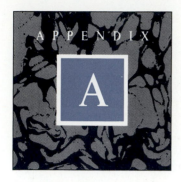
Record/ Cassette Selections

Record/Cassette 1, A: Chapters 1–2

1. Handel: "Hallelujah" chorus from *Messiah* (3:56). Philadelphia Orchestra; Eugene Ormandy, conductor; Mormon Tabernacle Choir; Richard Condie, director. (Example of note values in chapter 1, texture in chapter 2; can also be used in chapter 5 as an example of baroque music.)

2. Chopin: *Waltz,* op. 34, no. 2 (4:52). Dinu Lipatti, piano. (Example of note values and rubato in chapter 1; can also be used in chapter 8 as an example of solo piano music.)

3. Haydn: Symphony no. 101, first movement (7:47). New York Philharmonic; Leonard Bernstein, conductor. (Example of note values in chapter 1; sonata-allegro form in chapter 3. Can also be used to exemplify the classical symphony in chapter 7.)

4. Scott Joplin: "The Entertainer" (excerpt) (2:24). David Frost, piano. (Example of note values and syncopation in chapter 1, rag form in chapter 3.)

5. Palestrina: "Agnus Dei" from the mass *Veni Sponsa Christi* (2:18). Copenhagen Boys' and Men's Choir; Niels Moller, conductor. (Example of texture in chapter 2, Renaissance Mass motet in chapter 11.)

6. J. S. Bach: C Minor Fugue from *Well-Tempered Clavier,* vol. 1 (1:33). Glenn Gould, piano. (Example of imitative counterpoint in chapter 2; also useful in chapter 5 as an example of a baroque keyboard fugue.)

7. J. S. Bach: *Brandenburg Concerto* no. 2 in F Major, first movement (4:13). Marlboro Festival Orchestra; Pablo Casals, conductor. (Example of beat and steady tempo in chapter 1; can also be used in chapter 5 as an example of concerto grosso.)

Record/Cassette 1, B: Chapters 2–3

1. Barber: *Adagio for Strings* (7:42). Philadelphia Orchestra; Eugene Ormandy, conductor. (Example of string ensemble in chapter 2, "Americana" style in chapter 9.)

2. Beethoven: Symphony no. 6 in F Major, op. 68, "Pastorale"—third movement (5:28). New York Philharmonic; Leonard Bernstein, conductor. (Example of woodwinds in chapter 2.)

3. Mussorgsky: "Promenade" from *Pictures from an Exhibition* (1:50). New York Philharmonic; Leonard Bernstein, conductor. (Example of brass in chapter 2.)

4. Varèse: *Ionisation* (4:49). Robert Craft conducts. (Example of percussion in chapter 2.)

5. Chopin: Mazurka, no. 44 in C, op. 67, no. 3 (1:34). Alexander Brailowsky, piano. (Example of *ABA* form in chapter 3.)

6. Chopin: Mazurka, no. 41, op. 63, no. 3 (2:01). Alexander Brailowsky, piano. (Example of *ABA* form in chapter 3.)

7. J. S. Bach: "Allemande" from French Suite no. 1 in D Minor (2:36). Glenn Gould, piano. (Example of *AABB* form in chapter 3.)

Record/Cassette 2, A: Chapter 3

1. Haydn: Piano Sonata in D Major (3:11). Arthur Balsam, piano. (Example of rondo in chapter 3; also can be used as an example of a classical piano sonata in chapter 7.)

2. Beethoven: Piano Sonata in C Minor, op. 13, "Pathetique," second movement (4:43). Glenn Gould, piano. (Example of rondo in chapter 3.)

3. J. Baird: "I'm a Stranger Here" (2:06). Sonny Terry and Brownie McGhee. (Example of twelve-bar blues in chapter 3.)

4. Mozart: Symphony no. 40 in G Minor, first movement (8:43). Bavarian Radio Orchestra; Rafael Kubelik, conductor. (Example of sonata-allegro form in chapter 3, of classical symphony in chapter 7.)

5. Beethoven: Piano Sonata no. 12 in A♭ Major, op. 26, first movement (7:25). Paul Badura-Skoda, piano. (Example of theme and variations in chapter 3.)

6. Tchaikowsky: "March" from Nutcracker Suite op. 71a (2:28). New York Philharmonic; Leonard Bernstein, conductor. (Example of ABA form in chapter 3.)

Record/Cassette 2, B: Chapters 3-4

1. Tchaikowsky: "Overture Miniature" from *Nutcracker Suite,* op. 71a (3:15). New York Philharmonic; Leonard Bernstein, conductor. (Example of ABAB form in chapter 3.)
2. Haydn: *Sonata* in E minor, first movement (3:57). Arthur Balsam, piano. (Example of sonata-allegro form in chapter 3.)
3. Vivaldi: "Spring" Concerto, first movement, from *The Four Seasons* (3:36). St. Paul Chamber Orchestra; Pinchas Zukerman, violinist/conductor. (Example of descriptive music in chapter 4.)
4. C. M. von Weber: *Der Freischütz,* final portion of the "Wolf's Glen Scene" (3:48). Karl Kohn, Rudolph Schock, Lisa Otto, Elisabeth Grummer; Berlin Philharmonic Orchestra; Joseph Keilberth, conductor. (Example of descriptive music in chapter 4.)
5. Ives: *The Unanswered Question* (5:24). New York Philharmonic; Leonard Bernstein, conductor. (Example of philosophical program music in chapter 4; also useful in chapter 9.)
6. Beethoven: *Symphony no. 7* in A Major, op. 92—second movement (9:05). New York Philharmonic; Leonard Bernstein, conductor. (Example of philosophical program music in chapter 4.)

Record/Cassette 3, A: Chapters 5, 6, 8

1. Handel: Trio Sonata in F Major, first and second movements (5:07). (Example of a baroque trio sonata in chapter 5.)
2. F. Couperin: "Le Croc-en-jambe" from Ordre no. 22 (2:10). Sylvia Marlowe, harpsichord. (Example of the rococo style in chapter 6.)

3. J. C. Bach: Symphony in D Major, op. 18, no. 1, first movement (5:15). Philadelphia Orchestra; Eugene Ormandy, conductor. (Example of style galant in chapter 6.)
4. C. P. E. Bach: Symphony in B Minor (excerpt) (4:35). Martin Galling, harpsichord; Mainz Chamber Orchestra; Gunter Kehr, conductor. (Example of *Sturm und Drang* in chapter 6.)
5. Berlioz: *Roméo et Juliette* Dramatic Symphony, op. 17, "Love Scene" (excerpt)(5:46). New York Philharmonic; Leonard Bernstein, conductor. (Example of a dramatic scene from a choral/dramatic symphony in chapter 8.)
6. Berlioz: *Roméo et Juliette* Dramatic Symphony, op. 17, Scherzo "Queen Mab" section (excerpt) (2:46). New York Philharmonic; Leonard Bernstein, conductor. (Example of brilliant orchestration in chapter 8.)

Record/Cassette 3, B: Chapter 8

1. Brahms: Symphony no. 2, op. 73, first movement (15:13). New York Philharmonic; Leonard Bernstein, conductor. (Example of classically oriented nineteenth-century symphony.)
2. Borodin: *In the Steppes of Central Asia* (7:19). New York Philharmonic; Leonard Bernstein, conductor. (Example of a tone poem.)
3. Chopin: Polonaise in A♭ Major, op. 53, "Heroique" (5:14). Philippe Entremont, piano. (Example of a dance fashioned into a character piece for piano.)

Record/Cassette 4, A: Chapter 8

1. Chopin: Étude in G♭ Major, op. 10, no. 5 (1:34). Vladimir Horowitz, piano. (Example of nineteenth-century virtuoso keyboard work.)
2. Brahms: Intermezzo in A Major, op. 118, no. 2 (5:47). Stephanie Brown, piano. (Example of a character piece for piano.)

3. Fanny Mendelssohn-Hensel: *Andante con moto* (2:05). Virginia Eskin, piano. (Example of character piece for piano in chapter 8.)
4. R. Schumann: Concerto in A Minor for piano and orchestra, op. 54, first movement (14:41). Murray Perahia, piano; Bavarian Radio Orchestra; Andrew Davis, conductor. (Example of a romantic piano concerto.)

Record/Cassette 4, B: Chapters 8-9

1. Rossini: *The Barber of Seville,* Act I, scene i (15:53). Simone Alaimo, Paolo Barbacini, Leo Nucci; Orchestra and Chorus of Teatro alla Scala Milan; Riccardo Chailly, conductor; Romano Gandolfi, chorus master. (Example of nineteenth-century Italian comic opera with set numbers.)
2. Schubert: Erlkönig (4:09). Dietrich Fischer-Dieskau, baritone; Gerald Moore, piano.
3. C. Schumann: "Liebst du um Schönheit" (2:53). Katherine Ciesinski, mezzo soprano; Rudolph Palmer, piano. (Example of a nineteenth-century lied.)
4. Debussy: *Danse bohémienne* (1:43). Beveridge Webster, piano. (Example of Debussy's earliest style.)
5. Debussy: "Brouillards" from *Preludes,* Book II (2:41). Walter Gieseking, piano. (Example of impressionism.)

Record/Cassette 5, A: Chapter 9

1. Debussy: "La Flute de Pan" from *Chansons de Bilitis* (3:01). Frederica von Stade, mezzo soprano; Martin Katz, piano. (Example of symbolist poetry set to music.)
2. Schönberg: "Mondestrunken" from *Pierrot Lunaire,* op. 21 (1:36). Bethany Beardslee, soprano; Isidore Cohen, violin/viola; Charles McCracken, cello; Robert Helps, piano; Ernest Bright, clarinet/bass clarinet; Murray Panitz, flute/ piccolo; Robert Craft, conductor. (Example of expressionism with *Sprechstimme.*)

3. Berg: *Wozzeck,* Act III, scene ii (excerpt) (4:31). Walter Berry, Isabel Strauss; Orchestra of the Paris National Opera; Pierre Boulez, conductor. (Example of expressionism.)

4. Berg: *Wozzeck,* Act III, scene v (excerpt) (1:26). Childrens' Chorus of the Paris National Opera; Orchestra of the Paris National Opera; Pierre Boulez, conductor. (Example of expressionism.)

5. Milhaud: *Le Boeuf sur le Toit (The Bull on the Roof)* (excerpt) (3:12). Minneapolis Symphony Orchestra; Dimitri Mitropoulos, conductor. (Example of polytonality.)

6. Prokofiev: *Concerto no. 3* in C for piano and orchestra—first movement (8:48). Gary Graffman, piano; Cleveland Orchestra; George Szell, conductor. (Example of neoclassicism.)

7. Glass: "Train 1" from *Einstein on the Beach*—Act I, scene i (3:38). Philip Glass Ensemble. (Example of minimalism.)

Record/Cassette 5, B: Chapters 11, 12

1. Josquin des Prez: Motet *Ave Maria* (3:51). Copenhagen Boys' and Men's Choir; Niels Moller, conductor. (Example of Renaissance motet with imitative counterpoint.)

2. William Byrd: *Christ Rising Again* (3:20). Judith Nelson, Barbara Pearson, soloists. (Example of English verse anthem.)

3. Marenzio: *S'io parto, i'moro* (2:02). Madrigal Choir of the Danish State Radio; Mogens Wöldike, conductor. (Example of Italian madrigal.)

4. Morley: *Now Is the Month of Maying* (1:41). The Deller Consort. (Example of Elizabethan madrigal.)

5. G. Gabrielli: *Gloria in Excelsis Deo* (excerpt) (3:19). The Ambrosian Singers with Strings and Brass conducted by Denis Stevens. (Example of the mixture of vocal and instrumental elements in the late Renaissance.)

6. Stephen Foster: "Jeanie with the Light Brown Hair" (3:33). Jean Lemonds, soprano; Jay Fuller, piano. (Example of a parlor song in the genteel tradition.)

7. S. Stept: "Please Don't Talk about Me when I'm Gone" (1:59). The Side Street Ramblers, vocal. (Example of barbershop quartet with chromatic harmony.)

8. J. McHugh, D. Fields: "I'm in the Mood for Love" (2:53). Frances Langford, vocal. (Example of idealized romantic love song.)

9. H. Ruby, B. Kalmer: "Three Little Words" (3:01). Ethel Waters. (Example of up tempo love song.)

Record/Cassette 6, A: Chapter 12

1. H. Arlen: "Stormy Weather" (2:29). Ivie Anderson, vocal with Duke Ellington and His Famous Orchestra. (Example of unrequited love song.)

2. Fletcher Henderson: "Down South Camp Meeting" (3:17). Benny Goodman band. (Example of white swing.)

3. "Auld Lang Syne" (2:07). Guy Lombardo and His Royal Canadians. (Example of sweet band sound.)

4. M. Gordon, H. Revel: "Stay as Sweet as You Are" (3:06). Lanny Ross, vocal. (Example of tenor or "clean" style.)

5. Jimmy Durante: "Can Broadway Do without Me?" (2:58). Clayton, Jackson, and Durante. (Example of talking style.)

6. Arthur Johnson, Sam Coslow: "Learn to Croon" (2:36). Bing Crosby, vocal. (Example of crooning.)

7. Irving Berlin: "White Christmas" (2:27). Andy Williams, vocal. (Example of "straight," nonswing performing.)

8. Irving Berlin: "White Christmas" (4:04). Charlie Parker, alto sax. (Example of swing and improvisation.)

Record/Cassette 6, B: Chapter 13

1. Scott Joplin: "Maple Leaf Rag" (3:14). Scott Joplin, piano. (Example of ragtime [nonswing] style.)

2. Scott Joplin: "Maple Leaf Rag" (2:34). Jelly Roll Morton, piano. (Example of swinging style.)

3. Joe Oliver: "Dippermouth Blues" (2:19). King Oliver, trumpet. (Example of New Orleans style jazz.)

4. Oliver-Williams: "West End Blues" (3:14). Louis Armstrong, trumpet. (Example of solo-oriented 1920s jazz.)

5. Lillian Hardin-Armstrong: "Hotter Than That" (3:00). Louis Armstrong, trumpet. (Example of solo-oriented 1920s jazz.)

6. Parish, Carmichael, Mills: "Riverboat Shuffle" (3:07). Frank Trumbauer, C-melody sax; Bix Beiderbecke, cornet; Bill Rark, trombone; Don Murray, clarinet; Doc Ryker, alto sax; Itzy Riskin, piano; Eddie Lang, guitar; Chauncey Morehouse, drums. (Example of white jazz players.)

7. Fats Waller: "Numb Fumblin'" (2:56). Fats Waller, piano. (Example of stride piano.)

8. Charlie Parker: "Ornithology" (2:40). Charlie Parker, alto sax. (Example of bop.)

9. Paul Desmond: "Take Five" (excerpt) (2:12). The Dave Brubeck Quartet. (Example of cool jazz.)

10. Ornette Coleman: "Happy House" (excerpt) (2:08). Ornette Coleman, alto sax; Dewey Redman, tenor sax; Don Cherry, pocket trumpet; Bobby Bradford, trumpet; Charlie Haden, acoustic bass; Ed Blackwell, drums; Billy Higgins, drums. (Example of new jazz.)

Babbitt, Milton (b. 1916): American composer of serial and electronic music.

Bach, Carl Philipp Emanuel (1714–88): Son of J. S. Bach, a composer of chamber music, symphonies, and keyboard works, many of them in either *empfindsamer* or *Sturm und Drang* style.

Bach, Johann Christian (1735–82): Youngest son of J. S. Bach, composer of symphonies, concertos, and other works in the style galant of the preclassic era.

Bach, Johann Sebastian (1685–1750): Great master of the late baroque and of contrapuntal techniques. Best known works include the six *Brandenburg* Concertos, *St. Matthew Passion, Well-Tempered Clavier, Goldberg Variations.*

Barber, Samuel (1910–80): American composer of songs, opera, keyboard, and orchestral music. Best known works include *Adagio for String Orchestra, Knoxville, Summer 1915.*

Bartók, Béla (1881–1945): Hungarian composer much of whose music reveals his fascination with native folk music. Best known works are *Music for Strings, Percussion and Celesta, Concerto for Orchestra,* the six String Quartets.

Beethoven, Ludwig van (1770–1827): Great master of the late classical and early romantic eras, and probably the consummate master of the developmental process. Best known works: Symphony no. 5, Symphony no. 9, Symphony no. 3, the *Moonlight* and the *Pathetique* piano sonatas, the *Missa Solemnis.*

Berg, Alban (1885–1935): Student of Schönberg and a leading expressionist composer. Best known work: *Wozzeck* (opera).

Berio, Luciano (b. 1925): Italian composer whose music combines elements of chance and theater.

Berlioz, (Louis) Hector (1803–69): French romantic composer, especially prominent in the fields of dramatic and programmatic music. Best known work: *Symphonie Fantastique.*

Bizet, Georges (1838–75): French composer, primarily of operas. Best known work is the opera *Carmen.*

Borodin, Alexander (1834–87): Russian composer with nationalist leanings. Best known works: *Prince Igor* (opera) and *In the Steppes of Central Asia* (tone poem).

Brahms, Johannes (1833–97): One of the central romantic composers, tempered by classicism; a master of counterpoint. Best known works: the Four Symphonies, *German Requiem,* numerous songs and shorter works for piano.

Britten, Benjamin (1913–76): Foremost British composer of the twentieth century. Works in a somewhat dissonant tonal style.

Byrd, William (ca. 1540–1623): Foremost British composer of the Elizabethan era. Best known for his Masses and verse anthems.

Caccini, Giulio (ca. 1550–1618): One of the central figures in the development of Camerata opera.

Cage, John (b. 1912): American composer known chiefly for his use of aleatoric procedures and other kinds of experimental music.

Carter, Elliott (b. 1908): American composer who works in an intensely personal style. Much of his music is harmonically and rhythmically complex.

Chopin, Frédéric (1810–49): Polish composer of the romantic era; generally regarded as the consummate master of romantic solo piano music. Best known works: Twenty-Four Preludes, "Revolutionary" etude, *Heroic Polonaise.*

Copland, Aaron (b. 1900): American composer and a central figure in the "Americana" school. Some of his music is influenced by jazz. Best known work: *Appalachian Spring* (ballet).

Corelli, Arcangelo (1653–1713): Early baroque composer of trio sonatas.

APPENDIX

B

A
Brief
List
of
Composers
and
Their
Works

Couperin, François (1668–1733): Composer of elegant and often fanciful keyboard works in the rococo era.

Crumb, George (b. 1929): American composer best known for mystical works such as *Ancient Voices of Children.*

Debussy, Claude (1862–1918): Innovative French composer of the late nineteenth and early twentieth century; some of his works have been labeled "impressionistic." Best known works: *Prélude à l'Après-midi d'un faune, Clair de lune,* "Nuages," *La Mer.*

Delius, Frederick (1862–1934): British impressionist composer. Best known works are tone poems such as *Brigg Fair: an English Rhapsody* and *On Hearing the First Cuckoo in Spring.*

Donizetti, Gaetano (1797–1848): Italian romantic opera composer. Best known work: *Lucia di Lammermoor.*

Dufay, Guillaume (ca. 1400–74): Flemish composer of the early Renaissance. Best known for his polyphonic Masses.

Dunstable, John (ca. 1370–1453): Important British composer of the early Renaissance.

Dvořák, Antonin (1841–1904): Prolific Czech romantic composer. Best known work: Symphony no. 9 *(From the New World).*

Falla, Manuel de (1876–1946): Spanish nationalist composer.

Farnaby, Giles (1560–1600): Elizabethan composer best known for his works for the keyboard instrument known as the virginal.

Feldman, Morton (1926–87): American composer whose music reflects his fascination with tone color and subtle nuances. Developed his own brand of minimalism.

Franck, César (1822–90): Composer-organist-teacher. Many of his works are rich in chromatics. Best known works: Symphony in D Minor, and the oratorio *Les Béatitudes.*

Gabrieli, Andrea (ca. 1510–86): Composer of colorful works for voices with instruments and for organ.

Gershwin, George (1898–1937): American composer of popular music and works that combine elements of jazz and art music.

Gibbons, Orlando (1583–1625): English Renaissance composer of madrigals, keyboard works, and other pieces.

Glass, Philip (b. 1937): Preeminent composer of minimalist music.

Grieg, Edvard (1843–1907): Norwegian composer. Best known works: Piano Concerto in A Minor, *Peer Gynt* suite.

Handel, George Frederic (1685–1759): Great master of the late baroque and the central composer of opera seria, though today he is best known for works other than his operas. Best known works: *Messiah, Royal Water Music.*

Haydn, Franz Joseph (1732–1809): A consummate master of the pure classical style; sometimes called "the father of the symphony." Best known works include several of his 104 symphonies, such as the no. 101 (*The Clock*) String Quartet, op. 76, no. 3, and the oratorio *The Seasons.*

Hindemith, Paul (1895–1963): German composer and educator who developed a unique variety of expanded tonality.

Honegger, Arthur (1892–1955): A member of the so-called "French Six," best known for works such as the oratorio *Le Roi David* and the tone poem *Pacific 231.*

Ives, Charles (1874–1954): American composer, boldly innovative in his day. Best known works: *The Unanswered Question,* Fourth Symphony.

Josquin des Prez (ca. 1450–1521): Known to some of his contemporaries as "the prince of music," he was a preeminent composer of the middle Renaissance; best known for his Masses and motets.

Liszt, Franz (1811–86): A prolific composer of many kinds of music and one of the greatest of the nineteenth-century piano virtuosos. Best known works: the tone poem *Les Preludes,* many shorter works for piano.

Lully, Jean Baptiste (1632–87): The founder and leading practitioner of French opera in the middle baroque.

MacDowell, Edward (1861–1908): American composer. Best known work: *Woodland Sketches* (piano).

Machaut, Guillaume de (ca. 1305–77): Preeminent composer of the Ars Nova period, he was both a priest and trouvère and wrote both secular and sacred music.

Mahler, Gustav (1860–1911): Composer of several very large-scale works and a master orchestrator. Best known works: *Kindertotenlieder* (for voice and orchestra), Symphony no. 9.

Marenzio, Luca (ca. 1560–99): Important composer of Italian madrigals during the late Renaissance.

Mendelssohn, Felix (1809–47): A classically oriented romantic who wrote in nearly all genres except opera. Best known works: Symphony no. 4 *(Italian), Hebrides* Overture, *Elijah* (oratorio).

Mendelssohn-Hensel, Fanny (1805–47): Older sister of Felix Mendelssohn and composer of songs and piano works.

Menotti, Gian Carlo (b. 1911): Italian-American composer of operas such as *Amahl and the Night Visitors.*

Messiaen, Oliver (b. 1908): French composer and organist. Many of his works are imbued with mysticism and exoticism.

Milhaud, Darius (1892–1974): A member of the "French Six," his music is eclectic, showing the influence of American jazz, Latin rhythms, and several folk melodies. Best known works: *Le Boeuf sur le toit, La Création du Monde.*

Monteverdi, Claudio (1567–1643): The preeminent Italian composer of the early baroque. Best known work: *Orfeo* (opera).

Morley, Thomas (ca. 1557–1603): An important composer of English madrigals during the Elizabethan era. Best known madrigal: *Now is the Month of Maying.*

Mozart, Wolfgang (1756–91): A master composer in virtually all genres of music, instrumental and vocal. Among his best known works: *Don Giovanni*, Symphony no. 40 in G Minor, several piano concertos, and several piano sonatas.

Mussorgsky, Modest (1835–81): Russian nationalistic composer. Best known works: *Pictures at an Exhibition* (orchestrated by Maurice Ravel), *Boris Godunoff* (opera).

Okeghem, Joannes (ca. 1430–95): A master composer of the early Renaissance and the teacher of Josquin des Prez. Best known works are Masses and motets, especially the Mass *L'homme armé.*

Palestrina, Giovanni Pierluigi da (ca. 1526–94): The dominant composer in the field of sacred music during the late Renaissance. He is best known for his Masses such as the *Missa Papae Marcelli* and *Aeterna Christi munera.*

Prokofiev, Sergei (1891–1953): Eminent and prolific Russian composer. Best known works include: *The Love for Three Oranges* (opera), *Peter and the Wolf*, Piano Concerto no. 3.

Puccini, Giacomo (1858–1924): Very popular Italian opera composer, some of whose works are imbued with *verismo*. Best known works: *La Bohèmme, Madame Butterfly.*

Purcell, Henry (1659–95): The leading British composer of the middle baroque era. Best known work: *Dido and Aeneas* (opera).

Rachmaninoff, Sergei (1873–1943): Russian composer and piano virtuoso best known for luxuriant melodies as found in his piano concertos.

Ravel, Maurice (1875–1937): French composer, often cited as an impressionist. Best known works: *Gaspard de la Nuit, Daphnis et Chloé, Boléro.*

Reich, Steve (b. 1936): A leading minimalist composer, some of whose works reflect his interest in a process called "phasing."

Riley, Terry (b. 1935): Composer of minimalist music, including *In C.*

Rossini, Gioacchino (1792–1868): One of the giant composers of nineteenth-century Italian opera. Best known works: *Il barbiere di Siviglia, William Tell* overture.

Satie, Erik (1866–1925): Associated with the dadaist movement for part of his career. Best known works: *Gymnopédie* no. 1 (for piano solo or for orchestra as orchestrated by Debussy), *Parade* (ballet).

Schönberg, Arnold (1874–1951): Inventor of the twelve-tone system. Best known work: *Pierrot Lunaire.*

Schubert, Franz (1797–1828): Prolific composer of Lieder, orchestral music, chamber music, and piano works. Best known works: *Die Erlkönig*, Symphony no. 8 *(Unfinished).*

Schumann, Clara (1819–96): Piano virtuoso and composer of lieder and short works for piano; wife of Robert Schumann.

Schumann, Robert (1810–56): Gifted, tragic romantic figure. Best known works: *Kinderscenen*, Piano Concerto in A Minor.

Stamitz, Johann (1717–57): Important in the development of the early symphony in Mannheim.

Still, William Grant (b. 1895): Black-American composer.

Stockhausen, Karlheinz (b. 1928): Important composer in the development of electronic music. Best known work: *Gesang der Jünglinge.*

Strauss, Richard (1864–1949): Composer of tone poems, German operas, and other works. Best known works: *Also sprach Zarathustra, Der Rosenkavalier* (opera).

Stravinsky, Igor (1882–1971): Russian-American composer, one of the giants of the twentieth century. Best known works: *Le Sacre du Printemps, Petrushka.*

Tchaikovsky, Peter (1840–93): Very popular Russian composer from the late romantic period. Several of his melodies have been made into popular songs. Best known works: *The Nutcracker, Symphonie Pathétique, Swan Lake.*

Torelli, Giuseppe (ca. 1650–1708): Important composer in the development of the concerto grosso in the middle baroque era.

Varèse, Edgar (1883–1965):
Important composer in the fields of
experimental and electronic music.
Best known works: *Ionisation,
Poème Electronique*.

Verdi, Giuseppe (1813–1901): The
preeminent Italian opera composer
of the nineteenth century. Best
known operas: *Rigoletto, Aïda*.

Villa-Lobos, Heitor (1887–1959):
Brazilian nationalist composer.

Vivaldi, Antonio (ca. 1675–1741):
Prolific composer of concerti grossi
in the late baroque era. Best known
work: the four concerti grossi
comprising *The Seasons*.

Wagner, Richard (1813–83):
Foremost composer of German
opera in the nineteenth century.
Developed the music drama with its
system of leitmotifs. Best known
works: *Tristan und Isolde, Die
Meistersinger von Nürnberg*.

Weber, Carl Maria von (1786–1826):
Early romantic composer of German
operas and other works. Best known
work: *Der Freischütz*.

Webern, Anton (1883–1945): Early in
Webern's career, he was an
expressionist and student of
Schönberg. Later, he developed
serial techniques in works of
emotional density, many of which
are quite brief. Best known work:
Variations (piano).

absolute music music that is not based on a program or story; the opposite of program music.

accelerando a speeding up of tempo.

accent stress or extra emphasis given to a beat.

accidental a ♯ placed in front of a note raises that note in pitch by a half step; a ♭ placed in front of a note lowers that note by a half step.

acid rock a heavily amplified and electronic form of rock that emerged in the mid-1960s; it reflected the mores of the then-current psychedelic subculture.

adagio a slow tempo.

adi tala a particular tala in classical Indian music, consisting of a four-beat anga, followed by a two-beat anga, followed by another two-beat anga.

akshara a beat in classical Indian music.

aleatory *see* chance music.

allegro a fast tempo.

allemande a dance of moderate tempo, in duple meter, found in the dance suite of the baroque era, as in J. S. Bach's French Suites.

andante a moderately slow tempo that moves at a walking pace.

andantino a tempo that is somewhat faster than andante.

anga a smaller collection of beats within a tala in classical Indian music.

anthem a choral work with English text sung with or without accompaniment.

aria an elaborate solo song (with accompaniment) found in operas, cantatas, and oratorios.

Ars Nova the style period of the fourteenth century, at the end of the Middle Ages and just preceding the Renaissance, characterized by rhythmic complexity and secular attitudes.

art rock a branch of rock music that blends rock beats and instruments with instruments and thematic materials associated with art music.

atonal music not in a key, as in some of the works of Schönberg and Webern. Generally atonal music is more dissonant than music written in functional harmony.

ballade (1) a type of character piece for piano in the nineteenth century; (2) a fixed poetic-musical form of the trouvères.

bar a single unit of a metrical pattern; the same thing as a measure.

bar line in notating music, a bar line is drawn at the end of each repetition of a meter.

baroque the period from ca. 1600–1750.

basso continuo a bass line instrument such as a cello, and a chord-playing instrument such as harpsichord or organ; the basso continuo was used in most types of baroque music.

beat the basic rhythmic pulse of music, especially metrical music.

bebop *see* bop.

bel canto the "beautiful" style of singing associated principally with Italian opera.

binary a two-part form having the design *AB, AABB,* or *ABAB.*

bitonality music performed in two different keys simultaneously.

blues both a form and a manner of performance that grew out of southern black folk music, elements of which are used in pure blues singing, jazz, rhythm and blues, and other types of American popular music.

blues rock a type of rock from the early 1970s in which one senses the direct influence of pure blues singing and playing.

boogie-woogie an energetic style of piano playing that relentlessly plays on a pattern of 8 eighth notes to the 4/4 bar—the so-called "eight to the bar" style. The style developed in the 1920s and reached a pinnacle of popularity in the 1940s.

Glossary

bop (bebop)   a wild, aggressive style of jazz from the 1940s and 1950s. Charlie Parker and Dizzy Gillespie were important performers of this style.

bowing   pulling the bow across the strings of a stringed instrument.

break   a short, solo improvisation found in many kinds of jazz; in a break, the beat of the rhythm section is temporarily suspended.

bridge   a connective, often modulatory passage that leads from one theme to another, as in *A* theme . . . bridge . . . *B* theme.

cadenza   a passage (often elaborate and showy) for the soloist at the end of recapitulation of the first movement of a concerto, as in the cadenza of a piano or violin concerto.

cantata   a multisectional piece for voices and instruments, often with vocal solos (arias) and choruses. Many cantatas are based on sacred texts, some on secular texts. The history of the cantata began in the baroque.

chamber music   small ensemble music, such as string quartets.

chance (aleatory) music   music ordered by some kind of random directions; chance or aleatory music was developed by John Cage and others in the years following World War II.

chant   a melody set to words (either scriptural or nonscriptural) designed for use in the early Christian church.

character piece   a relatively short work for solo piano often with a descriptive or programmatic title; developed in the nineteenth century.

choral (dramatic) symphony   a type of symphony developed in the nineteenth century that adds solo and/or choral voices to the symphony orchestra.

chorale   text and melody of a Lutheran hymn, developed in the Renaissance and richly employed by J. S. Bach and others in the baroque.

chorale prelude   a type of organ music based on a chorale melody.

chord   three or more pitches sounding simultaneously.

chord progression   a succession of chords from which the sense of progression in a piece emerges.

chorus   in jazz, an improvised solo, usually thirty-two bars in length.

chromatic   nondiatonic pitches of a given key. Chromaticism may be used as a means of creating dissonance.

classical era   the years roughly 1770–1810, best typified in the works of Haydn and Mozart, as well as the earlier works of Beethoven.

coda   a section at the end of a movement. In many styles and works the coda serves as a kind of musical "stop sign"—it indicates that the movement is about to conclude.

comic opera   a lightweight form of opera that developed in the mid-eighteenth century. Comic opera in England was called ballad opera; in France, opéra-comique; in Italy, opera buffa; in Germany, Singspiele.

concertino   the solo group in the concerto grosso.

concerto   a work (usually) for one soloist and orchestra.

concerto grosso   the dominant form of orchestral music in the baroque, often in three movements (fast-slow-fast) as played by tutti (full orchestra) and concertino (small group of soloists) with basso continuo.

concerts spirituels   public concerts in Paris in the preclassic era.

consonance   the sense of tonal stability and restfulness; the opposite of dissonance.

contrapuntal   a musical texture containing counterpoint.

cool jazz   a sophisticated, mellow kind of jazz that developed in the 1940s and 1950s, almost simultaneously with the more aggressive bop style.

countermelody   a subsidiary melody in a contrapuntal texture.

counterpoint   a musical texture in which two or more different melodic lines are equally prominent and compelling.

country music   a brand of white music formerly called hillbilly music. In some ways it resembled black rhythm and blues.

courante   one of the basic movements of the baroque dance suite, with moderate tempo and triple meter.

crescendo   a systematic, gradual increase in loudness; it appears as ◁ .

crooning   one of the dominant singing styles of American popular music in the 1930s and 1940s. The style is breathy and filled with vocal "scoops."

da capo aria   aria in ternary form—*ABA*. Opera singers in the baroque usually ornamented or varied the repetition of the *A* section.

dadaism   a radical, antiestablishment artistic movement that focused on and reflected the insanity of humankind. The movement emerged principally in Paris after World War I.

dance suite   a collection of dances performed consecutively to form the larger whole. Nearly all of the dances in a suite have the binary form *AABB*.

decrescendo   a gradual, measured decrease in volume; it appears as ▷ in musical notation, and first became prominent in the preclassic era.

development   the middle portion of a sonata-allegro form in which materials presented in the exposition section are elaborated.

diatonic   tones that are "family members" of a key; the opposite of chromatic tones. Each key has seven diatonic members; for example, in the key of C only the pitches C, D, E, F, G, A, and B are diatonic—all others are chromatic.

dissonance   harmonic tension or instability; the opposite of consonance.

dominant seventh   one of the three basic chords in the system of functional harmony; it both resists and leads to the tonic chord.

double exposition   a term used to describe the special nature of the exposition section in the classical concerto. The orchestra plays the exposition section first, then the soloist joins the orchestra for the repetition (a nonliteral repetition) of the material in the exposition.

downbeat   a stressed or accented beat, such as the first beat in a metrical measure.

duplum   the voice above the tenor in twelfth- and thirteenth-century polyphony.

dynamics   levels of loudness and softness.

electronic music   music in which some or all of the sounds are electronically generated.

Elizabethan madrigal   the dominant form of secular vocal music in England in the late sixteenth century; Elizabethan madrigals tended to be lighthearted.

empfindsamer stil   the "sensitive style"; the melancholy, sentimental style of the preclassic era. A principal exponent of this style is C. P. E. Bach.

étude   literally "a study," Chopin's études for solo piano present the performer with specific technical difficulties.

exposition   the opening portion of a sonata-allegro form that introduces the dominant thematic materials.

expressionism   an artistic movement that emerged in the early decades of the twentieth century. The deeply emotional and introspective style was fostered mainly by Schönberg, Berg, and Webern.

fermata   the symbol ⌢ placed over a note indicating that the note is to be held for longer than its normal duration.

figured bass   a kind of musical shorthand used by continuo players in the baroque era; it consisted of a notated bass line and a series of numbers and figures above it.

finalis   the stable, ending pitch of a medieval church mode, somewhat analogous to the tonic pitch in tonal music.

flat   notated as ♭, it lowers by a half step the pitch it accompanies.

folk rock   a type of rock from the late 1960s and early 1970s that stressed less volume and electronics, and more politically oriented texts.

frequency   the number of times per second a sound-producing body vibrates.

fugue   a very important type of imitative counterpoint in which one or more "following" voices imitate the theme or subject of the "lead" voice.

functional harmony (tonality)   a system of organizing chords to produce the sense of being in a key. Tonic, dominant, and subdominant chords are the principal functional elements of the system.

gamelan   an Indonesian orchestra (specifically Bali).

genteel tradition   an era of American popular music from the mid-nineteenth century, consisting mainly of sentimental songs for voice and piano. Many of the songs of Stephen Foster belong to this tradition.

Gesamtkunstwerk   Wagner's version of the synthesis of the arts—music, drama, poetry, dance, and architecture.

gigue   one of the dances in the baroque dance suite, characterized by a lively tempo.

glissandos   sliding from one note to another.

glitter rock   a branch of rock music that features elaborate sets and costumes in live performances.

gospel music   black religious music from the early twentieth century that had much in common with blues performance practice.

Gregorian chant   the sanctioned (monophonic) music of the early Christian church; named after Pope Gregory I (Pope from 590–604).

ground bass   a particular kind of ostinato much favored in the baroque era.

guru   master performer/teacher of classical Indian music.

harmony   in the broadest sense, harmony refers to the chords in music. One harmonic language differs from another because of differences in the types of chords employed.

hayashi   the instrumental ensemble that accompanies Japanese Noh drama.

heavy metal   a more tightly controlled and less extravagant relative of acid rock; it emerged in the 1970s.

homophonic   a musical texture in which one line—the melody—is clearly more prominent than any of the other accompanying or "harmonizing" voices or lines.

hot jazz   a kind of jazz that emerged about 1917, featuring more solo improvisation than group improvisation.

humanism   an ideal born in the Renaissance in which humanity took new and special pride in its own achievements.

imitative counterpoint   texture in which a lead voice is echoed or imitated in one or more following voices, as, for example, in a fugue.

impressionism   a late nineteenth-century movement in French painting, dominated by Monet, Renoir, and others. Some find the musical analogue to this movement in certain works by Debussy.

improvisation   a musical creation in which the concept and the performance thereof occur almost simultaneously.

infinite melody   Wagner's continuous flow of melody as used in his music dramas.

intermezzo   a form of light musical entertainment that occurred between the acts of an opera seria in the late baroque. It was the earliest form of comic opera.

interval   the distance between two pitches. Such intervals have names; for example, the distance or interval between the pitches c and d is called the interval of a major second or whole step.

inversion   the upside down version of a melody or tone row.

isorhythm   the repetition of the rhythm of one section of music in other sections of the same work; a practice of the fourteenth century.

Italian madrigal   the dominant form of secular vocal music in sixteenth-century Italy; Italian madrigals tended to be more dramatic and emotional than Elizabethan madrigals.

jazz rock   a type of rock from the mid-1960s in which the influence of jazz improvisation and swing are apparent.

key   the proper ordering of tonic, dominant, and subdominant chords in functional harmony. A given key takes the name of its tonic chord; for example, the key of C major; the key of B minor, etc.

koto   a zither-like instrument from Japan.

largo   a very slow tempo.

legato   playing a musical line in a smooth, connected fashion; the opposite of staccato.

leitmotif   a musical motive (or even just a special chord) that is associated with a particular person, place, thing, or idea. Leitmotifs abound in the music dramas of Richard Wagner but are also employed by others, Strauss among them, in orchestral works.

lento   a slow tempo.

Les Six   a group of then radical young composers active in Paris just after World War I. One of them, Milhaud, was noted for his use of polytonality.

libretto   the story and complete text of an opera.

Lied   German word for art song; plural is Lieder.

line   synonym for a single voice or instrumental part of a musical texture.

liturgical item   a melody, text, or bit of ceremony officially sanctioned for use in the Church.

liturgy   the music, prayers, readings, and ceremony of a church, particularly the Roman Catholic church.

madrigal   a piece usually for unaccompanied vocal ensemble set to pastoral texts or love lyrics in the sixteenth century.

major second (whole step, whole tone)   comprises two minor seconds. On a piano keyboard, a whole step is produced by playing two keys that are separated from each other by one intervening black or white key.

Mass   the Roman Catholic worship service consisting of Ordinary and Proper parts.

measure   *see* bar.

melismatic   a type of text setting in which some syllables of text are sung to more than one melodic note.

melody   a succession of pitches which form a continuity and create a sense of self-contained completeness.

meter   a succession of beats organized into a pattern.

meter signature   a meter signature has two factors: in simple meters the upper factor tells the number of beats in the pattern; the lower factor tells what note value is to serve as the basic pulse of the meter.

metrical modulation   a systematic transition from one musical speed to another.

metrical psalm (psalmody)   music used in the early Calvinistic church that consisted of simple melodies and/or harmonizations set to metered translations of the texts from the 150 Psalms of the Bible.

minimalist music   a type of music that developed in the 1960s; it is created from a limited fund of uncomplicated musical materials.

minor second (half step, semitone)   the smallest interval in conventional (i.e., nonelectronic) Western music.

minuet   a dance in 3/4 meter, with moderate tempo. The minuet and trio is the third movement of a classical symphony.

mode   (1) the special quality or sound of the minor mode as distinct from the sound of the major mode. A minor tonic triad establishes minor mode; a major tonic triad establishes major mode. (2) The several church modes of the Middle Ages and Renaissance, each mode having its distinctive or characteristic intervallic structure.

moderato   a moderate tempo.

modified strophic   a composition that incorporates both strophic and through-composed elements.

modulation   changing from one key to another in the course of tonal composition.

monophonic   a texture consisting of one voice line or a single line of music without accompaniment, as in a Gregorian chant.

motet   a work for voices, usually with a sacred text. The motet was developed in the thirteenth century and reached a high artistic level in the Renaissance.

motive a brief musical figure, as in the opening measures of Beethoven's Symphony no. 5. A motive is shorter than a phrase and usually consists of just a few notes.

movement a unit of a larger work, as in the four movements of a classical symphony.

musical description music that imitates things beyond itself, such as babbling brooks, rain, thunder, bird calls, etc.

music drama Wagner's form of opera.

musique concrète an early form of electronic music that emerged after World War II. Natural and conventional sounds are captured on tape and manipulated in various ways.

neoclassicism a movement (ca. 1920–50) that emerged after World War I and featured a return to forms and genres of eighteenth-century music; seen in some of the works of Stravinsky, for example.

new jazz a broad label applied to several kinds of jazz that emerged in the 1960s after the fade of bop and cool.

Noh drama an ancient form of Japanese theatrical entertainment employing dialogue, songs and traditional instruments.

nonimitative counterpoint a texture in which there are two or more different and equally compelling musical lines, as distinct from imitative counterpoint in which one dominant line is echoed or imitated in several voices.

note value sounds in music have durational values. These values are expressed in a set of symbols which are called note values.

novelty song a type of popular song that developed in the 1930s, featuring lyrics that were faddish.

nuclear melody the basic melody played by some instruments in a Balinese gamelan, elaborated in various ways by other groups of instruments.

octave the duplication of a pitch eight diatonic tones higher, as in the octave C-c.

opera a musical-dramatic genre that employs singers, orchestra, stage sets, and costumes.

opera seria a highly elevated and virtuosic brand of Italian opera from the early eighteenth century consisting of three acts, a small cast, da capo arias, recitatives, and small ensemble numbers.

opus literally, "a work." Composers often assign opus numbers to their works, such as Beethoven's opus (op.) 14, etc.

oratorio a large-scale work for soloists, chorus, and orchestra, the text of which is usually sacred. Unlike opera, the oratorio is not staged but is presented as a concert piece.

Ordinary Kyrie, Gloria, Allelulia, Credo, Sanctus, Agnus Die. Each of these has a prescribed text that is sung (or spoken) in a specific place in each celebration of the Mass.

ordres a French term for a collection or suite of short pieces for harpsichord, introduced by François Couperin in the rococo.

organum the earliest known form of polyphony, from about the ninth century, in which the two parts move parallel to one another.

ostinato a musical passage (sometimes just a rhythmic figure) that is repeated doggedly throughout a movement or a large portion of a movement.

parlor song a simple, often sentimental kind of song for voice and piano from the genteel tradition in nineteenth-century North America.

philosophical program music a kind of music that expresses the essence and power of ideas and attitudes, such as nobility, integrity, love, etc.

phrase an internal division of a melody. A phrase is to a melody as a clause is to a sentence. Many phrases end with a temporary pause.

pitch determines the relative highness or lowness of a sound.

pizzicato plucking the strings of a stringed instrument with the finger tips, as opposed to bowing the strings.

polonaise a Polish dance arranged for solo piano, most notably by Chopin.

polyphonic a texture with more than one voice line. There are two major types of polyphony: homophony and contrapuntal.

polyrhythms two or more different rhythms operating simultaneously.

polytonality music written in three or more simultaneously sounding keys.

prelude (1) sometimes used as the first piece in a late baroque dance suite. (2) A short character piece for solo piano, introduced by Chopin in the mid-nineteenth century.

presto a very fast tempo.

program music instrumental music that is connected to or inspired by something beyond its acoustical self, such as a painting, a poem, a character, or a scene from nature.

Proper texts and chants of the Mass that are proper to and performed at specific times of the church year, as opposed to the Ordinary, whose texts never change.

punk rock an aggressively antiestablishment, nihilistic form of rock that developed in the late 1970s and carried over into the early 1980s.

rag (ragtime) a syncopated kind of popular music that emerged in the late 1890s in the hands of Scott Joplin and others.

raga a collection of pitches used in a classical Indian composition; roughly similar to a scale in Western music.

range the range of a melody is the distance between its lowest note and its highest note.

recapitulation the third portion of a sonata-allegro form, in which the turmoil of the development section is resolved.

recitative   a kind of heightened speech utterance, usually quite static melodically; unlike the more active aria, both of which are found in operas, oratorios, and cantatas.

reciting tone   in a church mode, the tone on which the bulk of a psalm or other text is sung. The reciting tone ultimately moves to the finalis of the mode.

reggae   a type of music from Jamaica that blends elements of Afro-Jamaican and rock music.

Renaissance   a cultural/artistic era comprising roughly the years 1450–1600.

Renaissance motet   a large-scale, one-movement work with Latin text, often featuring imitative counterpoint.

rest   silence in music.

retrograde   the backwards version of a melody, moving from the last note of the original melody to the first.

retrograde inversion   the backwards and upside-down version of a melody.

rhythm   having to do with all of the temporal aspects of music, such as beat, meter, tempo, and durational values.

rhythm and blues (R & B)   a type of music that emerged in the 1940s which, with certain modifications, became the basis for rock and roll.

riff   a brief melodic or rhythmic figure that is repeated over and over throughout a large section of a (if not the entire) jazz or rock piece. Its equivalent in art music in the ostinato.

ritardando   a gradual slowing of tempo.

ritornello   a patch of music that recurs several times in the course of a movement; often used in the baroque concerto grosso.

rocking and reeling (rocking and rolling)   terms from certain types of black music from the early twentieth century, used to denote ecstasy.

rococo   period between the baroque and classical styles (roughly 1730–50), generally characterized by lightness, polish, wit, and a lack of profundity.

rondo   a musical form consisting of the alternation of an *A* section with two or more contrasting sections, such as *ABACABA*.

root   the pitch upon which a chord is built; for example, the C major chord consists of C (root), E (third), G (fifth).

rubato   a flexible tempo in which there is extensive use of accelerando and ritardando.

saraband   one of the dances in the baroque dance suite that employs slower tempo and triple-meter form.

scherzo   a dance in triple meter at a fairly fast tempo; the scherzo and trio replaced the minuet and trio as the third movement of a symphony, beginning with Beethoven.

semitone   *see* minor second.

sequence   a liturgical chant proper to the Easter season.

serial music   the roots of serialized music are found in Schönberg's twelve-tone system, in which the twelve chromatic pitches are presented as a series in a tone row. Later composers have also serialized such elements as rhythm, dynamics, and instrumentation.

set number   a self-contained unit of a larger scene in nineteenth-century Italian opera.

seventh chord   a triad with an additional third on top of the stack. Reading from the bottom up, the members of the chord are root, third, fifth, seventh.

sharp   notated as ♯, it raises by a half step the pitch it accompanies.

slashing   a method of guitar playing found in reggae music in which the strings are strummed forcefully, producing a percussive sound.

soft rock and roll   a less abrasive and more insipid style of rock and roll that emerged in the late 1950s. It sometimes used violins as accompanimental background.

sonata   a genre of music—usually for one instrument, as in a piano sonata, or for two instruments, as in a sonata for violin and piano. A sonata usually consists of three or four movements with contrasting tempos, moods, and content.

sonata-allegro   a structure consisting of exposition-development-recapitulation-coda. In classical and many romantic symphonies, concertos, sonatas, and string quartets, the first movement is in this form; other movements may also be in the form.

song cycle   a collection of poems set to music (voice and piano) that develop a central narrative theme.

soul   a type of secularized gospel music.

Sprechtstimme   a type of utterance somewhere between speech and singing; used in Schönberg's *Pierrot Lunaire*.

staccato   a manner of playing a musical line crisply; the opposite of legato.

stage (talking) style   a singing style in American popular music that featured rough, raspy vocal quality and periodically lapsed into speech.

standard   an American popular song such as "Night and Day" that retains a measure of mass appeal over a long period of time.

stride piano   a piano style that established four-beat patterns in the left-hand, rather than the two-beat patterns of earlier jazz.

strophic   a composition in which a number of stanzas or verses of a poem are sung to one strand of music, as is the case with most church hymns.

Sturm und Drang literally "Storm and Stress"; a somewhat violent movement in the late preclassic era, a reaction against the lighthearted rococo style.

style galant an elegant, often lighthearted style from the preclassic era of the mid-eighteenth century.

subdominant chord one of the three primary functional chords in functional harmony; its function is to lead to the dominant.

sweet dance bands bands of the 1930s and 1940s that did not play swing music.

swing a type of rhythmic performance in jazz.

swing era the years from the early 1930s to about 1945.

syllabic a type of text setting in which each melodic note is sung to one syllable of text.

symbolism an essentially French literary movement of the late nineteenth century in which words were often used for their sonorous rather than their syntactical value. Some of Debussy's works can be seen as the musical counterpart of this movement.

symphony the dominant form of orchestral music in the classical and romantic eras.

syncopation a rhythmic disturbance in which accent is given to some beat other than the downbeat of a measure.

synthesizer an electronic instrument capable of producing sounds and modifications of sounds in a variety of ways.

tala a rhythmic cycle in classical Indian music.

tempo the pace at which a piece of music progresses.

tenor (1) a high range male voice. (2) Lower voice, usually in long note values, in twelfth- and thirteenth-century polyphony.

tenor (clean) style a singing style in American popular music in the 1930s and 1940s that stressed pure vocal quality and precise diction.

ternary three-part musical form—*ABA*.

texture having to do with the number and activity of voices in a musical fabric.

theater music a type of music that developed in the 1960s and exploited the visual aspects of live music performances.

theme a dominating, memorable melody of a section or movement in instrumental music.

through-composed a composition in which new strands of music are created for each verse or stanza.

tie a tie connects one note to the next, thereby increasing the durational value of the note.

timbre the characteristic tone color of a given instrument, as the special color of a flute is distinct from the color of an oboe, trumpet, bassoon, etc.

Tin Pan Alley the hub of the popular music business in New York City in the late nineteenth century.

tonality functional harmony; the sense of being in a key.

tone (symphonic) poem an orchestral piece in one movement with some programmatic basis; a product of the nineteenth century.

tone row the basic set of twelve pitches in serial form found in music written in the twelve-tone system.

tonic the tonic chord is the center of harmonic gravity in tonal music, the chord to which all others must ultimately resolve if the piece is to sound as if it has ended decisively.

tragedie lyrique a form of French opera established by Lully in the late seventeenth century; it combined music, drama, and ballet.

triad a stack of major and/or minor thirds; the members of a triad, reading consecutively from the bottom of the stack upwards, are root, third, fifth.

trio sonata the dominant form of chamber music in the baroque era, typically consisting of two continuo instruments and two solo instruments.

triplum the voice above the duplum in twelfth- and thirteenth-century polyphony.

trouvères wandering poet-musicians of the later Middle Ages.

tutti the entire orchestra in a baroque concerto grosso.

twelve-bar blues has the structure and harmony:

A	A'	B
1 2 3 4	5 6 7 8	9 10 11 12
I	IV I	V₇ I

twelve-tone system Arnold Schönberg developed this system in which the twelve chromatic pitches of the octave are organized in a logical but nontonal way. The twelve chromatic pitches are expressed in a tone row, no pitch being repeated until all the others have been presented.

upbeat the last beat in a measure, usually unaccented.

variations in a composition, the occurrence of an initially stated theme followed by a number of sections where, either the theme is embroidered upon, or the environment of the theme undergoes changes.

verse and refrain the standard American popular song format from the 1890s to the mid-twentieth century.

verse anthem similar to an anthem, but with one or more solo voices featured, along with the chorus.

volume (amplitude) the degree of loudness or softness of sounds.

worried notes in blues, notes played or sung with a quiver, while slightly and deliberately out of tune.

Index

Absolute music, 77, 80
Absolutism, 87, 111, 116
Academic Festival Overture, 169, 180
Accelerando, 18
Accidental, 27
Adagio, 18
Adagio for Strings, 25, 40, 69, 229,
    261–62
Adi tala, 390
Aerosmith, 375
Aeterna Christi munera, 297, 302
Affection, 89, 90
Africa, 382–85
Afro-American Symphony, 229, 274
Age of Charlemagne, 280, 289
Agnus Dei, 284
"Agnus Dei," 25, 37
"Ain't That a Shame," 359, 367
Akshara, 390, 394
"Alabama," 341, 355
Alceste, 85, 103
Alcina, 49, 55, 85, 94, 104–5
Aleatory music, 270–72
Alisa, 207
Allegro, 18, 22
Allemande, 55, 56, 100
"Allemande," 129
Allman Brothers, 375
Almaviva, Count, 207–14
Also sprach Zarathustra, 169, 189
Alto, 38, 300
Amahl and the Night Visitors, 229,
    274
"Amazing Grace," 25, 30, 33, 61, 359
Amplitude, 26
Ancient Voices of Children, 229,
    274–75
Andante, 18
Andante con moto, op. 2, no. 2, 169,
    195
Andantino, 18
Anderson, Laurie, 377
An die Musik, 169, 201–2
"And the Angels Sing," 313, 325
Anga, 390, 394
Anglicanism, 301
Anka, Paul, 367
Anna, Donna, 159–65
Années de Pèlerinage, 169, 194
Anthem, 300, 301, 309
    verse, 301
Anthology of African Music, An, 385
Antiphon, 36
Appalachian Spring, 229, 261
Apples, 70
L'Apprenti Sorcier, 169, 189
"April in Paris," 313, 327
Arabic and Druse Music, 382

Aria, 25, 102, 112
    baroque, 55, 94, 100, 103, 104,
        106–7
    cantata, 107
    da capo, 55, 104, 110
    opera, 102, 206, 207, 214, 221
    oratorio, 106–7
    ternary form, 55
Arlen, Harold, 313
    Hooray for What?, 313, 328
Armed Man, The, 297, 302
Armstrong, Harry, 313, 319
    "Sweet Adeline," 313, 319, 320
Armstrong, Louis, 313, 356
    "Hotter Than That," 341, 348
    influence of, 335
    in New Orleans and Chicago, 346,
        347, 348, 349
    "West End Blues," 341, 348
Ars Nova, 8, 280, 289–92, 293
    composer, 291–92, 293
    sacred music, 8, 289–92
    secular music, 8, 292
Art
    baroque, 87–89, 112
    impressionist, 231
    public, 122
    Renaissance, 87–89
    rococo, 117
Art music, 6–7, 132
    American, 276
    historical periods, 8–9
    rock, 376
    stylistic periods, 8–9
    twentieth century, 230–31, 275, 277
    since World War II, 265–75
Art song, 8, 200–205, 226. *See also*
    Lied
Asia, 385–89
As Thousands Cheer, 313, 328
"As Time Goes By," 313, 323
Atonal music, 239, 276, 277
"At the River," 229, 250
"Au bord d'une source," 194
Audience participation, 315
Augmented fourth, 28
"Au lac de Wallenstadt," 194
"Auld Lang Syne," 313, 332
Auric, Georges, 253
Avalon, Frankie, 367
Ave Maria, 297, 305

Babbitt, Milton, 266, 268, 277
Ba-Benzélé Pygmies, 384–85
Babinga, 384–85
"Baby Please Don't Go," 341, 344
Bach, Anna Magdalena, 97

Bach, Carl Philipp Emanuel, 96, 115, 125
    Berlin school, 127, 128
    Fantasia in C Minor, K. 475, 115, 123
    Sturm und Drang influence on, 123
    Symphony in B Minor, 115, 123, 127–28
Bach, Johann Christian, 96, 115, 122–23, 125
    Symphony in D Major, op. 18, no. 1, 115, 122, 128
Bach, Johann Sebastian, 13, 25, 37, 49, 85, 96–97, 115, 131, 274
    Brandenburg Concerto no. 2, 13, 18, 19, 85, 93, 95–96, 98, 112, 115, 131
    Brandenburg Concerto no. 5, 85, 94
    Cantata no. 80 (*Ein' feste Burg ist unser Gott*), 85, 108–11, 297, 300
    C Minor Fugue, 25, 37, 85, 93
    concerto grosso, 95
    flute sonata, 42
    French Suite no. 1 in D Minor, 49, 55–56, 115, 129
    "Grief and Pain," 55
    "Jesu, Joy of Man's Desiring," 85, 94
    "A Mighty Fortress Is Our God," 85, 108–11, 297, 300
    Saint Matthew Passion, 49, 55, 85, 96
    Six English Suites, 85, 100
    Six French Suites, 85, 100
    trio sonata, 98
    Well-Tempered Clavier, 25, 37, 85, 93
Bach-Abel concerts, 122
Baez, Joan, 373, 378
Baker, Laverne, 359, 363
    "Jim Dandy," 359, 363
Bali, 388–89, 394
Ballad, 324, 325
Ballade, 191, 292
Ballet, 103
    nationalistic, 171
    romantic era, 8, 171, 182
    Stravinsky, 243–45
    twentieth century, 243–45, 252, 255, 261, 276
Band
    black, 351–52, 356
    dance, 316, 331–32, 336
    era, 329–32
    marching, 345, 356
    New Orleans, 346–47, 349, 356
    recordings, 337

    sweet, 329, 331–32
    swing, 329–31, 350, 356
    white, 351–52, 356
Band, The, 359, 373
    "Like a Rolling Stone," 359, 373
Banjo, 346
Bar, 17
Bar line, 17
Barber, Samuel, 25, 69, 229, 259, 276
    Adagio for Strings, 25, 40, 69, 229, 261–62
Barber of Seville, 169, 206, 207–14
Baritone, 38
Barnet, Charlie, 313
    "Cherokee," 313, 331
Baroque, 8, 9, 87
    aesthetic creed, 89
    aria, 55, 94, 100, 103, 104, 106–7
    art, 87–89, 112
    bassoon, 41
    beat, 93
    cantata, 8, 100, 107–11
    chamber music, 86, 98, 112
    characteristics, 86, 90–91, 92–94, 112, 129
    chords, 86
    composers, 94–111, 112
    concerto, 86, 94–96, 112, 145
    concerto grosso, 8, 94–96
    dance suite, 55
    decline of, 116
    emotion, 89
    flute, 40
    fugue, 37
    genres, 99–111, 112
    harmony, 32, 86, 92, 112
    keyboard music, 8, 86, 99–100, 112
    meter, 86
    musical recipes, 90–91
    music in, 84–113
    opera, 8, 86, 100–106, 112
    oratorio, 8, 91, 100, 106–7, 112
    orchestra, 39
    orchestral music, 94–100
    trio sonata, 8, 98–99, 112
    variations, 100
    vocal music, 91, 100–111
Bartók, Béla, 25, 69, 229, 245–48
    counterpoint, 247, 276
    Fourth String Quartet, 229, 246–47
    Music for Strings, Percussion and Celesta, 44, 247–48, 276
    "Night's Music, The," 69, 76, 247
    Out of Doors, 69, 76, 229, 247
Basie, Count, 313, 330, 336
    "One O'Clock Jump," 313, 330, 331
Bass, 38, 300, 346, 372
Basso continuo, 92, 96, 98, 112
Bassoon, 40–43, 92, 125, 183, 256

"Battle Hymn of the Republic," 49, 61
Beach, Amy, 25, 259
    "Elle et Moi," 25
Beach Boys, The, 359, 368
    "Fun, Fun, Fun," 359, 368
    "Little Deuce Coupe," 359, 368
    "Surfin' U.S.A.," 359, 368
Beat, 16, 23
    back beat, 363
    baroque, 93
    Indian, 390, 394
    meter and, 17, 23
    rhythm and blues, 363
    rock and roll, 365–66
Beatles, The, 359, 368–71, 378
    "Being for the Benefit of Mr. Kite!," 359, 370
    "Come Together," 359, 369
    "A Day in the Life," 359, 369, 371
    "Eleanor Rigby," 359, 369
    "Fixing a Hole," 359, 370
    "Getting Better," 359, 370
    "Good Morning," 359, 371
    "A Little Help from My Friends," 359, 370
    "Lovely Rita," 359, 371
    "Love Me Do," 359, 366
    "Lucy in the Sky with Diamonds," 359, 370
    "Polythene Pam," 359, 369
    Sgt. Pepper's Lonely Hearts Club Band, 359, 370–71
    "She's Leaving Home," 359, 370
    "Taxman," 359, 369
    "When I'm Sixty-Four," 359, 371
    "Within You, Without You," 359, 370
    "Yesterday," 359, 369
"Beau Soir," 49, 61
"Beautiful Dreamer," 313, 317, 318
Bebop, 352
Beethoven, Ludwig van, 25, 49, 69, 124, 131, 139–45, 169
    concertos, 148, 166
    Eroica, 49, 55, 131, 141–44, 145, 154, 169, 175, 184
    Lieder, 200
    Moonlight Sonata, 131, 155–56
    Pastoral, 25, 43, 69, 73, 78, 169, 175
    Piano Concerto no. 1, 131, 148
    Piano Concerto no. 4, 131, 148
    piano sonata, 152, 153–56, 166
    Piano Sonata in A♭ Major, no. 12, op. 26, 49, 60, 131, 153–55
    Piano Sonata in F Minor, op. 2, no. 1, 49, 62

Piano Sonata no. 8 in C Minor, op. 13, 49, 57
Piano Sonata no. 14, op. 27, no. 2 (*Moonlight Sonata*), 131, 155–56
programs, 80
scherzo, 53
Sonata no. 13, 131
String Quartet, op. 18, 131, 151
string quartets, 151, 166
symphonies, 141, 166, 176, 180, 184
Symphony no. 1, 131, 141
Symphony no. 3 (*Eroica*), 49, 55, 131, 141–44, 145, 154, 169, 175, 184
Symphony no. 5, 25, 30, 43, 169, 175, 184
Symphony no. 6, *Pastoral*, 25, 43, 69, 73, 78, 169, 175
Symphony no. 7, 69, 78–80
Symphony no. 9, 169, 175, 186
Beggar's Opera, The, 157–58
"Begin the Beguine," 313, 331
Beiderbecke, Bix, 335, 348–49, 351
"Being for the Benefit of Mr. Kite!," 359, 370
Bel canto, 104, 173
Bellini, Vincenzo, 169, 206
Norma, 169, 206
"Benny and the Jets," 359, 375
Berg, Alban, 229, 238
Wozzeck, 229, 239–42, 276
Berigan, Bunny, 351
Berio, Luciano, 229, 274
Circles, 229, 274
Berlin, Irving, 313, 316
As Thousands Cheer, 313, 328
"Easter Parade," 313, 322, 323
"God Bless America," 313, 327
Berlin School, 127–28, 129
Berlioz, (Louis) Hector, 25, 169, 172, 173, 185–86, 192
Harold in Italy, 25, 39
program symphonies, 80, 225
Roméo et Juliette, 169, 186–87
Symphonie Fantastique, 169, 185
Berry, Chuck, 359, 369
"Roll over Beethoven," 359, 365
"School Days," 359, 365
Best of the Blues, 58, 344
B52s, 376
Big band era, 329–32
Big Brother and the Holding Company, 374
Binary, 51, 55–56
Bitonality, 245, 276
Bizet, Georges, 169, 173
Carmen, 169, 205
Blackboard Jungle, 360

Black Key Étude, 193
Black music. *See* Blues, Gospel music, Jazz, Rhythm and blues
Black Sabbath, 359, 375
"A National Acrobat," 359, 375
Blood, Sweat, and Tears, 376
Blues, 344–45, 355
recording of, 58
rock, 374–75, 378
twelve-bar, 51, 57–58, 322, 344, 362–63, 366, 377
"Blues before Sunrise," 341, 344
Boccherini, Luigi, 125
Boeuf sur le toit, Le, 229, 254
Bohème, La, 169, 206
Boléro, 25, 43
Boleyn, Anne, 307
Boogie woogie, 58, 366
"Boogie Woogie," 313, 331, 349
Bookkeeping, structural, 50–59, 65
Boone, Pat, 359, 367, 378
"Ain't That a Shame," 359, 367
"I Almost Lost My Mind," 359, 367
"Love Letters in the Sand," 359, 367
Bop, 342, 352–54, 356
Boris Godunoff, 169, 171, 205
Borodin, Alexander, 25, 169, 173, 225
In the Steppes of Central Asia, 25, 43, 169, 171, 188–89
Boulanger, Nadia, 25, 259, 275
"Je garde une médaille dèlle," 25
"Bourgeois Blues, The," 341, 344
Bowie, David, 359, 375
"Fame," 359, 375
Bowing, 39
Boyce, William, 125
Bradamante, 104
Brahms, Johannes, 169, 175, 179–82
Academic Festival Overture, 169, 180
character pieces, 191, 195
classicism and, 180–82
concertos, 196
contrapuntal tradition, 173
influence of, 238
Intermezzo, op. 118, no. 2, 169, 191, 195
Lied, 200
piano sonata, 190
solo songs, 172
symphonies, 225
Symphony no. 2, op. 73, 169, 180, 181–82, 183
Brandenburg, Margrave of, 96
Brandenburg Concerto no. 2, 13, 18, 19, 85, 93, 95–96, 98, 112, 115, 131

Brandenburg Concerto no. 5, 85, 94
Brass, 39, 43, 46, 371
Break, 349
"Break on Through," 359, 373
Bridge, 58
Britten, Benjamin, 25, 229, 274
Ceremony of Carols, A, 229, 274
Serenade for Horn, Tenor, and Strings, 229, 274
Young Person's Guide to the Orchestra, 25, 43
Broadway, 262, 316
Broonzy, Big Bill, 341, 374
"Baby Please Don't Go," 341, 344
"I Got Up in the Mornin' Blues," 341, 344
"Brother Can You Spare a Dime?," 313, 328
"Brouillards," 229, 232–33, 234
Brown, James, 359, 372, 378
"Good, Good Lovin'," 359, 372
"Please, Please, Please," 359, 372
Brownie and Sonny, 49, 344
"I'm a Stranger Here," 49, 58, 344
Brubeck, Dave, 341, 354
"Take Five," 341, 354
Bubonic plague, 289
Buddhism, 391
Bull, John, 308
Bull on the Roof, The, 229, 254
"Burning Down the House," 359, 377
Byrd, William, 297, 301, 307, 309
Christ Rising Again, 297, 301, 308
"By the Light of the Silvery Moon," 313, 321

"C. C. Rider," 359, 363
Caccini, Giulio, 85, 102
Le Nuove musiche, 85, 102
Cadenza, 146
Cage, John, 229, 271–72
Concerto for Prepared Piano and Orchestra, 229, 272
4' 33'', 229, 271–72
HPSCHD, 229, 272
Imaginary Landscape no. 4, 229, 271
Calvin, John, 300, 301, 309
Calvinism, 300–301
Camerata, 102
"Camptown Races," 313, 317, 318
"Can Broadway Do without Me?," 313, 333
Canonical Hours, 282, 293
Cantata, 8, 100, 107–11, 112
Cantata no. 80 (*Ein' feste Burg ist unser Gott*), 85, 108–11, 297, 300

"Caravan," 313, 323, 341, 352
Carmen, 169, 205
Carnival of Animals, 25, 40
Carter, Elliott, 229, 275
    Cello Sonata, 229, 275
    Piano Concerto, 229, 275
    Sonata for Flute, Oboe, Cello, and
        Harpsichord, 229, 275
    Three String Quartets, 229, 275
Caruso, Enrico, 333, 334
Castanets, 44–45
Casulana, Maddalena, 307
Celesta, 45, 247–48
Cello, 39–40, 92, 99, 148–51, 187, 189
    concerto, 196
    rock, 376
Cello Sonata, 229, 275
Ceremony of Carols, A, 229, 274
Cézanne, Paul, 70
Chamber music, 43
    baroque, 86, 98, 112
    classical, 148, 166
    contemporary, 8
Chance music, 270–72, 274, 275, 277
Chant, 280
    Gregorian, 8, 275, 280–85, 293
Character piece, 191–95, 225
Charles, Ray, 49
    "Someday," 49, 58
Charon, 103
Checker, Chubby, 359, 368
    "The Twist," 359, 368
"Cherokee," 313, 331
Chicago, 376
Chicago, Ill., 347
Chimes, 44
Chopin, Frédéric François, 13, 49, 173,
        175, 190, 191–95, 225
    character pieces, 191–92, 193–95
    concertos, 196
    études, 193
    Études, op. 10, 169
    Étude, op. 10, no. 5 in G♭ Major
        (Black Key Étude), 169, 193
    Mazurka, op. 63, no. 3, 49, 53
    Mazurka, op. 67, no. 3, 49, 52–53
    piano preludes, 172
    Polonaise in A♭ Major, op. 53
        (*Heroic*), 169, 192–93
    Prelude no. 1 in C Major, 169, 192
    Prelude no. 4 in E Minor, 169, 192
    Prelude no. 7 in A Major, 169, 192
    Prelude no. 20 in C Minor, 169, 192
    Prelude no. 21 in B♭ Major, 169,
        192
    Twelve Études, op. 10, 193
    Twenty-Four Preludes, op. 28, 169,
        191, 192
    Waltz, op. 34, no. 2, 13, 19, 22, 25

Chorale, 8, 107–11, 300, 309
    cantata, 107, 108
Chorale prelude, 100, 107, 112
Chord, 31–34, 46, 221
    baroque, 86
    consonant, 34
    harmony and, 32
    I, 33
    IV, 33
    progression, 31, 376
    seventh, 33, 46
    subdominant, 33, 46
    tonic, 33, 46
    V$_7$, 33
Chorus, 106, 107, 112, 175, 343
    opera, 206
Christ, 109
Christ Rising Again, 297, 301, 308
Church
    Middle Ages, 280
    modes, 281–82, 293
    music with soul, 372
Church of England, 301
Circles, 229, 274
"Ciribiribin," 313, 331
Clapton, Eric, 359, 374
    "Lay Down Sally," 359, 374
Clarinet, 40–43, 188, 196, 245, 255,
        256, 346
Clarinet Concerto, 229
Classical era, 9, 86
    composers, 133–45
    concerto, 8, 145–48
    opera, 8, 157–66
    oratorio, 8, 134
    piano sonata, 152–56
    sonata, 8, 58
    string quartet, 8, 148–51, 166
    symphony, 8, 124–25, 132–33,
        134–37, 138–39, 141–44
Classical music, 132. *See also* Art
    music
Classicism, 141, 144, 166
    Brahms and, 180–82
Clock, The, 13, 22, 131, 136–37
"Clouds," 69, 76, 229, 234–35, 275
C Minor Fugue, 25, 37, 85, 93
Cocteau, Jean, 252
Coda, 53, 59, 66, 143
Coleman, Ornette, 341, 354
    "Happy House," 341, 354
Coletrane, John, 341, 354
    "Alabama," 341, 355
Cologne, Germany, 266
Coloratura, 38
Colors of the Celestial City, 229, 275
Columbia-Princeton Music Center, 266
"Columbia the Gem of the Ocean,"
    229, 250

Comedy, musical, 316, 333
"Come Home Father," 313, 317
Come Out, 229, 273
"Come Together," 359, 369
"Come Where My Love Lies
    Dreaming," 313, 317
Commendatore, 160
Composers
    Americana, 259–62
    Ars Nova, 291–92, 293
    baroque, 94–111, 112
    cantata, 107–11
    character piece, 191–95
    classical era, 133–45
    concerto grosso, 94–96, 196–200
    galant style, 122
    jazz, 352
    keyboard music, 99–100
    nationalistic, 171
    opera, 101–6, 173, 206
    oratoria, 106–7
    piano sonata, 190
    romantic, 172–75
    symphony, 124–28
    trio sonata, 98–99
    viols, 308
    virginal, 307–8
    women, 9, 119, 259
Concertino, 94, 97, 112, 145
Concerto
    baroque, 86, 94–96, 112, 145
    Beethoven, 148, 166
    Brahms, 196
    cello, 196
    classical, 8, 134, 145–48, 166
    contemporary, 8
    grosso, 8, 94–96, 112, 145
    Mozart, 145–48
    nineteenth century, 196–200, 226
    preclassic, 8
    romantic era, 8, 196–200, 226
    Tchaikovsky, 196
    twentieth century, 258–59, 262,
        274–75
    violin, 25, 39, 69, 74, 131, 148,
        196–200, 226
Concerto for Cello and Orchestra, 25,
    39–40
*Concerto for Prepared Piano and
    Orchestra,* 229, 272
Concerts spirituels, 123
Concord Sonata, 229, 250
Consonance, 34
Constantine, 280, 293
Contemporary era, 8. *See also*
    Twentieth century
Continuo, 92, 98, 127
Contrabassoon, 41
Contralto, 38

Copland, Aaron, 229, 259, 260, 276
Appalachian Spring, 229, 261
Music for the Theatre, 229, 260–61
Corelli, Arcangelo, 85, 94, 98
Trio Sonata in F Minor, op. 3, no. 9, 85, 98, 112
Correa, Chick, 376
Cosi fan tutte, 131, 158
Couleurs de la cité céleste, 229, 275
Countermelody, 36, 59
Counterpoint, 35–36, 37, 129, 180, 274
Bartók, 247, 276
imitative, 36, 37, 299, 302, 308
nonimitative, 35–36, 291, 293
Renaissance, 299
Sturm und Drang, 123
Country music, 360, 377
Couperin, Francois, 115, 119, 128
"Le Croc-en-jambe," 115, 119, 121, 129
Courante, 55, 56, 100
Cream, 374
Creation, The, 131, 134
Création du Monde, La, 229, 255
Creation of the World, 229, 255
Credo, 284
Crescendo, 125
"Croc-en-jambe, Le" 115, 119, 121, 129
Crooning, 333–35, 337
Crosby, Bing, 313, 335, 337, 351
"Learn to Croon," 313, 335
Crumb, George, 229, 274
Ancient Voices of Children, 229, 274–75
Cymbals, 44–45

Dadaism, 250–53, 276
"Daily Bread," 313, 327
Danbury, Connecticut, 249
Dance, 53, 99, 132, 192–93
American, 315, 316. *See also* Band, Dance
Renaissance, 308, 309
sixties, 368
suite, 55, 99–100, 112
"Dance of the Sugar Plum Fairy," 25, 45
"Dancing on the Ceiling," 313, 323
Danse bohémienne, 229, 232–33
Danse profane, 25, 40
Danse sacrée, 25, 40
Dark Ages, 280, 289
"Darkness on the Delta," 313, 326
Davis, Miles, 376
"Day in the Life, A," 359, 369, 371
Debussy, Claude, 25, 49, 69, 73, 80, 229, 232–37
"Beau Soir," 49, 61

"Brouillards," 229, 232–33, 234
Danse bohémienne, 229, 232–33
Danse profane, 25, 40
Danse sacrée, 25, 40
Images, 229, 233
"La Flute de Pan," 49, 61, 229, 236–37, 276
La Mer, 25, 40, 229, 233
Nocturnes, 69, 76, 191, 229, 233
"Nuages," 69, 76, 229, 234–35, 275
Pelléas et Mélisande, 229, 236
Prélude à l'Après-midi d'un faune, 25, 40, 42, 229, 233, 236
Preludes, 229, 232
Sonata for Flute, Viola, and Harp, 25, 40
Decrescendo, 125
Degas, Edgar, 231, 275
Delius, Frederick, 237
Depression, 328
Descartes, René, 89
Description, 72–76
Dessicated Embryos, 229, 251
Detroit, 367
Development, 66, 184–85
concerto, 146
sonata-allegro, 58, 59
symphony, 184
Diagram, musical structure, 50–59
Dido and Aeneas, 85, 104
"Dippermouth Blues," 341, 346–47
"Dirty Trick, The," 115, 119, 121, 129
Dissonance, 34, 37, 254, 276
Bartók, 247
Brahms, 180
Schönberg, 239
Sturm und Drang, 123
Doctrine of Affections, 89, 104, 113
Doggett, Bill, 359
"Honky Tonk," 359, 363
Dominant seventh, 33
Domino, Fats, 359, 365, 367
"I'm Walkin'," 359, 365
Don Giovanni, 131, 158–66
Donizetti, Gaetano, 169, 206, 207
Lucia di Lammermoor, 169, 206, 207
"Quando rapito in estasi," 207
"Donna e mobile, La," 214
"Don't Be That Way," 313, 331
"Don't Blame Me," 313, 323
Doors, The, 359, 373, 378
"Break on Through," 359, 373
"Light My Fire," 359, 373
Dorsey, Jimmy, 329, 351
Dorsey, Tommy, 313, 329, 330, 336, 351
"Boogie Woogie," 313, 331, 349
"Marie," 313, 331
"Opus One," 313, 331

Double bass, 39
Double exposition, 145, 146
Downbeat, 17, 363
"Down in the Valley," 49, 61
"Down South Camp Meeting," 341
"Dreaming," 194
Drifters, The, 359, 367
"Fools Fall in Love," 359, 365
"Searchin'," 359, 363
Drones, 272
Drug culture, 373–74, 378
Drums, 44–45, 308, 346
African, 382, 384
Balinese, 388, 389
Indian, 391
Japanese, 392
rhythm and blues, 363, 377
rock, 376
soul, 372
Dudevant, Aurore-Lucie, 191–92
Dufay, Guillaume, 302
Duff, 382
Dukas, Paul, 169
L'Apprenti Sorcier, 169, 189
Dunstable, John, 302
Duplum, 286
Durante, Jimmy, 313, 333, 337
"Can Broadway Do without Me?," 313, 333
Durey, Louis, 253
Dvořák, Antonin, 25, 37, 169
Concerto for Cello and Orchestra, 25, 39–40
Slavonic Dances for Orchestra, 169, 171
Symphony no. 9 (*From the New World*), 25, 37
Dylan, Bob, 359, 372, 378
"Like a Rolling Stone," 359, 373
"The Times They Are A-Changin'," 359, 373
Dynamics, 26

"Easter Parade," 313, 322, 323
Eighteenth century, 87. *See also* Classical era, Preclassic era
clarinet, 42
rationalism, 124
symphony, 53
"Eight to the bar," 366, 378
Ein' feste Burg ist unser Gott, 85, 108–11, 297, 300
Einstein on the Beach, 229, 273
Eisenstadt, Austria, 133
"Eleanor Rigby," 359, 369
Electric Flag, 376
Electric Light Orchestra, 376
Electronic music, 8, 266–68, 273, 275, 277
rock, 371, 373, 375, 377

"Elephants," 25, 40
Elizabethan Age, 306
Elizabeth I, 306
"Elle et Moi," 25
Ellington, Edward Kennedy "Duke,"
    313, 336, 337, 341, 352
    "Caravan," 313, 323, 341, 352
    "Mood Indigo," 341, 352
    "Solitude," 341, 352
    "Sophisticated Lady," 341, 352
    "Take the A Train," 313, 331
Emerson, Lake and Palmer, 376
Emmett, Dan, 315
Emotion, 89, 238, 239, 276
Empfindsamer stil, 123, 128
English horn, 40–43, 189
Enlightenment, 86–87, 111–24
Eno, Brian, 377
Ensemble, 125, 221
"Entertainer, The," 13, 17, 22, 49, 57
Erlkönig, Die, 49, 61, 169, 200, 202–4
Eroica, 49, 55, 131, 141–44, 145, 154,
    169, 175, 184
Essays before a Sonata, 77
Esterhazy estate, 133–34
Étude, 193–95, 226
Étude, op. 10, no. 5 in G♭ Major
    (Black Key Étude), 169, 193
Études, op. 10, 169
Euridice, 103
Evans, George, 313, 319
    "In the Good Old Summertime,"
    313, 319, 321
Exposition, 58–59, 66, 145–46
Expressionism, 238–45, 275, 276

f, 26
Fabian, 367
Falla, Manuel de, 274
"Fame," 359, 375
Fantasia, 100, 112
Fantasia in C Minor, K. 475, 115, 123
Farewell, 131, 135–36, 150
"Farmer in the Dell," 25, 30
Farnaby, Giles, 297, 308
    Loth to Depart, 297, 308
Feldman, Morton, 273
Fermata, 19
ff, 26
fff, 26
Fiddle, 364, 377, 388
Fifteenth century. *See* Renaissance
Figaro, 208, 213–14
Figured bass, 92–94, 98, 112
Film music, 237, 316
Filters, 266
Finalis, 282

Fingal's Cave, 75–76, 169, 172
Fiorello, 207–14
Firebird, The, 229, 243
Fitzgerald, Ella, 313
    "A Tisket-a-Tasket," 313, 331
Five movements for string quartet, 229,
    239
"Fixing a Hole," 359, 370
Flabby Preludes, 229, 251
Flat, 27
Fliegende Holländer, Der, 169, 206
Florence, Italy, 103
Flute, 40–43, 95, 98, 187, 255
    African, 384
    Mannheim orchestra, 125
    neoclassic, 256
    trio sonata, 98
"Flute de Pan, La," 49, 61, 229,
    236–37, 276
Flying Dutchman, The, 169, 206
"Foggy Day in London Town, A," 313,
    327
Folk music, 6, 7
    modal scales, 29
    in rock music, 360
    romantic age, 171
    twentieth century, 243–45, 246,
    258, 260, 276
Folk rock, 372
"Fools Fall in Love," 359, 365
Form
    AA, 322, 336
    AAB, 66
    AA'B, 57–58
    AABA, 51–55, 336
    AABB, 55–56, 66, 99
    AB, 55–56, 66
    ABA, 51–55
    ABACA, 56–57, 66
    ABACABA, 56–57, 66
    ABACADA, 56–57, 66
    ABACD, 57
    binary, 51, 55–56, 66, 99
    boogie, 366
    bookkeeping, 50–59
    diagram, 50–59, 234
    length and, 51
    music and, 48–67
    operatic, 103–5
    rhythm and blues, 362
    rondo, 51, 56–57, 66
    sectional, 234
    sonata-allegro, 51, 58–59, 66, 74–76
    song, 322–23, 336
    ternary, 51–55
    twelve-bar blues, 51, 57–58, 66,
    362, 366
"For Unto Us a Child is Born," 107

Foster, Stephen, 313, 314, 315, 317–18,
    336, 337
    "Beautiful Dreamer," 313, 317, 318
    "Camptown Races," 313, 317, 318
    "Come Where My Love Lies
    Dreaming," 313, 317
    "Jeanie with the Light Brown
    Hair," 313, 317, 318
    "Laura Lee," 313, 318
    "Massa's in the Cold, Cold
    Ground," 313, 318
    "My Old Kentucky Home," 313,
    317, 318
    "Oh! Susanna," 313, 317, 318
    "Old Black Joe," 313, 318
    "Old Folks at Home," 313, 317, 318
    "Ring, Ring the Banjo," 313, 318
    "Way Down upon the Swannee
    River," 313, 317
4' 33'', 229, 271–72
"Fourth of July, The," 229, 250
Fourth String Quartet, 229, 246–47
Fourth Symphony, 229, 250
Franck, César, 173
Frankenstein, 170
Franklin, Aretha, 359, 372, 378
    "Satisfaction," 359, 371, 372
    "You Make Me Feel (Like a
    Natural Woman)," 359, 372
Freischütz, Der, 69, 72, 169, 171
French horn, 43, 125, 143
French Suite no. 1 in D Minor, 49,
    55–56, 115, 129
Frequency, 26, 45
Friml, Rudolph, 49
    "Indian Love Call," 49, 62
"Froggie Would A-Courtin' Go," 49, 61
From the New World, 25, 37, 43
Fugue, 36, 37, 100, 112, 248
"Fun, Fun, Fun," 359, 368
Futurism, 251, 276

Gabrieli, Andrea, 297, 308
    Gloria in Excelsis Deo, 297, 308
Gabrieli, Giovanni, 308
Galant style, 121–23, 128, 149, 151,
    166
    Haydn, 134, 152
    Mozart, 138
"Gallis Pole," 341, 344
Gamelan, 388, 394
Garfunkel, Art, 4, 5, 373
Gavotte, 265
Gay, John, 157
Gay 90s, 319–21, 336
"General William Booth Enters
    Heaven," 229, 250
Generation gap, 365, 377

Genesis, 376
Genre
    baroque, 99–111, 112
    black, 361
    orchestral music, 94–100, 112, 145
    Protestant, 300–302
    secular, 101–5
    sonata, 58
    soul, 371–72, 378
    tone poem, 188–89
    vocal music, 100–111, 112
Genteel tradition, 314, 316–18, 336
    recordings, 337
Gershwin, George, 229, 259, 262–63,
        313, 316
    "I Got Rhythm," 313, 322
    Of Thee I Sing, 313, 328
    Piano Concerto in F, 229, 262, 263
    Porgy and Bess, 229, 262
    Rhapsody in Blue, 229, 262, 341,
        351
Gershwin, Ira, 322
Gesamtkunstwerk, 220–21
Gesang der Jünglinge, 229
"Get It While You Can," 359, 374
"Getting Better," 359, 370
Gibbons, Orlando, 297, 308
    Pavane Lord Salisbury, 297, 308
Gideon, Miriam, 259
Gigue, 55, 56, 99, 100, 265
Gilbert and Sullivan, 316
Gilda, 214–16, 219
Gillespie, Dizzy, 353, 356
Giorgione, 87, 88
Giovanni, Don, 158–66
Giraud, Albert, 238
Glass, Philip, 229, 277
    Einstein on the Beach, 229, 273
    "Knee Plays," 273
Glinka, Mikhail, 205
Glissando, 248
Glockenspiel, 44
Gloria, 284
"Gloria," 303–4
Gloria in Excelsis Deo, 297, 308
"God Bless America," 313, 327
Goethe, 202
Gongs, 44–45, 388, 389
"Good Golly Miss Molly," 359, 366
"Good, Good Lovin'," 359, 372
Goodman, Benny, 313, 329, 330, 337,
        351
    "Don't Be That Way," 313, 331
    "Down South Camp Meeting," 341
    "Sing, Sing, Sing," 313, 331
    "Well Get It," 313, 331
"Good Morning," 359, 371
"Good Morning Mr. Blues," 49, 58
Gospel music, 361, 372
Gossec, Francois Joseph, 125
Gothic Age, 8, 280, 289

Götterdämmerung, 222
Gourds, 44
Graham, Martha, 261
Gregory I, 281, 293
Grieg, Edward, 169, 173, 196
    Piano Concerto in A Minor, 169,
        198–200
Griffes, Charles, 237
Grimani, Maria Margherita, 125
"Groovin' High," 341, 354
Ground bass, 37
Guitar, 345, 346, 363, 378
    acoustic, 372
    electric, 373, 376, 377, 393
    rhythm and blues, 377
    rock and roll, 366
    soul, 372
Guru, 391, 394
"Gute Nacht," 49, 61
Guthrie, Arlo, 373
Gymnopédie no. 1, 229, 253

Haley, Bill, 359, 360, 377
    "Rock around the Clock," 359, 360
Half step, 28
"Halleluia I'm a Bum," 313, 328
"Halleluja," 13, 22, 25, 37, 85, 107
Hamburg, Germany, 179
Hammerstein, Oscar, 359
    "You Are Too Beautiful," 359
Hampton, Lionel, 351
Handel, George Frederic, 13, 25, 37,
        95, 98, 105–6, 131
    Alcina, 49, 55, 85, 94, 104–5
    "For Unto Us a Child is Born," 107
    "Halleluja," 13, 22, 25, 37, 85, 107
    "He was despised," 55
    Israel in Egypt, 85, 91
    Messiah, 13, 22, 25, 37, 49, 55, 85,
        103, 106–7, 112
    "Tonami a vagheggiar," 49, 55, 94
    Trio Sonata in F Major, op. 2, no. 5,
        85, 92, 98–99, 112, 131
"Happy House," 341, 354
Harmony, 31–34, 35, 45, 46
    African, 384
    baroque, 32, 86, 92, 112
    beginnings of, 285–88, 293
    boogie, 58, 366
    chordal, 302, 308
    functional, 33–34, 37, 46, 86, 92,
        112, 175, 230, 276
    genteel tradition, 318
    Middle Ages, 32, 285–88, 289–90,
        293
    organum, 285–86
    Renaissance, 32, 37, 299
    rhythm and blues, 362
    Tin Pan Alley, 318–19
    twelve-bar blues, 58
    twentieth century, 245

Harold in Italy, 25, 39
Harp, 39, 40, 247, 382, 391
Harpsichord, 42, 92, 99–100, 112
    displaced by piano, 152
    Renaissance, 307
    rococo, 119
Harrison, George, 370
Hayashi, 392
Haydn, Franz Joseph, 13, 25, 49, 85,
        124, 131, 133–37, 180
    The Clock, 13, 22, 131, 136–37
    The Creation, 131, 134
    Farewell, 131, 135–36, 150
    minuet, 53
    "Minuet," 49, 53–54
    piano sonata, 152, 166
    Piano Sonata in E Minor, 49, 65
    Piano Sonata no. 37 in D Major, 49,
        56, 131, 152
    The Seasons, 131, 134
    String Quartet, op. 1, 149
    String Quartet, op. 3, no. 5, 131,
        149
    String Quartet, op. 20, no. 5, 131,
        150
    String Quartet, op. 33, no. 2, 25,
        40, 131, 151
    String Quartet, op. 50, no. 1–6, 131,
        151
    String Quartet, op. 54, no. 1–3, 131,
        151
    String Quartet, op. 76, no. 1–6, 151
    String Quartet, op. 76, no. 3, 49, 60
    String Quartet, op. 77, no. 1–2, 131,
        151
    string quartets, 149–50, 166
    Sturm und Drang quartets, 150
    Surprise Symphony, 85, 94
    symphonies, 176, 184
    Symphony no. 10 in D Major, 131,
        134
    Symphony no. 45 in F♯ Minor
        (Farewell), 131, 135–36, 150
    Symphony no. 92, 49, 53–54
    Symphony no. 101 (The Clock), 13,
        22, 131, 136–37
"Heading for the Last Roundup," 313,
        326
Hearing, 26
"Heartbreak Hotel," 359, 360
Heavy metal, 375, 378
Hebrides Overture, 69, 74, 75–76, 176
Hedonism, 116
Heine, Heinrich, 187
Henderson, Fletcher, 330
Hendrix, Jimi, 359, 373–74, 378
    "Manic Depression," 359, 373
    "Purple Haze," 359, 374
    "The Star Spangled Banner," 359,
        373
Henry VIII, 307

Herbert, Victor, 316
Herman, Woody, 313
  "Woodchopper's Ball," 313, 331
Heroic, 169, 192–93
"He was despised," 55
Hiller, Lejaren, 272
Hindemith, Paul, 274
Historical Anthology of Music in Performance, 291, 292, 308
History of Music in Sound, 291
Holidays, 229, 250
Holly, Buddy, 359, 369
  "Peggy Sue," 359, 365
L'homme armé, 297, 302
Homophony, 35, 37
Homosexuality, 182
Honegger, Arthur, 229, 253, 254, 276
  Jeanne d'Arc au bûcher, 229, 254
  Pacific 231, 229, 254
  Le Roi David, 229, 254
"Honky Tonk," 359, 363
"Honky Tonk Train," 359, 366
Hooker, John Lee, 341
  "Blues before Sunrise," 341, 344
Hooray for What?, 313, 328
Hope, 103
Horn Concertos, 25, 43
"Hotter Than That," 341, 348
"Hound Dog," 49, 58, 359, 366
Houston, Whitney, 376
HPSCHD, 229, 272
Hugo, Victor, 219
Humanism, 298, 308
Hungarian Rhapsodies, 169, 171
Hymns, 61

"I Almost Lost My Mind," 359, 367
Ibert, Jacques, 43
"If I Ever Get a Job Again," 313, 328
"If You Are in Love with Beauty," 204
"I Got Rhythm," 313, 322
"I Got up in the Mornin' Blues," 341, 344
Images, 229, 233
Imaginary Landscape no. 4, 229, 271
"I'm All Shook Up," 359, 365
"I'm a Stranger Here," 49, 58, 344
"I'm in the Mood for Love," 313, 323, 324
Impressionism, 231–35, 275
Improvisation, 231, 343–44, 346, 354–55, 356
  African, 382, 385, 394
  Indian, 390, 394
  Noh drama, 392, 394
"I'm Walkin'," 359, 365
"I'm Walkin' the Floor over You," 359, 364
In C, 229, 273
India, 389–91

"Indian Love Call," 49, 62
Instrumental music
  Balinese, 388
  Renaissance, 307–8, 309
Instruments, 37–45, 46
  African, 382, 384
  Balinese, 388
  country, 364
  double reed, 41
  Indian, 391
  Jamaican, 393
  Japanese, 392
  jazz, 42, 345
  keyboard, 45, 99–100, 152
  Renaissance, 307–8
  rhythm and blues, 363
  rock and roll, 366
  single reed, 42
  voice, 38–39
Intermezzo, 157, 167, 265
Intermezzo, op. 118, no. 2, 169, 191, 195
Interval, 27–31
  electronic, 267
  motet, 288
"In the Good Old Summertime," 313, 319, 321
"In the Mood," 49, 58, 313, 330, 331
"In the Shade of the Old Apple Tree," 313, 320
In the Steppes of Central Asia, 25, 43, 169, 171, 188–89
Inversion, 264–65
  retrograde, 264–65
Ionisation, 25, 44, 229, 273
Islam, 382, 385
"Isle of Capri," 313, 327
"Isn't She Lovely," 25, 39
Isorhythm, 291
Israel in Egypt, 85, 91
Italian Symphony, 69, 74, 169, 176–79, 180
"It Happened in Monterey," 313, 327
"It's Only a Paper Moon," 313, 323
"I've Been Lovin' You Too Long," 359, 372
"I've Got My Love to Keep Me Warm," 313, 323
"I've Got You under My Skin," 313, 323
Ives, Charles, 25, 69, 229, 249–50, 276
  "At the River," 229, 250
  Concord Sonata, 229, 250
  "The Fourth of July," 229, 250
  Fourth Symphony, 229, 250
  "General William Booth Enters Heaven," 229, 250
  Holidays, 229, 250
  program music, 77, 80
  texture, 275

The Unanswered Question, 25, 43, 69, 78, 229, 250, 275
Universe Symphony, 229, 249
Variations on "America," 229, 250
"I Was So Wrong," 49, 58
"I Wouldn't Trade the Silver in My Mother's Hair," 313, 327

Jacob of Liege, 3–4
Jagger, Mick, 371
Jamaica, 393
James, Harry, 313
  "Ciribiribin," 313, 331
Jank, 382
Japan, 392
Japan, 392
Jazz, 6, 7, 260, 262
  black and white, 351–52, 356
  bop, 352–54, 356, 342
  Chicago style, 349
  composers, 352
  cool, 342, 352–54, 356
  early, 344–45, 349
  European-African heritage of, 345–47, 355
  hot, 347–50, 356
  improvization, 343–44, 355, 356
  instruments, 42, 345
  modal scales, 29
  nature of, 342–44
  new, 342, 354–55
  New Orleans, 342, 344, 345, 346–47
  1920s, 342, 348–49, 356
  players, 350–51
  post-1960s, 356
  rock, 376, 378
  swing and, 328, 342–43, 350–52, 355, 356
  trombone, 43
  trumpet, 43
Jeanne d'Arc au bûcher, 229, 254
"Jeanie with the Light Brown Hair," 313, 317, 318
Jefferson Airplane, 359, 373
  "White Rabbit," 359, 373
"Je garde une médaille dèlle," 25
Je puis trop bien, 279, 292
"Jesu, Joy of Man's Desiring," 85, 94
"Jim Dandy," 359, 363
Joel, Billy, 49, 376
  "Just the Way You Are," 49, 51
John, Elton, 359, 375
  "Benny and the Jets," 359, 375
Joplin, Janis, 359, 374
  "Get It While You Can," 359, 374
  "Me and Bobby McGee," 359, 374
  "Piece of My Heart," 359, 374

Joplin, Scott, 13, 49, 341
    "The Entertainer," 13, 17, 22, 49, 57
    "Maple Leaf Rag," 49, 57, 341, 345, 350
Joshua Tree, 359, 377
Josquin des Prez, 297, 302, 309
    Ave Maria, 297, 305
    "Gloria," 303–4
    Pange Lingua, 297, 303–4
Jukebox, 331
Juliet, 187
Jupiter, 131, 139
"Just the Way You Are," 49, 51

Kafka, Franz, 238
Kansas, 376
Kansas City, 345, 347
Karnatic tradition, 389–91, 394
Kern, Jerome, 316
Key, 33, 46, 245
Keyboard music
    baroque, 8, 86, 99–100, 112
    Renaissance, 307–8, 309
    rock, 376
Keyness, 33, 46
Kinderscenen, 169, 191, 194
"King of Jazz," 350
"King of Swing," 329
King Oliver's Creole Jazz Band, 346, 341
Kingston Trio, The, 359, 372
    "Tom Dooley," 359, 372
"Knee Plays," 273
Köchel number, 138
Koto, 392
Kraftwerk, 377
Kyrie, 283, 284

Largo, 18
"Laudate pueri," 25, 36
Lauper, Cindy, 376
"Laura Lee," 313, 318
"Laus Deo Patri," 25, 36
"Lay Down Sally," 359, 374
Leadbelly, 341
    "The Bourgeois Blues," 341, 344
    "The Gallis Pole," 341, 344
"Learn to Croon," 313, 335
LeBrun, Charles, 89
Led Zeppelin, 359, 375
    "Stairway to Heaven," 359, 375
Legato, 39, 193
Lehar, Franz, 316
Leitmotif, 221–25
Lennon, John, 369, 370
Lento, 18, 22
Léonin, 286
Leporello, 158–65

"Let Me Wah-hoo, Wah-hoo, Wah-hoo," 313, 326
"'Leven Pounds of Heaven," 313, 327
Lewis, Jerry Lee, 366
Lewis, Meade Lux, 359, 366
    "Honky Tonk Train," 359, 366
Liberty, 124
Libretto, 101
"Liebst du um Schönheit," 169, 204–5
Lied, 8, 200–205, 226
Lieder, op. 12, 204–5
"Light My Fire," 359, 373
"Like a Rolling Stone," 359, 373
Liszt, Franz, 169, 173, 192
    Années de Pèlerinage, 169, 194
    "Au bord d'une source," 194
    "Au lac de Wallenstadt," 194
    character pieces, 191, 193, 194
    concertos, 196
    études, 191
    Hungarian Rhapsodies, 169, 171
    piano sonata, 190
    tone poems, 188, 225
    Wagner and, 175, 220
"Little Brown Jug," 313, 331
"Little Deuce Coupe," 359, 368
"A Little Help from My Friends," 359, 370
Little Richard, 49, 359, 366, 369, 377
    "Good Golly Miss Molly," 359, 366
    "Lucille," 359, 366
    "Tutti Frutti," 49, 58, 359, 360
"Little Sir Echo," 326
Liturgical item, 280
Liturgy, 280, 293
Liverpool, England, 368
Lohengrin, 169, 206
Lombardo, Guy, 313, 329, 332, 336
    "Auld Lang Syne," 313, 332
"Long Lonely Nights," 359, 367
"Lord Randall," 313, 314
"Lord's Prayer, The," 327
Los Angeles, 352
Loth to Depart, 297, 308
Louis XIV, 87, 116
Louis XV, 116, 128
Louÿs, Pierre, 236–37
Love, 306, 317, 318, 324–25
"Love Letters in the Sand," 359, 367
"Lovely Rita," 359, 371
"Love Me Do," 359, 369
"Love Walked In," 313, 323
Lucia di Lammermoor, 169, 206, 207
"Lucille," 359, 366
"Lucy in the Sky with Diamonds," 359, 370
Ludwig of Bavaria, 220
Lully, Jean Baptiste, 85, 103
    Alceste, 85, 103
    "When I Am Laid in Earth," 104
Lute, 92, 382

Luther, Martin, 297, 300, 309
    Ein' feste Burg ist unser Gott, 85, 108–11, 297, 300
Lutheran church, 97, 107
Lutheranism, 300
Lyrics, 324–28, 362, 364–65

McCartney, Paul, 369
MacDowell, Edward, 169, 173
    character pieces, 191, 194
    Woodland Sketches, 169, 171, 194
Machaut, Guillaume de, 279, 291–92, 293
    Je puis trop bien, 279, 292
    Ma fin est ma commencement, 279, 291
    Messe de Notre Dame, 279, 291–92
    S'il estoit nulz, 279, 291
Macon, Georgia, 372, 375
McPhatter, Clyde, 359, 367
    "Long Lonely Nights," 359, 367
    "Money Honey," 359, 367
    "The Treasure of Love," 359, 367
Maddalena, 214, 217–19
Madonna, 376
Madrigal, 306–7
    Elizabethan, 306, 307
    English, 8, 306
    Italian, 8, 91, 306–7
    Renaissance, 306–7, 309
Maeterlinck, Maurice, 236
Ma fin est ma commencement, 279, 291
Magic Flute, The, 25, 39, 131, 158
Mahavishnu Orchestra, 376
Mahler, Gustav, 173, 175
Major, 28–29. *See also* Interval
Mallarmé, Stéphane, 236
Manhattan, 368
"Manic Depression," 359, 373
Manilow, Barry, 376
Mannheim School, 125–27, 129
"Maple Leaf Rag" (Joplin), 49, 57, 341, 345, 350
"Maple Leaf Rag" (Morton), 341, 345, 350
Maqam, 382
Maracas, 44–45
"March," 49, 63
Marenzio, Luca, 297, 306, 309
    S'io parto, i' moro, 297, 306
Marie, 240–42
"Marie," 313, 331
Marley, Bob, 393
Marriage of Figaro, The, 131, 158
"Mashed Potatoes," 359, 368
Mass, 8, 282–85, 291, 293, 302, 305, 309
    Aeterna Christi munera, 297, 302
    Gregorian chant in, 282

L'homme armé, 297, 302
Pange Lingua, 297, 303–4
Veni sponsa Christi, 25, 37
"Massa's in the Cold, Cold Ground," 313, 318
Masterpieces of Music Before 1750, 36, 100, 286, 308
Mazurka, 191
Mazurka, op. 63, no. 3, 49, 53
Mazurka, op. 67, no. 3, 49, 52–53
"Me and Bobby McGee," 359, 374
Meaning, 70–71
    African music, 384
    Western music, 68–81
Measure, 17. *See also* Bar
Medieval era. *See* Middle Ages
"Meet Me in St. Louis, Louis," 313, 320
Melismatic setting, 62
Melisso, 104
Mellencamp, John Cougar, 376
Melody, 29–31, 45, 60
    African, 382, 384
    baroque, 93–94
    diatonic, 272
    Gregorian, 281
    infinite, 221
    Noh drama, 392
    nuclear, 388–89, 394
    reggae, 393
    rococo, 121
    subsidiary, 36
Mendelssohn, Felix, 25, 69, 72, 74, 169, 172, 173, 175–79, 180
    Bach and, 96
    concertos, 196
    Fingal's Cave, 75–76, 169, 172
    Hebrides Overture, 69, 74, 75–76, 176
    Italian Symphony, 69, 74, 169, 176–79, 180
    program music, 80
    Scotch Symphony, 176
    Songs without Words, 169, 191
    symphonies, 225
    Symphony no. 4 (*Italian*), 69, 74, 169, 176–79, 180
    Violin Concerto, 69, 74
    Violin Concerto in E Minor, 25, 39
Mendelssohn, Moses, 175
Mendelssohn-Hensel, Fanny, 169, 173, 176, 204
    Andante con moto, op. 2, no. 2, 169, 195
    The Year, 195
Menotti, Gian Carlo, 229, 274
    Amahl and the Night Visitors, 229, 274
Menuet, 155
Mer, La, 25, 40, 229, 233

"Merry-Go-Round Broke Down, The," 313, 326
Messe de Notre Dame, 279, 291–92
Messiaen, Oliver, 229, 275
    Couleurs de la cité céleste, 229, 275
Messiah, 13, 22, 25, 37, 49, 55, 85, 103, 106–7, 112
Meter, 9, 17–18, 23
    baroque, 86
    compound, 21, 22
    signature, 21
    simple, 21, 22
Mezzo soprano, 38
mf, 26
Middle Ages, 8, 280
    Ars Nova, 289–90
    ballade, 292
    brass, 43
    church, 280
    church modes, 281–82
    Gregorian chant, 8, 275, 280–85, 293
    harmony, 32, 285–88, 289–90, 293
    mass, 291–92
    ordinary and proper, 282–85, 291–92, 293, 302
    rhythm, 290
    texture, 289
"Midnight in Paris," 313, 327
"Mighty Fortress Is Our God, A," 85, 108–11, 297, 300
Miles, Kerry, 313
    "Meet Me in St. Louis, Louis," 313, 320
Milhaud, Darius, 229, 253, 254–55, 276
    Le Boeuf sur le toit, 229, 254
    La Création du Monde, 229, 255
Miller, Glen, 49, 313, 329, 330, 336
    "In the Mood," 49, 58, 313, 330, 331
    "Little Brown Jug," 313, 331
"Miller's Beautiful Daughter," 169, 201
Minimalism, 266, 272–73, 277, 377
Minor, 28–29. *See also* Interval
Minuet, 53, 132, 133, 139, 265
"Minuet," 49, 53–54
Mitchell, Joni, 373
Mode
    church, 281–82, 293
    Dorian, 29, 282
    Lydian, 29, 282
    major, 34
    minor, 34
    Mixolydian, 29, 282
    Phrygian, 29, 282
    pitch, 282
Moderato, 18
Modern era. *See* Twentieth century
Modulation, 34
    metrical, 275

Modulators, 266
Moments musicaux, 169, 172, 191
Monet, Claude, 231, 275
"Money Honey," 359, 367
Monn, Matthias Georg, 125
Monody, 102
Monophony, 35, 36, 382
Montesquieu, 124
Monteverdi, Claudio, 85, 102
    Orfeo, 85, 102–3
"Mood Indigo," 341, 352
"Moon Coming over the Mountain," 313, 326
"Moondrunk," 239
Moonlight Sonata, 131, 155–56
"Moon of Spain," 313, 327
Morley, Thomas, 297, 307, 309
    Now Is the Month of Maying, 297, 307
Morrison, Jim, 373
Morton, Ferdinand "Jelly Roll," 328, 341, 345
    "Maple Leaf Rag," 341, 345, 350
Moten, Bennie, 330
Motet
    Ave Maria, 297, 305
    Renaissance, 305, 309
    thirteenth century, 8, 286–88, 293
"Mother Song," 313, 327
Motive, 30, 46, 221
Motown, 367, 378
Movement, 53
    concerto grosso, 95
    string quartet, 149
    symphony, 53, 125, 126, 132–33, 145
Mozart, Wolfgang Amadeus, 25, 49, 85, 124, 131, 138–39, 169
    concertos, 145–46
    Cosi fan tutte, 131, 158
    Don Giovanni, 131, 158–66
    Horn Concertos, 25, 43
    Jupiter, 131, 139
    Lieder, 200
    The Magic Flute, 25, 39, 131, 158
    The Marriage of Figaro, 131, 158
    minuet, 53
    opera, 158–66, 167
    Piano Concerto no. 17 in G Major, K. 453, 131, 145, 146–48
    piano sonata, 152, 153, 166
    Piano Sonata in Bb Major, K. 333, 49, 64–65, 131, 153
    Queen of the Night aria, 25, 39
    String quartets, 151, 166
    symphony, 138–39, 166, 176, 184
    Symphony, K. 16, 131
    Symphony no. 26, K. 184, 131, 139
    Symphony no. 40 in G Minor, K. 550, 49, 54–55, 59, 66, 85, 94, 131, 138, 169, 184, 257

Symphony no. 41, K. 551 (*Jupiter*), 131, 139
Violin Concerto in A Major, K. 219, 131, 148
mp, 26
Mridanga, 391
Muffat, Georg, 94
Musette, 265
Musgrave, 229
Clarinet Concerto, 229
Music
absolute, 77–80
baroque, 84–113
between wars, 250–65, 276
categories, 6–7
chance, 270–72
classical era, 130–67
continuity in, 50
cultural differences, 381
definition of, 4–5
description, 72–76
drama, 206, 221–25, 226
evil in, 3
form and, 48–67
impressionist, 232–37
integration with other arts, 172
language of, 71–80
language of the soul, 171–72
meaning, 68–81
Middle Ages, 278–94
morality and, 3–4
movie, 237, 316
non-Western, 380–95
Plato's Republic and, 3
popular, American, 312–38
preclassic, 114–29
public, 122–23
Renaissance, 296–309
rock, 358–79
rococo, 121
romantic, 168–226
serial, 265
soul, 371–72
sound and, 24–47
style reflecting culture, 124–28
theater, 272
time and, 12–23
twentieth century, 228–77
after World War II, 265–75
Musical Traditions in Asia, 389
Music for Strings, Percussion and Celesta, 44, 247–48, 276
Music for the Theatre, 229, 260–61
Musician, 384, 391, 394
Music Man, The, 313, 333
Musique concrète, 266
Mussorgsky, Modest, 25, 169, 173, 175
Boris Godunoff, 169, 171, 205
"Coronation Scene," 205
Night on Bald Mountain, 169, 189

opera, 205
Pictures at an Exhibition, 25, 43
Mute, 39, 43
"My Country 'Tis of Thee," 49, 61, 62
My End Is My Beginning, 291
My Fair Lady, 313, 333
"My Mom," 313, 327
"My Old Kentucky Home," 313, 317, 318
"My Sweetheart's the Man in the Moon," 313, 321
Mythology
Greek, 102–3
Teutonic, 221, 226

"National Acrobat, A," 359, 375
Nationalism, 171, 205, 221, 274
Nature
baroque, 88
eighteenth century, 124
music, 76
rococo, 117–18, 128
romantic concept of, 170, 225
worship, 385
Nay, 382
"Nearer My God to Thee," 229, 250
Nelson, Ricky, 367
Neoclassicism, 255–59, 275, 276
New Orleans, 342, 344, 347, 356
New York City, 315, 347, 352
Nichols, Red, 351
"Night and Day," 313, 322, 323
Night on Bald Mountain, 169, 189
"Night's Music, The," 69, 76, 247
Nineteenth century. See also Romantic era
arts and philosophy, 170–71, 225
art song, 200–205, 226
English horn, 41
nationalism, 171
opera, 205–25
piano music, 189–95, 225
symphony, 53, 175–87, 225
tone poem, 188–89, 225
Nocturnes, 69, 76, 191, 229, 233
Noh drama, 392, 394
Nokan, 392
Non-Western music, 381
Asia, 385–89
Ba-Benzélé Pygmies, 384–85
Bali, 388–89, 394
India, 389–91, 394
Indonesia, 385–89
Jamaica, 393–94
Japan, 392, 394
North Africa, 382, 394
reggae, 393–94
Sub-Saharan Africa, 382–85
West Indies, 393–94

Norma, 169, 206
North Africa, 382, 394
Norton Anthology of Western Music, 284
Nostalgia, 325–26
Notation, 9, 17, 92
intervals in, 28
Note
accented, 16
dotted, 21, 23
duration, 21, 23
eighth, 19, 20
half, 19, 20
quarter, 19, 20, 23
sixteenth, 20
value, 9, 19–22, 29
whole, 20
worried, 344
Notre Dame Cathedral, 286, 293
Now Is the Month of Maying, 297, 307
"Nuages," 69, 76, 229, 234–35, 275
Nuove musiche, Le, 85, 102
"Numb Fumblin'," 341, 350
Nutcracker, The, 25, 45, 49, 63, 169, 182

Oboe, 40–43, 95, 125
Octave, 27, 28, 281, 288
Octet, 229, 256–57, 276
Ode to Joy, 175
Office Hours, 282
Of Thee I Sing, 313, 328
"Oh! Susanna," 313, 317, 318
Okeghem, Joannes, 302
"Old Black Joe," 313, 318
"Old Folks at Home," 313, 317, 318
"Old Oaken Bucket, The," 313, 316–17
Oliver, King, 341, 346
"Dippermouth Blues," 341, 346–47
"Once in a Lifetime," 359, 377
"One O'Clock Jump," 313, 330, 331
"On the Banks of the Wabash," 313, 319
Opera, 8, 157–66
aria, 102, 206, 207, 214, 221
ballad, 157–58, 205–25
baroque, 8, 86, 100–106, 112
buffa, 157
chorus, 206
classical, 8, 134, 157–66
comic, 106, 157–58, 167, 207–14
composers, 101–6, 173, 206
English, 103–4
folklore in, 171
form, 103–5
German, 206, 220–21, 226
grand, 205
history, 102
Italian, 104, 106, 206–19, 226

merging of comic and serious, 158–66
nationalistic, 171
nineteenth century, 205–25
opéra-comique, 157, 205
preclassic, 8
romantic era, 8, 171, 205–25
seria, 104, 106, 157, 167
tragedie lyrique, 103
twentieth century, 239–42, 262, 274
Opus, 52
"Opus One," 313, 331
Oratorio
baroque, 8, 91, 100, 106–7, 112
classical, 8, 134
twentieth century, 254
Orchestra, 39–45, 106, 112, 124
Balinese, 388, 394
brass, 43, 46
Mannheim, 125–27, 129
music drama, 221, 226
percussion, 44–45, 46
preclassic, 125
seating, 39, 40
strings, 39–40, 46
symphony, 37, 46
woodwinds, 40–43, 46
Orchestral music, 94–100, 112, 233
Ordinary, 282–85, 291–92, 293, 302
Ordres, 119
Orfeo, 85, 102–3
Organ, 92, 107, 112, 250
baroque, 98, 99–100
reggae, 393
Renaissance, 308, 309
rhythm and blues, 363
Organum, 285–86
"Ornithology," 341, 353
Ostinato, 37, 272, 363
Ottavio, Don, 162–65
Out of Doors, 69, 76, 229, 247
"Over the Rainbow," 313, 323
Overture, French, 103, 106
"Overture Miniature," 49, 63

p, 26
Pacific 231, 229, 254
Palestrina, Giovanni Pierluigi da, 25, 37, 297, 302
Aeterna Christi munera, 297, 302
"Agnus Dei," 25, 37
Veni sponsa Christi, 25, 37
Pange Lingua, 297, 303–4
Papillons, 169, 191
Parade, 229, 252–53
Parallel Organum, 37
Parker, Charlie, 341, 343, 353, 356
"Groovin' High," 341, 354
"Ornithology," 341, 353
"White Christmas," 341, 343–44

Parlor song, 316–17, 336
Passions of the Soul, The, 89
Pastoral, 25, 43, 69, 73, 78, 169, 175
Pathétique, 169, 183–85, 199
Patriotism, 327–28
Patronage system, 140
Pavane Lord Salisbury, 297, 308
Pavane pour une Infante défunte, 49, 64
Peachum, 158
"Peggy Sue," 359, 365
Pelléas et Mélisande, 229, 236
"Pennies from Heaven," 313, 323
Pentatonicism, 318, 385
Peppermint Lounge, 368
Pepusch, Johann-Christoph, 157
Percussion, 39, 44–45, 46, 247–48, 273, 308
African, 384
Perfect fifth, 28. See also Interval
Perfect fourth, 28. See also Interval
Pérotin, 286
Peter, Paul, and Mary, 373
Petrushka, 229, 243–45, 247, 276
Phasing, 272–73
Philip, Duke of Orleans, 116–17
Phones, 269
Phrase, 30
Piano, 39, 145, 152, 166, 247, 253, 346
blues, 345
boogie woogie, 366
character piece, 191–95, 225–26
concerto, 196–200, 226, 258–59
jazz, 345, 356
keyboard, 27
prepared, 272, 277
rhythm and blues, 363, 377
rock, 375
rock and roll, 366
romantic era, 8, 172, 189–95, 225
solo music, 189–95
sonata, 134, 152–56, 190–91, 225
soul, 372
stride, 349–50, 356
Piano Concerto, 229, 275
Piano Concerto in A Minor (Grieg), 169, 198–200
Piano Concerto in A Minor (Schumann), 169, 197–98
Piano Concerto in F, 229, 262, 263
Piano Concerto no. 1, 131, 148
Piano Concerto no. 4, 131, 148
Piano Concerto no. 17 in G Major, K. 453, 131, 145, 146–48
Piano prelude, 172
Piano sonata, 134, 152–56, 166, 190
Piano Sonata in A♭ Major, no. 12, op. 26, 49, 60, 131, 153–55
Piano Sonata in B♭ Major, K. 333, 49, 64–65, 131, 153
Piano Sonata in E Minor, 49, 65

Piano Sonata in F Minor, op. 2, no. 1, 49, 62
Piano Sonata no. 8 in C Minor, op. 13, 49, 57
Piano Sonata no. 14, op. 27, no. 2 (Moonlight Sonata), 131, 155–56
Piano Sonata no. 37 in D Major, 49, 56, 131, 152
Picasso, Pablo, 252
Pictures at an Exhibition, 25, 43
"Piece of My Heart," 359, 374
Pierrot Lunaire, 229, 238–39, 276
"Pinetop's Boogie Woogie," 49, 58
Piston, Walter, 43, 259, 276
Pitch, 26, 27–31, 45
chromatic, 33
diatonic, 33
key and, 33
modal music, 282
twelve-tone system, 238, 263–65
Pizzicato, 39, 246
Plato, 3
Platoon, 262
"Please Don't Talk about Me When I'm Gone," 313, 319
"Please, Please, Please," 359, 372
Poem, symphonic, 188–89, 262. See also Tone poem
"Poet of the piano," 191
Poland, 191
Police, 377
Polly, 158
Polonaise, 192–93, 226
Polonaise in A♭ Major, op. 53 (Heroic), 169, 192–93
Polyphony, 8, 37, 286–88
Polyrhythms, 345, 356
"Polythene Pam," 359, 369
Polytonality, 245, 254, 275, 276
Pompadour, Madame, 119
"Pony, The," 359, 368
"Popeye," 359, 368
Popular music, American, 7
crooning, 333–35
dance bands, 316, 329–32
depression and, 328
dissemination, 314–16
genteel tradition, 314, 316–18, 336
love in, 324–25
1930s, 322–28, 332–35
nostalgia in, 325–26
novelty songs, 326–27
parlor song, 316, 336
patriotism in, 327–28
rock, 360. See also Rock
singing, 332–35
swing. See Swing
Tin Pan alley era, 314, 315, 318–21, 336, 337

Porgy and Bess, 229, 262
Porter, Cole, 313, 316
    "I've Got You under My Skin,"
       313, 323
    "Night and Day," 313, 322, 323
Poulenc, Francis, 253, 254, 276
pp, 26
ppp, 26
Preclassic era, 86, 114–29
    empfindsamer stil, 123, 128
    musical styles of, 116–24
    orchestra, 125
    Sturm und Drang, 123–24
    style and culture, 124–28
    symphony, 8, 124–28
Prelude, 100, 191, 265
Prélude à l'Après-midi d'un faune, 25,
    40, 42, 229, 233, 236
Prelude no. 1 in C Major, 169, 192
Prelude no. 4 in E Minor, 169, 192
Prelude no. 7 in A Major, 169, 192
Prelude no. 20 in C Minor, 169, 192
Prelude no. 21 in B♭ Major, 169, 192
Preludes, 192, 229, 232
Presbyterianism, 300
Presley, Elvis, 49, 360, 364, 369, 377
    "Heartbreak Hotel," 359, 360
    "Hound Dog," 49, 58, 359, 366
    "I'm All Shook Up," 359, 365
Presto, 18, 22
Prince, 376
"Prince of Music," 303
Printing, invention of, 298
Program music, 77, 80, 97
    philosophical, 77–80
    romantic age, 172, 175, 183–85
    symphony, 183–86, 225
Prokofiev, Sergei, 229, 257–59, 276
    Third Piano Concerto in C Major,
       op. 26, 229, 257, 258–59
Proper, 282–85, 293
Psalmody, 301, 309
Psalms, metrical, 301, 309
Puccini, Giacomo, 169, 173, 274
    La Bohème, 169, 206
Purcell, Henry, 25, 37, 85, 103–4
    Dido and Aeneas, 85, 104
    Variations for Harpsichord, 85, 100
    Variations on a New Ground Bass,
       25, 37, 85, 100
"Purple Haze," 359, 374

"Quando rapito in estasi," 207
Quartet, 150, 214, 318–19
Queen Mab, 187
Queen of Soul, 372
Queen of the Night aria, 25, 39
Quintet, woodwind, 43

Rachmaninoff, Sergei, 173, 196
Radio, 315
Rag, 57, 345, 346, 356
Raga, 390–91
Ragtime, 345, 356
Rameau, Jean-Philippe, 92
R & B. *See* Rhythm and blues
Range, 30
Ras Tafari, 393
Rastafarianism, 393, 394
Rationalism, 124
Rattle, 384
Ravel, Maurice, 25, 49, 237
    Boléro, 25, 43
    Pavane pour une Infante défunte,
       49, 64
    Pictures at an Exhibition, 25, 43
Realism, 206
Reason, 124, 129
Rebab, 388
Recapitulation, 59, 66, 146
Recipes, musical, 90–91
Recitative, 100, 102, 112
    cantata, 107, 109, 111
    opera, 102, 206, 221
    oratorio, 106–7
    Orfeo, 103
Recorder, 308
Recording, 333–34
Redding, Otis, 359, 372, 378
    "I've Been Loving You Too Long,"
       359, 372
    "Try a Little Tenderness," 359, 372
"Red Sails in the Sunset," 313, 323
Reed, Jimmy, 49
    "I Was So Wrong," 49, 58
Reed pipe, 382
Reformation, Protestant, 298, 299–302,
    309
Regals, 380
Regency, 116
Reggae, 393–94
Reich, Steve, 229, 272–73
    Come Out, 229, 273
Reicha, Anton, 43
Renaissance, 8, 86, 298
    art, 87–89
    characteristics of music, 299
    counterpoint, 299
    dance, 308, 309
    harmony, 32, 37, 299
    humanism, 298
    instrumental music, 307–8, 309
    instruments, 307–8
    keyboard music, 307–8
    madrigal, 306–7, 309
    mass, 302–4, 305
    motet, 305, 309
    rhythm, 299
    sacred music, 8, 299–305, 308

    secular music, 8, 306–8
    texture, 299, 308
Renoir, Pierre Auguste, 231, 275
Republic, 3
Rest, 20–21
Retrograde, 264
Revolution, 124
Rhapsody in Blue, 229, 262, 341, 351
Rheingold, Das, 222
Rhythm, 15, 23, 45
    African, 345, 384
    atomic, 93, 95
    Bartók, 246–47
    beat and, 16, 23
    bop, 353–54
    electronic, 267
    meter and, 17
    metrical modulation of, 275
    Middle Ages, 290
    note value and, 19–22
    reggae, 393
    Renaissance, 299
    Stravinsky, 243
    tempo and, 18–19
    time and, 15–23
    twentieth century, 246–47
Rhythm and blues (R & B), 360,
    361–63, 377
Rhythm Boys, 351
Ricciardo, 104
Riff, 330, 363, 375
Rigoletto, 169, 214–19
Riley, Terry, 229
    In C, 229, 273
Ring des Nibelungen, Der, 169, 206,
    222–25
Ring of the Nibelungen, 169, 206,
    222–25
"Ring, Ring the Banjo," 313, 318
Ritardando, 18
Rite of Spring, 25, 43, 229, 243
Ritornello, 95
"Riverboat Shuffle," 341, 348, 349
Roach, Max, 353
Rock
    acid, 373–74, 375, 378
    art, 376, 378
    Beatles, 368–71, 378
    blues, 374–75, 378
    cello, 376
    Detroit style, 367
    era, 360
    folk, 372–73, 378
    glitter, 375, 378
    group, 37
    heavy metal, 375, 378
    jazz, 376, 378
    late 1980s, 377
    modal scales, 29
    Motown, 367, 378

New Wave, 376
punk, 375–76, 378
rock and roll, 364–67, 377, 378
Rolling Stones, 371
roots of, 360–64, 377
singers and songwriters, 376
sixties, 367–68, 373, 378
soul, 371–72, 378
structure, 58, 66
style, 360
surf, 368
way of life, 373
West Coast, 373–74
Rock and roll, 361, 364–67, 378
soft, 366–67, 377
"Rock around the Clock," 359, 360
Rocking and reeling, 361
Rocking and rolling, 360
Rock-steady, 393
Rococo, 8, 116–21
art, 117
characteristics, 118–19, 128, 129
music, 121
texture, 121
trends, 116
Rodgers, Richard, 316
Roi David, Le, 229, 254
Rolling Stones, The, 359, 371
"Satisfaction," 359, 371, 372
"Roll over Beethoven," 359, 365
Roman Catholic church, 280–81, 289,
293, 299
music of, 302–5
"Romantic classicist," 176
Romantic era, 9
art song, 200–205
ballet, 8, 171, 182
composers, 172–75
concerto, 196–200
nationalism, 171
opera, 8, 171, 205–25
piano music, 8, 172, 189–95, 225
symphony, 8, 172, 175–87, 225
Romanticism, 141, 144, 170, 225
Romeo, 187
Romeo and Juliet, 169, 182
Roméo et Juliette, 169, 186–87
Rondeau, 292
Rondo, 51, 56–57
"Roots, Rock, Reggae," 393
Rosina, 207
Ross, Diana, 367
Rossini, Gioacchino, 169, 173, 206
Il barbiere di Siviglia, 169, 206,
207–14
Rousseau, 124
Rubato, 19
Rubens, 87, 88, 93, 112
Ruckert, Friedrich, 204, 205
Rugged individualist, 249–50

Ruggiero, 104, 105
"Run, Run, Run," 359, 367
Russell, Henry, 315, 337

Saarinen, Eero, 14
Sackbut, 308
Sacred music, 8. See also Mass, Motet
African, 384
Ars Nova, 8, 289–92
Balinese, 388
Christian, 8
Indian, 389
Jamaican, 393
Japanese, 392
Middle Ages, 8, 280
Renaissance, 8, 299–305, 308
Sacre du Printemps, Le, 25, 43, 229,
243
Sahara Desert, 382
St. Louis, 345
St. Louis Arch, 14
St. Mark's Cathedral, 308, 309
Saint Matthew Passion, 49, 55, 85, 96
St. Petersburg, 182
St. Petersburg Conservatory of Music,
182
Saint-Saens, 25
Carnival of Animals, 25, 40
"Elephants," 25, 40
Salomon, 136
Salon, 119
Saltarello, 176, 179
Sammartini, Giovanni, 125
Sanctus, 284
Sand, George, 191
San Francisco, 373
Santana, 376
Saraband, 55, 56, 100
Sarons, 388
Satan, 109
Satie, Erik, 229, 251–53, 276
Dessicated Embryos, 229, 251
Flabby Preludes, 229, 251
Gymnopédie no. 1, 229, 253
Parade, 229, 252–53
Second to Last Thoughts, 229, 251
Three Pieces in the Form of a Pear,
229, 251
"Satisfaction," 359, 371, 372
Saxophone, 40–43, 255, 349
reggae, 393
rhythm and blues, 363, 377
rock, 376
Scale
African, 382
blues, 344
chromatic, 29
church modes, 29
diatonic, 29

European, 344
Indian, 390–91
major, 29
minor, 29
modal, 29
Noh drama, 392
"Scarborough Fair," 4, 5, 25, 32
Scarlatti, Alessandro, 125
Scenes from Childhood, 169, 191, 194
Schaeffer, Pierre, 266
Scherzo, 53, 142
Schiller, Friedrich, 175
Schönberg, Arnold, 229, 238–39, 263,
276
Pierrot Lunaire, 229, 238–39, 276
Suite for piano, op. 25, 229, 264,
265
Schöne Müllerin, Die, 169, 201
"School Days," 359, 365
Schubert, Franz, 49, 172, 173, 175,
200–204
An die Musik, 169, 201–2
Die Erlkönig, 49, 61, 169, 200,
202–4
"Gute Nacht," 49, 61
Lieder, 200–204
Moments musicaux, 169, 172, 191
piano sonatas, 190
Die schöne Müllerin, 169, 201
Trout Quintet, 169, 201
Unfinished Symphony, 169, 201
"Who is Sylvia?," 49, 61
Die Winterreise, 49, 61, 169, 201
Schumann, Clara, 173, 179, 200, 204–5
character pieces, 191
"Liebst du um Schönheit," 169,
204–5
Lieder, op. 12, 204–5
Schumann, Robert, 169, 172, 173, 175,
179, 190, 196–200
character pieces, 191, 192, 194
concertos, 196–98
"Dreaming," 194
Kinderscenen, 169, 191, 194
Papillons, 169, 191
Piano Concerto in A Minor, 169,
197–98
piano music, 225
"Traumerei," 194
Scotch Symphony, 176
Scrapers, 384
"Searchin'," 359, 363
Seasons, The (Haydn), 131, 134
Seasons, The (Vivaldi), 69, 72, 85,
97–98
Second to Last Thoughts, 229, 251
Secularism, 289, 293, 298

Secular music
    African, 384
    Ars Nova, 8, 292
    Balinese, 388
    baroque, 101–5
    Japanese, 392
    Renaissance, 8, 306–8
Seeger, Ruth Crawford, 259
Selassie, Haile, 393
Semitone, 28
"Send in the Clowns," 49, 51
Sentimentality, 123, 317, 326
"September by the River," 195
Sequence, 284
Serenade for Horn, Tenor, and Strings,
    229, 274
Serial music, 265, 277
Sessions, Roger, 259, 276
Set number, 207
Sex Pistols, 376
Sextet, 214
*Sgt. Pepper's Lonely Hearts Club
    Band,* 359, 370–71
"Shake, Rattle and Roll," 359, 363
Shakespeare, William, 70, 219
"Shall We Gather at the River?," 229,
    250
Sharp, 27
Shaw, Artie, 313, 329, 330
    "Begin the Beguine," 313, 331
Shawm, 308
Sheet music, 314–15, 336
Shelley, Mary, 170
"She's Leaving Home," 359, 370
Shields, Ron, 321
    "In the Good Old Summertime,"
        313, 319, 321
"Shine on Harvest Moon," 313, 319,
    321
Siegfried, 222
Sieglinde, 223–25
Siegmund, 223–25
S'il estoit nulz, 279, 291
Simon, Carly, 376
Simon, Paul, 4, 5, 373
"Simple Gifts," 261
Sinfonia a 8, 115, 125, 126–27
"Sing, Sing, Sing," 313, 331
Singing
    baroque, 100–111
    bel canto, 104, 173
    country music, 364
    crooning style, 333–35, 337
    1930s, 332–35
    rhythm and blues, 363
    talking style, 333, 337
    tenor style, 332–33, 337
Singspiele, 157
S'io parto, i' moro, 297, 306
Six, Les, 253–55
Six English Suites, 85, 100

Six French Suites, 85, 100
Sixteenth century. *See* Renaissance
Ska, 393
Skaggs, Boz, 376
Slashing, 393
Slavonic Dances for Orchestra, 169,
    171
"Slop, The," 359, 368
Smith, Bessie, 374
Smith, Pinetop, 49
    "Pinetop's Boogie Woogie," 49, 58
Smithson, Henrietta, 186
Social Contract, 124
"Solitude," 341, 352
Solo, 100, 101, 112
    cadenza, 146
    concerto, 146
    piano music, 189–95
    opera, 102
"Someday," 49, 58
Sonata, 58
    Beethoven, 153–56. *See also*
        Beethoven
    Brahms, 180, 190
    classical, 8, 58
    Haydn, 152. *See also* Haydn
    Mozart, 152, 153, 166. *See also*
        Mozart
    piano, 134, 152–56, 190–91, 225
    romantic era, 8, 180
    trio, 8, 98–99, 112
Sonata-allegro, 51, 58–59, 66, 74–76
Sonata for Flute, Oboe, Cello, and
    Harpsichord, 229, 275
Sonata for Flute, Viola, and Harp, 25,
    40
Sondheim, Stephen, 49
    "Send in the Clowns," 49, 51
Song
    art, 61
    best seller, 331
    cycle, 61, 201, 370
    depression, 328
    exotic, 326–27
    family, 327
    folk, 61
    form, 322–23, 336
    gay 90s, 319–20
    genteel tradition, 316–18
    modified strophic, 61–62
    1930s, 322–28
    novelty, 326–27
    parlor, 316, 336
    patriotic, 327–28
    popular, 61
    strophic, 61
    structure, 61–62
    through-composed, 61
    Tin Pan Alley, 318–21
    twentieth century, 250
"Song of India," 313, 327

Song of the Youths, 268–69
Songs without Words, 169, 191
Sonny and Brownie, 49, 344
"Sophisticated Lady," 341, 352
Soprano, 38, 300
Sorcerer's Apprentice, The, 169, 189
Soul, 371–72
Sound, 26, 27–31
Sound and sense
    ABA form, 53–55
    American School, 261–62
    ballet, 243–45
    Berlin School, 127–28
    binary *ABAB* form, 63
    character piece, 195
    classical style symphony, 136
    classic Renaissance motet, 305
    complex *ABA* form, 53
    dadaist style, 253
    electronic music, 269–70
    études, 193
    jazz soloists, 348
    minimalist music, 273
    minuet, 54
    minuet-trio-minuet, 54
    Music for the Theatre, 260–61
    neoclassic (neobaroque) Stravinsky,
        256–57
    neoclassic piano concerto, 258–59
    New Orleans style jazz, 347
    nineteenth-century symphony,
        176–79
    offshoot of American art music, 263
    piano concerto, 197–98, 199–200
    piano sonata, 153–55, 155–56
    polonaise, 192–93
    preclassic symphony, 126–27
    Renaissance choral music, 303–4
    romantic symphony, 181–82
    rondo, 56, 57, 64
    sonata-allegro form, 64–65, 75–76
    structure of nonprogram music, 79
    Sturm und Drang features, 135–36
    Sturm und Drang quartet, 150
    ternary *ABA* form, 62, 63
    tone poem, 188–89
    twentieth-century sectional form,
        234–35
Spaan, Otis, 49, 51, 341, 344
    "Good Morning Mr. Blues," 49, 58
    "Worried Life Blues," 341, 344
Sparafucile, 216
Speranza, 103
Sprechtstimme, 238
"Spring," 69, 72, 85, 97–98
Springsteen, Bruce, 376
Staccato, 193
"Stairway to Heaven," 359, 375
Stamitz, Johann, 115, 125
    Symphony in D Major (*Sinfonia a
        8*), 115, 125, 126–27

Standard, 322
Stanza, 61, 66
"Star Spangled Banner, The," 49, 61
"Star Spangled Banner, The"
    (Hendrix), 359, 373
"Stay as Sweet as You Are," 313, 333
Sterling, Andrew, 313
    "Meet Me in St. Louis, Louis," 313,
        320
Still, William Grant, 229, 274
    Afro-American Symphony, 229,
        274
Stockhausen, Karlheinz, 229, 268–70
    Gesang der Jünglinge, 229, 268–70
Storeyville, 347
"Stormy Weather," 313, 323, 325
Stradella, Alessandro, 94
Strauss, Johann, 316
Strauss, Richard, 169, 173, 225
    Also sprach Zarathustra, 169, 189
Stravinsky, Igor, 25, 229, 243–45, 276
    The Firebird, 229, 243
    neoclassicism of, 255–57
    Octet, 229, 256–57, 276
    Petrushka, 229, 243–45, 247, 276
    Le Sacre du Printemps, 25, 43, 229,
        243
    Symphony in C, 229, 257
String quartet, 8, 40
    Bartók, 229, 246–47
    Beethoven, 131, 151, 166
    classical, 8, 148–51, 166
    Haydn, 134, 149–51. *See also*
        Haydn
    Mozart, 151, 166
String Quartet, op. 1, 149
String Quartet, op. 3, no. 5, 131, 149
String Quartet, op. 18, 131, 151
String Quartet, op. 20, no. 5, 131, 150
String Quartet, op. 33, no. 2, 25, 40,
    131, 151
String Quartet, op. 50, no. 1–6, 131,
    151
String Quartet, op. 54, no. 1–3, 131,
    151
String Quartet, op. 76, no. 1–6, 151
String Quartet, op. 76, no. 3, 49, 60
String Quartet, op. 77, no. 1–2, 131,
    151
Strings, 39–40, 46, 125, 189, 371
Strophic structure, 61
Structure. *See also* Form
    Bartók, 246–47
    strophic, 61
    through-composed, 61, 66
Sturm und Drang, 127, 128, 149, 150,
    152, 166
    characteristics, 123–24, 128
    Haydn and, 134–36, 150, 166

Mozart and, 139, 166
    quartets, 150
    theme, 134
Style, Viennese, 116, 128
Style galant. *See* Galant style
Sub-Saharan Africa, 382–85
Suite, 99, 119
Suite for piano, op. 25, 229, 264, 265
Sulings, 388
Supremes, The, 359, 367, 378
    "Run, Run, Run," 359, 367
    "You Can't Hurry Love," 359, 367
"Surfin' U.S.A.," 359, 368
Surprise Symphony, 85, 94
"Sweet Adeline," 313, 319, 320
Swing, 314, 328–31, 336
    band, 329–31, 350, 356
    era, 329, 337
    jazz and, 328, 342–43, 355
    thirties and forties, 350–52
Syllabic setting, 62
Symbolism, 235–37, 276
Symphonie Fantastique, 169, 185
Symphony, 8
    Beethoven, 141, 166. *See also*
        Beethoven
    Berlin School, 127–28, 129
    Brahms, 180–82. *See also* Brahms
    choral, 175, 186–87, 225
    classical, 8, 124–25, 128, 132–33,
        188
    dramatic, 186–87
    eighteenth century, 53
    Haydn, 134–37, 166. *See also*
        Haydn
    Mannheim School, 125–27, 129
    movements, 53, 125, 126, 132–33,
        145
    Mozart, 138–39, 166. *See also*
        Mozart
    preclassic, 8, 124–28
    program, 183–86, 225
    romantic era, 8, 172, 175–87, 225
    twentieth century, 8, 257
    Vienna School, 128, 129
Symphony, K. 16, 131
Symphony in B Minor, 115, 123,
    127–28
Symphony in C, 229, 257
Symphony in D Major, op. 18, no. 1,
    115, 122, 128
Symphony in D Major (*Sinfonia a 8*),
    115, 125, 126–27
Symphony no. 1, 131, 141
Symphony no. 2, op. 73, 169, 180,
    181–82, 183
Symphony no. 3 (*Eroica*), 49, 55, 131,
    141–44, 145, 154, 169, 175, 184
Symphony no. 4 (*Italian*), 69, 74, 169,
    176–79, 180

Symphony no. 5, 25, 30, 43, 169, 184
Symphony no. 5, *From the New World,*
    25, 43
Symphony no. 6 (*Pastoral*), 25, 43, 69,
    73, 78, 169, 175
Symphony no. 6 (*Pathétique*), 169,
    183–85, 199
Symphony no. 7, 69, 78–80
Symphony no. 9, 169, 175, 186
Symphony no. 9 (*From the New
    World*), 25, 37
Symphony no. 10 in D Major, 131, 134
Symphony no. 26, K. 184, 131, 139
Symphony no. 40 in G Minor, 49,
    54–55, 59, 66, 85, 94, 131, 138,
    169, 184, 257
Symphony no. 41, K. 551 (*Jupiter*),
    131, 139
Symphony no. 45 in F♯ Minor
    (*Farewell*), 131, 135–36, 150
Symphony no. 92, 49, 53–54
Symphony no. 101, 13, 22, 131, 136–37
Syncopation, 17, 22, 23, 350
Synthesizer, 266, 277, 377

Tabl, 382
Tailleferre, Germaine, 253
"Take Five," 341, 354
"Take the A Train," 313, 331
Tala, 390, 391, 394
Talking Heads, The, 359, 377
    "Burning Down the House," 359,
        377
    "Once in a Lifetime," 359, 377
Talma, Louise, 259
Tambourine, 44–45, 382
Tangerine Dream, 377
Tannhäuser, 25, 43
"Taxman," 359, 369
Tchaikovsky, Peter, 25, 49, 169, 173,
    182–83
    concertos, 196
    "Dance of the Sugar Plum Fairy,"
        25, 45
    "March," 49, 63
    The Nutcracker, 25, 45, 49, 63,
        169, 182
    "Overture Miniature," 49, 63
    Pathétique, 169, 183–85, 199
    Romeo and Juliet, 169, 182
    Symphony no. 6 (*Pathétique*), 169,
        183–85, 199
Teagarden, Jack, 335
Telemann, Georg Philipp, 98
Tempo, 18–19, 23, 93, 133
Temptations, 367, 378
Tenor, 38, 286, 300
Ternary, 51–55

426 Index

Text
    opera, 101
    setting, 62, 91
Texture, 34–37, 45
    African, 382
    contrapuntal, 35, 36, 46
    homophonic, 35
    Middle Ages, 289
    monophonic, 35, 46
    polyphonic, 35–37, 46
    Renaissance, 299, 308
    rococo, 121
Theater music, 272, 274
Theme, 30, 46
    development, 59, 184–85
    Sgt. Pepper, 370–71
    Sturm und Drang, 134
    variation and, 60–61, 66
Third Piano Concerto in C Major, op. 26, 229, 257, 258–59
This parting kills me, 306
Thomson, Virgil, 259, 276
Thornton, James, 313, 319
    "On the Banks of the Wabash," 313, 319
"Three Little Words," 313, 324
Three Pieces in the Form of a Pear, 229, 251
Three String Quartets, 229, 275
Tie, 21, 23
Timbre, 26, 45
Time
    movement and, 14
    music and, 12–23
    rhythm and, 15–23
"Times They Are A-Changin', The," 359, 373
Timpani, 44–45, 247
Tin Pan Alley, 314, 315, 318–21, 336
    recordings, 337
"Tisket-a-Tasket, A," 313, 331
Toccata, 100, 112
"Tom Dooley," 359, 372
"Tonami a vagheggiar," 49, 55, 94
Tonality, 33, 92, 230, 239, 264, 274
Tone
    poem, 8, 171, 182, 188–89, 225, 254
    reciting, 282
    row, 264, 277
Tonic, 33, 92
Torelli, Giuseppe, 94
Tragedie lyrique, 103
"Traumerei," 194
"Treasure of Love, The," 359, 367
Treatise on Harmony, 92
Triad, 33
Triangle, 44–45
Trio sonata, 8, 98–99, 112

Trio Sonata in F Major, op. 2, no. 5, 85, 92, 98–99, 112, 131
Trio Sonata in F Minor, op. 3, no. 9, 85, 98, 112
Triplum, 286
Tristan und Isolde, 169, 206
Trombone, 43, 256, 309, 346, 376, 393
Trout Quintet, 169, 201
Trouvères, 8, 291, 292
Trumbauer, Frankie, 341, 348, 349
    "Riverboat Shuffle," 341, 348, 349
Trumpet, 43, 95, 256, 309, 346, 376, 393
"Try a Little Tenderness," 359, 372
Tuba, 43
Tubb, Ernest, 359
    "I'm Walkin' the Floor over You," 359, 364
"Turkey in the Straw," 229, 250
Turner, Joe, 359
    "Shake, Rattle and Roll," 359, 363
Tutti, 94, 112
"Tutti Frutti," 49, 58, 359, 360
Twelve-bar blues, 51, 57–58, 322, 344
    boogie, 366
    rhythm and blues, 362–63, 377
Twelve Études, op. 10, 193
Twelve-tone system, 238, 263–65, 275, 276
Twentieth century
    adaptions and expansions, 274–75
    Americana composers, 259–62
    art music, 230–31, 275, 277
    ballet, 243–45, 252, 255, 261, 276
    chance music, 270–72, 274, 275, 277
    dadaism, 250–53, 276
    electronic music. *See* Electronic music
    experimentation, 249, 254–55, 275
    expressionism, 238–45, 275, 276
    folk music, 243–45, 246, 258, 260, 276
    harmony, 245
    impressionism, 231–35, 275
    minimalism, 266, 272–73, 277, 377
    neoclassicism, 255–59, 275, 276
    opera, 239–42, 262, 274
    oratorio, 254
    rhythm, 246–47
    rugged individualist, 249–50
    symbolism, 235–37, 276
    symphony, 8, 257
    tone poem, 254
    twelve-tone system, 238, 263–65, 275, 276
Twenty-Four Preludes, op. 28, 169, 191, 192
"Twist, The," 359, 368

Ud, 382
Unanswered Question, The, 25, 43, 69, 78, 229, 250, 275
Unfinished Symphony, 169, 201
Universe Symphony, 229, 249
Upbeat, 17
U2, 359, 377
    Joshua Tree, 359, 377

Vallee, Rudy, 334, 337, 338
Varèse, Edgar, 25, 229
    Ionisation, 25, 44, 229, 273
Variations, 60–61, 66, 100
Variations for Harpsichord, 85, 100
Variations on "America," 229, 250
Variations on a New Ground Bass, 25, 37, 85, 100
Venice, 97
Veni sponsa Christi, 25, 37
Verdi, Giuseppe, 169, 173, 206, 226, 274
    "Donna e mobile, La," 214
    Rigoletto, 169, 214–19
Verismo, 206
Versailles, 116–17
Verse
    and refrain, 319–21
    anthem, 301
Vibraphone, 44
Victimae paschali laudes, 279, 284–85, 293
Vienna School, 128, 129
Vietnam War, 369, 373
Villa-Lobos, Heitor, 274
Vina, 391
Viola, 39–40, 148, 189, 196, 226
Violent Femmes, 376
Violin, 39–40, 95, 98, 145, 148–51
    concerto, 25, 39, 69, 74, 131, 148, 196–200, 226
    Indian, 392
    rock, 376
    rock and roll, 366–67
Violin Concerto, 69, 74
Violin Concerto in A Major, K. 219, 131, 148
Violin Concerto in E Minor, 25, 39
Violoncello, 39
Viols, 308, 309
Virelai, 292
Virginal, 307–8
Vivaldi, Antonio, 69, 80, 95, 97–98
    Seasons, The, 69, 72, 85, 97–98
    "Spring," 69, 72, 85, 97–98
Vocal ensemble, 214–19
Vocal music
    African, 382, 384–85, 394
    baroque, 91, 100–111
    genres, 100–111, 112

Voice, 38–39, 384
"Volga Boatmen, The," 229, 258
Voltaire, 124
Volume, 26, 45
Von Bulow, Cosima, 220
Von Köchel, Ludwig, 138
Von Martinez, Marianne, 125
Von Meck, Mme., 183
Von Schober, Franz, 201
Von Weber, Carl Maria, 169
  Der Freischütz, 69, 72, 169, 171

Wagenseil, Georg Christoph, 125
Wagner, Richard, 25, 169, 172, 173,
  220–25
  Brahms and, 180
  Der fliegende Holländer, 169, 206
  Götterdämmerung, 222
  influence of, 238
  leitmotif, 221–25
  Liszt and, 175
  Lohengrin, 169, 206
  music drama, 221–25, 226
  opera, 206, 220–21
  Overture from *Tannhäuser,* 25, 43
  Das Rheingold, 222
  Der Ring des Nibelungen, 169, 206,
    222–25
  Siegfried, 222
  Tristan und Isolde, 169, 206
  Die Walküre, 222
Walden, 249
Waller, Fats, 341, 350
  "Numb Fumblin'," 341, 350
  "Whispering," 341, 354
Walküre, Die, 222
Waltz, op. 34, no. 2, 13, 19, 22, 25
Watteau, Jean Antoine, 118, 128

"Way Down Upon the Swannee River,"
  313, 317
Webern, Anton, 229, 238, 265, 277
  Five movements for string quartet,
    229, 239
Weick, Clara, 196, 197
Weight, musical, 132
"Well Get It," 313, 331
Well-Tempered Clavier, 25, 37, 85, 93
"West End Blues," 341, 348
West Indies, 393–94
"What Are Little Girls Made Of?,"
  313, 327
"When I Am Laid in Earth," 104
"When I'm Sixty-Four," 359, 371
"Where Have You Been, Billy Boy?,"
  313, 314
"Whispering," 341, 354
Whistle, 384
"White Christmas," 341, 343–44
Whiteman, Paul, 350–51
"White Rabbit," 359, 373
"Who is Sylvia?," 49, 61
Whole step, 28
Whole tone, 28
Willis, Chuck, 359
  "C. C. Rider," 359, 363
  "Mashed Potatoes," 359, 368
  "The Pony," 359, 368
  "Popeye," 359, 368
  "The Slop," 359, 368
  "Work with Me Annie," 359, 362,
    364
Wilson, Teddy, 351
Winterreise, Die, 49, 61, 169, 201
Winter's Journey, 49, 61, 169, 201
"Within You, Without You," 359, 370
Women composers, 9, 119, 259
Wonder, Stevie, 25, 39, 376
  "Isn't She Lovely," 25, 39

"Wondrous Things of Thee Are
  Spoken," 49, 60
Wood blocks, 44–45
"Woodchopper's Ball," 313, 331
Woodland Sketches, 169, 171, 194
Woodwinds, 39, 40–43, 46
Woodworth, Samuel, 313, 316–17
  "The Old Oaken Bucket," 313,
    316–17
Word painting, 306
Work, Henry C., 313, 337
  "Come Home Father," 313, 317
"Work with Me Annie," 359, 362, 364
World War I, 238, 257
World War II, music after, 165–75,
  277, 337
"Worried Life Blues," 341, 344
Worried notes, 344
Wozzeck, 229, 239–42, 276

Xylophone, 44, 247, 384, 388

Year, The, 195
"Yesterday," 359, 369
"You Are Too Beautiful," 359, 362
"You Call It Madness, But I Call It
  Love," 313, 325
"You Can't Hurry Love," 359, 367
"You Go to My Head," 325
"You Make Me Feel (Like a Natural
  Woman)," 359, 372
Young Person's Guide to the Orchestra,
  25, 43
"You! You're Driving Me Crazy," 313,
  325

Zimmerman, Robert, 372